PAUL

PIONEER FOR ISRAEL'S MESSIAH

PAUL

PIONEER FOR ISRAEL'S MESSIAH

JAKOB VAN BRUGGEN

TRANSLATED BY
ED M. VAN DER MAAS

PUBLISHING
P.O. BOX 817 • PHILLIPSBURG • NEW JERSEY 08865-0817

Page design and typesetting by Lakeside Design Plus

Printed in the United States of America

Library of Congress Cataloging-in-Publication Data

Bruggen, J. van, 1936–

[Paulus. English]

Paul : pioneer for Israel's Messiah / Jakob van Bruggen ; translated by Ed M. van der Maas.

p. cm.

Includes bibliographical references (p.) and indexes.

ISBN-13: 978-0-87552-648-5 (paper)

ISBN-10: 0-87552-648-9 (paper)

1. Paul, the Apostle, Saint. 2. Christian saints—Turkey—Tarsus—Biography. I. Title

BS2506.B75713 2005

225.9'2—dc22

[B] 2005042984

CONTENTS

ANALYTICAL OUTLINE

Part 2: Paul the Apostle

FIGURES

MAPS

PREFACE

Paul is a person who has fascinated me for a long time and whose life and thought I have studied for many years. In this book, which is the fruit of these studies, I try to describe Paul's life in such a way that the reader will find Paul's life as exciting to read about as it was in fact. I have also analyzed the main motives behind Paul's actions. In doing so I continuously interacted with modern theories about the person and meaning of this sometimes rather mysterious apostle. I am thankful to the Lord that he gave this book a wide acceptance in my own country.

Now that the book is published in English, it is my wish that also many English-speaking readers will become fascinated, again or for the first time, by this exceptional servant of the Messiah Jesus Christ.

The translation was done by my friend Ed van der Maas (Grand Rapids, Mich.). I am thankful that he was willing to take upon himself this task in a difficult period of his life. I was assured of an expert and careful translation, and I remember with pleasure the many contacts we had in that period of cooperation.

I am thankful to Allan Fisher for accepting my book for publication by P&R Publishing; it will feel itself quite at home in this environment.

Last but not least, I mention our friends Henk and Joan Berends-VanderPol (Lynden, Wash.). They stimulated the translation of this book and generously sponsored the work. I am thankful for their friendship and support!

INTRODUCTION

aul is, with Peter, the best known of the apostles. They even share a feast day: June 29, the day of Saint Peter and Saint Paul. But unlike Peter, Paul is one of the most controversial personalities in the first generation of the Christian church.

On the one hand, Paul is admired as the pioneer for Christianity, the new religion in the Roman Empire. As a preacher he traveled through many lands. With great zeal he established Christian communities. With great self-denial he helped build them up through his letters. To this he owes his place in the history of the church as the acclaimed preacher to the nations.

On the other hand, many blame Paul for causing the break between church and synagogue, between Jews and Christians. They see it as his fault that Christianity became a new religion among the nations of the world.

It seems that this ambivalence in understanding the apostle Paul already existed during his lifetime. On the one hand we find in the book of Acts an almost heroic picture of the converted persecutor of the church, who preached the gospel as far away as Rome, with great results and with the moral support of the Christians in Jerusalem.

On the other hand we encounter in Paul's letters someone who frequently has to speak out forcefully against personal criticism and against attacks on his work. Apparently Paul did not only have admirers like Luke and Timothy, but also detractors, among whom were some of his Jewish fellow-Christians in Jerusalem.

Attempts have been made more than once during the last two centuries to resolve this ambivalence by silencing part of the sources. Acts then is viewed as presenting a flattering picture of the apostle Paul that promotes him—incorrectly—to the successful and undisputed leader in the preaching of the gospel to the nations. Also, some letters traditionally attributed to Paul that present a relatively undisputed picture of the apostle are thought not to have been written by Paul himself. The few remaining sources then show us an individual who tried to come up with a radical alternative for Jewish Christianity. The church later found a compromise between the authentic Christianity of Peter, the shepherd, and the aggressive criticism of that Christianity on the part of this troublesome Paul.

It is, however, rather unsatisfactory to silence part of the historical sources simply because they do not agree with an image of Paul we have established in a later era, at a far remove. Why should we avoid the challenge of listening to *all* the sources in order to arrive on the basis of the *diversity* of these sources at a cautious reconstruction of the real Paul, to the extent that it can indeed be recovered?

The image of Paul then becomes more complicated—but reality is often more complex than we might suspect on the basis of later, simplified perceptions of that reality.

In this book Paul appears as a pioneer for the Messiah, Jesus Christ.

Part 1 describes the course of his life. It appears that Paul's life proceeded by fits and starts and with a measure of restlessness that is reflected not only in his letters but in fact also in Acts. In a variety of ways all sources converge to present a pioneer life: adventurous, unpredictable, nonlinear, full of risks.

Part 2 discusses the place Paul occupies in the historical development of the Christian church. How is Paul's gospel related to the message of the other apostles? How does Paul's vision of the Christian community relate to the place of the nation of Israel? In discussing this we shall find that Paul was not a marginal figure, operating out of reaction, but a driven pioneer for a Christianity that is aware of Christ's kingship but that realizes at the same time that it is not a new religion but the fulfillment of the promises to Abraham.

To avoid overloading the chapters in part 1 with details, appendix 1 discusses the chronological data and some cardinal issues in the reconstruction of Paul's life, while appendix 2 presents a chronological bibliography of Paul's correspondence. Similarly, part 2 is supplemented by appendix 3, which presents a brief discussion of the place the law occupied in Judaism.

Many books have already been written about Paul. Many of these works complement one another, and it is unavoidable that topics covered in this book are also discussed elsewhere. What then makes this book unique?

In the first place, this study distinguishes itself from the majority of current Pauline studies by adopting a positive stance toward the *totality* of the historical sources.

Second, this book seeks to present Paul's life, letters, and historical position as an integrated whole. Frequently books about Paul deal with individual aspects of his life and work (e.g., introduction to Paul's letters, Paul's biography, or Pauline theology).[1] This scattering of the various aspects over a variety of books, without integration, easily causes us to miss the overall picture that is the aim of this book.

Third, there is a strong emphasis on calling to account some current reconstructions of the first-century history. After more than nineteen centuries of Pauline studies there are sometimes solutions in circulation that are all too readily accepted as certain and definitive, even though they turn out to be untenable on closer inspection. Cases in point deal, for example, with the problems surrounding the relationship between Acts 15 and Galatians 2, the date of 1 Timothy and Titus, the relationship between Paul's gospel and his Jewish background, and the manner in which Paul writes about the law.

It is my hope that this book will be of help to all those who want to get a clearer perspective on the moving target that was the apostle Paul. I have tried to write in such a way that this book can be used as an integrated textbook on the apostle Paul, but also as a resource for the reading of commentaries on Acts or the letters of Paul.

Over the many years in which I looked from a distance at the mysterious and sometimes irritating figure of the Jewish Christian Paul, I have often felt that he would forever remain elusive. I have learned that this elusiveness is related to his calling as a pioneer—and also to the invisible guiding Hand in his life. Whoever looks at Paul for any length of time, ultimately sees Jesus Christ—which is precisely how Paul himself wanted to fade from the picture!

PART ONE

PAUL
THE PIONEER

1

GONE FROM TARSUS

Paul, both in his early life and in his later years, presents something of a moving target. When we look for him in one place, we find that he has already moved on to the next.

Saul was born in Tarsus, a city on the east end of the southern coast of modern Turkey. It was a flourishing commercial center, situated on a river in a fertile region. Although the city remained linked to the culture of the East, it was also known for its openness toward Hellenistic culture and education.[1] Saul spent his earliest years there, but he left this Greek city some time before reaching adulthood. Our knowledge of this early period of Paul's life is fragmentary; all we know about it comes from the years Paul lived or traveled elsewhere.

1.1 Saul the Tarsian

We know from the book of Acts that Saul was born in Tarsus. In a speech to the Jewish crowd that threatens him in the temple at Jerusalem he says, "I am a Jew, born in Tarsus of Cilicia, but brought up in this city [i.e., Jerusalem]. Under Gamaliel I was thoroughly trained in the law of our fathers" (Acts 22:3).

Why does Paul mention his place of birth at the beginning of this speech? The rumor was circulating among the crowd that he had brought Greeks into the temple, and thus Paul is going to great lengths to make it clear that he is not a renegade Jew or an enemy of the Jewish way of life. By presenting himself as a true Jew, by both descent and education, he defends himself against the charge that he holds the temple in contempt.

But under these circumstances, would it not have been better to leave out the fact that his birthplace lay far outside Palestine? This would certainly have been the case had it not been common knowledge among his hearers that he came from Tarsus. Saul was known in Jerusalem as "the Tarsian," as Acts 9:11 shows. Jesus instructs Ananias in Damascus to visit a "Saul named 'the Tarsian' " (*Saulon ono-*

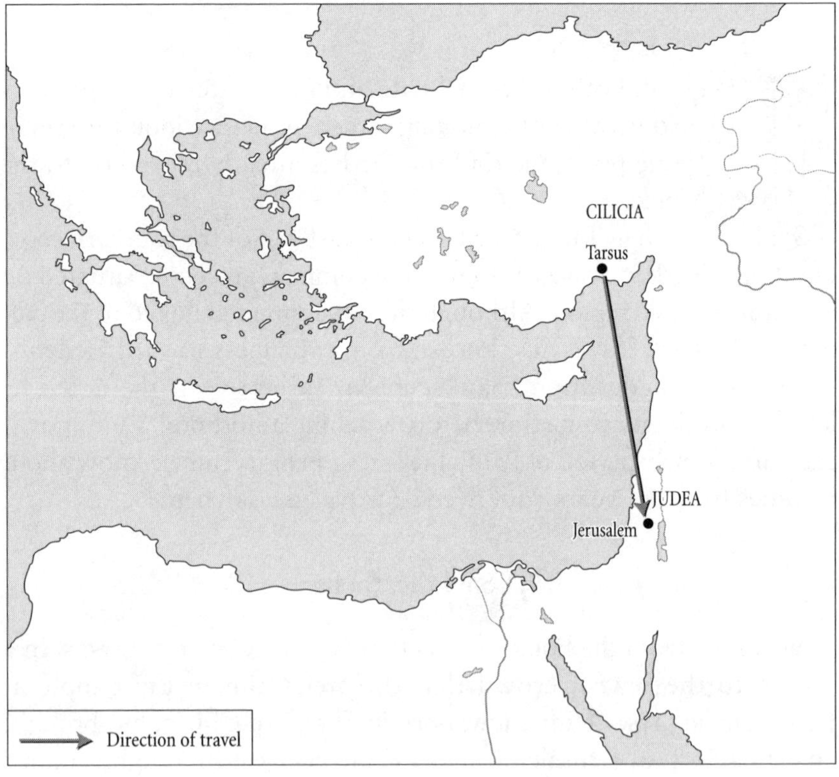

Map 1: *The Cities of Paul's Youth*

mati Tarsea; many English versions [e.g., NASB, NIV, NRSV] incorrectly translate this phrase as if it read *Tarsea onomati Saulon*, "a man from Tarsus named Saul"). There were undoubtedly other people named Saul in Jerusalem, and he was apparently distinguished from other Sauls by being called "Saul the Tarsian."

The fact that *this* Saul was known in Jerusalem as "the Tarsian" provides fertile soil for the accusation that as a Christian he had brought Greeks into the temple. The man who is known as hailing from Tarsus is apparently a crypto-Hellenist, a secret friend of Greeks and Greek culture. Doesn't his nickname alone betray his real intentions? It is at this point that Paul explains the true facts behind the name "Tarsian": Yes, he was born in Tarsus, but he is a Jew in the fullest sense of the word, born and raised in Judaism, and from his earliest years its confirmed proponent (Acts 22:3–5).

While Paul minimizes the significance of his birthplace when addressing his fellow Jews in Jerusalem, he capitalizes on it that very same day in his meeting with the commander of the Roman military contingent in Jerusalem. The commander thinks that Paul is simply an Egyptian rebel on the run. But the apostle corrects him and states, in full awareness of who and what he is, "I am a Jew, from Tarsus in Cilicia, a citizen of no ordinary city" (Acts 21:39). Paul distances himself from the idea that he might be an Egyptian: he is a *Jew*. And furthermore, he distances himself from the suspicion that he might be an antisocial individual: he is a citizen of an important Greek city in Cilicia!

But there is an additional element: not only was Paul born in Tarsus, he also has its citizenship. This could be acquired by birth only if the parents already were citizens. Because Saul was still young when he left Tarsus, he must have received its citizenship through his parents. This then implies that Saul's parents must have had a prominent position in the city and must have acquired the privilege of citizenship—a remarkable occurrence in a world in which the Jews were often excluded from such urban privileges.

Because Paul was a citizen of Tarsus, it is not surprising that he was known as "the Tarsian" in Jerusalem. His citizenship enabled Paul to impress a Roman soldier, but ever since his childhood he himself considered it more important that he belonged to the Jewish people, and later, as a Christian, he attached more importance to the fact that we "do not have an enduring city, but we are looking for the city that is to come" (Heb. 13:14).

The man known among the Jews as "the Tarsian" did not make himself comfortable in this citizenship of an earthly city: Saul of Tarsus becomes a champion of the Jerusalem of God!

1.2 A Greek Education?

More than once the fact of Paul's birth in Tarsus has been used as the basis for the assumption that in Tarsus Paul gained an extensive knowledge of Hellenistic culture and a familiarity with Greek philosophy and literature. The apostle then stood with one leg in the Greek world (having grown up in Tarsus) and with the other in the Jewish world (as a student of Gamaliel's).[2] Moses was raised at the Egyptian court and later benefited greatly from this background. Did Tarsus serve a similar function for Paul?

W. C. van Unnik rejects this notion. In his study *Tarsus or Jerusalem: The City of Paul's Youth* he comes to the conclusion that Paul grew up, not in Tarsus but in Jerusalem. He bases this on Acts 22:3. Traditionally this verse has been understood to mean "I am a Jew, born in Tarsus of Cilicia, but brought up in this city under Gamaliel. I was thoroughly trained in the law of our fathers and was just as zealous for God as any of you are today." On this reading of the verse, Paul mentions Jerusalem only in connection with Gamaliel, which means that he grew up in Tarsus but later went to Jerusalem to study under Gamaliel. Van Unnik, however, thinks that Paul's early youth was also spent in Jerusalem. According to him, the phrase "brought up in this city" should be read as followed by a period, and thus not connected with "under Gamaliel": ". . . born in Tarsus of Cilicia, but brought up in this city [Jerusalem]. Under Gamaliel I was thoroughly trained. . . ." Gamaliel is thus mentioned as the one who trained Paul "in the law of our fathers." If we read Acts 22:3 in this manner, then Paul was in Jerusalem when he was (1) raised by his parents and (2) instructed by Gamaliel. More recent editions of the Greek New Testament and some more recent Bible versions place a comma (NASB) or period (NIV) between "brought up in this city" and "under Gamaliel."[3]

The Greek sentence structure, however, makes it more plausible to maintain the connection between "brought up" and "under Gamaliel." The reason is that Luke uses three verbs, each followed by an elucidation ("*born* in Tarsus of Cilicia; *brought up* in this city under Gamaliel; *trained* in the law of our fathers"). Paul can compare his training by Gamaliel to the work of parents; he feels that he was "brought up" by this rabbi. The use of a term from the parental realm of child rearing provides an emotional touch. Paul uses the term to show what Gamaliel's instruction has meant to him. True, he was "born in Tarsus," but he was "brought up in this city," at the feet of Gamaliel who "trained him in the law of our fathers." The apostle does not say that he grew up as a child in Jerusalem, but he does say that as a Jew he received his all-important training at the feet of the teacher Gamaliel, who was, in a sense, Paul's foster father!

All this leaves room for the assumption that Paul spent his youth in Tarsus. The fact that he was given the nickname "Tarsian" when he arrived in Jerusalem also argues in favor of this assumption: apparently he was at that time no longer an infant or toddler. In Tarsus Paul became intimately acquainted with the culture and education of a Greek city. To be sure, even in Palestine we cannot speak of an absolute separation between the Jewish and Hellenistic worlds; the people in Jerusalem were not unacquainted with Hellenism.[4] Nevertheless, the interaction is more intense and more complete in a city such as Tarsus than in Jerusalem. Even if Paul, as the child of orthodox Jewish parents, participated in the culture of the city only in limited measure and was not molded by it, we can say with certainty that he was at least exposed to, and hence acquainted with Hellenistic education, sports, and culture.[5] This may explain why in his letters he draws images from the world of sports with such ease and why he occasionally quotes classical authors.

Nevertheless there is little reason to call Paul a man of two worlds on the basis of his youth in Tarsus. In the first place, he really grew up in three worlds: (1) the world of regional and national cultures and religions (Judaism among them); (2) the world of Greek or Hellenistic international culture; and (3) the governmental and juridical world of the Roman Empire.[6] Second, Paul calls himself a man of one world: the Jewish world! He views his life among his people in Jerusalem not as something he found only as an adult. From birth he lived as a member of the people of Israel, and his stay in Jerusalem merely served to enhance that way of life.[7] Thus he speaks of the way he lived ever since he was a child, from the beginning of his life among his own people and also in Jerusalem (see Acts 26:4).[8] But the ease with which he can move in the Greek world, first as a Jew and later as a Christian, may be due in part to his youth as a citizen of Tarsus. This enabled the pioneer of Christianity to be not only "to the Jews, a Jew" but also "to the Greeks, a Greek."

1.3 Roman Citizen

Being born a citizen of Tarsus did not make one automatically a citizen of Rome. The commander of the garrison, when he heard that Paul was a citizen of Tarsus, did not know that this prisoner had Roman citizenship as well. He received a shock when he discovered a little later, while Paul was already being tied up to be flogged, that Paul was a Roman citizen (Acts 22:25–29; 23:27). Earlier, the magistrates of Philippi also had not suspected that Paul and Silas, the two Jews they had thrown in prison, were Roman citizens (Acts 16:37–38).

The commander of the Roman garrison in Jerusalem is curious how Paul obtained the privilege of Roman citizenship. He himself had had to pay a large sum of money to get his. When questioned, Paul replies that he was born a citizen of Rome (Acts 22:28)! This means that his parents were citizens of both Tarsus *and* Rome. Young Saul was born into a family that had managed to reach a prominent social position in the world of that time!

Nevertheless, Paul used his Roman citizenship only occasionally, and only in situations where it would be of help in the spread of the gospel. Otherwise he saw it as being far inferior to his true citizenship. As he writes to the church in Philippi, where many had Roman citizenship, "our citizenship is in heaven. And we eagerly await a Savior from there, the Lord Jesus Christ, who [has] the power that enables him to bring everything under his control" (Phil. 3:20–21). Paul here uses terms that were familiar from the worship of the emperor, who was lord (*kyrios*), savior (*sōtēr*), and brought the world "under his control."

Paul did not disdain his Roman passport; he knew how to give it a positive place in his life, but without considering it something to brag about.[9] As a young man he was proud of his citizenship in Jerusalem, and as an older man he knew himself to be a citizen of the Jerusalem above. He used his earthly passport appropriately but sparingly.

1.4 Departed for Jerusalem

Saul did not stay in the city from which he derived the nickname "Tarsian." Jerusalem became his spiritual city of origin. There he let himself be trained by Gamaliel in the law of God and the traditions of the fathers (Acts 22:3).

Whenever the apostle speaks of his life before becoming a Christian, he depicts himself, in a variety of contexts, as a man who was fanatically zealous for God's law and for the people of Israel.[10]

In Galatians 1, Paul wants to show that the gospel must be believed because it originated with God himself, not with any human being. From a human perspective Paul would seem to have been an utterly unlikely candidate for the Christian faith. God himself revealed the gospel to him—before that, Paul's own preference had been a Jewish nation without Jesus (Gal. 1:13–14)!

In Philippians 3 the apostle warns his readers against the allure of the centuries-old synagogue, which, with its historical roots and venerable traditions, seems far superior to the small, not yet fully established Christian community. Yet Christians must find their joy in the Lord, not in an imposing earthly synagogue. Paul himself had to learn this. From birth he had been deeply impressed by Israel's history and traditions.[11] Only when he came to realize that Jesus means even more than all of Israel, both past and present, did he surrender, and ever since, that which had been imposing to him in earthly Israel was surpassed by his joy in Christ. But this does not alter the fact that before his being called by Christ Paul was a committed Jew! From birth he was not a man of two worlds, but of one city: not Tarsus, but Jerusalem:

"If anyone else thinks he has reasons to put confidence in the flesh, I have more: circumcised on the eighth day, of the people of Israel, of the tribe of Benjamin, a Hebrew of Hebrews; in regard to the law, a Pharisee; as for zeal, persecuting the church; as for legalistic righteousness, faultless" (Phil. 3:4–6).

1.5 Known from His Mother's Womb

In Galatians 1:15 Paul writes that "God . . . set me apart from birth." He was born a citizen of a well-known Greek city. He also was a Roman citizen from birth. In his early years he could become acquainted with Greek culture. He was not ashamed of the world in which he grew up, nor of his earthly citizenship papers, but he apparently felt drawn from the first by the Almighty, which is why he went to study in Jerusalem, with Gamaliel. Saul of Tarsus was from childhood known by God. His life before becoming a Christian was not a negative or even a neutral period. On the contrary! He was connected with God from the womb. Later, standing before the Sanhedrin, he called out, "I am a Pharisee, the son of a Pharisee" (Acts 23:6). Not only was he himself a Pharisee, his father was also. He was indeed a Pharisee by birth![12]

Paul's connection with God from his mother's womb is the most determining factor in the rest of his life. His social circumstances are of secondary importance. According to some, he grew up in well-to-do circumstances and learned the tent-making trade only because a teacher of the law was supposed to know a trade (at least in later times). Because Paul as apostle was truly dependent on the income from his trade, it would seem, however, that he did not come from a well-to-do family.[13]

Saul was probably born into a family of tanners, who had to work hard to make a living. He grew up in the fear of the Lord, like young Samuel. He did not want to be something else. That is why he left Tarsus to become a devoted servant of the Most High in the Roman Empire, a driven zealot for the God of Israel. Thus he also believed that his having been set apart from the womb required a special effort on his part, in the name of his God, with regard to the new, emerging sect of the Nazarenes.

2

FROM PERSECUTOR TO DESERTER

In Jerusalem, Saul gained a reputation as a persecutor of Christians, supported by the high priest and feared by the Christians. But just when he is on the verge of his most successful raid yet, he suddenly disappears from sight. The Sanhedrin is faced with a deserter. And Saul turns his back not only on Tarsus, he also disappears from his beloved Jerusalem.

What moved him to defect?

2.1 Radically Pro-Jerusalem

Saul the Tarsian found his spiritual home in the temple-city of Jerusalem. There he distinguished himself through zealous devotion to the service of Israel's God.

His dedication to Judaism was outstanding, even among his fellow-students. To the Galatians he writes, "I was advancing in Judaism beyond many Jews of my own age" (1:14). Many take the words *en tōi genei mou* to mean "among my countrymen" (NASB), that is, "Jews" (NIV). But the context shows that he refers more specifically to those in his own age group, and the word *genos* adds something: it indicates "persons of the same kind." This may refer to the Jews who belong to the same group of people as Paul himself: the other students of Gamaliel or the other young Pharisees. Paul then indicates that even among the spiritual elite he stood out because of his fanatical zeal for the tradition.

In Jerusalem this exacting Pharisee encountered the Jesus revival that was taking place after this miracle worker from Nazareth had been executed for blasphemy (he, a human being, had dared to make himself equal with the Almighty, blessed be his Name!). For Saul this new sect was an abomination, a great evil in the Holy City.

Because he came from Cilicia, Saul certainly was not ignorant of the debates in Jerusalem between the Greek-speaking Christian Stephen and "the Jews . . . of Cilicia and Asia" (Acts 6:9). If Saul, as a fervent exponent of the traditions, personally took part in these debates, he and his allies would have experienced that "they could not stand up against [Stephen's] wisdom or the Spirit by whom he spoke" (Acts 6:10). Perhaps Saul was among those who resorted to the same tactic that had been used at the trial of Jesus—the use of false witnesses (Acts 6:11). In any case, young Saul is prominently present at the stoning and is willing to take care of the clothes of these witnesses when they stone Stephen (Acts 7:58). Luke writes that Saul fully endorsed this execution (Acts 8:1).

The trial of Stephen marks the beginning of Saul the persecutor of Christians. In his youthful zeal he takes the (for him) logical next step. The sentencing of Stephen made clear, in his opinion, that the "Jesus sect" is guilty of incessantly speaking blasphemous words against the temple and the law. Because of the name of Jesus, respect for the holy place diminishes and ancient traditions are changed (Acts 6:13–14).

It is easy to understand that such a negative view of the Christian church developed. The Jews who belonged to the party of the so-called Nazarenes acknowledged Jesus as authoritative lawgiver. He gave new interpretations of portions of the Torah (Sabbath laws, laws on ceremonial cleanness and uncleanness), and his pronouncements sometimes superseded the words of Moses (in the case of marriage laws). But this did not mean that the Torah as a whole had lost its validity for Jesus. On the contrary, he did not annul the law and the prophets in Israel (Matt. 5:17), and he continued to tell the people to listen to what the teachers of the law told them (Matt. 23:2–3). It is therefore incorrect to seek the reason for Saul's persecution of the Christians in the notion that their confession of Jesus led them to a wholesale rejection of the law.[1] Saul the persecutor used "aggression against the law" as an inflammatory argument for his persecution, but the central issue was not rejection of the Torah but rather the acknowledgment of Jesus as the Son of God. Saul came out in support of the earlier decision of the Sanhedrin to remove Jesus from Israel as a false prophet, a blasphemer. He felt it to be his obligation to implement this decision, on God's behalf, when unexpectedly after Jesus' death thousands of Saul's fellow-Jews appeared to be infected by the Crucified One, giving the impression that they considered Jesus to be more important than Moses, the prophet of the Lord.

For a young religious radical such as Saul it was self-evident, not only that Stephen had to die, but that this apostate sect had to be rooted out and destroyed. Saul lacked the maturity of his teacher Gamaliel, who had advised to leave the disposition of this new movement to God himself: a movement that is not from God will die out and disappear of its own accord (Acts 5:34–40). Saul is probably an exponent of the Greek-speaking Jews of the Diaspora (cf. Acts 6:9)—emigrants from the fatherland are often more radical than those who stay at home. In any case, Paul later describes his persecution of the Christians as proof of his great zeal for the traditions of the fathers (Gal. 1:13–14). History provides many examples of fanatics who manage to turn a latent distaste into aggressive persecution. There is therefore no reason to seek an explanation of Saul's zeal in some traumatic experience in his own life.[2]

In a short time, Saul, out of conviction, emerged as the leader of the pogrom against the members of the sect of the Nazarenes. Although the impetus for the persecution came from the death of Stephen (who belonged to the group of Greek-speaking Christians), the persecutions targeted not only those Greek-speaking Christians but the whole church, with the exception of the apostles (Acts 8:1, 3; 9:1). Saul, as Ananias said, turned against "all who call on your name."[3]

2.2 Systematic Persecutor of Christians

The new element Saul introduces into the persecution of Christians is a systematic approach and planning. Until the death of Stephen there had been only some incidental actions against a few Christians (first against Peter and John and then also against all the apostles). The Jewish leaders acted only to the extent that increasing unrest in the temple gave them reason to act.

It is Saul who turns this policy of repression into one of systematic aggression that finds expression in several ways.

1. In Jerusalem, Christians are actively persecuted when they gather as believers, that is, not only when they create a disturbance but when it is known that they participate in the worship of Jesus the Nazarene as the Messiah. There is now a policy of actively tracking down Christians. In Jerusalem Saul organizes raids in which people are arrested and jailed. We read in Acts 8:3 that Saul "going from house to house . . . dragged off men and women and put them in prison." This description leads us to suspect that these were homes where Christians met to eat Jesus' Supper and to receive instruction (Acts 2:46; 5:42); the women present at these meetings are also arrested. The mere fact of assembling in a small group of Christians could, for strict Pharisees, serve as prima facie evidence to support the accusation that these men and woman participated in a blasphemous sect that spurned the synagogue. In this manner Saul "made havoc of the church" (Acts 8:3a KJV; "began ravaging the church" NASB). He dismantled the sect in Jerusalem. As a result, individual Christians took refuge outside the temple city and were scattered throughout Judea and Samaria (Acts 8:1).

The apostles are exempted from this expulsion from Israel; they can stay in Jerusalem (Acts 8:2). This may seem strange, but it is due to the fact that they had already been on trial before the Sanhedrin. The verdict had been that they no longer could spread the gospel, but at the same time they had been released only after having been flogged (Acts 5:40). The Sanhedrin could not reopen their case without good cause. The apostles were not in danger until a new Herod, who had the royal prerogative of initiating his own action against them, became king over Jerusalem (Acts 12:1–4).[4]

2. Not only are Christian gatherings raided, but Paul, together with others, also puts heavy pressure on individuals in the synagogues who confess that Jesus is the Messiah. Thus he forces them to abandon the Christian faith by making them blaspheme Jesus and renounce him (Acts 26:11). We find a late echo of these events in a letter of the apostle when he says that "no one who is speaking by the Spirit of God says, 'Jesus be cursed.' " He remembers all too well how often he had forced the words "Jesus be cursed" from fellow Jews in the synagogues.[5]

3. An active policy of persecution outside Jerusalem further prevents the exiles from perpetuating the sect. In the book of Acts, Paul's trip to Damascus to persecute the Christians there receives a great deal of attention, since it turned out to be the turning point that determined the rest of his life. This gives the impression that the persecution suddenly jumped from Jerusalem to Damascus. But the region between these two cities did not escape persecution. We can deduce this from a comment Paul makes in speaking to Agrippa: "Many a time I went from one synagogue to another to have them punished, and I tried to force them to blaspheme. In my obsession against them, I even went to foreign cities to persecute them" (Acts 26:11). The way this is phrased indicates that an active policy of persecution against Christians was implemented in the synagogues inside Palestine before plans were made for similar persecutions outside Palestine (in Damascus). This explains why the Christians who left Palestine did not settle elsewhere but led an itinerant life: they were hunted and scattered as they were fleeing (Acts 8:1, 4; 11:19).

4. Finally the persecution expands even beyond the borders of Palestine. It would appear that this step is due entirely to the initiative of the radical Saul. He personally asks the high priest for written authorization to expand the policy of persecution to include the synagogues in Damascus (Acts 9:1–2). If Christians are found there, they may be deported to Jerusalem to be tried by the Sanhedrin. This is necessary because a false prophet must be tried in Jerusalem, and the same applies to all those who are guilty of participating in his false teachings.

In fact, the charge against the Christians is the same as the charge against Jesus. They accept Jesus' view of himself: that he has come from God and is equal to God, the manifestation of the Lord himself in Israel—whereas for Saul and others he is no more than a human being. In the eyes of the persecutor, the sect of the Christians fails to honor the Holy One, and this teaching must therefore not gain a foothold in Israel, nor in Palestine, nor in the Diaspora. Judaism may have a pluralistic character—but all movements within Judaism must remain within the boundary set by the words "Hear, O Israel: the LORD our God, the LORD is one" (Deut. 6:4).

2.3 Persecutor out of Ignorance

Most of what we know about Paul's activities as a persecutor comes from Paul himself. As a historian, Luke devotes several sentences to the topic (Acts 8:1–3; 9:1–2, 14, 21), but in his report of two of Paul's speeches we find more details. The apostle does not suppress his past! He reminds the Jews in Jerusalem of his past when they want to lynch him because he has become a Christian apostle to the nations (Acts 22:4–5). And he elaborates further in his speech to King Agrippa (Acts 26:9–12). In both cases he uses his past to make clear to non-Christian Jews that he was originally even more fiercely opposed to Christianity than his audience now is opposed to his gospel.

From Paul's letters we can gather that his past as persecutor was also known among the non-Jewish churches. He briefly alludes to it in Galatians 1:13: his readers have undoubtedly heard about it! The same is true of Philippians 3:6. In both places Paul uses his past to reinforce his argument that from birth he was a devout non-Christian Jew, whose aversion to Christianity was a matter both of conviction and of action.

It is striking that Paul, writing to Timothy, characterizes this activity as done "in ignorance and unbelief" (1 Tim. 1:13). Did Paul not know anything about Jesus? This is not likely. If nothing else, he must have gained much information about the faith of the Christians during the interrogations of the apostles. Furthermore, the stories about the mass movement surrounding Jesus' ministry were generally known. Saul was undoubtedly well informed. What is at issue here is not *lack of knowledge* but *lack of intent*. In the laws of Moses a distinction is made between sinning in ignorance and sinning "with a raised hand." Sins committed with a raised hand are a result of apostasy and recalcitrance; the sin is committed intentionally. But sins committed in ignorance are not committed intentionally and can therefore be forgiven more readily when there is repentance. Thus Peter tells the Jews in Jerusalem that they and their leaders killed Jesus in ignorance (Acts 3:17). Paul thus can equate his unbelief with ignorance. He was of course aware of Jesus' claim, but he could not believe that this man, Jesus, was the manifestation of God on earth. In spite of his unbelief, Paul acted in good faith. His intent was to serve Israel's God in purity and sincerity. In this he distinguishes himself from traitors and defectors, who know better but betray both their experience and their faith.

In this connection we can ask whether Saul personally had seen Jesus' ministry in Jerusalem. There is a very good possibility that he had. Shortly after the ascension, Saul already appears to be an influential student of Gamaliel's. This means that he must have been in the city in his preceding years of study, when Jesus appeared at the feast of tabernacles or at the feast of the dedication of the temple or during the Passover. He was then able to observe from a distance the deliberations of the Sanhedrin to put Jesus to death. Did Paul himself ever stand in the crowd, listening to Jesus in the temple court?

There are no personal, biographical reminiscences of Jesus in Paul's letters, although they do show a familiarity with the tradition concerning him (his words, the institution of the Lord's Supper, the appearances after the resurrection, etc.).[6] But the absence of personal reminiscences does not necessarily mean that Saul did not personally see Jesus in action or follow Jesus' career. Paul's letters are occasional writings and do not lend themselves to biographical reminiscences. Besides, it is understandable that Paul the Christian modestly concurs with the traditions of the other apostles where the history of Jesus is involved. He himself, after all, viewed Jesus during his life on earth through the lenses of an unbeliever and enemy.[7] There is little reason to remember the time when Saul viewed the person of Jesus from the perspective that Beelzebub was using Jesus to endanger the holy nation.

Saul's unbelief during the ministry and death of Jesus made him a persecutor "in ignorance." One who does not believe that Jesus Christ is the Son of God cannot but think that he is a blasphemer. Driven by this thought the young radical Jew from Tarsus became responsible for the first systematic aggression on the part of non-Christian Judaism against the members of the sect of the Nazarenes.

2.4 Confrontation with Christ

How could this fanatical persecutor ever have become the pioneer of Christianity? He was certainly the least qualified for that role! It is impossible to explain this radical reversal on the basis of some kind of inner development.[8] Besides, the time for this turnaround is too short to allow for a gradual process of change. Within the span of a few days, Saul changes from Jesus' opponent to his exponent, a preacher of his gospel.

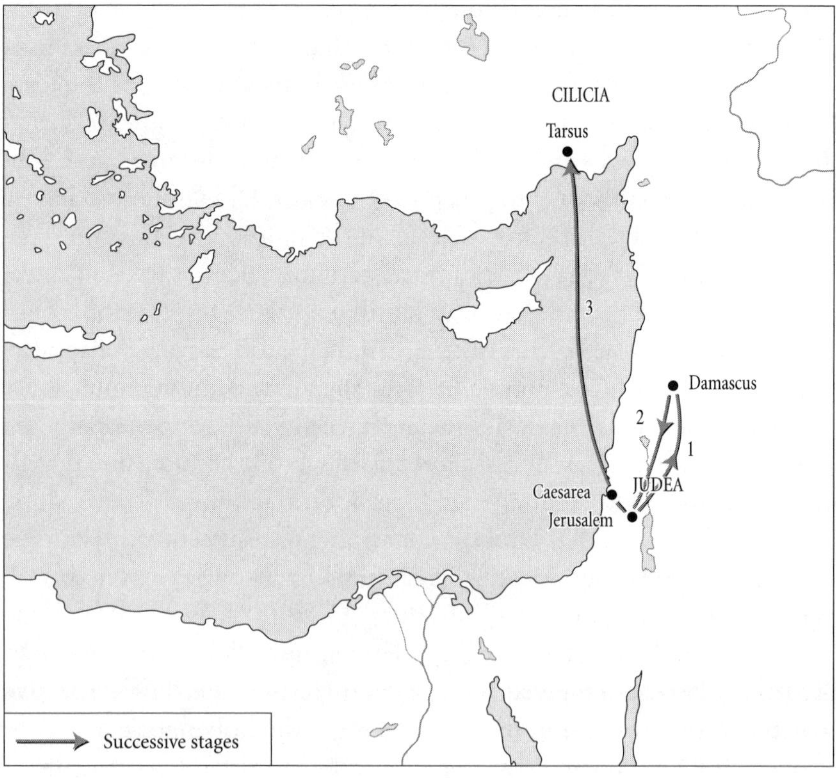

Map 2: *From Persecutor to Persecuted*

Who brought this about? Jesus Christ himself confronted the leader of his opposition. Shortly before Saul reaches Damascus, Jesus puts him in a blinding heavenly light and speaks to him: "Saul, Saul, why do you persecute me?" (Acts 9:4). He stands in Saul's way and lets Saul hear His name: "I am Jesus, whom you are persecuting." Saul is no match for this light and this voice. Like a blinded prizefighter he stumbles into Damascus; others lead him by the hand, and Saul, humbled, prays to God during three days of complete fasting (Acts 9:8–9, 11).

Saul's turnaround presupposes the reality of the ascended Jesus of Nazareth. Those who reject this possibility cannot give a satisfactory explanation for the swift, radical change in this persecutor.

Luke tells the story of this change in such a way that the contrast between light and darkness is prominent. On the one hand he emphasizes the darkness out of which Saul must be called. He is "breathing threats and murder" (9:1 NASB) and even asks for warrants for Damascus (9:2). Jesus calls him his "persecutor" (9:4: "Saul, Saul, why do you persecute me?"; cf. 9:5: "I am Jesus, whom you are persecuting"). Ananias reminds the Lord of the threat Saul poses, first to the Christian community in Jerusalem (9:13) and now, with his warrants, to Damascus (9:14).

On the other hand, Luke emphasizes the unexpected light that envelops Saul. Immediately he lets himself be baptized (9:18), and immediately he begins to preach in the synagogues (9:20). The people see the new Paul against the background of his very recent history as persecutor (9:21). The people in Jerusalem are afraid of him (9:26), but after he is introduced to them, Paul joins them and is active in the synagogues (9:28–29). The radical thoroughness of his conversion is emphasized especially by the fact that his conversion leads the Jews to making plans to kill him (Damascus, 9:23; Jerusalem, 9:29). The roles have been completely reversed: the Christians now must take *Paul* to safety (9:25, 30).

The result of all this is that the church experiences peace (9:31). The engine that drove the persecution suddenly quits. This is the result of Jesus' personal intervention (9:3–9), in which Ananias is asked to assist (9:10–12, 17–19). The inner freedom with which Paul preaches is the result of the gift of the Spirit (9:17). On a single day, the day of Pentecost, thousands of Jews were converted through Christ and the Spirit and manifested the fruits of faith; now this same process takes place, with intense focus, in one very specific life.

In Acts 9 we do not find specific instructions that Jesus gave Paul. Paul is directed to go to the city, where he will be told what to do (9:6), which apparently involves "coming to faith" as a Christian and the public confession of that faith "by letting himself be baptized." Ananias says that Paul must be filled with the Spirit by opening himself up to the Spirit (9:17). This is thus his call to the Christian faith. The persecutor of Jesus is called to become a worshiper!

Saul was unable to resist this call from God. In his letters Paul characterizes this event as his "calling": "God . . . called me by his grace" (Gal. 1:15). The verb "to call" and the noun "calling" are used frequently in the New Testament. They constitute the standard terminology for coming to faith in Christ. The thought behind it is that the lost unbeliever hears the voice of God calling with such power that he or she cannot do anything but turn around and become a disciple.[9]

For the apostle Paul this confrontation with Christ is the impetus to let go of his opposition to Jesus. For him this does not mean conversion to another religion. In Galatians 1:15 Paul sees his life as having always been under the control of the Almighty: "God, who set me apart from birth, . . . called me by his grace." God was in his life from the beginning, but Saul seriously erred in his rejection of the Messiah. It is the God of his youth who at this point brings him to repentance and faith. As persecutor, Saul had failed to keep pace with God's timetable, but now he is brought back into God's present—the dawning for Israel of the time of the Messiah from heaven! The calling of Saul shows the reality of Jesus' resurrection and ascension.

The attempts to explain the radical change in Paul's life as resulting from a more immanent process merely shift the locus of the miracle but do not explain it. Thus, the Jewish historian of religion Alan Segal has provided a complex reconstruction of Paul's radical change of heart. His transition from Pharisaic Judaism to apocalyptic and mystical Judaism is supposed to have led to the experiencing of ecstasies and revelations, which he now interprets in the light of the (Christian-) apocalyptic community he has joined. This community consisted of both Jewish and Gentile Christians, and Paul ended up with a (Gentile-) Christian interpretation of the visions. Thus the social context influenced the interpretation of his religious experience.[10]

This complicated reconstruction from the perspective of a socially influenced depth-experience shifts the problem to the question how this community of Christians within Judaism could ever have come into existence without the resurrection and ascension. Something similar applies to the idea that Paul saw Jesus in an apocalyptic vision and thereby "arrived at the insight that Jesus was alive." This interpretation, then, does not follow from the facts but from the circumstance that this vision could for Paul the apocalyptic visionary (which, after all, he was in his later years) mean nothing other than that the Crucified One had been raised by God from the dead.[11] Why would an apocalyptic visionary think in this situation of a resurrection from the dead rather than of Jesus having been taken up into heaven after his death? We must add to this the general observation that both the book of Acts and Paul himself do not describe the event near Damascus as a vision but as an actual event and as a calling!

2.5 Evangelist among the Jews

From the perspective of the Sanhedrin, Saul appeared to be a deserter and traitor. He deserted from his post as persecutor and even went over to the enemy by appearing soon thereafter as a preacher in the camp of the Nazarenes.

In Damascus, Saul goes into the synagogues a few days after his baptism to proclaim that Jesus is the Son of God and to show from the Scriptures that Jesus is the Messiah (Acts 9:20, 22). He already knew much about Jesus, and he knew the content of the gospel. Up to this point he had rejected this content in unbelief, but now that he has come to faith in Christ, he can quickly emerge as evangelist among his fellow Jews. Suddenly he finds that the arguments used by Stephen and others (which he possibly had tried to refute in the synagogue of the Jews from Cilicia) now have become his own.

It is understandable that the non-Christian Jews in Damascus want to catch this deserter in his own net: they guard the gates so they can kill him. But Saul does not let himself be intimidated by this ambush attempt—any more than the Christians whom he had chased from Jerusalem had been intimidated. He departs for Jerusalem. This trip took courage, for Saul now has to return to a city where his former friends despise him as a deserter and his former enemies will still shrink from him. But thanks to Barnabas's mediation, Saul is accepted into the circle of the apostles. And he himself makes every effort to convince his erstwhile friends of the reality of Messiah Jesus, even though this means that he now becomes a victim of the very persecution he himself had fostered, so that he has to retreat to Tarsus, where as a citizen of the city he is safe (Acts 9:26–30).

2.6 Paul's Task

From the moment of his turning toward Christ, Saul has a task. Ananias, the Christian, must tell Paul that Jesus sees him as "my chosen instrument to carry (*bastazein*) my name before the Gentiles and their kings and before the people of Israel. I will show him how much he must suffer for my name" (Acts 9:15–16).

The verb *bastazein* means "to bear, to carry." It is sometimes incorrectly translated as "to bring." The image is that of a basket or jug in which one carries something to someone. Jesus wants to bring his name to many, and Saul appears to be the right vessel in which to transport that name. In 2 Corinthians 4:7 Paul describes himself as a "jar of clay" (KJV, "earthen vessel") for the gospel.

The suffering for the name of Jesus flows from the fact that Jesus wants to carry his own name "before the Gentiles and their kings and before the people of Israel." The Crucified One is also a Rejected One: with that name one cannot appear before the authorities or before the Jews who had him crucified. In practice Paul's task, therefore, will mean that he has to appear as prisoner and accused before kings and Jews. Christ needs a martyr to carry his name into palaces and before the Sanhedrin. This will become clear in the second half of Acts.

Saul, better than many others, can witness to the fact that Jesus lives: Paul himself is living proof of it. He was allowed to see Jesus in the light of heaven, and he was allowed to hear directly Jesus' voice and his words (Acts 22:14). It now becomes his task to "be [Jesus'] witness to all men of what you have seen and heard" (Acts 22:15), to be "a servant and . . . a witness of what you have seen of me" (Acts 26:16).

From the outset this task was not limited to the Jews but encompassed the nations who are still in the grip of Satan (Acts 26:17–18). This is not really surprising, since Jesus had already told his disciples before his resurrection to make all nations his disciples (Matt. 28:19) and to preach the gospel to "all creation" (Mark 16:15). What is peculiar is not that Paul's mission will take him to the nations—but that he will come there as the great persecutor who is now a suffering apostle for the same Jesus he once persecuted.

It is important to make a distinction here between "the preaching of Jesus to the nations" and "the preaching to those nations without imposing the requirement of circumcision." Paul's task does not enter into the question that would later become a burning issue—the question of the uncircumcised Christians from the nations. His assignment is limited to this: bearing witness worldwide to what he has heard and seen. That is why the Jews are also included in this task. And Paul makes every effort to bring the gospel to them first: "I was not disobedient to the vision from heaven. First to those in Damascus, then to those in Jerusalem and in all Judea . . . I preached that they should repent and turn to God and prove their repentance by their deeds" (Acts 26:19–20).

2.7 Exemplar of Grace

The manner in which Saul was called made him an exemplar of the grace of God that he would preach. He later writes to Timothy: "Here is a trustworthy saying that deserves full acceptance: Christ Jesus came into the world to save sinners—of whom I am the worst. But for that very reason I was shown mercy so that in me, the worst of sinners, Christ Jesus might display his unlimited patience as an example for those who would believe on him and receive eternal life" (1 Tim. 1:15–16).

Paul's conversion is sometimes erroneously described as the acceptance of a new perspective on the law or on Israel.[12] But Paul was not set free from legalism but from an aversion to the gospel.[13]

At that point he had to leave his life as persecutor of Christians, because Christ made him his prisoner of war and called him into a new service. The secret of Saul's turnaround is the reality of Christ's ascension. The image of the ex-persecutor symbolizes for Christianity the essence of each individual Christian life: God grants grace, at Jesus' request!

GONE TO ARABIA

Saul has barely become a Christian and begun to work as an evangelist among the Jews in Jerusalem and Judea when he disappears after having to flee to the city of his birth, Tarsus.

We would expect that the next time we get news of Paul it will come from this city. And this is indeed true in the book of Acts, where we read that a few years later Barnabas goes looking for Saul and leaves for Tarsus (Acts 11:25). But when we read Galatians 1, we suddenly find the apostle in Arabia. In comparison with the description in Acts, Paul would seem to be completely off course in Galatians 1. From the very beginning it is not easy to follow the tracks of the pioneer for the Messiah.

Furthermore, the chronologies during this first period of Paul's life as a Christian appear to be inconsistent. Almost immediately after his calling Saul is an active evangelist, but after he has fled from Jerusalem to Tarsus (Acts 9:30) there is suddenly a long period of silence. In Acts it seems as if Saul does not start preaching again until many years later, when Barnabas comes to find him and takes him to Antioch (Acts 11:25–26). According to many interpreters, Saul's calling is soon followed by a period often referred to as the "silent years." But how could this active man suddenly quit preaching for a long time, right after having been called to spread the name of Christ everywhere? The silent years involve a period of at least four to seven years (depending on the calculation of the year of Jesus' death and the year of Paul's calling).

Did he need a number of silent years for a gradual spiritual reorientation? Many interpreters feel that Paul had to mature before he could continue preaching.[1] But this assumption does not fit the fact that immediately after his conversion Saul already could be a formidable debater for Christianity in the synagogues in Damascus and Jerusalem.

It would seem more plausible that Saul after his flight to Tarsus continued without interruption to be an evangelist. Was he at that time active in the regions of Syria and Cilicia? In Galatians 1:21 we read that from Jerusalem he went to those areas to spread the Christian faith there. Yet it seems impossible that these activities should be dated during the period following his flight from Jerusalem, shortly after his conversion to Christ. For in Galatians 1:17–21 we read that there were at least three years between Saul's calling and this ministry in Syria and Cilicia—three years during which he worked in Arabia. But how can the trail to Arabia fit into the chronology of Saul's first years as a Christian?

3.1 Arabia

In the first century A.D., Arabia was Israel's neighbor. It included not only the Sinai Peninsula and part of modern Saudi Arabia, but also a large portion of the Transjordan region: the former countries of Ammon, Moab, and Edom. From the highest point of the temple in Jerusalem one could with the naked eye see in the distance one neighboring country: Arabia![2]

Herod Antipas was married to a princess from this country. He was painfully reminded of the close proximity of his father-in-law, King Aretas, when he sent his wife away. Aretas organized a punitive expedition against the country of his former son-in-law, and Herod Antipas was ignominiously defeated. This would indicate that Palestine and Arabia were indeed neighbors.[3]

For the Jews, Arabia was not a remote country. There were Jews and proselytes who lived in Arabia; on the day of Pentecost there were Cretans and Arabs present in Jerusalem (Acts 2:11)![4]

3.2 The Gospel for Arabia

Apparently Saul worked for several years in Arabia as a Christian preacher. His letter to the Galatians makes this clear, and virtually no one doubts the genuineness of this epistle.[5] His preaching apparently led to tension in this region. In 2 Corinthians 11:32–33 we read how the secular authorities even took action against him: "In Damascus the governor under King Aretas had the city of the Damascenes guarded in order to arrest me. But I was lowered in a basket from a window in the wall and slipped through his hands."[6]

Damascus almost certainly was outside (to the north of) the realm of Aretas. It is not a city of Aretas, but rather a "city of the Damascenes."[7] The "governor" (Gr.: *ethnarchēs*) is not in charge of Damascus, as the term "governor" might suggest. Rather, the *ethnarchēs* is in charge of a group of people, so that this "governor" may have been the local leader of the Arabian residential and commercial quarter in Damascus.[8] In that function he could not issue arrest warrants within the city of Damascus. He could, however, post guards outside or inside the city to ambush Saul and murder or kidnap him.[9] The apostle escapes this trap set inside or outside the gate by climbing out of a window in the city wall.[10]

This casual comment in 2 Corinthians shows that highly charged tensions had developed between Aretas of Arabia and Saul the Jewish Christian. This indicates that he must indeed have been active in this region as a preacher. The turmoil that appears to have developed in Arabia has been cause for the authorities to pursue this "agitator" even beyond their borders, all the way to the gates of Damascus.

In Acts we do not read anything about this early preaching of the gospel in Arabia. The topic apparently falls outside the scope and intent of Luke in the composition of his book: Luke describes above all the spread of the gospel in the Roman Empire.

3.3 Ishmael First

For Saul, the journey to Arabia was the first journey of his mission to "the nations." In Galatians 1 he tells how God revealed to him that he was to preach Christ among the Gentiles, and he continues by writing how he immediately departed for Arabia (Gal. 1:16–17).

What moved Paul, in spearheading the preaching to the Gentiles, to start there rather than elsewhere? This may become clearer when we consider the origins of the Arabian people: they are the descendants of Ishmael, Isaac's half brother! Thus they, of all the nations, have the closest links to the patriarch Abraham.[11] And the God of Abraham also gave a promise to Ishmael (Gen. 16:10–12; 21:18).

For Paul this background is important. In his letter to the Galatians he writes about two covenants (Gal. 4:24), represented by Sarah and Hagar respectively. About Hagar he writes, "Now Hagar stands for Mount Sinai in Arabia" (Gal. 4:25). Apart from the playful connections Paul makes between various historical data, we can see that for him there is a direct connection between Arabia and Hagar.

This leads us to surmise that Saul as preacher of the gospel began his journey to the Gentiles at the oldest crossroads—there where the people of Ishmael and the line of Isaac and Israel parted ways. We don't know for sure whether many came to faith through Saul's missionary work, but the fact that his work led to much negative reaction would indicate that his preaching did not go unnoticed. It is usually success that provokes jealousy and enmity! In any case, Saul had to flee after a period of time. The obvious place to go to was across the northern border of Arabia, back to the city he knew both as a Jew and as a Christian: Damascus. He could not have suspected that Aretas would try to kidnap and kill him even there.

3.4 The Mystery of Christ for the Gentiles

The apostle mentions Arabia as the first place where he began to preach to the Gentiles. But how was it that Paul came to work among the Gentiles? What is the origin of this mission to the nations?

Various answers have been given to this question, answers that frequently have something in common. The traditional explanations usually start with the idea that all distinctions between Israel and the nations have been eliminated. According to some interpreters, Paul struggled already before Damascus with the law, and his calling by Christ caused him to abandon permanently the law as the demarcation of a special people.

According to others, the origin of Paul's mission lies especially in the Damascus experience itself. The righteous Pharisee found himself to be a sinner who was made alive by grace—and this becomes emblematic for all people, without distinction. In short, through a radical theological reversal from faith in particularistic grace (through the law, via Israel) to faith in universal grace (through Jesus Christ, for all humanity), the road to the Gentiles opened up quite naturally. On this view, Paul's mission to the Gentiles is a rather unproblematic implication of his Christ experience.[12]

Although this theological explanation seems to make sense—certainly in light of Paul's later epistles—it is nevertheless in conflict with the historical data. Why is Paul after his calling near Damascus a preacher *only to the Jews* and not to the Gentiles? And why, relatively shortly thereafter, does he suddenly and abruptly begin to preach to non-Jews, and then specifically in Arabia? There appears to be a distinction between the moment when Paul became a Christian and the moment when he began to exert himself in mission to the Gentiles.[13]

The fact that some time elapsed between the two forms of preaching could be explained on the basis of the development of the apostle's thinking. But against this argue both the fact that that period is short and the fact that Paul departs for Arabia quite suddenly. Especially the latter does not fit well with the notion of a gradual transition to a different way of working. Rather it would seem that (after his calling) another external factor played a role in Paul's life that suddenly made him a preacher among the Gentiles, beginning in Arabia.[14]

We lack the data to add further details to the period of Saul's activity in Arabia, but the context in which he mentions his journey to the descendants of Ishmael helps us here. The letter to the Galatians deals with the gospel for the Gentiles: the good news that God has mercy on all nations, without the requirement that they must first be circumcised or become members of the Jewish nation. In the first chapter Paul emphasizes that this gospel is not a human invention (Gal. 1:1, 11). He received it himself by revelation (Gal. 1:12), as the data we have would support. Originally he was a persecutor of Christians and a fanatical defender of the Jewish way of life (Gal. 1:13–14). Only God could transform this zealot for Judaism into a preacher to the nations.

It pleased God to do just that (Gal. 1:15a). The Bible reader usually thinks immediately of the events on the road to Damascus: was that not the place where Paul was called and sent? But there is reason to introduce a distinction here between Saul's being called to faith in Jesus the Messiah and the revelation of the gospel without circumcision. A careful translation shows that Galatians 1:15 distinguishes three things:

1. The setting apart from birth that allowed Saul to be from childhood a devoted servant of the God of Israel.
2. The calling to the faith whereby God pardoned the persecutor of Christians.
3. The revelation of God's Son (to preach the good news about him among the Gentiles).

The third event presupposes the first two. The verse reads, "But when God—who [1] set me apart from birth and [2] called me by his grace, was [3] pleased to reveal his Son in me so that I might preach him among the Gentiles . . ." The third comes *after*, and is based on, the first two, yet is distinct from them.[15]

God's revelation of his Son in the apostle Paul is the direct cause of his immediate departure for Arabia (Gal. 1:16–17). This shows that in Galatians 1:17 Paul is not thinking of the time immediately after his calling to the Christian faith (near Damascus). At that point he began first to function as an evangelist among the Jews. The perspective on a worldwide ministry had already opened up, but Paul takes the first step toward a nation outside Israel only after God revealed his Son to him in a special manner.

In this Paul can be compared with Peter. Peter knew that he would be a witness to both Jews and Greeks, but it took a special revelation

(Acts 10) to make Peter enter the home of a Gentile to preach Christ there and even to baptize uncircumcised Gentiles there. Apparently Paul also received a special revelation that made it clear to him that he could bring the good news unconditionally to the Gentiles: he did not first need to make the Gentiles Jewish proselytes, but he could incorporate them directly in Christ through the work of the Spirit.

This gospel without circumcision is what is discussed in Galatians. In the first chapter Paul makes it clear that he received this gospel through "revelation" from Jesus Christ (Gal. 1:12). His calling at Damascus is never called a "revelation" (*apokalypsis*). Galatians 1:12 speaks of a special revelation, which he received after his call at Damascus.

At Damascus Christ had promised Saul that he would receive further revelation about his future task. Thus we read in Acts 26:16 that Jesus says, "I have appeared to you to appoint you as a servant and as a witness of what you have seen of me and what I will show you." Paul speaks of such a later appearance or revelation in Acts 22:17–21:

> When I returned to Jerusalem and was praying at the temple, I fell into a trance and saw the Lord speaking. "Quick!" he said to me. "Leave Jerusalem immediately, because they will not accept your testimony about me." "Lord," I replied, "these men know that I went from one synagogue to another to imprison and beat those who believe in you. And when the blood of your martyr Stephen was shed, I stood there giving my approval and guarding the clothes of those who were killing him." Then the Lord said to me, "Go; I will send you far away to the Gentiles."

Apparently Paul was from time to time allowed to see and hear Jesus via direct visions. This is mentioned only sporadically. Paul generally is silent on matters that cannot be verified. But he hints that he is familiar with "visions and revelations from the Lord" (2 Cor. 12:1). On one of these occasions he was even "caught up to the third heaven . . . to paradise. He heard inexpressible things, things that man is not permitted to tell" (2 Cor. 12:2–4).[16]

Galatians 1 deals with the revelation of the Son in Saul that he "might preach him [as good news] among the Gentiles." And it is precisely about this special revelation that the apostle speaks elsewhere as well, albeit without many details. Thus we read in Ephesians 3:1–13 about the mystery that had long remained hidden, "that through the gospel the Gentiles are heirs together with Israel, members together of one body, and sharers together in the promise in Christ Jesus" (v. 6). This mystery, Paul says, has been "made known to me by revelation" (v. 3).

The same mystery of the salvation of the Gentiles through faith in Christ is mentioned as well in the doxology at the end of Romans, where we also read that it has been made known "through revelation" (Rom. 16:25).

Apparently God has thus given Saul, sometime after his call to faith and after his first work as an evangelist among the Jews, a special revelation. This revelation is the reason why he suddenly knew with certainty that he could preach Jesus Christ as unconditional good news to the Gentiles. After this revelation he left immediately for the nations. And Arabia (Ishmael's descendants) was the first to be given the opportunity to share in this blessing. Thus Paul became the vanguard of the preaching of the gospel to the Gentiles.

3.5 Back in Tarsus—without "Silent Years"

When did this mission to Arabia take place? In any case not immediately after Saul's being called to faith near Damascus. It is impossible to fit Paul's work in Arabia between the first departure from Damascus as a Christian and the first arrival as a Christian in Jerusalem, as some have tried (i.e., between Acts 9:25 and 9:26).[17]

Riesner even questions whether Paul ever preached in Arabia at all.[18] He is of the opinion that Paul followed a prophetic scheme in his journeys and entered the Gentile world from Jerusalem.[19] If that is correct, a missionary journey to Arabia that does not begin in Jerusalem is in effect an a priori impossibility. In any case, according to Riesner, such a journey is out of the question immediately after Paul's flight from Damascus. He thinks that it was already during this flight that Aretas of Arabia guarded the gates (2 Cor. 11:32–33), which would leave little opportunity to preach immediately thereafter in the territory of this king. Yet Paul states emphatically in Galatians 1:16–17 that his assignment to "preach him [as good news] among the Gentiles" is his motivation to travel to Arabia without consultation with Jerusalem. The mention of Arabia in this context would be irrelevant if all this trip entailed was a brief, inactive stay in Arabia during which Paul did not act as bringer of the good news in the land of King Aretas.[20] There is thus reason for asking whether Aretas did not guard the gates until a later occasion and whether the visit to Arabia took place immediately after Paul's calling near Damascus.

Some try to come up with a reconstruction that lets Paul, after his first flight from Damascus (Acts 9:23–25), via the detour of a working stay in Arabia (Gal. 1:17), make his first visit to Jerusalem as a Christian (Acts 9:26–30). The visit to Arabia then concludes again with a flight from Damascus, where Aretas puts guards at the gates. This time Paul escapes again via the wall and he now goes immediately to Jerusalem, where he finally arrives, three years after his conversion and after an active stay in Arabia (Gal. 1:18; Acts 9:26).

But this conflation of Acts 9 and Galatians 1 runs into many problems. If Saul the persecutor of Christians did not return to Jerusalem until three years after his conversion and after a public ministry in Damascus and Arabia, it is strange that the Christians in that city are still afraid of him and still cannot believe that he has become a follower of Christ (Acts 9:26). And why then can Barnabas tell the fearful Christians only of Saul's public actions in Damascus—and of nothing else? Furthermore, preaching to the Gentiles in Arabia would not fit in with the continuity of his preaching to the Jews in Damascus and to the Jews in Jerusalem (Acts 9:20–22, 28–29).[21] Besides, the temple vision in Jerusalem, in which Christ appears to Paul to tell him that he is being sent to the Gentiles (Acts 22:17–21), must be placed before the preaching of the gospel in Arabia, so that it is impossible to place the work mentioned in Galatians 1:17 between Paul's call at Damascus and his first return to Jerusalem.[22]

It is more likely that the preaching in Arabia took place during the period referred to as the "silent years." This is the period between the time when Saul fled from Jerusalem to Tarsus (Acts 9:30) and the time when Barnabas goes looking for him there to involve him in the work in Antioch (Acts 11:25–26).[23]

This leads to the following reconstruction of Paul's movements during this period (see also fig. 1).

1. Saul flees from Jerusalem to Tarsus. Shortly before his flight he had been allowed to see Jesus in a vision in the temple court and he had heard that he would be sent to the Gentiles (Acts 22:21). His flight to Tarsus can therefore not be viewed as a discontinuation of his activities; this city is a safe haven because he holds its citizenship. From there he can, once the danger has passed, undertake new activities.

2. After his flight from Jerusalem, and probably during his stay in Tarsus, Saul receives a new revelation in which it becomes clear to him that the good news of Jesus may be preached to the Gentiles unconditionally. It would seem that this vision fell in approximately the same period as Peter's vision of the clean and unclean animals that gave him

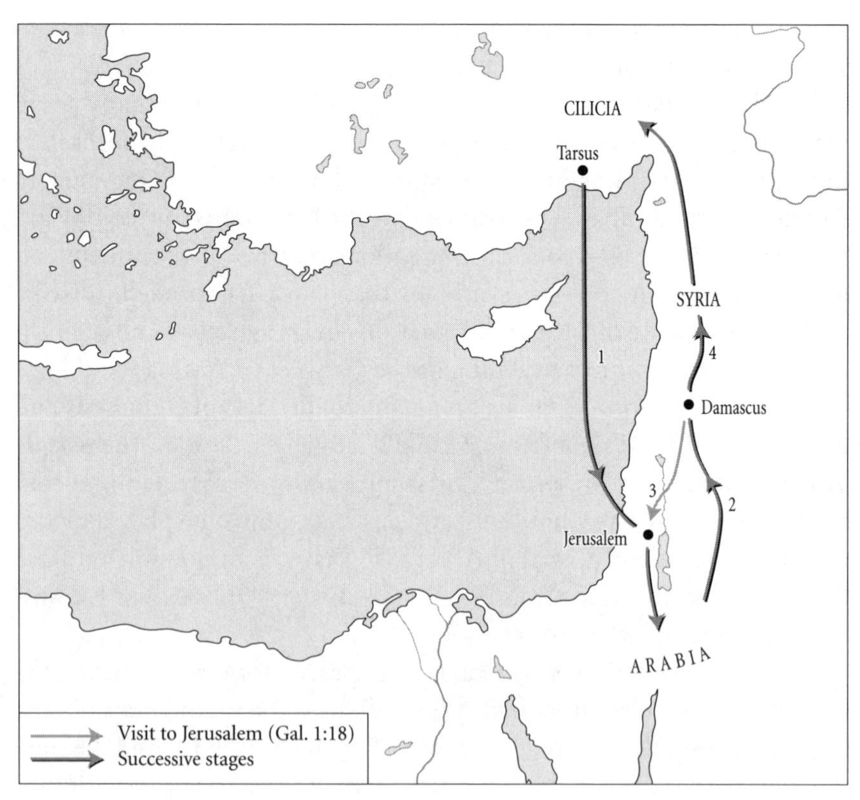

Map 3: *Paul's First Missionary Labors among the Nations*

freedom to cross the threshold of Cornelius the Gentile's home. For it is striking that Peter's vision is told in Acts 10—after the narrative of Saul's conversion and his departure for Tarsus. On the other hand, Paul, when he comes back into the picture in Acts 11, is being sought to help with the preaching to the Gentiles (in Antioch). This means that in the period in between he must have become known as a preacher to the uncircumcised. The revelation that led him to do this then falls in the same period as the vision that moved Peter to baptize uncircumcised believers.

3. While those in Jerusalem still weigh the implications of the events in the house of Cornelius (Acts 11:1–18), Paul, after receiving his revelation, goes without delay directly to Arabia. He misses the deliberations in Jerusalem because he travels directly to his primary mission field without first visiting Jerusalem (Gal. 1:17). Although the paths of Peter and Paul run parallel—both now baptize Gentiles who have come to faith, without circumcision—they have arrived at this position independently. For both, their conviction is based on direct revelation and not on people, nor on each other.

4. The preaching in Arabia puts Saul once again in the position of a fugitive. After a period of work in Arabia he escapes the hostility of King Aretas by fleeing to Damascus. It is not the first time he arrives there, which is why he writes in Galatians 1:17, "I went immediately into Arabia and later returned to Damascus."

5. When the representative (*ethnarchēs*) of Aretas puts guards around Damascus, Saul once again uses the escape route he had used before. When the Jews threatened him during his first visit, he escaped because fellow-Christians let him down in a basket over the wall (Acts 9:25). This proven method is later used again to let him escape Aretas's ambush (2 Cor. 11:32–33). Perhaps a fellow Christian (Ananias?) lived in a house on the wall with a window on the outside that could easily be used as an emergency exit as often as necessary.

6. Paul then goes to Jerusalem for a brief visit. It has by now been three years since he has been with the apostles, and therefore also three years since he had to leave in a great hurry to flee to Tarsus. It seems to make sense for Paul to visit Cephas (Peter) and to speak with him (Gal. 1:18–20). In the meantime, Paul will have heard of the events at

Cornelius's house and the discussions they set off in the church in Jerusalem. There was reason for Paul to visit his fellow-apostle Peter after the radical changes of the preceding years.

7. Two weeks later Paul leaves again, this time to spread the Christian faith in Syria and Cilicia (Gal. 1:21). There he does not remain the solitary preacher he had been—the first preachers from Jerusalem begin to penetrate the region. The persecutions have caused them to travel ever farther, "as far as Phoenicia, Cyprus and Antioch," but "telling the message only to Jews" (Acts 11:19). This changes in Syrian Antioch. There a few men from Cyprus and Cyrene begin "to speak to Greeks also, telling them the good news about the Lord Jesus" (Acts 11:20). Apparently Saul, during his work in Syria and Cilicia at that same time, did not visit the city of Antioch. It is nevertheless possible that his example (in conjunction with Peter's vision) served as a stimulus. For it is striking that Barnabas, from Antioch, goes looking specifically for Saul. Thus it is known that as "preacher to the Gentiles" Saul can be an excellent helper in the city where the Christians from Jerusalem only now are making a first beginning with taking the gospel to the Gentiles.

8. Barnabas goes looking for Saul in Tarsus; he locates Saul, who is put to work in Antioch. Because in the book of Acts Luke says nothing about Saul after he fled to Tarsus until Barnabas finds him, the appearance is created that Saul spent all those years waiting until Barnabas would come to get him. But this cannot be the case. The book of Acts provides hints that lead us to surmise that Saul must have been active after his departure for Tarsus. Otherwise, what reason could Barnabas have had to go looking for Saul to enlist his help specifically for a mission to the Gentiles in Antioch? Even though Luke does not mention it, he leads us to conjecture that in some way Saul, after going to Tarsus, earned a reputation as preacher among non-Jews. Note that Luke does not say that Barnabas went to "get" Saul in Tarsus. He writes only that Barnabas goes there to look for him—but not that he actually finds him immediately in that city. In Acts 11:25–26 we read, "Then Barnabas went to Tarsus to look for Saul, and when he found him, he brought him to Antioch." Barnabas had arrived in Antioch from Jerusalem (Acts 11:22). This means that he likely knew what all the churches of Christ in Judea knew: Saul,

after his brief visit with Peter, preached the gospel in Syria and Cilicia (Gal. 1:21–23). Barnabas knew that he might be able to find Saul "the Tarsian" in the vicinity of Cilicia, and it therefore made sense for him to travel first to Tarsus, Saul's birthplace and temporary place of residence; if Saul was not there, his acquaintances would most likely know where he could be found.

From the moment Saul begins to work with the church in Antioch he is once again within the scope of Luke's narrative. From here on out the paths Paul travels remain complicated, but they are generally easier to follow because we now have the epistles as well as the data from Acts.

FIG. 1
GALATIANS 1 AND ACTS 9

Galatians 1 as a report of Paul's calling in Acts 9	Acts 9	Galatians 1 as the report of a revelation later than Acts 9
"God's Son revealed in me" (1:15–16)	Paul's calling (9:2–19)	Called by grace (1:15a)
Stay/preaching in Arabia (1:17a)		
Return to Damascus (1:17b)	Preaching in the synagogues in Damascus (9:20–25)	
Two-week visit to Cephas in Jerusalem (1:18–19)	Stay with the apostles in Jerusalem; preaching in Jewish territory (9:26–29)	
Preaching in Syria and Cilicia (1:21)	Flight to Tarsus (9:30)	
	(Acts 10: revelation to Peter to go to Cornelius, the Gentile)	Revelation to Paul as the beginning point of his preaching to the nations (1:16)
		Preaching in Arabia (1:17a)
[Silent Years]		Flight to Damascus (1:17b; cf. 2 Cor. 11:32–33)
		Two-week visit to Cephas in Jerusalem (1:18–19)
	(Acts 11:25: Barnabas looks for Saul for help in the mission to the Gentiles in Antioch)	Preaching to the nations in Syria and Cilicia (1:21–24)

3.6 Pioneer in Mercy

On a map of the spread of the gospel, Paul's preaching in Arabia is little more than a blank that cannot be filled in. But the existence of this blank is a significant characteristic of Paul as pioneer for the Messiah. He later writes to Timothy: "God . . . wants all men to be saved and to come to a knowledge of the truth" (1 Tim. 2:4). Saul the persecutor of Christians himself experienced intensely the mercy of God, and he places himself in the service of this mercy from the beginning.

It must have cost Saul the fanatical Jew much self-denial to preach the unconditional gospel of God's mercy to, of all people, the oldest enemies of Israel, the Arabs. Saul follows here in the footsteps of his Master, who prayed even for his enemies. When through revelation Paul is made aware how great the mystery of God's love for this world is, he does not hesitate. He immediately crosses the border into hostile territory: Arabia!

"For Christ's love compels us, because we are convinced that one died for all" (2 Cor. 5:14–15).

4

WANDERING THROUGH SOUTHERN TURKEY

From Antioch, Paul travels with Barnabas through Cyprus and southern Turkey. For Jews this was not a problem. Throughout this region there were synagogues where Jews were welcome, and this is what Paul and Barnabas take advantage of. They visit the synagogues on Cyprus and go to the synagogues in Pisidian Antioch and Iconium (Acts 13:5, 14; 14:1). But they increasingly encounter hostility on the part of the Jews, until they finally become wanderers who must constantly take refuge, from Pisidian Antioch to Iconium (Acts 13:50–51) and from Iconium to Lystra (Acts 14:4–7), from where they are chased in the direction of Derbe (Acts 14:19–20).

The result of this trip is that God opens a door of faith for the Gentiles as well (Acts 14:27). Paul and Barnabas are guided on their journey by the Holy Spirit who had sent them (Acts 13:2). Again and again Paul the wandering pioneer is driven from a city—but new disciples of Christ remain behind after his forced departure (Acts 14:22).

Usually this first period of wandering is called the first missionary journey because it is the first time in the book of Acts that Luke describes a period of Paul's traveling. But it is in fact not Paul's first missionary journey; rather, it may already be his third. The first journey took him to Arabia, the second to the regions of Syria and Cilicia. We know little or nothing about either of these two. Luke's report of this journey to Turkey allows us to surmise to some extent the apostle's missionary strategy.

Paul, like Barnabas, was already familiar with preaching to the Greeks. But are the Jews henceforth passed over in this missionary effort aimed at the Gentiles? The report of the wanderings in southern Turkey shows that this is not the case.

4.1 Not Apart from Jerusalem

When the gospel is brought to the Gentiles in Syrian Antioch, many come to faith, and here they are called "Christians" for the first time (Acts 11:20–21, 24, 26). But this does not mean that ties with the mother church in Jerusalem are severed. On the contrary!

1. When they hear about the conversion of the Greeks in Antioch, the church in Jerusalem sends Barnabas to that city to evaluate what is happening (Acts 11:22). Barnabas is a man full of faith and the Holy Spirit. Through that Spirit he can, as a Jew, rejoice in God's grace, and he encourages the uncircumcised Christians to persevere in their faith in Jesus Christ (Acts 11:23–24). The Christians accept his visit and his initiative to involve Saul. Thus the Greek Christian community is from the very beginning connected with the church from Israel.

2. The Greek Christian community also is aware of its obligation to stand in solidarity with the believers in Palestine. When prophets arrive from Jerusalem and one of them, Agabus, prophesies that a famine is coming, the church in Antioch decides to organize a collection to help the brothers in Judea. Barnabas and Saul, with their strong ties to Jerusalem, deliver this financial aid to the elders in Jerusalem (Acts 11:27–30; 12:25).

This shows that the new community of Greek Christians remains rooted in the older church from the Jews. The Christians in Jerusalem watch over the new converts, who in turn show their love for the ancient people of God.

Thus, when Barnabas and Saul, as instructed by the Holy Spirit, are sent out from Antioch, it does not mean that there is to be a second preaching initiative side by side with the first: the mission to the Gentiles as distinct from the mission to the Jews. The gospel remains targeted at the Jews, but is no longer limited to them. The vision is not changed—it is broadened.

4.2 In the Service of the Spirit

Some studies describe the so-called first missionary journey as a typically Antiochian matter.[1] Not until the second and third journeys would Paul work as an independent apostle, without ties to Antioch and entirely according to his own lights. On the first journey he must function within the strategy of the church in Antioch. More than once this has been linked to the notion that it was the break with that church that forms the background of the later tensions in Galatia.[2]

But it is not correct to call this first journey an Antiochian project.

1. In Acts 13:1–3 we read how the journey of Barnabas and Saul began. During a period of praying and fasting, the Holy Spirit spoke (probably through one of the prophets): "Set apart for me Barnabas and Saul for the work to which I have called them." It is not the church that decides to send out missionaries, but the Spirit asks the church to relinquish two of its prophets (cf. Acts 13:1).
2. The work Barnabas and Saul are to perform is the work to which the Spirit had called them earlier. We see here not the program of a church but the calling of two people.
3. With fasting and prayer the church lays hands on them and lets them go. There is no question here of a sending by the church but rather of a making available to the Spirit. They are "committed to the grace of God" for the work to which the Spirit had called them earlier (Acts 14:26).

Barnabas and Saul thus do not go out into the world to start a new, Antiochian project. They are given the freedom by their brothers and sisters in Antioch to continue their task as preachers elsewhere. Saul was called to preach Christ without restrictions in this world, and

Barnabas was in wholehearted agreement with this generous offer of grace through the preaching of the Christian faith.

4.3 First the Jews

The first missionary journey is often viewed as the first preaching directed exclusively at the Gentiles. But this is a one-sided perspective. Barnabas and Saul, as they penetrate deeper into the world of the Gentiles, turn consistently to the Jews first.

On Cyprus none less than the Gentile proconsul Sergius Paulus comes to faith in Christ. This is so amazing that the story is told in detail (Acts 13:6–12), but the fact of the matter is that the work in Cyprus consisted mostly of preaching the Word of God in the synagogues (Acts 13:5).

At Pisidian Antioch Gentiles accept the Word of God, and in the entire region non-Jews come to the faith (Acts 13:48–49), but this happens only after the Jews have rejected the gospel in their synagogues (Acts 13:45–46). Besides, the core of the new Christian community as a whole still consists of Jews and worshipers of God (Acts 13:43). These "worshipers of God" lived in the shadow of the synagogue and worshiped the God of Israel. They did not let themselves be circumcised and thus did not belong to the people of Israel, but they stood in close spiritual kinship with Israel.

At Iconium a large crowd comes to faith, but this happens because of the manner in which Barnabas and Paul speak in the synagogue. And the believers include "Jews and Gentiles" (Acts 14:1).

But many Jews closed themselves to the gospel. They began persecuting Barnabas and Paul and expelled them from the synagogues. But this did not put an end to their preaching, for these apostles were convinced that the gospel was not limited to the Jews. Therefore they could, so it seems, speak directly to the Gentiles in Lystra, until their Jewish enemies overtook them there also (Acts 14:7, 19–20).

From the course of events during Paul's wanderings through southern Turkey we can deduce that "preaching to the nations" does not mean that Israel was passed over. The reverse is true. As Paul later states in his letter to the Romans, "The gospel . . . is the power of God

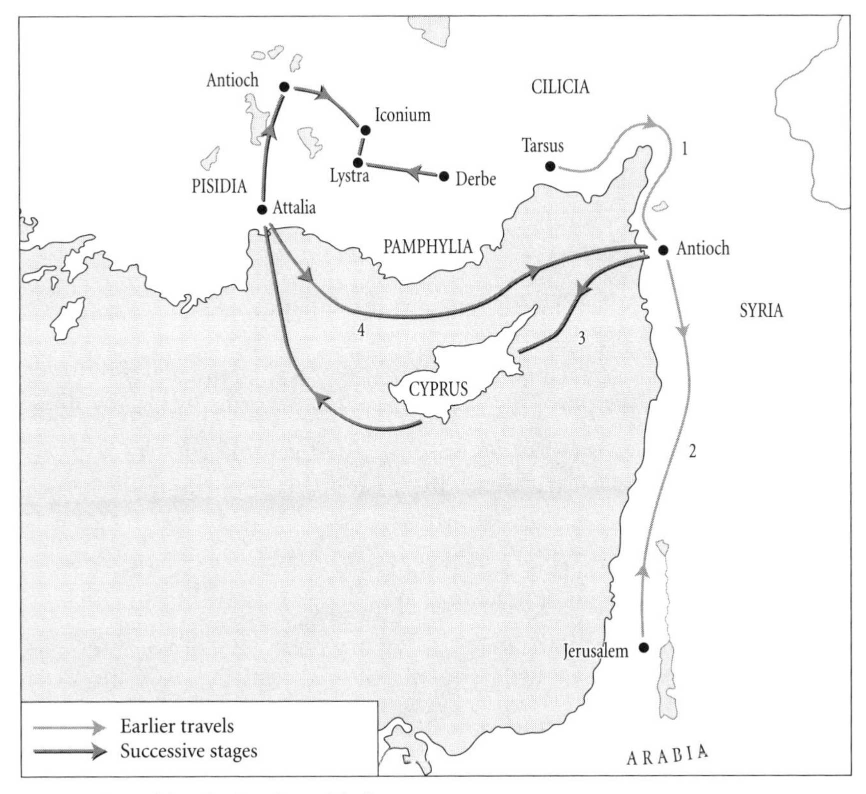

Map 4: *Preaching in Southern Turkey*

for the salvation of everyone who believes: first for the Jew, then for the Gentile" (Rom. 1:16).

We continue to see this same pattern in Paul's work again and again. On his later journeys he also goes first to the synagogues (Acts 16:13, Philippi; 17:1–4, Thessalonica; 17:10–11, Berea; 17:17, Athens; 18:4, Corinth; 19:8–9, Ephesus). Even in Rome, where in the meantime a Gentile Christian community has been established, Paul contacts already on the third day after his arrival the Jewish leaders to speak with them about the gospel (Acts 28:17–29). Paul also takes into consideration the feelings of the Jews in a given region: thus he lets Timothy be circumcised because of the Jews in the area of Lystra and Iconium, since everyone knew that his father was a Greek (Acts 16:3).

As a pioneer for Christianity, Paul, together with others, makes it clear that Christianity is not a second religion that stands side by side with, or replaces, the Israelite religion. Christianity is the fulfillment of the Old Testament faith. Therefore Christianity always begins with Israel, even when it captures a place in the hearts of the Gentiles. Among all nations, Paul is a messenger of the Messiah of Israel!

4.4 The Energy of the Gospel

In the synagogues, Barnabas and Paul preach the appearing of God's Messiah, Jesus, and they show how his coming is the fulfillment of the promises to Abraham (Acts 13:32–33). At the same time they prove the kingship of this Lord Jesus Christ by performing many amazing miracles in his name. For the Gentiles the energy of the gospel is striking, especially because it is a healing energy, superior to the feats of various kinds of miracle workers of that day.

Thus Barnabas and Paul meet on Cyprus the Jewish sorcerer Bar-Jesus, also called Elymas. When he attempts to turn Proconsul Sergius away from the Christian faith, the apostles strike him with temporary blindness, against which this false prophet is powerless (Acts 13:6–11). For the proconsul this is an impressive event that shatters the allure of Elymas's magic. Sergius now listens to the teaching of the Lord Jesus (Acts 13:12).

In Iconium the Lord also bears witness to the word of his grace: he enables Barnabas and Paul "to do miraculous signs and wonders" (Acts 14:3).

In Lystra a man is healed who had been paralyzed from birth and could not walk. This miracle proves that the Lord of the gospel has divine power. Barnabas and Paul are even thought to be the greatest gods in the Greek pantheon: Zeus and Hermes (Acts 14:8–18).

Also in Lystra a miracle takes place that gives the impression that Paul is "untouchable": after being stoned and left for dead, he gets up and walks into the city (Acts 14:19–20).

When Barnabas and Paul return from this journey, they have much to tell about "all that God had done through them" (Acts 14:27; 15:4).

These signs and wonders are accompanied by a notable display of weakness and by the experience of much suffering on the part of the apostles. This sets them apart from the magicians of that day: individuals with power liked to assert themselves and did not want to be underappreciated. And the people did not dare interfere with them out of fear of retaliation by the divine powers these individuals controlled. But Barnabas and Paul, with all their miracles, are still "wanderers" and "hunted men" in southern Turkey. And they calmly let this suffering happen to them, thus setting themselves apart from the accepted norm. They show that what they do is not about them, as if they were some kind of "supermen" (cf. Acts 14:11–12, 15), but about the Lord Jesus Christ, for whose sake they accept suffering.

On the later journeys we find this same curious combination of power used on behalf of others and weakness borne by themselves. In this the apostles reflect the likeness of their Master, who also went about doing good and who also suffered.[3] For example, in Ephesus Paul is famous as a miracle worker. Even the handkerchiefs and aprons of this preacher can be used to heal the sick and to cast out demons (Acts 19:11–12). On the other hand, no lightning from heaven strikes the people when they form a mob to lynch this opponent of the ancient gods (Acts 19:23–40). Paul is forced to retreat and leave Ephesus!

On Malta Paul appears to be invulnerable to the revenge of the gods when he survives the bite of a poisonous snake. Yet he remains a prisoner who is being taken to Rome (Acts 28:1–10).

In his letters Paul more than once points back to the powers that accompanied the coming of the gospel. "The things that mark an apostle—signs, wonders and miracles—were done among you with great perseverance" (2 Cor. 12:12). The power demonstrated alongside the preaching validates its content. Thus the apostle writes, "My message and my preaching were not with wise and persuasive words, but with a demonstration of the Spirit's power, so that your faith might not rest on men's wisdom, but on God's power" (1 Cor. 2:4–5). And in Romans 15:18–19 he sums it up by speaking of "what Christ has accomplished through me in leading the Gentiles to obey God by what I have said and done—by the power of signs and miracles, through the power of the Spirit. So from Jerusalem all the way around to Illyricum, I have fully proclaimed the gospel of Christ."[4]

4.5 Christian Communities New and Old

It is striking that the wanderings through southern Turkey suddenly change into a return to Antioch, and that Barnabas and Paul do not take the most direct route (from Derbe to Antioch) but retrace their steps and travel back via a long detour to first visit the churches they have founded and to encourage them. The newly converted Christians know that Barnabas and Paul are on their way back to Antioch and that they want to tell the church there what the Lord has done among the Jews and Gentiles in this region. The young communities can thereby gain awareness of their connectedness with the older churches. The "frontier" joins the "settled region" in this growth phase of Christianity.

However, the new churches are not incorporated into an organizational structure or made to join the Jewish people through circumcision. They are, with prayer and fasting, "committed . . . to the Lord, in whom they had put their trust" (Acts 14:23b). Barnabas and Paul encourage them to be steadfast in that faith and to realize that "we must go through many hardships to enter the kingdom of God" (Acts 14:22). The apostles themselves have endured much persecution during their wanderings through southern Turkey, and they now teach these new Christians that this is part of what it means to serve the Crucified One (Acts 14:22).

The group of believers in each city is given a form of local organization through the appointment of elders: responsible leaders comparable to those found in other groups and voluntary associations (Acts 14:23a). It is therefore incorrect to characterize the churches in this region as Antiochian churches with which Paul then lost contact after his break with Antioch (as some infer from Gal. 2).

4.6 The Work Completed

In Acts 14:27 we read that Barnabas and Paul give a report to the church in Antioch about "all that God had done through them and how he had opened the door of faith to the Gentiles." This wording shows how little the preaching of the gospel followed a systematic plan.[5]

The return to Antioch is rejected in some of the more recent reconstructions of Paul's life. It is assumed that it was Luke who turned the journey to southern Turkey into a single journey with a clear beginning and end. In reality Barnabas and Paul then traveled from Turkey on into Greece.[6] What Luke presents as the first and second journeys is thought to have been in fact one long journey. However, the historicity of this first journey is convincingly defended by Breytenbach.[7]

1. In retrospect we might get the impression that Barnabas and Paul had a plan for this first journey. Their route as drawn on maps might suggest this to some extent. But in actual fact the journey through southern Turkey was determined mostly by "time and chance" or by "incidents and aggression." It is the Spirit of Christ who "had opened the door of faith to the Gentiles" (Acts 14:27), but Barnabas and Paul had to discover day by day the path that led to that door. They did not set out with an itinerary that they then followed.

2. Apparently they felt at some point that their task had been finished, perhaps because, as they traveled east to Derbe, they came near Cilicia where the gospel had been brought before. In any case, they return from a journey that for them was not the first of three, but a work complete in itself. There is no indication that another journey is being considered or planned. Paul is the pioneer of Christianity, but not its strategist!

5

CALLED TO ACCOUNT

The earliest history of the Christian church was stormy. Within a short time there were thousands of believers in Jerusalem. Not much later Peter baptized the first Gentiles. And in the period immediately following, the Christian faith soon gained an increasingly large number of adherents in the Gentile world outside Palestine. The outpouring of the Holy Spirit was followed by an unforeseen and surprising series of developments.

During those early years the Christians were more than once hard put to keep up with those developments. The rapid growth of the church in Jerusalem led after some time to internal conflicts, which became the impetus for the appointment of an administrative council of seven wise men (Acts 6:1–7). The reports of Peter's actions at the home of the Gentile Cornelius received a critical response in the mother church in Jerusalem. Only after Peter explained how the Spirit guided his steps did peace return among the believers (Acts 11:1–18). The large increase in the numbers of uncircumcised Christians outside Palestine also led to reactions from the circle of the first disciples (Acts 15:1).

The leaders in the preaching to the Greeks are accused of neglecting a critical step. They bring the new Christians only halfway. Is accepting Israel's Messiah not supposed to lead to incorporation into the people of God? How can one belong to the King of Israel without joining the people of that King?

It is understandable that those who had taken the lead in preaching to the Greeks (Barnabas and Paul) end up, after their return from southern Turkey, at the center of this conflict in Antioch (Acts 15:2). The time for accountability has come. How do the actions of Paul and Barnabas outside Palestine relate to the revelation of God to his people Israel?

5.1 What Happens to Godliness?

The unrest begins in Antioch when Christians from Judea arrive who teach the uncircumcised Christians that "unless you are circumcised, according to the custom taught by Moses, you cannot be saved" (Acts 15:1). They do not say that circumcision is the way to salvation. Salvation is through faith in Christ. But that faith can, according to these teachers, not be separated from Moses.

This reaction is quite understandable. What happened in those days was revolutionary. There are already uncircumcised adherents of Messiah Jesus far beyond Antioch! Does this not cause Moses to lose his significance? Are not the law and the prophets sacrificed for the sake of Jesus? The Jewish Christians are of the opinion that the new development (the gospel for the Gentiles) must be a continuation and extension of the past relationship that God had built with mankind (making Israel the gate to becoming his people).

It is not necessary to describe this conflict as a collision between legalism and grace. The plea for the circumcision of the new Christians has nothing to do with a disdain for Messiah Jesus. On the contrary. These Christians from Judea cannot imagine that Messiah Jesus would want to have subjects who refuse to become part of God's people.

Joining God's people finds expression especially in a particular lifestyle. Judaism is not built on confessional documents but on conduct. The question that is always at the center of attention is, What is the right conduct to honor God? Characteristic are matters such as Sabbath observance, circumcision, dietary laws, and sacrifices. These are the forms that give expression to godliness. How could one possibly be saved without godliness and the expressions of godliness? How could one serve the Lord while at the same time giving the appearance of neglecting his law, which he gave at Sinai? In Jerusalem, some Christians from the party of the Pharisees state the matter this way: "The Gentiles must be circumcised and required to obey the law of Moses" (Acts 15:5).

Thus the crisis that develops in Antioch is religio-ethical in nature.[1]

5.2 Being a Christian without Becoming a Jew

Like earlier conflicts, this one also ends up being discussed in Jerusalem (Acts 15:1, 6), where the apostles and the elders are (the disciples from the time of Jesus' life on earth). To them Jesus gave the power to bind and to loose, to make authoritative pronouncements (Matt. 16:19).

As with earlier conflicts, it is Peter who speaks the words of resolution on behalf of the apostles (Acts 15:7–11; cf. 11:4–17). Before Peter spoke, Barnabas and Paul had already talked about what God had done through them, but their report met with severe criticism (Acts 15:4–5). But after Peter speaks, the climate changes. Again Barnabas and Paul relate the signs and wonders God has done through them among the Gentiles. This time the whole assembly is quiet and listens attentively (Acts 15:12).[2]

What did Peter say? He reminded those present of two things. (1) God himself gave his Holy Spirit to uncircumcised believers. He did not make a distinction between circumcised and uncircumcised but cleansed through faith the hearts of Greeks as well as Jews (Acts 15:7–9). (2) The godliness of the nation of Israel has been so disappointing through the centuries that there is no reason to put the yoke of the law on new fellow-believers (Acts 15:10–11). The first argument reminds Peter's hearers of the events at Cornelius's home and the vision that preceded them. The second argument fits in with Stephen's speech (Acts 7) and also with Jesus' diatribe against the Pharisees and teachers of the law (Matt. 23). Peter here in fact also incorporates the significance of the baptism of repentance of John the Baptist. He, the last prophet of the old covenant, had already said that there is little reason left to say "We have Abraham as our father," for "out of these stones God can raise up children for Abraham" (Matt. 3:9).

What is at issue here is the humbling of oneself about one's past and present, combined with the joy over the new beginning that God now makes with both Greek and Jew!

Jesus' brother James from the circle of the earliest disciples lends support to Peter's words. He does so with proof from the Scriptures (Amos 9:11–12): in the latter days God will restore the house of David, and then "all the nations that bear my name" will seek the Lord. The extraordinary element here is that it is the *Gentiles* (lit.) "upon whom my name is called" (Acts 15:17 KJV).

Peter and James thus see continuity between past and present. The God of Israel gave the law and now gives the Messiah. His name remains decisive. But the nation of Israel has proven that it cannot live under the law nor live up to it. God intervened and gave the Messiah. A better way of salvation—but coming from the same Lord. God opens up a new way—but it remains the God of Abraham, Isaac, and Jacob who opens it up!

Anyone who accepts the Messiah of God therefore does not (any longer) have to become a Jew to gain a share in this God of Israel!

5.3 Being a Christian without Remaining a Gentile

James sees the Gentile Christians as people over whom the name of the God of Israel was spoken when they were baptized in the name of Jesus. This means that they can no longer continue to worship idols. Conversion to Christ implies turning around to the one God, the Creator of heaven and earth, the God of Abraham and the Father of the Son of David.

James's proposal is twofold. (1) He proposes to "not make it difficult for the Gentiles who are turning to God" (Acts 15:19); the Holy Spirit himself does not make it difficult! Therefore the final decision reads, "It has seemed good to the Holy Spirit and to us to impose on you no further burden than these essentials" (Acts 15:28 NRSV). (2) He also proposes the specific essentials that the Gentiles who turn to God must adhere to: abstention from anything contaminated by idols (Acts

15:20). Accepting the Christ of God implies a radical break with the idols of the Greek world which the Gentiles had served before.[3]

This requirement to make a break with idols is elaborated in a few brief points: "abstain from things [NIV: food] polluted by idols, from sexual immorality, from the meat of strangled animals and from blood" (Acts 15:20). In the book of Acts this list occurs three times. In all three lists the point about idols comes first, while the second, third, and fourth items are given in reverse sequence in the decree itself (Acts 15:29) and when the decision is cited later (Acts 21:25). This variation in order does not appear to be particularly significant. It may be that the last three items are in fact a more specific interpretation of the one that always comes first: "things polluted by idols."

In the pagan world sexual immorality or fornication was acceptable (1 Cor. 5:1), but in the eyes of Israel's God it was an abomination (1 Cor. 6:13–20), and this remains true after Pentecost.

In the world of idols the drinking of blood is given magical significance, but the people of Israel have learned not to rely in any way on animistic powers. The Jewish people were therefore forbidden to drink blood (Lev. 7:26–27). This prohibition is not part of the dietary laws; rather, it stands by itself and is directed against idolatry.

It is more difficult to determine the meaning of "things strangled" (KJV; the NIV gives an interpretive paraphrase: "the meat of strangled animals"). In one manuscript (D) the phrase has even been omitted in all three instances![4] The prohibition against "things strangled" is probably a refinement of the prohibition against the drinking of blood. In the case of strangulation, the blood remains in the meat. In idol worship the meat of strangled animals was sometimes thought to have special powers because the "soul" was still in the meat. But the phrase has also been interpreted as symbolic of all actions that cheat or shortchange one's neighbor so that the neighbor is in danger of being "strangled" by injustice.[5]

When we read the four items from the clearest to the most obscure, we can conclude that what is at issue here is in any case the avoiding of contamination with idolatry: not only direct participation in sacrificing to idols is prohibited from now on, but also the "natural" life related to idolatry, in which the powers of sex and blood are given unbridled free rein.

The uncircumcised Christian must make a break with the idols and with related superstition and immorality. The four items delineate a broad area of which only a few salient points are mentioned.[6]

These four points thus are directed against life in the world of idols. They do not put the Gentile Christians under the yoke of the law, but they do put them under the yoke of Israel's God. The law of Moses remains valid for the Jews themselves. James concludes his proposal with the comment, "For Moses has been preached in every city from the earliest times and is read in the synagogues on every Sabbath" (Acts 15:21). It looked as if preachers such as Barnabas and Paul were busy eradicating the law of Moses from the world. But they will not be able to do this, because this law for all Jews has long been read in the synagogues in the whole world.

Furthermore, Barnabas and Paul do not attack the Jewish way of life. The question is not how Jews must henceforth live, but whether Gentile Christians must be made subject to that same law of Moses. In a sense James establishes a bifurcation here to which he later refers when Paul arrives in Jerusalem at the end of his third missionary journey. James then asks Paul to make it clear that he most definitely does not "teach all the Jews who live among the Gentiles to turn away from Moses, telling them not to circumcise their children or live according to our customs" (Acts 21:21). Paul must show that, on the contrary, he himself is "living in obedience to the law" (Acts 21:24). And James goes on to say, "As for the Gentile believers, we have written to them our decision that they should abstain from food sacrificed to idols, from blood, from the meat of strangled animals and from sexual immorality" (Acts 21:25). Here it becomes apparent that the law has not been abrogated as the rule for Israelite godliness, but that the law is not imposed on Gentiles who let themselves be baptized in Christ's name and who come to faith in Israel's God.

According to some, these four points constitute a compromise. For the sake of the Jews, the Gentile Christians should take into consideration a few Jewish sensibilities: (1) things that have indirectly been "contaminated" by idols; (2) marriages in degrees of consanguinity that are unacceptable to Jews; (3) the consumption of blood; and (4) eating meat from strangled animals.[7] Jacob Jervell follows the same exegesis but does not want to speak of a compromise. According to him it was customary that Gentile Christians were exempted from circumcision but not from the law.[8] These "Judaizing" exegetical approaches to the four points move from unclear (blood and strangled animals) to clear (idolatry and fornication) and thereby detract from that which is clear.

1. The word fornication (*porneia*; NIV "sexual immorality") is much too general to serve without further clarification as a specific term for degrees of consanguinity in marital relationships.
2. The phrase "things polluted by idols" (Acts 15:20) is parallel to the phrase "food sacrificed to idols" (Acts 15:29); both cases involve idol worship as a whole, not secondary or derivative matters.
3. The terms "blood" and "strangled" do not relate to any dietary laws but to abstinence from superstition and excesses such as are connected with idol worship. The keeping of these commandments (which are also found in the Old Testament) has nothing to do with a compromise for the sake of some of the Jews, but rather with the permanent requirement to abstain—also for uncircumcised Christians—from all forms of idolatry.[9]
4. The four items listed are not presented as a compromise or as something to be added to the faith, but as essentials: they must be characteristic of everyone who turns to the one true God.
5. James's reference to the reading of the law of Moses in all the synagogues (Acts 15:21) cannot be used as an argument for urging Gentile Christians to be considerate toward the Jews. If this were the case, James would have had to point to the presence of Jews in the Christian church. Instead, he points to the synagogues, in which the Gentile Christians have no part. Furthermore, he does not point to any "sensibilities of Jews" but to the permanent significance of the law in the synagogues—which is not at issue here.

In his first letter to the Thessalonians Paul makes it very clear that conversion to Christ implies a turning away from idols and a return to the true God. He writes, "You turned to God from idols to serve the living and true God, and to wait for his Son from heaven, whom he raised from the dead—Jesus, who rescues us from the coming wrath" (1 Thess. 1:9–10). The apostolic decree asks of the idol-worshiping Gentiles who are baptized in Christ "the obedience that comes from faith" in the true God (Rom. 1:5).[10]

It is therefore understandable that there is a measure of correspondence between the apostolic decree and two kinds of rules in later Judaism:

1. The so-called Noachide commandments, which describe the characteristics of the "righteous Gentile" who does not belong to Israel but will nevertheless have a place in eternal life.[11]
2. Rules for the "alien living among you," derived from Leviticus 17–18.[12] Both involve (later) rules that apply to non-Jews and that formulate minimum requirements to be accepted as a righteous Gentile or resident alien.[13] Such rules naturally reflect the most essential aspects of the Jewish faith.[14] A decisive distinction between these two sets of rules and the apostolic decree, however, is that Acts 15 does not deal with unbelievers but with fellow-believers over whom the name of the Lord has been spoken. Besides, there are quite a few differences between the decree and the two sets of rules.[15]

5.4 Christian Ethics

The so-called apostolic decree has become the earliest fundamental tenet of Christianity. This decision is the first one that is distributed among all Christians as a "foundational document."

In Acts 16:4 we read that Paul, during a subsequent visit to the young churches in southern Turkey, "delivered the decisions reached by the apostles and elders in Jerusalem for the people to obey." Luke is not in the habit of repeating matters that are generally known. Thus he mentions the appointment of elders in the young churches once

(Acts 14:23), and in the rest of his book he assumes that this is a known fact (cf. Acts 20:17). There is therefore every reason to assume that Paul in his later work continued to give the apostolic decree to newly founded churches, as he immediately began to do in southern Turkey, according to Luke.

This is also apparent from the fact that Paul can allude to this decree in his letters. In his first letter to Thessalonica he writes about the manner in which we must live as Christians: "For you know what instructions we gave you by the authority of the Lord Jesus. It is God's will that you should be sanctified: that you should avoid sexual immorality" (1 Thess. 4:2–3). The reference to instructions that had been given earlier, combined with a striking similarity in wording with the apostolic decree (*apechesthai tēs porneias*), makes it likely that Paul reminds his readers here of part of that decree. In the same context we also see a statement that is reminiscent of the tenor of the decree as a whole: "For God did not call us to be impure, but to live a holy life. Therefore, he who rejects this instruction does not reject man but God, who gives you his Holy Spirit" (1 Thess. 4:7–8).

In his first letter to the Corinthians the apostle takes great pains to make clear to the stubborn Corinthians the necessity of the prohibition on the eating of "food offered to idols" (the term is the same as that used in the apostolic decree: *eidōlothyton*). His lengthy discussion in 1 Corinthians 8:1–11:1 leads up to the following statement: "Do I mean then that a sacrifice offered to an idol is anything, or that an idol is anything? No, but the sacrifices of pagans are offered to demons, not to God, and I do not want you to be participants with demons" (1 Cor. 10:19–20).

More than once we see idolatry and sexual immorality mentioned close together in Paul's epistles (1 Cor. 5:10–11; 6:9; 10:7–8; Eph. 5:5) along with forms of licentiousness (Gal. 5:19–21; Eph. 4:17–24). The lists of vices from which Christians should abstain can be viewed as more extensive variants of the short list in the apostolic decree.[16]

Familiarity with this apostolic decree became so general that the terminology would recur in a later letter to Thyatira, a church in western Turkey. There a false prophetess seduces the church into "sexual immorality and the eating of food sacrificed to idols." When the church condemns her, Christ "will not impose any other burden" on the church than to "hold on to what you have" (Rev. 2:20–25).

5.5 Exemplar of Godliness

The fact that the apostle Paul preached the gospel without restriction to all people and administered baptism also to those who came directly from paganism, without circumcision, led to evil rumors about Paul, from Jerusalem to Rome. In Jerusalem the rumor was spread that Paul taught "all the Jews who live among the Gentiles to turn away from Moses" (Acts 21:21), and in Rome allegations made the rounds that he supposedly taught "Let us do evil that good may result" (Rom. 3:8). Thus Paul gets caught between Jew and Greek. And he remains for the rest of his life a man "called to account."

But in reality this pioneer for Messiah Jesus is a champion of true godliness on the part of both Jews and Greeks. The redemption *through* Christ is a redemption *toward* God, the God whom Paul himself served from his youth. In his farewell to the elders of Ephesus the apostle voluntarily gives account of himself: "I have not hesitated to preach anything that would be helpful to you but have taught you publicly and from house to house. I have declared to both Jews and Greeks that they must turn to God in repentance and have faith in our Lord Jesus" (Acts 20:20–21).

6

VANISHED IN GREECE

After the conference in Jerusalem, Barnabas and Paul return to Antioch. At that point there are no plans yet for further journeys to other regions. During these weeks Paul certainly did not expect that within a few years he would make a journey through Macedonia, the birthplace of the world-conqueror Alexander the Great and the cradle of Hellenism, nor that he would give a speech on the Areopagus in the ancient cultural center, Athens. How did Paul end up so suddenly in Greece, and why did he stay there for an extended period of time?

6.1 The Meandering Trail to Greece

Without planning and via a roundabout way, Paul ends up in Greece, first in Macedonia in the north, then in Athens in the south.

There were no specific plans to go in this direction.[1] Paul's first plan for a new journey from Antioch was to go in the direction of Cyprus and southern Turkey—the regions that they had visited before. But the initiative to pay another visit with Barnabas to these churches failed. As preparations for the journey were being made, a conflict arose about whether or not to take along John Mark, who had given up halfway through the previous journey. Paul and Barnabas could not come to an agreement, and they decided to travel separately.[2] This second plan is implemented. Barnabas goes with John Mark to Cyprus. Paul and Silas also travel west, but over land, via Syria and Cilicia. Thus, Barnabas goes to the starting point of the previous journey (Cyprus), while Paul goes to the last stops on the previous trip (Derbe and Lystra). Here Timothy is added to the traveling party as "junior helper" (Acts 15:36–16:3).

Apparently Paul did visit a number of cities where he had already founded churches on his first journey. He leaves the apostolic decree with the churches in these cities (Acts 16:4); thus the young churches may know that they have been accepted by the Jewish Christian fellowship in Jerusalem and that as Christians they are encouraged to serve the God of Israel and to break with idolatrous practices.

It is unclear what Paul's further plans were. Apparently he does more than simply visit the existing churches. He appears to have made plans to push farther to the north or to the west in Turkey with the gospel. Thus he travels with Silas and Timothy through Phrygia and Galatia (Acts 16:6), two neighboring regions. After Paul visits Phrygia and then Galatia, he veers off into an easterly direction. This is not too surprising once we realize that Paul is not busy implementing the so-called second missionary journey. He has no plans whatsoever to go to Greece. He travels around in Turkey, and his wandering movements can be explained by more or less chance circumstances, such as whether a road that was blocked is open, the presence of contacts in a given region, the avoidance of obstacles, and unexpected illness. Thus it is also well possible that he intends to travel from Pisidia in the south, via its northern neighbor Phrygia, westward to Asia (along the western coast) to preach there. But the Holy Spirit prevents this (Acts 16:6), and they may have decided to go in a more easterly direction from Phrygia, toward Galatia. The way Luke phrases the narrative at this point makes this a likely course of events. He writes, "Paul and his companions traveled throughout the region of Phrygia and Galatia, having been kept by the Holy Spirit from preaching the word in the province of Asia. When they came to the border of Mysia, they tried to enter Bithynia" (Acts 16:6–7).

In some Bible versions the expression *tēn Phrygian kai (tēn) Galatikēn chōran* is translated as if *kai* ("and") were absent: the Phrygian-Galatian region. This is then thought to refer to a small, specific area, namely, that portion of the larger province of Galatia that was originally part of Phrygia. Paul then did not visit the original region of Galatia at this time. The Greek phrase, however, requires the rendering "the Phrygian *and* Galatian region." Luke does not use the newer terminology for the Roman provincial divisions here but refers to the original regions: Phrygia and Galatia.[3]

Paul preached in Phrygia and Galatia. This is apparent from the contrast between what is said about these regions and about Asia, where they were "kept by the Holy Spirit from preaching the word" (Acts 16:6). It also follows from the fact that on a subsequent trip Paul visits Galatia and Phrygia, "strengthening all the disciples" (Acts 18:23).

Encouraged by the opportunities for the gospel in Phrygia and Galatia, Paul and Silas try again to go in a westerly direction. Because a trip to Asia is not possible, they now travel in a more northwesterly direction and arrive in Mysia. Maps of Paul's second journey show a trajectory that continues smoothly to the coast from where the crossing to Greece can be made. But this is not Paul's plan at all. From Mysia they want to continue to work in Turkey, now more to the north, toward Bithynia. But the Spirit prevents them from visiting this area (Acts 16:7–8). Paul, Silas, and Timothy reach a dead end in their travels through Turkey. They cannot go south to Asia and they cannot go north to Bithynia. Behind them lies Phrygia, which they have already visited, and before them, at Troas, is the sea that separates Turkey from Greece.

Here at Troas a night vision gives the somewhat meandering travels through Turkey an unexpected turn. Paul sees a Macedonian man. This is the prototype of the valiant warrior. A few centuries before, Macedonian men led by Alexander the Great advanced from here to the east. Their generals had become the leaders of the new states that were established there. It was they who opened the gates for Greek

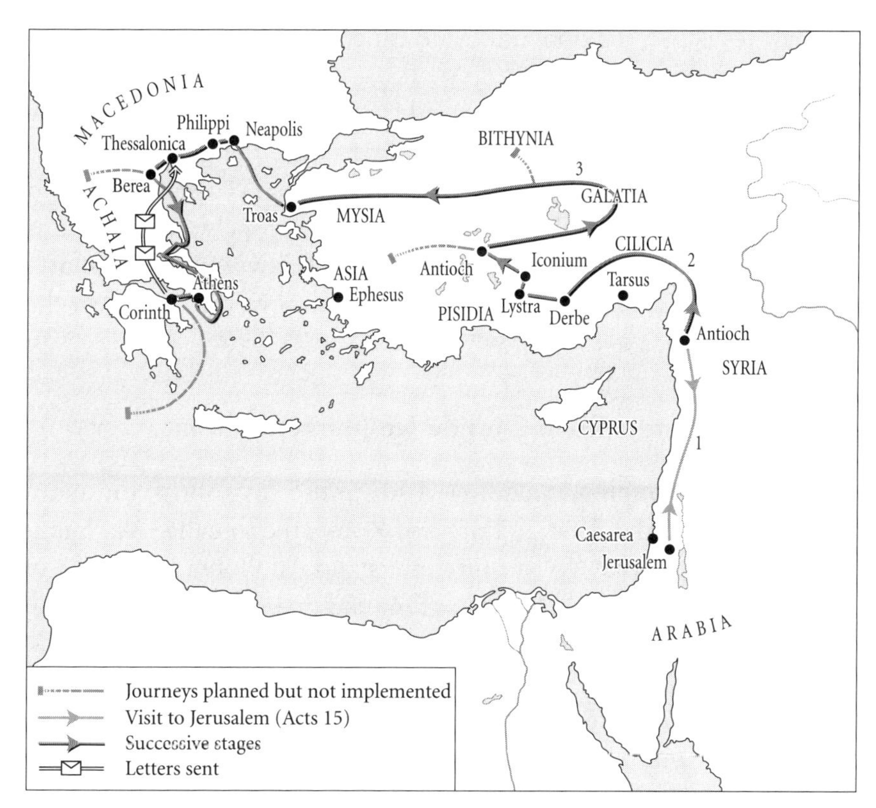

Map 5: *Preaching Westward*

culture to spread in the former territories of Asshur, Syria, and Egypt. Since the arrival of the Macedonian man in the east, everything had changed there. Hellenistic culture advanced and became for many Jews a temptation to secularization. The party of the Pharisees was, historically speaking, one of the most important countermovements to this Hellenism in Israel. In fact, in the vision in Troas, Paul the Jew meets his antipode: the believer from Israel sees the Gentile conqueror from Macedonia. The surprising thing is that the powerful man now cries for help. The world conqueror needs Christ: that is the reality revealed to Paul in the vision. The gospel of Christ is the reality that must now penetrate Macedonia.

Paul, Silas, and Timothy, used to revelations and visions, can easily draw the conclusion: they are called to preach the good news of

Messiah Jesus in Macedonia, the ancient center of power in the north of Greece.

It is surprising how their way is led. Later Paul will work for many years in Asia. When Peter writes his first letter, the gospel has also reached Bithynia. Why did these two regions remain closed at first and Macedonia get priority? The movements of the gospel seem circuitous and unpredictable. In any case, Paul and his fellow travelers are prepared to follow these meandering routes, and thus they arrive in the city of Philippi.

6.2 Stranded in Corinth: No Journey to Rome

Traveling through Macedonia, Paul and Silas follow the main through-route to the West, to Italy and Rome, the so-called Via Egnatia. From Philippi they go to Amphipolis and Apollonia and arrive in Thessalonica (Acts 17:1). After that they end up in Berea (Acts 17:10).

There is no indication that they were planning to go also to Achaia, the ancient center of Greek culture. They end up there in spite of their intent. Continuous, life-threatening opposition from the Jews in Macedonia forces Paul to leave the main highway to the west and to flee by sea in the direction of Achaia, to Athens (Acts 17:5–9, 13–15). By doing this they hope to throw their pursuers, who continue to look for them in a westerly rather than southerly direction, off their track.

At this point Paul himself certainly was not planning a stay in Achaia. He waits there for Silas and Timothy, who are to follow. But Paul gets stuck in Corinth. He meets Aquila and Priscilla there, who have recently arrived from Italy. Apparently this is very important news for Paul, for Luke writes that Paul moved in with his fellow tentmaker "because Claudius had ordered all the Jews to leave Rome" (Acts 18:1–3). This phrase is often connected with Aquila and Priscilla, but why would they leave Italy when the Jews had been ordered only to leave Rome? The phrase may also be understood as the reason why Paul settles in Corinth for now. He cannot continue. He hears from Aquila and Priscilla what the situation in Rome is, which is for them a reason to settle for the time being in Corinth. Rome appears to be closed to Jews at this moment. Paul sees in this an indication that he must temporarily stay in Achaia as well, since all other avenues are blocked. He had to leave Turkey, Macedonia proved too dangerous, Rome is closed. The Jewish tentmakers Aquila and Paul are drawn to each other. For both, Corinth becomes the place where they wait until Rome is open to Jews once again.[4]

On maps of Paul's missionary journeys, all we see are the journeys he actually made—but not the many plans that never came to fruition. They are forgotten, but they definitely had significance at that time.

Thus we read in the letter to the Romans that Paul himself wanted to bring the gospel to Rome: "I do not want you to be unaware, brothers, that I planned many times to come to you (but have been prevented from doing so until now) in order that I might have a harvest among you, just as I have had among the other Gentiles" (Rom. 1:13). When the apostle writes this letter, the gospel has already been brought to the city by others, and Paul only needs to make a visit of mutual encouragement (Rom. 1:11–12). But the Christians in Rome must know that Paul would have preferred for it to have been otherwise. He did not stay away from Rome because he would have been ashamed of the gospel in this the capital of the empire (Rom. 1:16), but he was hindered from being the first preacher there (Rom. 1:13). One of the things that hindered him was the temporary closing of Rome to Jews at the time when Paul could have made a trip there from Corinth.[5]

6.3 Active in Achaia—But No Return to Thessalonica

For more than a year and a half Corinth is the home base for Paul's work. He ended up here more or less accidentally, and he stays out of necessity. Yet this is exactly where he is supposed to be! One night the Lord Jesus says to him, "Do not be afraid; keep on speaking, do not be silent. For I am with you, and no one is going to attack and harm you, because I have many people in this city" (Acts 18:9–10). Until his stay in Corinth Paul's life had been one of constant motion: often hindered by the Spirit to preach in a given place, and also often chased by the hostility of the Jews. Now for the first time a longer, uninterrupted period of rest begins.

During this time, Corinth is his home base for preaching in Achaia; after Macedonia, the gospel now also reaches this province. Reports of the advance of the good news in Macedonia filter down to Achaia and encourage the new believers there. The brethren in Macedonia are an example to them because they (like the believers in Achaia) turned from idols to the living and true God and are waiting for his messiah from heaven (1 Thess. 1:7–9).

Paul's work in Macedonia had been abruptly interrupted. It is understandable that as time went on he increasingly wanted to visit the brothers there again. We find traces of this in the first letter to Thessalonica. This letter comes from Paul, Silas, and Timothy (the team of the second journey) and is written from Achaia.

Paul writes that he was unfortunately hindered from making a personal visit to Thessalonica. Timothy now comes in his stead, while Paul stays behind in Athens (1 Thess. 3:1–2).

When did this happen? This staying behind in Athens is often connected with Acts 17:15, where we read that Paul was left behind in that city when he fled Macedonia.[6] During this first stay of Paul in Athens, Timothy is thought to have made a brief round trip to Thessalonica (see fig. 2).

Fig. 2
Staying Behind in Athens during the First Visit

Paul	Stay in Berea (Acts 17:10–13)
and	Paul (alone) to Athens (Acts 17:14–15)
Thessalonica	Timothy to Athens and back to Macedonia without Paul (1 Thess. 3:1–5)
	Paul to Corinth (Acts 18:1–4)
	Timothy and Silas come from Macedonia to Corinth (Acts 18:5), and Timothy reports on the Thessalonians (1 Thess. 3:6–10)

This reconstruction is, however, very problematic.[7]

1. According to Acts 18:5, Silas and Timothy do not rejoin Paul until after he has left Athens and has gone on to Corinth. It is then

impossible for Paul to have already sent young Timothy back to Thessalonica from Athens.

2. Besides, what would have been the benefit of sending Timothy back immediately? Paul the fugitive was aware of the latest news from Thessalonica. At this point he could not very well write, "For this reason, when I could stand it no longer, I sent to find out about your faith" (1 Thess. 3:5). And why would Paul send someone back to a church to find out how things are when that person had just come from that church?

3. When Paul writes 1 Thessalonians 3, not only Paul and Timothy are in Athens, but there is a third person who stays with Paul when Timothy travels on to Thessalonica by himself. For Paul writes, "When *we* could stand it no longer, *we* thought it best to be left by *ourselves* in Athens" (1 Thess. 3:1). A few verses later he repeats the first phrase, but in the first person: "when *I* could stand it no longer, *I* sent to find out about your faith" (1 Thess. 3:5). Paul is in full agreement with the *joint* decision.[8] Since the letter is written by Paul, Silas, and Timothy, it would seem logical that Silas is the third person in Athens.

4. Paul and Silas's decision to stay behind when Timothy continues on alone was preceded by a series of attempts to travel from Achaia back to Macedonia. Each time Satan stopped them (1 Thess. 2:17–18). When they are once again at a standstill, in Athens, they decide that Timothy must go alone. At least they will know how things are with the brothers in Thessalonica.

We may conclude that Paul, Silas, and Timothy, as they traveled through Achaia, tried more than once to return to Macedonia but, with the exception of Timothy, never were able to do so. They were stranded in Achaia to be active there. During this period Paul can in the end communicate with the Christians in Macedonia only via two letters to Thessalonica.

These letters date from the second half of Paul's stay in Achaia. The first was not written until after the apostle had been active for some time in and around Corinth, and the second toward the end of his stay in Corinth (see fig. 3).

FIG. 3
STAYING BEHIND IN ATHENS DURING LATER VISIT

Paul	Stay in Berea (Acts 17:10–13)
and	Paul (alone) to Athens (Acts 17:14–15)
Thessalonica	Paul to Corinth (Acts 18:1–4)
	Timothy and Silas come from Macedonia to Corinth (Acts 18:5) Repeated attempts to return to Macedonia from Achaia fail (1 Thess. 2:17–18)
	A renewed attempt leads to "shipwreck" in Athens; Paul and Silas decide to stay behind together and to send Timothy alone to Macedonia (1 Thess. 3:1–5)
	Timothy returns to Paul and Silas with a report about Thessalonica (1 Thess. 3:6–10)

6.4 Appeal to the Greeks in Athens

Paul is now in the birthplace of Greek civilization and the home of many gods and goddesses. Here he gets every opportunity to work toward the implementation of the apostolic decree: let the Gentiles turn from the idols to the living God!

We owe an example of the preaching to the Greeks in Achaia to Luke, who has preserved for us a speech that Paul was able to give shortly after his arrival on the Areopagus in Athens. This speech serves more or less as a model for preaching to cultured Greeks, of whom there were also many in Corinth.

The reason behind the request to come and speak on the Areopagus is the amazement Paul generates in this city with the gospel of a resurrection from the dead. Yet this is not what Paul begins his speech with. Rather, he begins with an attack on the idols. His speech could in large part have been given by any Jew. The message of Israel's God is placed over against the world of the many known and unknown gods (Acts 17:22–30). Athens must turn away from the idols!

Only then does Paul speak of the most recent work of Israel's God: the sending of a man whom he raised from the dead and through whom he shall judge the world. The coming judgment through a human being who has been raised from the dead requires that people make haste to return to the one Creator of heaven and earth (Acts 17:31–32).

We find these central themes also in 1 Thessalonians 1:9–10. There Paul says that the Christians in Macedonia (1) have turned from the idols to the living and true God and (2) expect his Son from heaven, whom he has raised from the dead and who delivers us from the coming wrath.

6.5 Program for New Converts (1 and 2 Thessalonians)

How did the apostle go about preaching the gospel and founding churches? The book of Acts is helpful in providing information about Paul's itinerary and events that took place during his travels, but it does not say much about the way Paul approached his actual task of preaching and church planting. For this we must look at his letters.

The two earliest letters of Paul that we have date from the time of his first stay in Macedonia and Achaia. Both were written to Thessalonica, the church Paul would have liked to visit again. These letters are apparently from the team that worked together on this journey: Paul, Silas, and Timothy (1 Thess. 1:1; 2 Thess. 1:1).

Because this is a church that had been founded only recently, these letters contain a relatively large number of allusions to the basic instruction the church had received.[9] This is a welcome addition to the book of Acts: Luke gives us, with the exception of the speech to the elders of Ephesus, only Paul's earliest addresses to the church, from which we cannot infer the basic elements of early Christian catechetical instruction. And although we do not find these presented systematically in the letters to Thessalonica, we can nevertheless gain a fragmentary knowledge of the first teaching Greeks received when they came to accept Christ as their Lord.

1. The gospel is not simply empty words but a source of power and Spirit, as they have experienced (1 Thess. 1:5).
2. On earth, suffering and faith go hand in hand (1 Thess. 1:6; 2:14; 3:3–5).
3. The Christian life is governed by faith, hope, and love (1 Thess. 1:3), of which love is central (1 Thess. 4:9–10).

4. Believers must abide by the instruction they have received orally or in writing (2 Thess. 2:15). We must think here of Paul's own oral teaching during his visit to Thessalonica (when he also handed them a copy of the apostolic decree concerning the freedom and responsibility of Gentile Christians) and Paul's first letter to this church in which this teaching was written down.
5. This teaching includes instructions for the sanctification of life (1 Thess. 4:1–3), God's judgment on our sins (1 Thess. 4:6), the duty to earn one's own living (1 Thess. 4:11; 2 Thess. 3:6, 10), the coming of the Lord as a thief in the night (1 Thess. 5:2), and the reminder of the deceptive coming of the "lawless one" who will claim to be the coming redeemer (2 Thess. 2:3–4).
6. There already are responsible leaders in the church (1 Thess. 5:12–13).

From the start these elements were part of the instruction for new converts. According to some interpreters we can even detect in the sequence of 1 and 2 Thessalonians a measure of development of this initial instruction toward a later, corrected form. In 1 Thessalonians Paul still operates from the primary, naïve expectation of the imminent return of Jesus. Given the misunderstandings within the church he backtracks in his second letter to the Thessalonians. There Paul suddenly inserts an end-time scenario that includes the deceptive appearance of the "man of lawlessness" who presents himself as a god in the temple. Thus already in Greece the expectation of Jesus' imminent return had to give way to a complicated eschatology that projects the return of Christ into an unknown, distant future.[10]

But this reconstruction of an early evolution in the Christian expectation of the return does not do justice to the whole of the data in both letters.

1. The instruction concerning the time before the return of Jesus (2 Thess. 2:1–12) is not in any way linked to the warning in the same letter not to stop working (2 Thess. 3). It seems therefore not very likely that there would be a direct connection

between this instruction concerning the time before Jesus' return and the unwillingness to work.

2. Already in the first letter we find warnings against an unwillingness to work, and it appears that these warnings were already part of the first, oral teaching of Paul (1 Thess 4:11–12; 2 Thess. 3:10).
3. The second chapter of 2 Thessalonians is not directed against expecting Jesus' return too soon, but rather against the danger of a wrong expectation. The latter would lead to a being enamored of the "man of lawlessness" who performs many miracles but nevertheless must ultimately retreat when the true World Ruler appears.
4. The contents of 2 Thessalonians 2—concerning the appearing of the "man of lawlessness"—were already part of the initial instruction (2 Thess. 2:5).

These two letters thus do not present a later development of the teaching; instead, both letters remind frequently of the earlier instruction, already given at the time when the Christian community was founded. Back then the "full counsel of God" was already being taught. From the beginning, a variety of themes were present that later got more detailed, individual attention (faith, hope, love; the spiritual armor; the resurrection as reality; the danger of secularization; the building up of the church in love).

Paul's preaching in Greece was from the beginning aimed at establishing a new community, based on the apostolic tradition, led by its own spiritual leaders, persevering in sanctification. The gospel mobilizes Macedonians and other Greeks for a new Ruler and a different culture.

6.6 The Selfless Tentmaker of Christ

Macedonia is the land of ancient power, Achaia the region of ancient culture. Greece is a land of nobility in the new military world of the Romans!

The preacher of a crucified and resurrected Jesus is unacceptable in these regions. In Macedonia he is persecuted and in Athens ridiculed.

His presentation is, after all, strictly un-Greek. He does not have the style and presence of an orator or philosopher (1 Cor. 2:1–5), nor does he have the glamour of a *magus*, an oriental wonderworker. Stranger yet: he humbles himself to doing manual labor as a tentmaker, and he refuses to accept honoraria. How can an artisan who makes his living with his hands command any esteem in the Greek world where only new philosophies, wealth, or fame confers stature and popularity?

It is striking that Paul very intentionally does not ask for any kind of payment for his work or for himself. In Corinth he initially earned a living as tentmaker in the workshop of Aquila and Priscilla, and only later did he devote himself exclusively to preaching (Acts 18:3–5).[11] But in the meantime he already created a lasting impression![12]

Paul did not accept payment for his many signs and wonders, although in that day it was considered perfectly normal for magicians to be richly rewarded for their help. Nor did he as a rule accept financial support from the churches. Paul, Silas, and Timothy can write concerning this period in Macedonia, "We worked night and day in order not to be a burden to anyone" (1 Thess. 2:9). Paul, like the other apostles, certainly would have had the authority to let himself be supported by the churches, but he can later write to Corinth, "I have not used any of these rights" (1 Cor. 9:15).

The apostle has thus become the paragon of the gospel: Christ became poor to make us rich (2 Cor. 8:9). Paul does not look for honor from people, but he acts like a selfless mother who cherishes and cares for her children (1 Thess. 2:6–7). The apostle wants to be an example for the newly converted to imitate. Let them not be parasites but be prepared to work and earn their living (2 Thess. 3:7–12).

In the Greek world, full of pride and ambition, Paul demonstrates the humility, the selflessness, and the personal commitment of Christ's love. While he seems lost in the Greek world, by his actions he paves in fact the way for a new life.

7

REAPPEARANCE IN JERUSALEM

Paul's lengthy stay in Achaia ends abruptly and unexpectedly when he sets sail for Syria (Acts 18:18). It was not his intent to leave the region permanently. On a stopover in Asia he even promises the interested Jews in Ephesus solemnly that he will return to them, God willing (Acts 18:19–21).

Why did he have to leave Corinth at that particular time and why could he not spend more time in Ephesus? The reason was that he had taken a vow. This vow apparently went into effect in the Corinthian port city of Cenchrea, where Paul had his hair cut off. No razor would touch his head nor would he drink wine or strong drink during the rest of the trip (Acts 18:18). A vow to the Lord must be concluded with a Nazirite sacrifice in the temple in Jerusalem (Num. 6:1–21). It is therefore clear that Paul has obligated himself to God under oath to travel first to Jerusalem, without allowing himself to be held up in Ephesus or other cities. (In most manuscripts of Acts 18:21 this journey to Jerusalem is explicitly mentioned as taking place shortly before one of Israel's great feasts: "I must by all means keep this feast that cometh in Jerusalem" [KJV].)

From the perspective of Corinth this journey to Jerusalem and Antioch can easily be viewed as a trip to Syria (Acts 18:18). As a special protectorate under a Roman governor, Palestine was an exceptional area within the Roman province of Syria,[1] but viewed from the outside it was an integral part of this province. Besides, Palestine was part of the geographical area that was referred to as Syria in those days.[2]

Paul lands in the Jewish port city of Caesarea, "greet[s] the church," and leaves for Antioch (Acts 18:22). Luke does not describe the visit to Jerusalem; it is not relevant in the scheme of his book. According to some, Luke even assumed that Paul traveled directly from Caesarea to Antioch, without visiting Jerusalem.[3] But this cannot be the case.

1. Why would Paul have sailed past the more northerly region of Antioch and wait to disembark until he reached Caesarea, which meant that he had to backtrack over land to Antioch?
2. Luke writes that Paul disembarked (*katelthōn*) in Caesarea and then went up (*anabas*). This verb is generally used of the (festive) going up to the higher elevation of Jerusalem. Luke thus refers indirectly to the visit to Jerusalem.
3. Paul's greeting "the church" would in Judea most naturally refer to the church whose home base is Jerusalem, where the apostles and elders are.
4. Luke has already said that Paul was "under a vow"; a single word is then adequate for the reader to understand that he went up to Jerusalem, where he had to fulfill his vow.
5. After greeting the church, Paul goes down (*katebē*) to Antioch. Caesarea lies on the coast, and from there one has to go up to Antioch. The combination of going up and going down between Caesarea and Antioch makes it clear that Paul in the meantime visited a city generally known to be situated at a higher elevation.
6. Caesarea is the nearest large port city if one wants to travel by ship to visit Jerusalem.

What made the apostle decide to reappear rather suddenly in Jerusalem? Why did he pay a brief visit there before going to Antioch? We have more material at our disposal that can help us find an answer

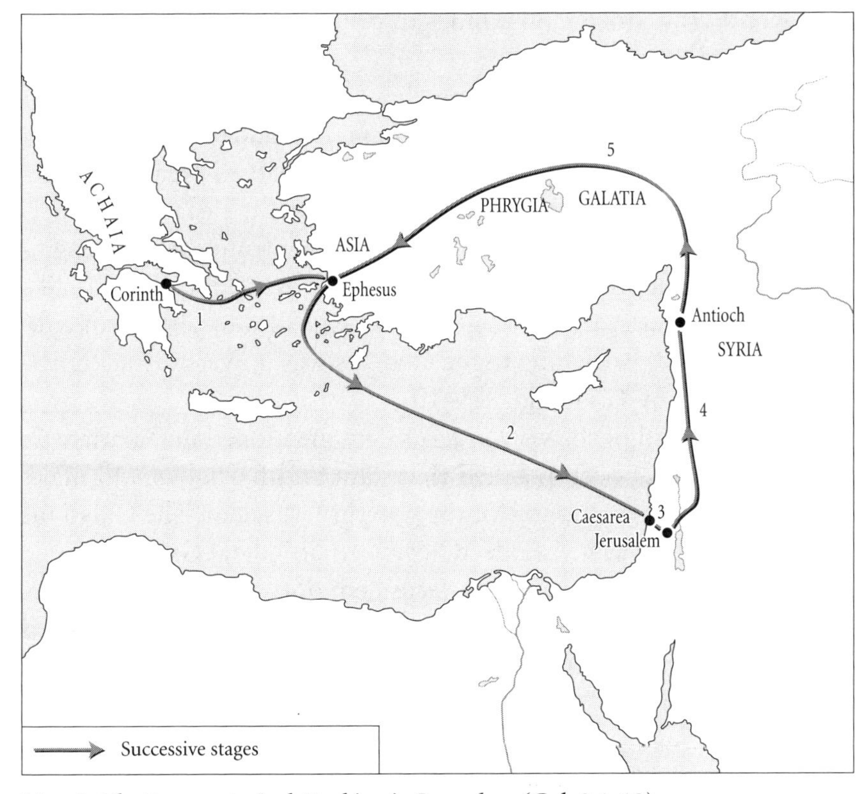

Map 6: *The Journey to Seek Backing in Jerusalem (Gal. 2:1-10)*

to these questions than is often assumed. It is specifically the letter to the Galatians that can shed light on the reason for the visit.

7.1 The Visit "Fourteen Years Later" (Galatians)

The letter to the Galatians was written during the so-called third missionary journey and thus dates from the period after Paul's first stay in Macedonia and Achaia. On his way there he had already had the opportunity to bring the gospel to the region of Phrygia and Galatia. And when he returns from his "vow visit" to Jerusalem, he travels again through this region on his way to Ephesus, with the purpose of "strengthening all the disciples" (Acts 18:23). We know that Paul did not write his well-known letter to the Galatians until after this second visit, since Paul alludes to previous first and second visits (Gal. 4:13).

In this letter the apostle pays much attention to the preceding history of the gospel. His readers in Galatia are suddenly in danger of straying from that gospel, even though the gospel Paul preaches comes from God himself. The story of Paul's life makes it clear how he personally received the gospel from God and how from the very beginning he acted as a preacher motivated directly by God (Gal. 1:11–24). Furthermore, in a recent deliberation the apostles in Jerusalem concluded that Paul's preaching to the Gentiles was universally acknowledged as willed by God (Gal. 2:1–10).

Toward the end of the visit to Jerusalem mentioned in Galatians 2, the agreement has been reached that Paul and Barnabas will make every effort to collect money for the poor in Jerusalem. The Galatians know from Paul that he is indeed "eager to do" that (Gal. 2:10).

This collection for the poor in Jerusalem does not play a role during Paul's first stay in Greece. We do not find traces of his efforts toward such a collection until the so-called third missionary journey (after the visit to Jerusalem of Acts 18, which is discussed in this chapter). From this we can draw the conclusion that in Galatians 2 the apostle talks about a visit to Jerusalem that immediately preceded the third missionary journey and that thus coincided with his "vow journey" to Jerusalem.[4]

The apostle dates the visit to Jerusalem he describes in his letter as having taken place "fourteen years later" (Gal. 2:1). In the immediately preceding section he has twice used the word "later" (*epeita*). He went to Arabia as the result of a revelation and *then* (three years later) to Jerusalem (1:18) and *then* to the region of Syria and Cilicia (1:21). When Paul now uses the word *epeita* again for the third time in this brief passage, it is most natural to think of an event that took place "fourteen years" after the event mentioned immediately before (i.e., fourteen years after the departure for Syria and Cilicia). Without entering into the details of the chronology, we can say that the "vow visit" of Acts 18 fits in well with this dating. The revelation that motivated Paul to preach to the Gentiles took place in A.D. 35, 36, or early 37. Paul's visit to Jerusalem three years later must be dated A.D. 38, 39, or early 40. The departure for Syria and Cilicia falls shortly thereafter in the same year, so that a new visit to Jerusalem that takes place fourteen years after that must be dated A.D. 51 or 52 if the beginning and ending years are counted. This leads to a date after the second missionary journey.[5]

What light does the report in Galatians 2 shed on Paul's sudden departure from Greece for a visit to Jersualem?

7.2 Threatened Freedom

For Luke it was interesting to relate how in the apostolic decree (Acts 15) the apostles and elders established freedom from the law for Gentile Christians. Because Luke does not talk about the period of building and conflict that followed in the young churches, he also skips over the details of Paul's later visit to Jerusalem (Acts 18). From the letter to the Galatians it appears that this visit had much to do with the tensions that later emerged in the young churches. In a pastoral letter occasioned by conflict and threat (Galatians) such a visit is very much worth mentioning, whereas Luke's purpose in writing Acts allows him to virtually ignore it.

Apparently Paul traveled to Jerusalem out of concern: the gospel he preached was endangered. His work was threatened. "Brothers" had infiltrated the church "to spy on the freedom we have in Christ Jesus and to make us slaves" (Gal. 2:4). Paul is not writing about the church in Jerusalem being infiltrated, but rather the Gentile churches founded by Paul. The freedom of Paul and his readers—our freedom—is spied on, and we are in danger of being made slaves. The danger exists here that the gospel will disappear from the Gentile Christian churches. This rearguard attack could obscure the truth of the gospel. Therefore Paul travels to Jerusalem, "so that the truth of the gospel might remain with you" (Gal. 2:5).

From these statements it appears that the gospel had already reached the Gentiles before this consultation in Jerusalem and that their freedom from the law had already been acknowledged. Thus the widely accepted equation of the discussion in Galatians 2 and the apostolic council of Acts 15 is not likely to be correct (apart even from the decision concerning the collection for the poor that was not reached during the Acts 15 council). The so-called apostolic decree of Acts 15 establishes the freedom of the uncircumcised Christians; the discussion of Galatians 2 is aimed at maintaining that freedom!

Paul travels to Jerusalem on the basis of a revelation he received personally (Gal. 2:2). At the time of Acts 15, Barnabas and Paul were delegated to Jerusalem by the church in Antioch, but the initiative for this visit in Galatians 2 comes entirely from Paul himself. *He* goes up to Jerusalem (Gal. 2:1a). He takes Barnabas with him and also Titus (Gal. 2:1b; *sumparalabōn*). Titus is a special guest of Paul's (Gal. 2:3; *ho syn emoi*). Apparently Paul (with Titus) and Barnabas meet in Jerusalem, but they arrive there from the different areas in which they work. They are no longer an inseparable team, as was the case on the first journey (which preceded Acts 15), but they emerge here as independent workers who go jointly to Jerusalem for a consultation. Paul thus can give a report of his part in the deliberations: *I* "set before them the gospel that *I* preach among the Gentiles . . . for fear that *I* was running or had run my race in vain"; "those men added nothing to *my* message"; and "God . . . was also at work in *my* ministry as an apostle to the Gentiles." In a summary statement it appears that the same applies to Paul and Barnabas ("*We* did not give in to them for a moment"; "gave *me and Barnabas* the right hand of fellowship"; "All they asked was that *we* should continue to remember the poor"), but in the report about the deliberations they appear as two independent persons who do not act as an inseparable duo. This points to the period in which Paul and Barnabas no longer worked and traveled together but each went his own independent way. This was true during the second missionary journey. The consultation of Galatians 2 reflects the situation between the second and third journeys—a situation in which the work among the Gentiles was under threat. It was a situation so serious that Paul and Barnabas agreed to both go to Jerusalem after Paul had received a revelation to make this trip.

According to many interpreters it would be difficult to imagine that Paul and Barnabas, after their conflict at the beginning of the second journey, would nevertheless appear jointly in Jerusalem at the end of that journey. But this is not as remarkable as it may seem.

1. The reason for the conflict was incidental and of limited significance: whether John Mark should go along. There is no question of a distancing with regard to the purpose or method of preaching.

2. Apparently Paul later changed his mind about the cause of the conflict: he came to see John Mark as a valuable helper (in Col. 4:10 he commends "Mark, the cousin of Barnabas"; when Paul writes to Philemon, Mark is with him [v. 24]; and in his last letter Paul even acknowledges that Mark is "helpful to me in my ministry" [2 Tim. 4:11]). Paul thus admitted later that he had been wrong in his negative assessment of Mark. And with this the grounds for the incident between him and Barnabas had disappeared.

3. In 1 Corinthians 9:6 Paul writes collegially and even with a touch of humor about Barnabas: "Or is it only I and Barnabas who must work for a living?" There is no reason, therefore, to assume that the incidental conflict between Barnabas and Paul (Acts 15:39) has led to a permanently disrupted relationship. They remain colleagues in the preaching to the Gentiles, even if they no longer travel together.

It is therefore not all that surprising that Barnabas and Paul both go to Jerusalem to address a shared concern. Paul's apparent feeling that he must be in Jerusalem at a particular time (the next feast) may relate to the possibility that Paul and Barnabas had agreed upon this particular date for their meeting in Jerusalem.

The two leaders of the mission among the Gentiles now both go to Jerusalem to discuss with the apostles who work primarily among the Jews, and with James, the leader of the Jewish Christians, the matter of the threatened freedom of the Gentile Christians.

7.3 The Decision of Acts 15 Apparently Inadequate

A comparison of Galatians 2 and Acts 15 raises for many a burning question: How can Paul in Galatians fail to mention the apostolic decree of Acts 15 and ignore his visit to Jerusalem during which the decree was agreed upon? After all, the decree already stated that circumcision was no longer obligatory for Gentile Christians! What would have been easier for Paul than simply to appeal in his letter to the apostolic decree of Acts 15! Yet he does not do so. Does this show (1) that this decision was *never* made, or (2) that it was *not yet* made, or (3) that the report in Galatians 2 of the visit to Jerusalem describes in fact (albeit in very different words) the meeting at which the apostolic decree was issued? For many, the absence of any mention of the apostolic decree in Galatians is such an overriding problem that they resort to the assumption that the consultation in Galatians 2 must be the same as that in Acts 15, in spite of the almost insurmountable differences between the reports of these meetings. Some try to explain away the sharp differences in description by assuming that Paul emphasized the bitter struggle of those days, whereas Luke glossed this over in a smooth narrative. Others try to achieve a measure of harmonization between Galatians 2 and Acts 15.

There are no explicit points of contact of any significance between Galatians 2 and Acts 15. The only elements they have in common are the names Paul, Barnabas, Peter, James, and Jerusalem. Although these names are specific, they occur frequently and also in combination with each other in the New Testament period. They don't therefore point to one specific time. Besides, there are so many differences between the two reports that they must either be played off against one another as biased and subjective representations, or we must assume that Galatians 2 contains the description of a kind of preliminary discussion while Acts 15 describes the plenary session at which the actual decision is made.

Some of the differences are minor (not mentioned in Acts 15 are John [Gal. 2:9] and the fact that Paul went up "in response to revelation" [Gal. 2:2]), but some are quite radical (the presence of the uncircumcised Titus [Gal. 2:3]; the fact that in Acts 15 Peter stands with Paul against the Pharisees who insist on circumcision, while in Galatians 2 Peter belongs to the other party with which Paul reaches an agreement [Acts 15:6–11; Gal. 2:7–9]).

It would appear that in Galatians 2 Paul describes a different meeting than the one in Acts 15. When the agreement on the collection is taken into account, Galatians 2 must refer to a later meeting. But the unavoidable question pops up again: Why doesn't Paul mention the earlier consultation of Acts 15?

It would seem that there are two reasons why Paul should have mentioned his visit at the time the apostolic decree was issued.

1. The first reason has to do with the argument of Galatians 1–2, in which Paul presents a continuous case to show that he is not dependent on (the apostles in) Jerusalem. After all, immediately after the revelation he went to Arabia and he did not go to Jerusalem until three years later. After that he preached outside Palestine until he returned to Jerusalem fourteen years later. Doesn't Paul in this argument characterize himself as an apostle independent from Jerusalem? In that case he could not afford to distort the record by sweeping one visit to Jerusalem under the rug!

This argument would be valid if Paul in Galatians 1 were indeed describing his independence as a person. But Galatians 1 deals with the divine origin of the gospel (see Gal. 1:11–12, 15). This argument concludes in 1:24 ("they praised God because of me"). Then, in chapter 2, begins a different argument: this divine gospel has also been defended by Paul in Jerusalem (Gal. 2:1–10) and in Antioch (Gal. 2:11–21). There was no reason for Paul to include Acts 15 in this line of reasoning, because during the apostolic consultation a case from Antioch was discussed. The apostolic decree does not fit in Galatians 1 (where the divine origin of Paul's gospel is at issue) or in Galatians 2 (where Paul personally defends that gospel). In the argument of Galatians 1 and 2 there was simply no reason to mention the apostolic consultation in Acts 15.

2. There is a second reason why it is thought that Paul could not leave the decision of Acts 15 unmentioned in Galatians 1–2. This reason relates to the argument of the letter as a whole. Galatians deals with the circumcision of Gentile Christians—which is what the apostolic decree addressed! Paul should at least have specifically mentioned this decision in his argument.

This line of reasoning would have validity if the issue in the churches in Galatia were the same as that which led to the apostolic decree. But this is not the case. The fronts have shifted, and the letter to the Galatians is necessary in spite of the apostolic decree. A new issue has developed that has similarities with the earlier problem but that cannot be solved simply by pointing to earlier decisions. It is this new issue that brings Paul (and Barnabas) to Jerusalem, several years after the apostolic decree was issued. The apostolic decree of Acts 15 is inadequate for the situation in Galatia: new agreements are necessary. This will become clear when we look at the threat in Galatia.

7.4 Fear of the Circumcised

In his letter to the Galatians Paul gives a clear example of the kind of threat that now confronts the Gentile Christians. After the consultation in Jerusalem, which proceeded harmoniously and where the threat appeared to be under control, things go wrong again in Antioch. A conflict arises, which involves Paul on one side and Peter, Barnabas, and many others on the other side (Gal. 2:11–21). It is a conflict generated by a highly specific situation.[6]

Until the incident in Antioch, Paul, Peter, and Barnabas and many Jewish Christians were used to eating together with Gentile Christians, both at the Lord's Supper and at other meals. They no longer called "unclean" what God had called "clean" (Acts 10:13–15). As observant Jews, however, they would not have participated in such shared meals. The food of the Gentiles was in many respects in conflict with the dietary laws, and the contact with Gentiles could also lead to other types of ceremonial uncleanness. For Jewish Christians such as Peter and Paul this had, however, been no reason to avoid contact with uncircumcised Christians. Even if they themselves still observed the laws of purity, they nevertheless considered the uncleanness that could result from contact with Gentiles as they ate with uncircumcised brethren less important than the unity that God had given through the Spirit: one in Christ, together at the table.

What caused the reversal of this open attitude? Some Christians arrive in Antioch who came "from James" (Gal. 2:12). This "James" is not further identified but is apparently *the* James, the brother of Jesus (cf. 1 Cor. 15:7; Gal. 1:19; 2:9). These Jewish brothers thus come from Jerusalem, where James is the leader of the church, and they belong to the group of Jewish Christians who are particular about the keeping of the law (cf. Acts 21:20). The Christians from Jerusalem certainly do not come and demand that the Gentile Christians must be circumcised in order to be saved (as was the case in Acts 15:1–2)! All they do is "separate themselves." They maintain their distance from the Gentile Christians. They are not aggressive toward these Gentile Christians—they are afraid!

The brothers from the circle of James and later also many Jewish Christians in Antioch (even Peter and Barnabas) distance themselves from their uncircumcised fellow-Christians. They do this out of fear "of those who belonged to the circumcision" (Gal. 2:12).[7] This cannot refer to the Jewish Christians, since it is the Jewish Christians who are afraid of "those of the circumcision"![8] Therefore, "those of the circumcision" refers to the non-Christian Jews.[9] The Jewish Christians let themselves be intimidated by their fellow-Jews. They do not want to compromise themselves vis-à-vis their fellow Jews by contact with uncircumcised people. They are apparently tolerated and left alone as followers of Messiah Jesus, but they would be persecuted if they would so much as give the appearance of making common cause with the Gentiles.

This is the dominant sentiment in Jerusalem at the end of Paul's third journey. James and the elders then point out to Paul that the thousands of Christians in Jerusalem are "zealous for the law" (Acts 21:20). They have heard rumors that Paul was teaching Jews in other countries to turn away from the law and to neglect circumcision (Acts 21:21). This rumor must be squelched! For the Christians in Jerusalem it is not a problem that the Gentile Christians, as stated in the apostolic decree, are not circumcised and are required only to abandon idolatry (Acts 21:25). But Jews must continue to observe the law, even after they have accepted Messiah Jesus!

Against this background it is not so strange that people from the circle of James do not participate in meals with uncircumcised Christians. They follow a policy of "ecclesiastical apartheid." The apostolic decree does not apply here, since the decree did not address the consequences of mission to the Gentiles for the behavior of Jewish Christians!

After the middle of the first century this becomes an increasingly important issue. After Palestine as a whole had become a Roman province in A.D. 44, religio-political tensions began to grow. Jewish nationalism became stronger and in Israel this always meant that religious tolerance could be viewed as collaboration with the enemy. In this period the fear of "those who belonged to the circumcision" becomes a significant factor for the Jewish Christians who do not want to be persecuted for unlawful contacts with ceremonially unclean Gentiles.

This separatism of the Jewish Christians led to the isolation of the uncircumcised Christians. The unintended and unintentional consequence of this separatism was that the Gentile Christians could feel themselves excluded. Were they in fact second-class citizens, in spite of their faith in Christ? They actually were indirectly invited to let themselves be circumcised for the sake of continuing the contact with Jewish brothers and sisters, even with Peter and Barnabas!

Paul was one of the few who realized that this matter threatened the very foundation of Christianity. Even though Peter and Barnabas acknowledged the legitimate position of the Gentile Christians, they in fact cast a shadow over it. When the unity of the church was broken because the Jewish Christians continued to withdraw behind the law and circumcision, there would be either a Christianity that was entirely separate from Israel or a Christianity that for the sake of peace was absorbed into Judaism.

Here "the freedom we have in Christ Jesus" is under scrutiny from the outside, so that the Gentile Christians, who are still weak and therefore easily threatened, can be tempted to let themselves be encapsulated in the perceived safety of the law, so that they become slaves of the law (Gal. 2:4–5).

It appears that these developments had already been in the making for some time. Jews from Jerusalem apparently had come into various Gentile Christian churches. They viewed these churches from the outside and held themselves separate from the gatherings of the Gentile Christians. Because of this the freedom these Gentile Christians had gained became in fact a problem, a burden, a dividing wall between brothers. We cannot trace historically which individuals played a leading role in this and which churches they entered, but this new development was in any case reason for Paul to go to Jerusalem.

When the epidemic nevertheless spreads a few years later and also threatens the churches in Galatia, Paul writes a letter about it. He tells the Galatians how forcefully he resisted this deformation within Christianity while he was in Antioch. For in Galatia we see the same problem as in Antioch: the freedom of the Gentile Christians is not called into question, but they are nevertheless implicitly encouraged to let themselves be circumcised—for the sake of the safety of their Jewish fellow-Christians. Paul writes, "Those who want to make a good impression outwardly are trying to compel you to be circumcised. The only reason they do this is to avoid being persecuted for the cross of Christ" (Gal. 6:12). The pressure toward circumcision does not come from the idea that no one can be saved without circumcision. The only reason this pressure is exerted is so that the Jewish Christians can gain honor from their fellow-Jews for bringing Gentiles into the fold of Israel: "Not even those who are circumcised [as Jews] obey the law, yet they want you to be circumcised that they may boast about your flesh" (Gal. 6:13).

In the earliest Christian church we see two successive problems. The first concerns the recognition of Gentile Christians; this issue is settled after the first missionary journey by means of the apostolic decree of Acts 15. But this recognition causes a second problem that surfaces during the second journey and that remains active afterward: How should Jewish Christians communicate with their uncircumcised fellow-Christians in daily life and especially in coming together and eating together the Lord's Supper? The Gentile converts were asked to break with their pagan past for the sake of Christ. Must Jewish Christians for the sake of their brothers in Christ now break to some extent with their Jewish background—or at least learn to change priorities at the point of the law of purity? Or should the new Gentile converts be charitable enough to join the Jewish people?

7.5 Backing from Jerusalem

When the second issue unexpectedly raises its head also in Galatia, Paul reminds the Galatians of the past history of his gospel: God gave him a personal revelation, many years ago, about the unrestricted preaching of the gospel to all people. Much has happened since then. During the most recent discussions in Jerusalem it became once again apparent how generally his gospel has been acknowledged. And when Peter and Barnabas had a moment of weakness in Antioch (an incident about which people in Galatia may have heard) Paul did not skirt the issue. He forcefully opposed them (Gal. 2:11–14) and reminded them of the implications of the gospel of grace (Gal. 2:15–21). Jesus ate with the prostitutes and tax collectors who came to him. That does not mean in any way that he became a "servant of sin" (Gal. 2:17 NRSV; *hamartias diakonos*, "minister of sin" [NASB]; "promotes sin" [NIV]). Should Jewish Christians then refuse to eat with uncircumcised Christians? What is at stake is in fact the gospel of grace and the unity of Christianity.

The report of the consultation in Jerusalem is revealing in what did not happen.

1. Titus, who was a Greek, was not forced to let himself be circumcised—even in Jerusalem (Gal. 2:3). He was accepted there in Christ, and the leaders did not let themselves be influenced by the indirect pressure on the part of some Jewish Christians (Gal. 2:4)! Nor was there fear in Jerusalem that the presence of Titus would compromise them vis-à-vis non-Christian Jews. How real this danger nevertheless was became clear a few years later when the presence of Trophimus, an uncircumcised Christian in Paul's group, almost led to Paul's lynching (Acts 21:27–36).
2. The leaders in Jerusalem did not impose anything on Paul and Barnabas (Gal. 2:6); they did not add anything to the apostolic decree (*ouden prosanethento*).
3. Missionary praxis does not change; Paul and Barnabas continue to go to the Gentiles, Peter and the others to the Jews (Gal. 2:7–9).
4. The only arrangement that is made concerns the collection as a sign of solidarity between the Gentile Christians and the poor in Jerusalem.
5. For Paul, the trip to Jerusalem provided good support. He now knew with certainty that the freedom of the Gentiles would continue to be accepted, even though it would still take a great

deal of effort to teach the Jewish Christians to deal with this in such a way that the unity in Christ was not endangered. In practice this could mean for Jewish Christians that they would be persecuted as unclean friends of Gentiles, even as their Master was rejected as a "friend of sinners and tax collectors."

7.6 Paul the Determined

Paul showed his determination during his "vow-journey" to Jerusalem. When the tide threatened to turn in some Gentile Christian communities, Paul did not side with his fellow Jews (Gal. 2:5). His trip to Jerusalem was an effort to safeguard the unity of the apostles before it was too late (Gal. 2:9). When that unity was nevertheless endangered by the actions of his closest friends, Peter and Barnabas, he even publicly contradicted and corrected them, in spite of their leadership positions (Gal. 2:11).

Paul lived out of the rock-solid certainty of that which he had received through revelation: "But even if we or an angel from heaven should preach a gospel other than the one we preached to you, let him be eternally condemned!" (Gal. 1:8). The vehemence with which Paul makes this statement hints at how difficult it is to defend a truth that is accepted in principle by all, yet later undermined by the actions of many.

EMBATTLED IN EPHESUS

After his "vow-visit" to Jerusalem, Paul was obligated to travel to Ephesus in Asia. When he had wanted to go to Asia on his previous journey through Turkey, the Holy Spirit had hindered him from going there (Acts 16:6). But when he made a stop in Ephesus on the way back from Greece to Jerusalem, there appeared to be an unexpected open door for the gospel: the Jews asked him to stay longer. Paul could not do so because of his vow to go to Jerusalem, but he promised to come back "if it is God's will" (Acts 18:21). It is therefore clear in which direction he must travel from Antioch: to Ephesus.[1] On his journey through central Turkey he can now revisit the Christian communities in Galatia and Phrygia (Acts 18:23). This time he does not find a closed door in Phrygia (cf. Acts 16:6) but can continue his trip to Ephesus without hindrance (Acts 19:1).

In Acts 19:1 we read that he arrives in Ephesus after a journey through *ta anōterika merē*. The definite article indicates that this expression refers to the previously mentioned (*ta*), higher (than Ephesus) (*anōterika*) regions of Galatia and Phrygia (see Acts 18:23).[2] Paul travels through the central mountains of Turkey and then descends to the coast, where Ephesus lies (see map 6).

This important city on the western coast of Turkey now becomes for many years the center of Paul's work.[3] Although we do not know much about this period, it is clear that they were very eventful years. On the one hand the gospel became known in the whole region of Asia during this period, among both the Jews and the Greeks (Acts 19:10). On the other hand, Paul later looks back on this period with these words: "We do not want you to be uninformed, brothers, about the hardships we suffered in the province of Asia. We were under great pressure, far beyond our ability to endure, so that we despaired even of life" (2 Cor. 1:8). And elsewhere he writes that he "fought wild beasts in Ephesus" (1 Cor. 15:32).

What is the significance of this period in Paul's pioneer life?

8.1 Three Years in and out of Ephesus

The apostle Paul was a traveler. He never stayed long in one place. His calling spurred him on, or he was chased by the persecutors. The length of his stay in the large city of Ephesus is therefore striking: no less than three years! He can later say to the elders of the Christian community there, "Remember that for three years I never stopped warning each of you night and day with tears" (Acts 20:31).

Paul does not say that he was in Ephesus for three years without interruption, but rather that over a period of three years he never ceased warning them. This does not preclude the possibility that he may have made a journey during this period. On the basis of other information we can say with certainty that he made at least one (longer) journey.

1. Luke describes the period in Ephesus in two stages. The first takes place primarily in the city of Ephesus and is characterized by two years of preaching in the lecture hall of Tyrannus. This was preceded by or began with a period of three months in which he (still) spoke in the synagogue (Acts 19:8–10). "After all this had happened," Paul decided to travel to Jerusalem and Rome via Macedonia and Achaia. But before setting out on this journey he "stayed in the province of Asia a little longer" (Acts 19:21–22). Thus the three-year period appears to consist of a rather lengthy stay in the city of Ephesus (two years plus) and a shorter period in the region of Ephesus, in Asia. We are given the

impression that between these two periods Paul made a journey outside the region of Ephesus and Asia.

2. This impression is confirmed and becomes a certainty when we read both letters to Corinth that have survived. At the end of the first letter Paul appears to be planning a journey from Ephesus through Macedonia and Achaia. He hopes to stay in Corinth for a while and perhaps even to spend the winter there. Apparently the latter did not happen, for we can infer from 2 Corinthians that the (disappointing) visit was cut short rather quickly with the promise to return in the not-too-distant future (2 Cor. 1:16; 1:23–2:2). In the end Paul's plan was not carried out in this form. He decided to postpone his third visit to Corinth (2 Cor. 13:1) and to go (back) to Macedonia before making his concluding visit to Corinth. This journey to Macedonia and Corinth (immediately preceding his departure for Jerusalem) is described in Acts 20:1–3. It is the journey after the definitive departure from Asia. Apparently the interim journey through Macedonia, with the interim visit to Corinth that did not go well, took place earlier, that is, within the three-year period in Ephesus. It is quite possible that Paul made this journey after he had worked for just over two years in Ephesus and before he spent some more time in Asia. In any case Paul thus made at least one journey from Ephesus (see fig. 4).

FIG. 4
PAUL'S MOVEMENTS IN AND OUT OF EPHESUS

Stay in Ephesus	Journeys
Three months in the synagogue (Acts 19:8)	
Two years in the lecture hall of Tyrannus (Acts 19:9–10)	Trip to Crete?
Care for Ephesus temporarily handed over to Timothy (1 Tim. 1:3; 3:14–15)	"Interim journey" (via Macedonia to Corinth and an earlier-than-planned return to Ephesus)
In Asia for some time (Acts 19:21–22)	
Demetrius incites a riot (Acts 19:23–20:1)	
	Farewell journey through Macedonia to Corinth (Acts 20:1–2)
	Departure from Corinth and a forced detour via Macedonia to Troas; by ship to Jerusalem (via Miletus) (Acts 20:3–6)

We can nevertheless speak of a three-year period during which Ephesus was the home base for Paul's work as an apostle—the longest time he spent in one place!

Although the apostle came to Ephesus at the request of the Jews, some of them later made life very difficult for Paul in this city. He speaks of "tears and . . . trials which came upon me through the plots of the Jews" (Acts 20:19 NASB). The instigator was probably one Alexander, a coppersmith (NIV: metalworker). Paul later writes in a passage in which his thoughts are in Ephesus and Troas, "Alexander the metalworker did me a great deal of harm . . . he strongly opposed our message" (2 Tim. 4:14–15). And in another letter to Timothy, which was also intended for Ephesus, he speaks of "Hymenaeus and Alexander, whom I have handed over to Satan to be taught not to blaspheme" (1 Tim. 1:20). It is striking that in the narrative of the riot caused by the silversmiths in Ephesus we read how the Jews push forward a certain Alexander to "make a defense before the people"—but he doesn't get a chance when the crowd notices that he is a Jew (Acts 19:33–34). The agitation of the crowd was directed against those who would undermine the trade in idolatrous souvenirs—specifically against Paul. But the people are not very familiar with the difference between Jews and Christians. It is possible that the Jews wanted to use a fellow craftsman, the coppersmith Alexander, to explain to the people that they should not hold the Jews as such responsible, but rather a new group that consisted of Christians. The people of Ephesus should not confuse Christianity with Judaism! During this dangerous riot the Jews apparently wanted to distance themselves emphatically from Paul and his fellow-Christians. Their opposition to him was so fierce that they would later in Jerusalem initiate a smear campaign that would almost lead to Paul being lynched by the crowds there (Acts 21:27–31; 24:18–19).

Before his imprisonment Paul was never able to work longer in one place without interruption than in Ephesus, but he apparently was nowhere as controversial as in this particular city!

8.2 Christianity and the Idols

As a flourishing Hellenistic city, Ephesus was also a center of paganism. Here the pioneer of Christianity collides even more intensely with the religiosity of the Gentiles than in other cities and regions, but the power of Christ in this charismatic figure appears to be in proportion to the challenge.

In Ephesus he gains such a reputation as a wonder-worker that people even try to get hold of handkerchiefs and aprons he has touched, because through these the sick are healed at home and evil spirits flee (Acts 19:11–12). Illness and demons cannot stand even the scent of Christ's messenger—they must flee from it. At the end of this period Paul can characterize his work with this image: "through us spreads everywhere the fragrance of the knowledge of him," and "we are to God the aroma of Christ among those who are being saved and those who are perishing" (2 Cor. 2:14–15).

The name Jesus becomes so popular that traveling Jewish exorcists want to make the name of this dynamic fellow-Jew part of their repertoire. But it quickly becomes clear that Jesus is not one name among many, but a unique name. An evil spirit chases would-be exorcists, the sons of a Jewish chief priest, naked out the door with the words "Jesus I know, and I know about Paul, but who are you?" (Acts 19:13–17). This incident proves beyond a shadow of a doubt that the amazing miracles demand faith in this new Lord!

When this incident becomes known among all Jews and Greeks, awe of the name of Jesus grows. Those who had already come to the faith no longer dare to secretly keep their books of magic; they burn them (Acts 19:17–20). This was a tremendous sign of courage: how much faith must these people, who until recently were so superstitious, have had that they dared to throw these books of magic into the fire. Apparently they were no longer in the least afraid of the powers that until then had held them under their spell!

The spectacularly superior power of Paul as servant of the gospel makes the name of Jesus known and honored in all of Ephesus and in the entire region of Asia (Acts 19:10). This is also precisely why Paul becomes a controversial figure. The idols do not allow themselves to be simply chased away—their servants protest. Demetrius, a prominent businessman in the souvenir trade connected with the temple of Artemis, incites his colleagues:

> And you see and hear how this fellow Paul has convinced and led astray large numbers of people here in Ephesus and in practically the whole province of Asia. He says that man-made gods are no gods at all. There is danger not only that our trade will lose its good name, but also that the temple of the great goddess Artemis will be discredited, and the goddess herself, who is worshiped throughout the province of Asia and the world, will be robbed of her divine majesty. (Acts 19:26–27)

What is exceptional in Paul's work in Ephesus is that Christianity becomes known here in the Gentile world and can no longer remain unnoticed. And this is due especially to the many wonders and signs that accompanied it and that proved Christ's superiority over the idols.

8.3 The Christianization of a Gentile World (1 Timothy)

In this period the apostle also wrote a letter to Timothy, and indirectly to the Christian community in Ephesus that was entrusted to Timothy's care at the time. It is known as 1 Timothy and is considered part of the Pastoral Epistles. It is primarily a letter for a pastor (Timothy), but at the same time it is a letter written to the church in which he works: Ephesus, where Paul left Timothy behind (1 Tim. 1:3). The letter is addressed to one person but is clearly not intended as a confidential, private communication. It deals continuously with what Timothy must teach the Christian community. The letter tells him "how people ought to conduct themselves in God's household" (1 Tim. 3:15). Sometimes the apostle goes over Timothy's head directly to the men and women in the Christian community in Ephesus (1 Tim. 2:8–15) or to the elders and their helpers in that community (1 Tim. 3:1–13). It is Timothy's duty to "point these things out to the brothers" (1 Tim. 4:6) and to "teach" (1 Tim 4:11; 6:3). In most manuscripts the letter ends with a personal blessing: "Grace be with you [singular]," but in a smaller number of manuscripts the "you" is plural and thus would include the Christian community: "Grace be with you [all]" (1 Tim.

6:21). This variant indicates that the letter written to one individual was nevertheless read as a letter to many.

In spite of the fact that at present many date this first letter sent to Timothy at Ephesus after the three years Paul worked in Ephesus,[4] there is reason to return to an earlier date that for some time has been virtually abandoned, namely, during the third journey:[5]

1. Timothy is still young and must be admonished to live in such a way that no one will look down on him because he is young (1 Tim. 4:12).

2. The Christian community in Ephesus is still in a phase in which various instructions about behavior and further organization of the work are meaningful (such as deportment in the worship service, requirements for the lifestyle of the elders, the position of widows). The letter points to a time of building, when not everything has taken shape and been formalized yet.

3. Paul is still actively involved in the work at Ephesus; he hopes to return there and to relieve Timothy (1 Tim. 3:14–15). But a direct involvement in the work at Ephesus after the three-year stay is out of the question. In his farewell address to the elders Paul says that he will not return to this area: "I know that none of you among whom I have gone about preaching the kingdom will ever see me again" (Acts 20:25; cf. 20:38). While it is true that Paul frequently changed his plans, in this case a word from the Spirit has shown him that he is traveling to Jerusalem to face "prison and hardships" (Acts 20:22–24). And even if this apostle did at a later date go through Asia on his way elsewhere, it is inconceivable that he once again would have spent a long period of time in the city (including an interim period during which Timothy takes his place). Paul made up the final balance sheet of his work in Ephesus when he said farewell to the elders after the three years there and placed the responsibility for the Christian community in their hands (Acts 20:26–35).

In earlier centuries this letter was often correctly dated during the so-called third missionary journey. This view fell out of favor when the then-customary narrowing of this dating appeared to be open to debate. The problem lay in the equating of 1 Timothy 1:3 ("As I urged you when I went into Macedonia, stay there in Ephesus") and Acts 20:1 (Paul leaves Ephesus definitively after the Artemis riot and departs for Macedonia). These cannot refer to the same departure for Macedonia, however, for after the Artemis riot Timothy travels with Paul and is not left behind in Ephesus (Acts 20:4). Because no other departure for Macedonia is mentioned in Acts, the more precise dating of this event during the third journey appeared to be problematic. But the problem can be resolved when we realize that Paul made a journey *during* his three years in Ephesus. Not only did this journey take him to Corinth (as is generally accepted), but he traveled to Corinth via Macedonia: "After I go through Macedonia, I will come to you—for I will be going through Macedonia" (1 Cor. 16:5).[6] What is involved here is not the last journey (Acts 20), when Paul had already been planning for some time to go to Jerusalem (Acts 19:21); at the time of the writing of 1 Corinthians 16 this was at best an option, certainly not a firm plan (1 Cor. 16:3–4).

In Acts we also find an indirect trace of this interim journey via Macedonia and Corinth. In the last period of Paul's stay in the region we suddenly read about Gaius and Aristarchus as "Paul's traveling companions from Macedonia" (Acts 19:29). How did the apostle suddenly acquire traveling companions from Macedonia? They certainly did not join Paul when, many years before, he had fled from this area to Athens. Apparently the apostle has more recently, during his stay in Ephesus, visited Macedonia again, and thus he can have traveling companions from that region with him during the last phase of his work in Ephesus.

The dating of 1 Timothy during the three years of Paul's work in Ephesus can be narrowed down to the period of his interim journey from Ephesus to Macedonia and Corinth. During this journey Timothy apparently stayed behind as vicar. This may also have been the reason why Paul waited with his departure for Macedonia until Timothy was once again in the city (1 Cor. 16:11).

We bypass here the question whether the linguistic usage of the letter allows for its authenticity. We limit ourselves to the question of dating the letter on the assumption that it was indeed written by Paul. However, the linguistic characteristics argue against authenticity to a lesser degree than has been assumed since Friedrich Schleiermacher.

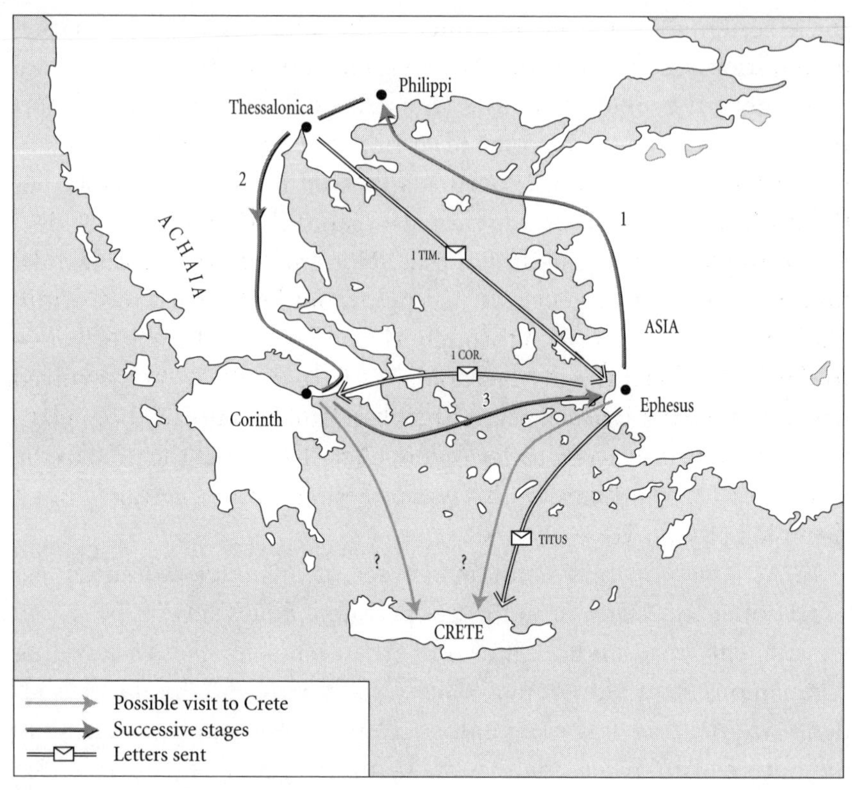

Map 7: *Journey from and back to Ephesus*

1. The letter is written to a person from Paul's immediate circle; this fact can have a bearing on word choice and phraseology and produce limited differences in word choice and sentence structure when compared with other letters that were written to Christian communities rather than to an individual.
2. It is difficult on the basis of modern stylistic analysis to maintain that the letter cannot have been written by Paul.[7]

Although the letter deals especially with the internal organization of the community, there are nevertheless traces of the encounter between the gospel and the world of Greek culture as it took place especially in Ephesus. Although it would be incorrect to view the letter primarily from the perspective of the contrast in Ephesus (since there are also connections with the positive elements in pagan culture and religion), there is nevertheless at least a measure of contact between the topics in this letter and the local surroundings.[8]

There was apparently a threatening danger that the Greek appreciation of "myths and genealogies" would continue to be an influence in Christianity—via the use of the writings of Israel, which the Gentile Christians encountered once they came to faith in the mighty Messiah of this nation. There was as yet too little awareness that the Scriptures are intended to convert the godless and not to support a continued indulgence in "fables and genealogies" that may appeal to the mind but do not touch the heart and spirit (1 Tim. 1:3–11).

The gospel has come for sinners and puts them in touch with "the King eternal, immortal, invisible, the only God" (1 Tim. 1:15–17). Among the first tasks of believers, therefore, is that they learn to pray for the salvation and conversion of all people, including those in authority (1 Tim. 2:1–7).

In a world of anger and strife, of luxury and ostentation, the Spirit of Christ urges an attitude toward life that is modest (1 Tim. 2:8–15). Quarrelsome men should unite in peaceful and holy prayer to God. To the extent that women in the temples of the idols were used to sober dress, few adornments, and hair worn down rather than in high or elaborate styles,[9] Christianity does not provide an excuse for suddenly changing to a less sober form of dress and behavior. On the other hand, the gospel is not to be misunderstood as an ascetic message, such as, for example, the Neo-Pythagoreans spread (1 Tim. 4:1–5).

In a world in which sports occupied a prominent place, people must learn that training in godliness brings greater gain than physical training (1 Tim. 4:8–10). Godliness is also more valuable than riches: Christianity values piety (*eusebeia*) above the orientation toward success and money, and this *eusebeia* is given a new direction through the person of Jesus Christ (1 Tim. 6:5–19).

In the background of the letter stands the image of a world that is on the one hand full of myths that have been passed on from grandmothers to their grandchildren (1 Tim. 4:7) and full of avarice, luxury, egoism, superstition, and a foolish preoccupation with sports—but a world that on the other hand still knows of piety, love for fellow human beings, and modesty. The gospel of the one God and his Redeemer, as well as the hope of eternal life—these are things that in this world bring about renewal toward living in love and modesty. On the one hand the power of the gospel hits Ephesus like a bomb. On the other hand, Christianization takes time and continued preaching by Paul and his replacement Timothy. The temple of Artemis stands majestic, rich, and imposing. Over against this, Christ builds "the house of God, which is the church of the living God, the pillar and ground of the truth" (1 Tim. 3:15 KJV). The enchantment of the idols is supplanted by the "mystery of [true] godliness" (1 Tim. 3:16). This mystery is great. It is as if Paul alludes to the well-known slogan "Great is Artemis of the Ephesians" (Acts 19:34).[10] The new motto, that of Christianity, is different:

> The mystery of godliness is great:
> He appeared in a body,
> was vindicated by the Spirit,
> was seen by angels,
> was preached among the nations,
> was believed on in the world,
> was taken up in glory. (1 Tim. 3:16)

9

LONG-DISTANCE PASTORATE

Toward the end of his second letter to Corinth Paul gives a list of the many calamities and persecutions that make his work difficult. At the end of the list he writes, "Besides everything else, I face daily the pressure of my concern for all the churches" (2 Cor. 11:28). Here it becomes evident how the growth of the gospel increasingly threatens to overwhelm the life of the apostle: he is overburdened with care and aftercare!

This is especially true during the so-called third missionary journey. While Paul is working in Ephesus for an extended period, there are, farther west, already Christian communities in Macedonia and Achaia. Those communities had been established by him and continue to demand his attention. Furthermore, the number of coworkers active in this region keeps growing, and they also ask for his support. These communities and colleagues are not located too far from where Paul is, and accessibility throughout the region is such that they can visit back and forth with relative ease. Thus the apostle remains fairly well informed about developments elsewhere. Fellow Christians and coworkers travel back and forth in the region and facilitate, intentionally or unintentionally, the exchange of information. The result is that Paul in Ephesus is closely involved in the ups and downs of Christian communities and people spread over a rather large area.

A few of the letters of the apostle that have been preserved give us a clear idea of his long-distance pastoral care. Both letters to Corinth were written in the context of an ongoing situation that required attention and care and are therefore very different from the letter to the Galatians, which is more an unexpectedly necessary crisis-letter. And the letter to Titus was clearly written to a coworker who must continue his work on Crete without the apostle's presence. This letter has a different character from the first letter to Timothy, which is in fact a letter written on the road and intended for the Christian community in Ephesus, Paul's own home church in those years.

In these three letters, two of which are intended for Corinth (in Achaia) and one for Titus (on Crete) we have examples of long-distance attention and care—care for a Christian community that had been established earlier in the region (Corinth) and care for a person who is one of Paul's closest associates and works elsewhere in the region to establish and build up new, independent communities (Titus). These three documents give us insight into the day-to-day worries of the apostle.

9.1 Attending to a Sound Beginning (Titus)

It is difficult to assign an exact date to the letter to Titus. It is not a prison epistle. Paul is a free man, since he can freely choose to (probably) spend the winter in Nicopolis (Titus 3:12). It is therefore not very likely that Titus was left behind on Crete when Paul was on his way to Rome as prisoner and experienced the stormy journey along the inhospitable south coast of Crete (Acts 27:7–12). Titus's work on this island must have preceded the period of Paul's captivity, because afterward there was no period when the apostle worked in the region of Greece, Asia, and Crete.

The letter then should be dated in the period when Paul's home base was Ephesus, from where he also made a longer journey through Macedonia and Achaia. Did he ever make a separate, short trip to Crete from Ephesus? If the apostle somehow visited Crete during the first two years of his stay in Ephesus, he entrusted the preaching of the gospel there to Titus when he left. This may be what the beginning of the letter alludes to: "The reason I left you in Crete was that you might straighten out what was left unfinished" (Titus 1:5).

It is, however, also possible, though less likely, that the apostle himself never visited Crete during those years and that he sent Titus there to preach. Against expectations, no one came to take over Titus's duties after he had been there for some time. On the contrary, he received instructions to stay on the island (even when, perhaps, other coworkers moved on or were allowed to return to Paul). In that case Paul alludes at the beginning of the letter to this continuing "posting" ("I left you in Crete"), and he describes in the letter the reason for this continuation of Titus's task in Crete.[1]

In any case, Titus will be relieved soon, either by Artemas or by Tychicus (Titus 3:12), and he will receive a visit of support from Zenas the lawyer and Apollos (Titus 3:13). These brief comments open a window on the time when many of the people around Paul were engaged in the preaching of the gospel (1 Cor. 16:11) and when there was an active traveling back and forth of preachers and helpers. The mention of Apollos also fits in with the middle portion of the third journey: Apollos is then in the vicinity of Paul and has his own itinerary (1 Cor. 16:12).

The apostle himself hopes to spend the winter in Nicopolis, where Titus can join him (Titus 3:12). There were many cities called Nicopolis, but this refers in all likelihood to a Nicopolis in the Greek world, of which Crete was also a part, specifically to Nicopolis in Achaia. During his stay in Ephesus Paul was planning to spend the winter in Achaia, as he writes to the Corinthians (1 Cor. 16:6). This plan was ultimately abandoned due to conflicts, but it is not impossible that the letter to Titus was written before the plan had been canceled. Paul was often forced to change his plans, which makes it difficult to determine in retrospect whether plans that are mentioned in passing were actually carried out (for a reconstruction of what Paul planned to do and what he actually did, see fig. 5). In any case, Paul wrote during (the middle of) the third missionary journey a letter of instruction to a colleague who worked elsewhere.

Fig. 5
Hypothetical Reconstruction of Planned and Actual Activities (Based on the Letter to Titus)

Planning Calendar	Diary
Spring A.D. 55 (The year ahead)	A.D. 55 (The year in retrospect)
Pentecost	**Pentecost**
Leave Ephesus (1 Cor. 16:5–9). Apollos wants (with Zenas) to stay and thereafter go to, among other places, Crete (1 Cor. 16:12; Titus 3:13). (Shall I send Tychicus or Artemas to relieve Titus soon on Crete [Titus 3:12]?)	Left Ephesus (1 Tim. 1:3). Hope that Apollos will carry out his plans! Another letter written to Titus.
Summer	**Summer**
Trip through Macedonia (1 Cor. 16:5; 1 Tim. 1:3).	Good reception in Macedonia; the collection is being taken up (2 Cor. 8:1–5). Two new coworkers taken along: Gaius and Aristarchus (Acts 19:29; cf. 20:4). Someone sent to Crete to relieve Titus. Letter written to Timothy in Ephesus.
Winter	**Winter**
Stay in Achaia (1 Cor. 16:6). Spend the winter in Nicopolis (Achaia) and let Titus come there (Titus 3:12).	Left Corinth and Achaia in a great hurry, the visit a failure; returned to Ephesus already before winter (2 Cor. 2:1–2; 13:2). Promised to return soon to visit Macedonia one more time from Achaia, and thereafter expected to be helped on the way from Achaia to Jerusalem (2 Cor. 1:15–16). Titus fortunately did find me! [Later addition: perhaps it will be better to go to Macedonia first, because the reports from Corinth continue to be bleak. Deploy Titus to improve the climate in Corinth first?]

In Paul's letter to Titus on Crete, we find topics of importance to the establishing of a Christian community. Elders must be appointed (Titus 1:5–9). This must be done "in every town"; this addition indicates that also on Crete the gospel spread rapidly.

But from the start this gospel must immediately distance itself from people who want to turn it into another philosophy among many or into an interesting new form of religiosity. Faith in Christ lives by God's grace, and this grace is aimed at the renewal of life (Titus 2:11–14; 3:4–7). This renewal must change young and old, man and woman (Titus 2:1–10). *That* is the point, and not speculative theories or a preoccupation with genealogies (Titus 1:10–16; 3:8–11). Greeks and Romans were interested in (mythological) genealogical connections between humans and (demi)gods[2] and apparently made avid use of the ancient stories and genealogies in the Scriptures of Israel with which they came in contact via the gospel. Thus Christianity is in danger of being devalued in the shortest possible time to a kind of pagan-Jewish syncretism that lacks obedience to God and renewal through the Spirit.

It is striking that these hazards do not surface later but immediately, at the very beginnings of the new Christian communities. This is probably due to the fact that up to this point the Jewish Bible had been a book for the synagogue, and it was easy for Greeks to simply pass over those identity papers of the Jews. But now that the power of Christ is entering the world, it appears to be possible to share in the book of this God, without circumcision and without becoming a Jew. Without conversion, people rapidly incorporated this book into the pagan conceptions they had been raised with, conceptions about gods and humans, myths and genealogies, speculations about the former Golden Age, and the discussions about rituals and taboos.

This is one of the day-to-day worries of the apostle Paul: the concern to make clear everywhere, as pioneer of Messiah Jesus, that the Christian faith seeks to call forth a new humanity and is not intended to confirm unchanged people in their self-confidence by means of genealogies. He writes to Titus, "I want you to stress these things, so that those who have trusted in God may be careful to devote themselves to doing what is good. These things are excellent and profitable for everyone. But avoid foolish controversies and genealogies and arguments and quarrels about the law, because these are unprofitable and useless" (Titus 3:8–9).

9.2 Community Growth and Humility (1 Corinthians)

Of all of Paul's letters, the two letters to Corinth that have been preserved are perhaps most concretely involved with the Christian community. This is due to the special circumstances that occasioned them. Paul was in Ephesus (in Asia), not too far away from Corinth (in Achaia) as the crow flies. This meant that he was kept rather well informed about the ups and down of this community by people who were coming and going ("some from Chloe's household"; Timothy; Stephanas, Fortunatus, and Achaicus; 1 Cor. 1:11; 16:10, 17). He himself was also able to stay in contact with the Christian community through others as well (1 Cor. 16:12), and the community could also send him a letter with questions (1 Cor. 7:1). These circumstances allow us to get a close-up view of the life of the Christian community in the letters to Corinth. The correspondence deals with more specifics than do the letters to Philippi or Ephesus, Galatia or Rome. The result is that the reader of Paul's correspondence gets the impression that the Christian community in Corinth was very different from the other Christian communities. But that is a premature conclusion. The "map" of the Christian community in Corinth is drawn to a different scale than the "maps" of the other churches. We should rather assume that these letters to Corinth present an "enlarged," more detailed picture and thus give a good impression of what all could be going on in still relatively young churches. And although in the other letters we get less detail, we may assume that the situation and the problems elsewhere were comparable (as is confirmed by the general pastoral instructions Paul gives Timothy and Titus).[3]

In 1 Corinthians many topics are addressed, varying from individual problems to very general teachings. Among the former are a serious case of adultery (1 Cor. 5), a case of brothers who take each other to court (1 Cor. 6), rich people who do not wait for the poor people at the communal supper (1 Cor. 11:17–22), and fathers who prefer not (or no longer) to give their daughters in marriage (1 Cor. 7:25–40). More general topics include the resurrection of the dead (1 Cor. 15), how to handle the gifts of the Spirit (1 Cor. 12–14), the question of eating meat offered to idols (1 Cor. 8–10), and others.

But all these issues involve a fundamental attitude, and it is with this that Paul begins his letter. The danger that threatened in Corinth was combining the new faith with ancient Greek, human pride. The believers preferred to be identified as supporters of superministers (Peter, Paul, Apollos, and even Christ) rather than as servants of the crucified Jesus Christ (1 Cor. 1–4). This explains why the believers in Corinth found it relatively easy to live their own lifestyles: pride keeps itself from submission to commandments that impact one's life.

The issues in the Christian community in Corinth show that there was a tendency to follow one's own ideas about marriage, or about the eating of meat sacrificed to idols, about the freedom of women or the manner in which the Lord's Supper was observed, or about the use of the gifts of the Spirit or the attitude toward fornication (1 Cor. 7–14). The Corinthians even held to a more Hellenistic view of the resurrection as not being bodily (1 Cor. 15).

Over against this mentality Paul chooses a position from the perspective of the cross of Christ (1 Cor. 1–4). The level of the groundwater of Hellenism is high in the Christian community in Corinth—but it is also the groundwater of human nature. The apostle avoids falling into the same trap. He does not speak highly of himself, but he shows by his own example the power of grace and the weakness of Christ, which are demonstrated in his selfless service and his preaching with its lack of rhetorical sophistication (1 Cor. 1:17; 2:1–5; 9:12–23). It is precisely from this "weakness" that he can write with outspoken directness. The shepherd goes ahead of his flock in humility to the foot of the cross! Paul is deeply concerned that the new Christian community be set free from the old traditions of human pride and self-will.

Since the nineteenth century, many see 1 Corinthians as written to a community divided into parties.[4] The following points argue against this notion of opposing factions. (a) The letter as a whole gives the impression that there was *one* community with *one* Lord's Supper (1 Cor. 11); (b) there were slogans in support of preferences or favorites (Peter, Paul, Apollos, Christ), but there was no clear division into two, three, or four groups; (c) the manner in which Paul handles the issue would rather point to the fact that he continually had to fight against a Hellenistic penchant for wisdom and individualism—exemplified in the first place by the way in which Corinthian Christians almost idolized individuals (1 Cor. 1–4).

Again and again the letter sounds a call to humility and modesty: as a new religion, Christianity is not triumphant—it is serving! "Brothers, think of what you were when you were called. Not many of you were wise by human standards; not many were influential; not many were of noble birth. But God chose the foolish things of the world to shame the wise; God chose the weak things of the world to shame the strong . . . so that no one may boast before him" (1 Cor. 1:26–29). "So then, no more boasting about men! . . . [for] you are of Christ, and Christ is of God" (1 Cor. 3:21–23). And, "[Let] no one of you . . . become arrogant in behalf of one against the other. . . . What do you have that you did not receive?" (1 Cor. 4:6–7 NASB). That is why Paul reproaches them: "Your boasting is not good" (1 Cor. 5:6), and "If anyone wants to be contentious about this, we have no other practice—nor do the churches of God" (1 Cor. 11:16). Or "did the word of God originate with you" perhaps? (1 Cor. 14:36).

In a note added in his own hand at the end of the letter (1 Cor. 16:21–24), Paul says in no uncertain terms, "If anyone does not love the Lord, let him be accursed. Maranatha" (NASB). The letter as a whole shows how passionately the apostle handled his long-distance pastorate, wanting also in this manner to be instrumental in making the crucified Christ manifest in the Greek world of human affairs.

9.3 The Servant of Christ under Attack (2 Corinthians)

Christianity is not founded on the spread of impersonal manifestos or theoretical systems. Its foundation is the faith of apostles and prophets. The gospel goes "from faith to faith" (Rom. 1:17 NASB). Believers, called by God and gripped by the good news, spread the gospel and may, thanks to the outpouring of the powers of the Spirit, receive others as brothers and sisters in that faith.

Paul says that God has made people "competent as ministers of a new covenant—not of the letter but of the Spirit; for the letter kills, but the Spirit gives life" (2 Cor. 3:6). These called servants reflect in their lives the glory of the Lord; they themselves change "from glory to glory" (2 Cor. 3:18–4:1 NASB). The Christian church follows the examples of saints and prophets. As the apostle follows his Lord Christ, so the believers may become followers of the apostles (1 Cor. 11:1). Preachers must consciously be examples to be imitated (2 Thess. 3:9).

This is the power of the gospel: it proves itself as a renewing power, in the first place in the life of its ministers. But here also lies the vulnerability of the gospel: in challenging the servant, the gospel is attacked as well. Thus Paul is not only slandered and persecuted from outside the Christian community, but within his own pastorate he has had to deal more than once with contempt for his person. This put his work as preacher of the gospel at risk! In the second letter to Corinth we get a close-up view of one instance of this.

Apparently there was in Corinth an individual who openly agitated against Paul. During the interim visit (after the first two years in Ephesus) there appears to have been an intense campaign against the person of the apostle instigated by this individual. The campaign raised emotions to the point where it seemed advisable to have a cooling-off period. At the end of this period the problems were not immediately solved; only after Titus's supplementary mission was Paul able to visit Corinth once again with pleasure (2 Cor. 2:5–11).

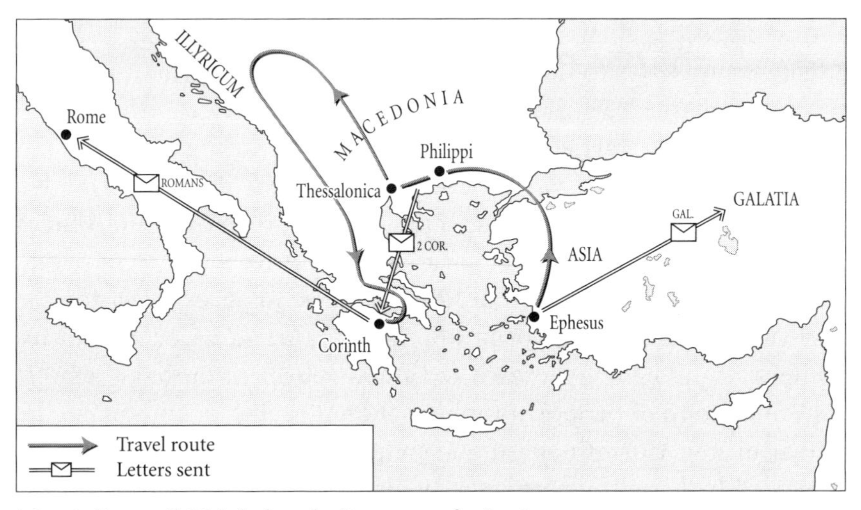

Map 8: *Farewell Visit before the Departure for Spain*

We don't know who this individual was and how the Christian community did Paul an injustice. It seems that Paul is intentionally vague about the matter after the issue has been settled. But we do know something of the final outcome.

In preparation for a pleasant third visit Paul had decided to go to Corinth via a detour and to send Titus ahead on a peace mission (2 Cor. 1:15, 23; 13:1–4). But the climate in Corinth was still so unfavorable that this change of plan on Paul's part was given a negative interpretation: he was undependable, a man whose yes and no didn't mean much to him (2 Cor. 1:17). This automatically cast a shadow on all his work: how dependable are the words of this man? The apostle must take great pains to make it clear that his gospel is an unqualified yes on God's part and that his own actions are congruent with that yes (2 Cor. 1:18–2:4).

Paul is in a bind. He does not want to commend himself to the church; the Christian community in Corinth must itself be an eloquent commendation for the apostle (2 Cor. 3:1–3). On the other hand, he must defend himself to prevent that his gospel becomes suspect. In 2 Corinthians we see Paul struggle with this heavy task which his love for the Christian community does not allow him to evade. The emotional tone of this letter betrays how difficult this was for him. As apostle he must set aside any feelings of having been personally misjudged, so that his focus remains on how his Master receives lasting honor.

The second letter to the Corinthians has a curious structure. In the first seven chapters Paul writes much about his service in the gospel: a glorious service carried out by a weak human being (2 Cor. 1–7). These chapters elicit a sympathetic attitude on the part of the reader. Then Paul writes, rather unexpectedly, about the collection that is being held for Jerusalem. He appeals to the Corinthians to cooperate intensively in this collection, and he expresses appreciation for the Christian community in Corinth in these chapters (2 Cor. 8–9). This is followed suddenly by a third section: a vehement outburst against a specific group of people. It looks as if Paul begins by embracing the community in Corinth again and by praising them, so that he can immediately thereafter permanently distance himself from the people who are trying to drive a wedge between him and the Christian community (2 Cor. 10–13). It is therefore very well possible that the more positive portions in the first half of the letter are formulated in part with the presence of opponents in mind, opponents who are frontally attacked only in the final chapters.[5]

Why does the apostle postpone this confrontation for so long? Probably because he dreads it. The sudden, almost unrestrained, vehemence in chapters 10–13 betrays a writer who is ill at ease. And no wonder. Paul must present himself in contradistinction to people who discredit his gospel by the impressive manner in which they present themselves. The apostle, by comparison, pales into insignificance (2 Cor. 10:10). Although Paul is not interested in impressing people as such, he cannot, in the interest of the Christian community, evade the confrontation. Thus he must write about a topic he does not really consider worth writing about: his own status and standing.

Apparently his opponents impressed the people in Corinth with their proud Jewish descent (2 Cor. 11:22–23). They also viewed the apostle Paul as inferior to the *real* apostles in Jerusalem—the "most eminent apostles" (2 Cor. 11:5 NASB).

The Jewish Christians who influence the Christian community in Corinth combine respect for the most eminent apostles in Jerusalem with contempt for the insignificant apostle Paul. This leads Paul to compare himself twice positively with those superapostles in Jerusalem (2 Cor. 11:5–11; 12:11–13): he has the signs of an apostle in common with them (2 Cor. 12:12), and the only thing in which he differs from them is that as a rule he does not wish to receive financial support. Bracketed between these comparisons with the superapostles we find a comparison of Paul with the false apostles in Corinth (they boast in their greatness, but Paul boasts in his sufferings, 2 Cor. 11:12–12:10).[6]

These Jewish Christians also bragged about revelations they received (2 Cor. 12:1–6). There are no indications that they brought any new teaching or insisted on circumcision. Yet Paul says that under the influence of these people the Christians in Corinth are in danger of switching allegiance to a different Jesus, a different Spirit, a different gospel (2 Cor. 11:4). Paul states his case very strongly. But it is appropriate in this situation, when "the simplicity and purity of devotion to Christ" (2 Cor. 11:3 NASB) are degraded to group support for special people of superior religious descent who can point to impressive relatives in Jerusalem. It would seem to be merely a matter of attitude and atmosphere—but attitude and atmosphere are intrinsic aspects of faith. The one thing that is appropriate here is losing oneself in Christ: people are merely servants who point to him. Paul uses the image of a bride who is joined to her husband: he, Paul, is the intermediary who joins the community of faith to Christ (2 Cor. 11:2). Once the relationship has been established, the intermediary is no longer of importance. The community in Corinth must not gaze in admiration at people. If they do, they in fact let go of their Master and the gospel of his grace.

How was it possible for the atmosphere in Corinth to become this poisoned? It happened in part because the Greek believers in that city were still susceptible to what is important by human standards (see 1 Corinthians), and in part because Paul himself was not a very imposing figure, whose resumé was in fact a source of some embarrassment to the Greeks. In this "weakness" of the apostle his opponents lodge themselves to flaunt their own, more imposing, resumés.

That is why the apostle writes at some length and bluntly about those things in his life that were a source of embarrassment to some: he has suffered the humiliation of being flogged (more than once), he was in prison, he was stoned once, he was shipwrecked three times, has been attacked by robbers, and often has not had enough to eat or drink (2 Cor. 11:23–29)—is that the apostle of the great Messiah? Paul has taken on the form of him who was "despised and rejected by men, a man of sorrows, and familiar with suffering" (Isa. 53:3).

In the Greek world such a life full of adversity was considered a sign that the gods apparently were ill disposed toward this man (cf. Acts 28:4)! And in the Christian community in Corinth, Paul the man fades into insignificance compared with the prosperous "pseudoapostles" (2 Cor. 11:13).

Paul was well aware of the negative impact of his image as one who seemed to attract bad luck. He felt that behind all his adversities there was an angel of Satan who tormented him (2 Cor. 12:7; 1 Thess. 2:18). The Lord gave this angel of Satan free rein in order to keep Paul small and humble. And when the apostle prayed for an end to this opposition, the answer was, "My grace is sufficient for you, for my power is made perfect in weakness" (2 Cor. 12:9). Thus, in the end, Paul learned to turn his troubles into a source of pride: "For Christ's sake, I delight in weaknesses, in insults, in hardships, in persecutions, in difficulties" because his strength as servant of the Crucified One lay precisely in his working as a servant bowed down by adversities (2 Cor. 12:10).

In 2 Corinthians the apostle tries to show the connection between the power of Christ and the weakness of the servant. The disciples during Jesus' life on earth were already focused on the question as to which one of them was the greatest, and in the history of Christianity this is the question that again and again siphons attention away from Christ and his gospel. With this letter Paul has given future servants of the gospel once and for all the model for a vision of service and servant, of ministry and minister. Ridiculed in his weakness, Paul became the pioneer for a Christendom that is guided by the word of the Master: "Come to me, all you who are weary and burdened, and I will give you rest. Take my yoke upon you and learn from me, for I am gentle and humble in heart, and you will find rest for your souls. For my yoke is easy and my burden is light" (Matt. 11:28–30).

10

ABSENT FROM ROME

After first preaching the gospel without the requirement of circumcision in Arabia, Paul was led ever farther west along a meandering route. After a first wandering journey through southern Turkey, it looked on a later journey as if the apostle would go to Rome sooner than he had expected. He traveled through Macedonia via the main highway that led to the center of the Roman world empire, the Via Egnatia. But he was diverted to Corinth, and after that he spent a long period in Ephesus. The westerly movement was interrupted and even changed into a slightly easterly direction.

Why did Paul not go on to Rome in those years? Was he ashamed of the gospel? Was he afraid to enter the city of the emperor with this humble, unimpressive news of the Crucified One? The apostle vehemently denies this in his letter to the Christians in Rome: "I am not ashamed of the gospel, because it is the power of God for the salvation of everyone who believes: first for the Jew, then for the Gentile" (Rom. 1:16). He had intended to bring this gospel to Rome much sooner, but he was prevented from carrying out his travel plans (Rom. 1:13). He may refer here to the plan to move on from Macedonia to Rome during the second journey, or to reach it by sea from the port city of Corinth. But these plans did not materialize because of the persecution by the Jews in Macedonia, which forced Paul to flee to Achaia, and because of Claudius's expulsion of the Jews from Rome, which at that point made it impossible for Paul to travel farther west from Achaia. Paul was "eager to preach the gospel also to you who are at Rome," but he was prevented from doing so until the end of the third journey (Rom. 1:13–15; 15:22).[1]

In the meantime the gospel has made its way to Rome, and there is already a group of people "called to be saints" in the city (Rom. 1:7). The banner of Christ has been planted in the center of the world empire, but the pioneer of Christendom was not there when it happened. This unique situation gave rise to a unique document: Paul's letter to a church that arrived before he himself could make the trip there.

It is a letter that goes into great detail and depth about the meaning of the gospel for both Jews and Gentiles. Paul had been much involved with both groups in Ephesus. Does he in this letter simply project his experiences in Ephesus onto people he has never met?[2] Or does he write specifically for the congregation in Rome? If the latter, why does he go on at such length about the meaning of the law, the importance of Israel, and so forth? The epistle to the Romans is something of a puzzle: Paul has never been in Rome, yet he writes one of his longest letters to this community. What moved him to do so?[3]

10.1 Rome: *First* the Greek

Some claim that the apostle Paul was afraid that the community in Rome would fall under Jewish-Christian influence and thus be brought under the yoke of circumcision and law. In this letter, Paul then makes every effort to secure this outpost and to keep it consonant with *his* gospel. His emphasis on themes such as "law" and "Israel" then would have been in reaction to the actions of the Judaizers, who wanted to make the young Christian community a messianic variant within Judaism.

If this were correct, however, we would expect some measure of confrontation with false teachers. But they are never mentioned, which gives Paul's discussion a somewhat abstract character. It is as if he speaks into the air—why does he not directly address those people he opposes if they were indeed active in Rome?

Only once does Paul warn against people who cause divisions and obstacles (*skandala*; Rom. 16:17–20). But he does so at the very end of his letter. The final chapter of Romans contains a remarkably large number of names, divided into two groups: the usual short list of personal greetings at the end (16:21–23), and a much longer list of greetings (16:3–15) after the commendation of Phoebe (16:1–2) and before the warning against false teachers (16:17–20). In this longer list the names are accompanied by notes of commendation concerning their merit in service to the gospel—which is unusual in a simple list of greetings at the end of a letter. Paul also uses an unusual formula: instead of the common "I greet" or "We greet" we find the command "Greet." The readers of this letter are instructed to greet these people whom Paul mentions and commends. These are people in Rome whom Paul knows from personal experience. Thus the apostle advises this Christian community, which he does not know personally, to maintain close contact with his friends and acquaintances who preach or support the gospel in their midst. This section then concludes with a general exhortation to accept one another in love and a universal greeting from all the churches of Christ (16:16).

By contrast, the warning against false teachers (16:17–20) does not mention anyone by name. It is probable that Paul simply gives a general warning: should people come into the community who teach anything different or act differently from the coworkers in Christ whom he has just commended, let the community beware! (The letter then concludes with the usual greetings and personal comments in vv. 21–23.)[4]

It is unlikely that at the conclusion of Romans Paul is thinking of the Judaizers. Rather, he has in mind people who "are not serving our Lord Christ, but their own appetites" (v. 18). This points to licentiousness and a worldly mentality rather than to Judaizers (cf. Phil. 3:18–19). There is no reason to project the exhortations at the end of the letter back onto the letter as a whole and to assume that the letter was written entirely in confrontation with (unmentioned) Jewish-Christian false teachers.

Some think that it is possible to find an explanation for the curious phenomenon of a letter purportedly combating Judaism—but without mentioning the infiltrating Judaizers. The history of the origin of the Christian community in Rome then is viewed as unique; it would have led to a situation in which the tensions between Jewish Christians and Gentile Christians escalated without any outside influence, so that apostolic intervention was called for.

In this explanation the origin of the community in Rome is located within the synagogue: the first Christian community in Rome was Jewish-Christian. Because of the unrest in the synagogues that was generated by the coming of the gospel of Christ in the synagogues in Rome, Claudius would have decided to expel all Jews from the city (ca. A.D. 49). In the Jewish vacuum that followed, a new Christian community then sprung up in Rome, but this time a Gentile-Christian community. When the Jewish Christians returned a few years later to the empire's capital, they found there a kind of Pauline community. And from that moment on there is suddenly tension within the Christian community in Rome.[5] It is a tension between two constituent elements of the community, each with its own history: the Jewish Christians and the Gentile Christians. They meet together in the city where they live, Rome, but it is difficult to arrive at a symbiosis. This is the situation to which the apostle writes an extensive discourse on the topics that form the background of this internal tension (law, circumcision, Israel).

Against this reconstruction stands the fact that Paul does not write about factions or parties within the community. Not until he is finished with his extensive discussion about the law and Israel does he mention a distinction in the community between the strong and the weak (Rom. 14:1–15:6). But this distinction is unrelated to the contrast between Jewish Christians and Gentile Christians.[6] Nor does it involve the distinction between non-Christian Jews and Christians.[7] It concerns people who have problems with the consumption of meat and wine (Rom. 14:21)—a difference of opinion concerning vegetarianism or asceticism, which fits in a non-Jewish context where Pythagorean religious influences also play a role.

Furthermore, there are insufficient grounds for the notion of the development of an early Jewish-Christian community in Rome.

Claudius did expel the Jews from Rome around A.D. 49, but Acts 18:2 does not in any way connect this expulsion with disturbances caused by the preaching of Christ. Such a link is also ruled out when we consider Gallio's attitude during that same period. He came to Corinth as governor, as the emperor's representative, and must have been fully conversant with the events in Rome during the preceding months and years. If he had shortly before experienced a sweeping removal of Jews on the basis of religious disputes involving Christ, he would have reacted very differently when the Jews, arguing with Paul, a Christian, came before his court (Acts 18:12–17). But Gallio "showed no concern whatever" (Acts 18:17b). This attitude would be incomprehensible if similar disputes had recently moved the emperor to drastic reprisals against the Jews. We see unconcern similar to Gallio's also in Claudius Lysias (Acts 23:27–30) and Festus (Acts 25:18–20). As long as religious disputes don't form a menace for the Roman government, they are ignored by that government! Another point is that the Jews are not familiar with such a conflict in their synagogues. When Paul arrives during Nero's reign as a prisoner in Rome, the Jewish community appears to have only second-hand information about the sect of the Nazarenes (Acts 28:21–22). These points prove that the Christian community in Rome did not have an explicitly Jewish-Christian origin.

When the Roman historian Suetonius writes that Claudius expelled the Jews from the city because they continuously caused trouble at the instigation of one *Chrestus*, it is not likely that this is a reference to Christ.[8] Suetonius was aware of the fact that the *christiani* were named after Christus, not after Chrestus.[9] Besides, the context of Suetonius's comment indicates that the disturbances took place in Palestine; the expulsion of the Jews from the city of Rome thus constitutes a reprisal intended to send a timely and unambiguous message to this nation in the far-away eastern border region.[10]

It is possible that around A.D. 49 the name of a prominent Jewish guerilla in Palestine called Chrestus was circulating in Rome. Perhaps his name was mentioned in some report or other from the governor in Palestine, and he came to be seen as the principal instigator of the disturbances of that moment.[11] The resurgence of Jewish nationalism in Palestine since A.D. 44 and the accompanying guerilla activities had in those years a growing influence on the Jewish Christians in Jerusalem: they became increasingly fearful of those who were "of the circumcision." Apparently Emperor Claudius felt that it was necessary to send a timely warning signal to the Jews in Palestine by depriving them of access to the city of Rome for a period of time. We ask too much of Suetonius's observation when we try to use it as the basis for the hypothesis of an early arrival of the gospel in Rome and of disturbances caused by the gospel of Christ in the synagogue in Rome.

There is thus every reason to continue reading Paul's letter to the saints in this city as a letter to a Christian community that was of predominantly Gentile-Christian origin (cf. Rom. 1:5, 13; 11:13). The apostle says, "I have written you quite boldly on some points, as if to remind you of them again, because of the grace God gave me to be a minister of Christ Jesus to the Gentiles with the priestly duty of proclaiming the gospel of God, so that the Gentiles might become an offering acceptable to God, sanctified by the Holy Spirit" (Rom. 15:15–16). The apostle who brought the gospel everywhere to the Jews first and then to the Gentiles has in the letter to the Romans the unusual task of writing to a Christian community in a city where the gospel reached the Greeks first!

10.2 Paul: *Also* the Greek

In Rome we find for the first time a situation that will occur quite frequently in later centuries: the gospel reaches the Gentiles directly and not via the synagogue. What will the identity of Christendom become in the end? Will it experience a rapid shift from a messianic Jewish group to a (new) Greek religion?

The letter to the Romans is intensely occupied with the position of the Greek Christian community. After the Reformation, this letter was read especially in the context of the doctrine of justification and as such became relevant in the discussions between Roman Catholic and Protestant Christians. But originally it did not address an intra-Christian debate. For Paul the relevant question was how the Christian community is related to God's people, Israel.

This was a topic of immense interest in Rome. There was a sizable Jewish community there, well-known throughout the city, some of whom were influential at the imperial court. The nation of Israel was present at the center of the Roman Empire. When Emperor Claudius expelled the Jews for a time from Rome because of disturbances in Palestine, it became clear to what extent the Jews in Rome were seen as citizens of faraway Jerusalem. As such they were admired as well as controversial. On the one hand they commanded respect because of their religion without images and their respectable lifestyle; on the other hand any misdeeds on the part of Jews in Rome were especially noted and elaborated on in the slander mills against them.[12]

When the Gentiles in Rome ("Greeks") come to faith in the power of the new Lord Jesus and let themselves be baptized in the name of Christ the King, a curious situation develops. These new Christians benefit from a Jewish Messiah without being tied to the Jewish background of that Messiah. They begin to use the Scriptures of Moses and the prophets without having identified themselves with Moses' people or living in accordance with Moses' law. At the very least this raises the question of an identity of its own for the Christian faith. This is perhaps difficult to imagine twenty centuries later. But a similar identity problem could occur in the Western world: if Islam were to seek adherents in North America among ethnic European groups, without these new adherents being required to study Islamic history, to assume Arabic ethnicity and cultures, or to formally become a Muslim, what kind of (new) religion would this be?

Add to this that the young church in those days did not have a history or tradition of its own. She stood in the world, bare, without spires or history books or any characteristics to mark her identity. The Christian community seemed to be an offspring of the synagogue that had fallen out of the nest—it lacked the imposing stature of Judaism with its ancient traditions, its branches in every city on earth, its magnificent past, and its venerable ancient Sacred Scriptures.

The apostle Paul writes his letter to further define and clarify the position of the Greek Christian community. It is not a new edifice, standing side by side with Israel; nevertheless it is entitled to exist in its own right.

1. It is not a new, separate edifice, standing side by side with Israel. Paul clarifies this with an image. If we view Israel as a tree, we can say that some branches have been cut from this tree (the Jews who do not yet want to believe in God's Messiah, Jesus). But the Greeks who have accepted him do not constitute a new tree; rather, they are branches that are grafted onto the old tree. There is therefore no reason to take a stand over against Israel: "Do not boast over those branches. . . . You do not support the root, but the root supports you" (Rom. 11:18). Christendom is a branch of the ancient tree!

2. At the same time the Greek community that does not live under the law of Moses exists in its own right. The gospel is "the power of God for the salvation of everyone who believes [in the Son of God]: first for the Jew, then for the Gentile" (Rom. 1:16). This faith is not something new: it connects both Jew and Greek with Abraham, who lived by faith in God, long before Moses and long before the coming of the law (Rom. 3:31–4:25). It is this period before Moses and before Israel became a nation, set apart under the law, to which Paul draws his readers' attention. From the perspective of the law and from the perspective of the Jewish people, the Gentiles are outsiders—and remain outsiders even as Christians. But viewed from the perspective of Adam, the father of all humanity, the Greeks who come to faith in the Messiah of the God of Israel are like the prodigal son who returns home. The road to God, which had narrowed beginning with Moses, opens up wide again: as in Adam all die, so in David's son, Christ, all are made alive again (Rom. 5:12–21). Lost children at last learn to say again "*Abba*, Father," through the Spirit of Jesus (Rom. 8:12–17). This obligates them to return also to the recognition of the one Creator (Rom. 1:18–25) and to living out of the Spirit of this one God (Rom. 12:1–2).

In a sense, the letter to the Romans is an elaboration of the apostolic decree ("Gentile Christians do not have to become Jews but cannot remain Gentiles"). Now that God's grace has appeared it is no longer necessary to take up the yoke of the law (which Israel was not able to keep). But it is necessary to serve with Israel the one Creator and to break with all idolatry in order to devote one's life henceforth to him, the almighty God of Abraham, Isaac, and Jacob.

Paul summarizes all this in the formula "first the Jew but also the Greek" (Rom. 1:16; 2:9–10; 3:9; 10:12). There is no distinction: "the same Lord is Lord of all and richly blesses all who call on him" (Rom. 10:12). The obedience of faith in the one God and the rejection of idolatry are what unite Jew and Greek. This one God is the Father of Jesus Christ, whose human ancestry is "from the Jews" (Rom. 9:5) and who "as to his human nature was a descendant of David" (Rom. 1:3). In Rome the Greeks are the first to come to faith in Christ. It is not until Paul arrives in Rome as a prisoner that the Jewish community in that city is confronted with the gospel. But for the identity of Christendom it is important that the Gentile Christians know their place: "*First* the Jew, then *also* the Greek"!

10.3 Exemplar from Afar

The apostle Paul wrote his letter to the believers in Rome toward the end of his stay in the region of Greece and Asia. He is about to go to Jerusalem with the collection for the poor and hopes to be able to travel after that via Rome to Spain (Rom. 15:23–26, 28–29).

Because Paul had never been to the far western reaches of the empire, he had not been able to involve the Christians there in his collection for Jerusalem. Nevertheless he holds up the collection as a "long-distance example" before the Christians in Rome. Even though the Christian community in Rome is not directly part of it, they nevertheless should know why Greeks would take up a collection for poor Jewish Christians in Jerusalem: "If the Gentiles have shared in the Jews' spiritual blessings, they owe it to the Jews to share with them their material blessings" (Rom. 15:27). The collection delineates the bond of Christian identity: Greeks are not linked with Jews through the law but through love and mutual recognition! The spiritual benefits the Greeks now enjoy were first given to Israel. Jesus Christ began his ministry, not in Rome but in Galilee! This is what must determine the attitude of the Gentile Christians: their right to exist in Christ is to give concrete shape to their spiritual connectedness with Jewish Christians in acts of love.[13]

Not only the collection, but also Paul's actions set an example—from a distance—for the believers in Rome. Paul has in the meantime experienced much opposition from the non-Christian Jews, especially in Ephesus, and he senses a tension between him and some Jewish Christians, especially from Jerusalem. Humanly speaking it would not have been strange if Paul had saved himself the trouble of writing the letter to the Romans. Why would he, persecuted as he was by the Jews, make such an effort to make it clear to a Greek-Christian community that they are in effect only a branch in the tree of Israel? And why would the apostle to the uncircumcised, whose actions were so heavily scrutinized by some Jewish fellow-Christians, mention his collection for Jerusalem with such emphasis and conviction to a community that was not even involved in it?

Despite the persecution Paul writes this letter, and he does not try to hide the tensions with which he has to live. He even asks the Roman Christians to pray for him: "I urge you, brothers, by our Lord Jesus Christ and by the love of the Spirit, to join me in my struggle by praying to God for me. Pray that I may be rescued from the unbelievers in Judea and that my service in Jerusalem may be acceptable to the saints there" (Rom. 15:30–31). The apostle fears that he will encounter a stiff headwind in Jerusalem, yet he goes there in love.

Paul writes very clearly about his basic attitude: "I have great sorrow and unceasing anguish in my heart. For I could wish that I myself were cursed and cut off from Christ for the sake of my brothers, those of my own race, the people of Israel. Theirs is the adoption as sons; theirs the divine glory, the covenants, the receiving of the law, the temple worship and the promises. Theirs are the patriarchs, and from them is traced the human ancestry of Christ, who is God over all, forever praised! Amen" (Rom. 9:2–5). Even as Jesus wept over Jerusalem—"O Jerusalem, Jerusalem, you who kill the prophets and stone those sent to you, how often I have longed to gather your children together, as a hen gathers her chicks under her wings" (Matt. 23:37)—so Paul prays for the same city. And he involves the Greeks in Rome in that intercessory prayer.

In this way he enables them to resist the imposing and demanding appeal of the Jewish synagogue, which looks down on the uncircum-

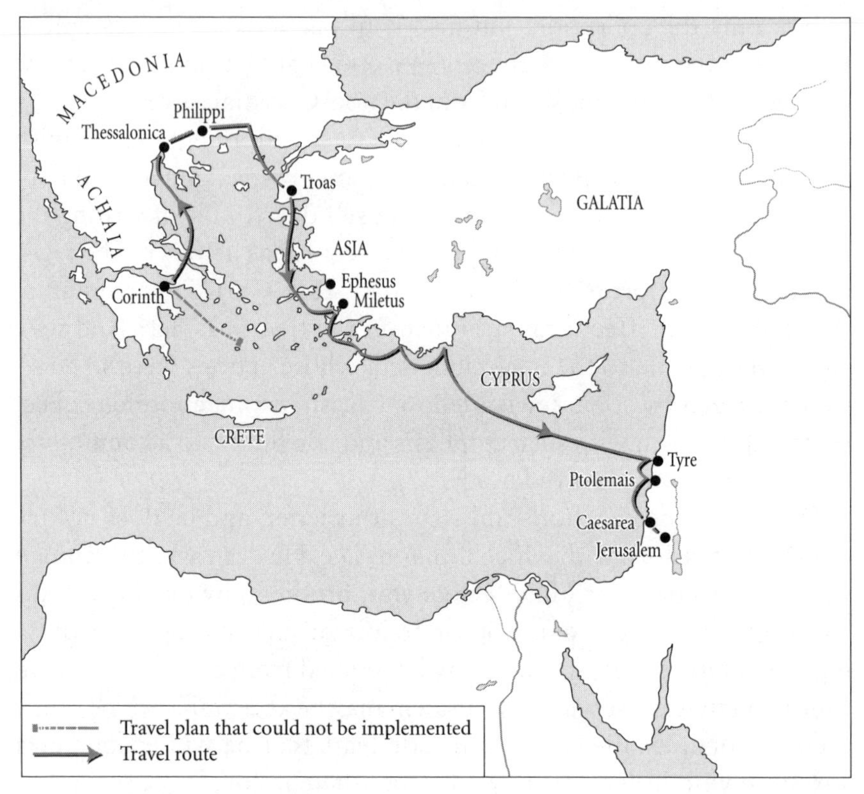

Map 9: *The Detour to Jerusalem*

cised Christians from the Gentiles. The synagogue emphasizes that in the law the Jews possess "the embodiment of knowledge and truth" (Rom. 2:17–20), and their pride and pretensions cast a shadow over the new Christian community. In his letter, however, Paul does not only show that the law without Christ is a dead-end road, he provides at the same time an example of love for the proud and of prayer for the unwilling. Love conquers the threat that emanates from pride. "Love does no harm to its neighbor. Therefore love is the fulfillment of the law" (Rom. 13:10).

Paul provides the Christian community in Rome with an example from afar. An example of involvement with Israel through help and prayer. Thus he is a pioneer for the Christendom in which two sons may once again live together in love and unity in their Father's house.

11

PRISONER OF HIS COUNTRYMEN

When Paul travels to Jerusalem with the collection for the saints, he is tense: how will his action be received there? It is intended as a symbol: the Gentile Christians look after the cradle of their faith and with their material gifts give thanks for the spiritual gift of the gospel that came to them from Jerusalem and Israel. Will the symbol be well received? Paul envisions two possible dangers: (1) the Jews who have remained disobedient to the gospel of Messiah Jesus constitute a threat to him, and (2) he is not certain how well disposed the Jewish Christians will be toward the collection from the Gentile world (Rom. 15:31). Paul's fears are confirmed. In Jerusalem he falls into the hands of the disobedient Jews and becomes their prisoner for a long period of time (Acts 21:27–25:12). And while the brethren in Jerusalem are not uncharitable, they nevertheless adopt a reserved attitude toward him (Acts 21:18–25).

Paul was not taken entirely by surprise. On the journey eastward the Spirit of Christ had continuously made it clear to him that "prison and hardships" were awaiting him (Acts 20:23). The prophet Agabus from Jerusalem makes it more concrete when the apostle arrives in Caesarea in Judea: "In this way the Jews of Jerusalem will bind the owner of this belt and will hand him over to the Gentiles" (Acts 21:11).

But the apostle does not let himself be deterred. He declares that he is prepared "not only to be bound, but also to die in Jerusalem for the name of the Lord Jesus" (Acts 21:13). He would not die in Jerusalem, but he was bound there and he was detained in Caesarea for a long time as prisoner of Jerusalem.

Although the apostle is willing to die for non-Christian Jews if it would mean that they would see the light of the gospel, many of his fellow Jews appear to shut themselves off from Christ Jesus and therefore also from Paul, the pioneer for this Messiah. His final visit to the temple city ends in rejection and hatred. Jerusalem rejects Rabbi Saul!

11.1 The Breaking Point

When the hostility toward Paul manifests itself violently in the temple court, where the mob almost lynches him, it is in fact a culmination of the persecution Paul had experienced from the Jews in the Diaspora. Many years ago Paul had left for Damascus as persecutor of the Christians. But when on the way there he was called by Christ and began to preach the gospel in the synagogues, the hostility of the non-Christian Jews immediately led to active persecution. When Paul fled to Jerusalem to get away from the persecution, it soon appeared that he was no longer safe there either. And working in the Diaspora in the years that followed, he was persecuted in all the cities and countries where he brought the gospel, first to the Jew and then to the Greek. He was systematically obstructed in Ephesus by Alexander, a Jew. And again it is the Jews from the Diaspora who fan the flames of persecution in Jerusalem.

When the Jews from Asia saw Paul in the temple, they rushed toward him, grabbed him, and accused him before the people in the temple court: "Men of Israel, help us! This is the man who teaches all men everywhere against our people and our law and this place. And besides, he has brought Greeks into the temple area and defiled this holy place" (Acts 21:27–28; 24:19).

This accusation was false. Paul had been seen in the city with Trophimus, a Gentile Christian from Ephesus, but he had not brought this uncircumcised brother into the temple court (Acts 21:29). Nevertheless, this accusation shows why the non-Christian Jews were so violently opposed to Paul: he in fact allowed uncircumcised Gentiles access to Israel's God. Granted that this was done in the name of Messiah Jesus and that his intent was not to alienate the Jews themselves from the law, Paul nevertheless undermined the exclusivity of the law and the temple. What was painful for the Jews was that Paul wanted to bring the Greeks to the God of Abraham without circumcision and the law—as if the way of Jesus was superior to the law of Moses. In fact, in all this Paul would seem to suggest to uncircumcised Greeks that they have access to the Holy One of Israel apart from the nation of Israel.[1] Is that not the same thing as bringing Greeks into the Holy Place?

Many Jewish leaders at the time of John the Baptist had refused his baptism of repentance for the forgiveness of sins and had closed themselves off from the coming of God himself in the person of Jesus of Nazareth. Their response to John's appeal to humble themselves as sinners, to surrender in faith to the Messiah of God, and to follow his way, was to hold on tightly to nation, temple, and law—which now take on a function they were never intended to have. Judaism does not remain what it was: it changes because it takes a position against God's work in Jesus (and thus closes itself off from this breaking in of the age to come). This brings with it, of necessity, a violent rejection of Paul, the pioneer of Christendom for Jew and Greek.

11.2 Prisoner and Outlaw

Paul now becomes the prisoner of his countrymen. This applies to the time when he was held in the military barracks in Jerusalem and to almost the entire period of his imprisonment in Caesarea.

The commander of the Roman garrison in Jerusalem has rescued Paul in the temple court and has kept him from being lynched. The apostle is merely placed in custody for an investigation into his (possible) guilt (Acts 21:31–33). Because of this preliminary investigation

Claudius Lysias organizes a hearing before the Sanhedrin (Acts 22:30; 23:28). He comes to the conclusion that there is no reason to make Paul a prisoner of Rome; the disturbance surrounding Paul is merely an internal Jewish religious matter (Acts 23:29). The only reason why he does not release Paul but transports him at night to Caesarea is that Paul's life is threatened by a Jewish conspiracy. It also has come to the commander's attention that Paul is a Roman citizen. In a sense Paul is thus held in protective custody by the Romans (Acts 23:12–13).

Also in Caesarea Paul is not a prisoner of Rome in the juridical sense. Governor Felix organizes a hearing to investigate why this Jewish Roman citizen is threatened with death by his fellow Jews (Acts 23:35–24:2).

Then follows a period during which the governor leaves the matter undecided (Acts 24:22). He hopes that Paul will pay him a bribe to be released in a safe manner, since a simple release would mean Paul's death at the hands of a Jewish execution squad. Paul thus needs (as Felix sees it) the help of the governor to be safe when he is released. And the governor expects to be paid a fair amount for giving this kind of help, which he is not obligated to offer.

The apostle has thus reached an impasse. His fellow Jews in fact prevent his release. He becomes a prisoner in Palestine for several years. He is a prisoner of the Jews, and when Felix, at least two years later, leaves Paul behind in prison for his successor to deal with, he does so "to grant a favor to the Jews" (Acts 24:27)!

11.3 Appeal to Compatriots

This somewhat dusky period in Paul's life leads to several speeches in his own defense. It is as if the aggression of his compatriots gives the apostle the opportunity to explain once again very clearly to all of them why, as a good disciple of Gamaliel, he now acts as a preacher of the gospel of Jesus of Nazareth.

Paul was able to give account of himself at least three times. (1) He defended himself in the temple, on the steps to the barracks, as the crowd that wanted to lynch him listened. He addressed them in their own language—not in Greek but in Aramaic (Acts 21:40–22:2).

(2) Paul had the opportunity to present his case before the Sanhedrin, where he used the theological differences between Pharisees and Sadducees (Acts 23:1–10). (3) And finally, Paul had an opportunity to defend himself before Governor Felix and the Jewish delegation from Jerusalem headed by Tertullus, a lawyer (Acts 24:1–21). This apologia led Felix (and his wife, Drusilla, who was a Jewess) to send frequently for Paul to talk with him about the new faith (Acts 24:24–26).

In all these cases Paul has to defend himself against Jews. He therefore emphasizes regularly that faith in Jesus Christ flows directly from faith in "the God of the fathers." Ananias of Damascus is here an unexpected witness: "a devout observer of the law and highly respected by all the Jews living there" (Acts 22:12). Ananias had said that "the God of our fathers" had chosen to have his Son appear to Saul and made him his witness to all men of what he had "seen and heard" (Acts 22:14–15). Paul was never disloyal to his faith in "the God of our fathers": "I worship the God of our fathers as a follower of the Way, which they call a sect" (Acts 24:14).

Paul also emphasizes that the Christian faith is in continuity with faith in the resurrection of the dead (a non-Greek perspective, believed by the Pharisees but abandoned by the Sadducees) and with the expectation of the coming judgment on both the righteous and the wicked (Acts 23:6; 24:15).

Paul sees in his own calling proof of the reality of Messiah Jesus: how could he, the most fanatical persecutor of Christians, have suddenly been changed so drastically if he had not heard a Voice and seen the Light (Acts 22:6–9)?

Finally, Paul describes his mission to the Gentiles as a consequence of the unwillingness of Jerusalem to accept this Messiah Jesus. Even the conversion of the most prominent persecutor of Christians was for them not reason enough to reconsider their position (Acts 22:17–21). It was their unbelief in Jesus that brought about his going elsewhere.

But as soon as Paul touches on his mission to the Gentiles, he appears to alienate his audience. The nations must come to Jerusalem and there be grafted into Israel! Anyone who does missionary work with his back turned on Jerusalem deserves to die. He holds the temple in contempt!

These three speeches in his own defense make it clear that Paul's abandoning his persecution of the Christians does not mean that he now fights Judaism. He has not turned anti-Jewish! To the contrary, the Christian faith is nothing but the fulfillment of all that is written in the law and the prophets (Acts 24:14). Jews who still refuse to accept the Risen Christ are thereby unintentionally disobedient to the God of the fathers, the one true God.

11.4 James and the Brothers

It is striking that we do not hear anything about Paul's Christian fellow-Jews in connection with his arrest and during his years in custody. Why do the Christians in Jerusalem not choose to side openly with Paul? Are they afraid to show their sympathy for fear of the non-Christian Jews? Or are they critical of the apostle?

James, the brother of Jesus, is during this period the leader of the believers in the temple city. Paul visits him the day after his arrival in Jerusalem. But James and the elders indicate that they have some reservations about his coming. They do support his mission-without-circumcision to the Gentiles (Acts 21:19–20a, 25), but the criticism of Paul as it circulates in Jerusalem (and makes an impression on the Jewish Christians who keep the law) makes them ill at ease (Acts 21:20). The persistent rumor is that Paul teaches defection from the law and from circumcision to the Jews in the Diaspora as well. The elders therefore ask Paul to act clearly as a Jew while in Jerusalem. He could do this by assuming the expense of a Nazirite sacrifice. James and the elders thus do not stand up for Paul, but they leave it up to him to make a better impression. This is at the very least a weak attitude: Paul did not experience much support from the saints in the capital.

Here James and the elders even imply a silent criticism of Paul. They know very well that Paul does not teach the Jews throughout the Diaspora to reject Moses. But when they mention this slander and consider it important to refute it, they give wide berth to the most important issue of those years. There is no difference of opinion between them and Paul on the question whether Gentile Christians should be circumcised. But the acceptance of Christian Greeks asks something from the Jewish Christians as well. The unity in Christ with uncircumcised believers brings with it the requirement that Jewish Christians must be prepared to place Christ and his new community above the dietary laws. Even if they themselves continue to live as Jews, in accordance with the law, they cannot let this be a hindrance to social interaction with Gentile Christians and to eating with them in the Christian community. For the Jewish Christians this means that they must be prepared to be somewhat flexible in their implementation of the dietary laws and the laws governing ceremonial cleanness. But this flexibility is interpreted by non-Christian Jews as a complete break with the law. Combating this slanderous accusation against Paul *without* saying anything about the right of Jewish Christians to view, in Christ, the dietary and cleanness laws as not applicable to their interactions with converted Gentiles bypasses the heart of the issue. James and the brothers turn in fact the clock back to the incident in Antioch (Gal. 2:11–14). But being tolerant of uncircumcised believers is not the same as accepting them as fellow-believers.

James and the elders are probably reticent because they fear persecution of Jewish Christians in Jerusalem. They keep therefore their distance when Paul becomes the object of that persecution. The apostle has to endure that his fellow Jews allow him to be held prisoner and that his fellow Christians among these Jews stay aloof from him. The pioneer for the Messiah—a lonely prisoner in Palestine!

It is not until many years later that James is forced to emerge from the shadows. In the early 60s, when Paul has gone to Rome, this other leader of the Christians, the brother of Jesus, is stoned. According to Eusebius, the Jews took out their anger against Paul on James.[2] He was not ashamed of his Master then, and he voluntarily accepted a martyr's death. His caution in the days of Paul ultimately did not help him to escape from the hostility of his non-Christian compatriots. And his faith made him willing to be killed for the sake of Jesus.

11.5 Compatriots and Coreligionists (Philippians)

From Caesarea Paul wrote a letter in which he speaks at length about his experience as a prisoner potentially under sentence of death. In the letter to Philippi Paul considers the possibility of his death (Phil. 1:20). It is therefore more likely that Paul wrote this letter from Caesarea than during his imprisonment in Rome, as has also been maintained but is less likely.[3] In the capital of the Roman Empire he did not have to be afraid that he would be executed: a letter of acquittal from Festus had traveled with him to the emperor (Acts 25:26; 26:32). But in Caesarea his situation was continuously uncertain, not so much because of the Roman authorities, who were careful in their dealings with a Roman citizen, but because of the real threat that lurked just outside the prison gate. The moment Felix sets him free, murderers will not rest until they have ambushed and killed him. That is why Paul from Caesarea can speak in such striking words about a choice: to die or to remain (Phil. 1:22–25). The apostle can influence whether he lives or dies. Thus in the end, by appealing to Caesar in order to avoid being transported to Jerusalem (where he almost certainly would have been attacked and killed), he chooses to stay alive.

In the letter to Philippi Paul shows how charitable his attitude can be toward the Jewish Christians in Jerusalem who maintain their distance from him. Some "preach Christ out of selfish ambition, not sincerely, supposing that they can stir up trouble for me while I am in chains. But what does it matter? The important thing is that . . . Christ is preached. And because of this I rejoice" (Phil. 1:17–18).

For the readers in Philippi it must have been strange that their preacher now is a prisoner in his own country. That is why Paul writes rather extensively about his suffering and about the Jews. His own suffering is a reflection of Christ, who took on the form of a servant and humbled himself unto death—and thus God exalted him! (Phil. 2:5–11). Through his suffering the apostle also sets an example for his fellow Christians to look after the interests of others.

As for the non-Christian Jews, Paul once was one of them as a Pharisee beyond reproach, but now he has found more in Christ: "I consider everything a loss compared to the surpassing greatness of knowing Christ Jesus my Lord, for whose sake I have lost all things" (Phil. 3:8). Paul now experiences "the fellowship of sharing in his sufferings," and when he becomes "like him in his death" he will also experience "the power of his resurrection" (Phil. 3:10–11). In this also the apostle is an example for the Christians in Philippi. They also must "rejoice in the Lord" (Phil. 3:1; 4:1, 4) and live as strangers among their compatriots: they are—like Paul—citizens of a heavenly kingdom (Phil. 3:20–21). They are fellow-citizens in Christ and therefore alienated from their unbelieving compatriots, be they Jews or Greeks. Ultimately Paul is prisoner for the sake of his citizenship in heaven, which he shares with all Christians, Jewish and Gentile, including those in Philippi.

11.6 Rulers and Authorities (Colossians)

The apostle saw this difficult period, when he was being held by the Romans as a prisoner of the Jews, as a kind of race he had to run for the sake of many in the world who did not even know him personally. As the bearer of the mystery of Christ he must persist in the face of the powers of aggression and death. He writes about this in a letter to the Christians in Colossae. He probably never visited Colossae, but his coworker Epaphras came from that city (Col. 4:12) and was well known there: he "is for you a faithful minister of Christ" (Col. 1:7 KJV). Among the mutual acquaintances were also Tychicus and Onesimus (Col. 4:7–9).

This letter was written during a period of imprisonment (Col. 4:3, 18), at the same time as the letter to Philemon. In the latter Paul refers to a possible release and envisions visiting Philemon (Philemon 21–22). Because he had already completed his ministry in the east before his imprisonment, it is not likely that he would later travel back from Rome toward present-day Turkey. A journey via Colossae assumes that Paul is released in the east and then visits the city on his way west, to Rome and Spain, when he travels the land route (in the winter time).

There are also chronological reasons why this letter cannot easily be assigned a later date (i.e., during the captivity in Rome). Paul did not arrive in Rome until about A.D. 61 (see fig. 6 at the end of appendix 1). But in A.D. 60 a severe earthquake hit Colossae; it is likely that Paul wrote his letter before the city was virtually wiped from the face of the earth—before A.D. 60.[4]

Paul writes to Colossae: "I want you to know how much I am struggling for you and for those at Laodicea, and for all who have not met me personally. My purpose is that they may be encouraged in heart and united in love, so that they may have the full riches of complete understanding, in order that they may know the mystery of God, namely, Christ, in whom are hidden all the treasures of wisdom and knowledge" (Col. 2:1–3). They must not forget his chains but remember them—this is the personal wish with which Paul himself signs the letter (Col. 4:18).

In the letter to Colossae (unlike the letter to Philippi) the apostle writes not so much about his future and about his attitude toward the Jews. Here he emphasizes much more the fact that Christ stands above all powers, rulers, and authorities (Col. 1:15–20). Paul himself seems to have fallen victim to the intrigues of the powers and authorities of this world, but he continues to see himself as the emissary of Christ, actively seeking to help also the believers in Colossae to grow in faith and love for this Messiah.

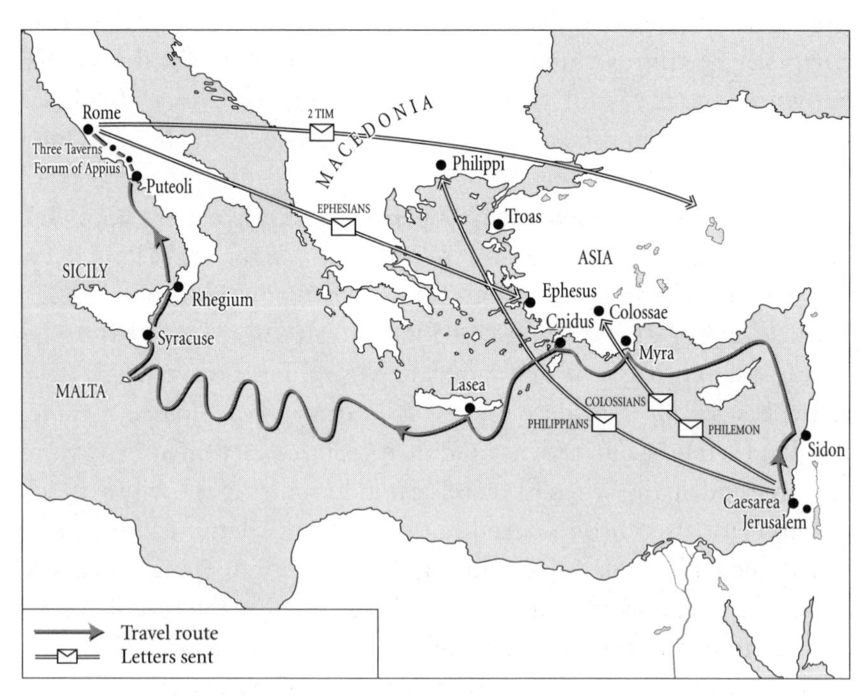

Map 10: *Imprisoned in Caesarea, Facing Possible Death in Rome*

11.7 A Good Temper Preserved (Philemon)

From this same time frame we also have a short letter that opens a window on Paul's mood during this long period as prisoner of the Jews.

Onesimus, a slave of a Christian master, Philemon, has run away and sought refuge with Paul. He had been, as Paul says with a smile and a play on words, of great usefulness to Paul as Mr. Useful (*Onēsimos*) (Philemon 11).

The overall situation in the letter is rather humorous. The prisoner sends back a useful slave to a rich man who lives in freedom! And, as a poor apostle, he even offers to pay for any losses (for which he would be repaid by Philemon's gratitude).

Paul proves here the truth he had formulated for himself elsewhere in these words: "I have learned the secret of being content in any and every situation, whether well fed or hungry, whether living in plenty or in want. I can do everything through him who gives me strength" (Phil. 4:12–13).

12

SENT IN SHACKLES TO THE EMPEROR

For many years, the apostle Paul was continuously a prisoner. This became his identity: "Paul, a prisoner of Christ" (Philemon 1; Eph. 3:1).[1]

This long period can be divided into segments. The first years he was a prisoner in Palestine, kept in protective custody as a result of the murderous intentions of his compatriots.

But this changed as soon as Paul made his appeal to Caesar. At that point he entered the Roman judicial system.[2] Festus, the new governor in Palestine, had wanted to please the Jews by having Paul transferred for questioning to Jerusalem (Acts 25:1–2, 9). But the apostle knew that if this happened, he would be killed (Acts 25:3, 11). At that point he chose for life and for a continued ministry from prison. To this end he appealed, as a Roman citizen, to Caesar. Festus then had little choice but to draw up a document for his superiors and to arrange for Paul's transport to Rome. It is only at this point that the Roman government sees fit to draw up a document concerning citizen Paul (Acts 25:26–27).

The apostle does not regain his freedom, but from now on he is on his way to Caesar, and therefore is safe and protected.

12.1 Innocent

Paul's life is full of unpredictable developments and paradoxical situations. His journey to the emperor certainly is an example. On the one hand he is a prisoner and shares this fate with enemies of the state and criminals. He once again is perceived negatively: "I am . . . chained like a criminal" (2 Tim. 2:9). On the other hand, again and again it becomes clear to those around him that he is innocent. Those who come in closer contact with Paul get the impression of someone who suffers innocently. For whom is he willing to go through this? That is the mystery of his patiently tolerating being chained and incarcerated. Those who come even closer discover here the mystery of the Crucified One: Paul voluntarily bears the chains of Christ. Thus he writes to Timothy: "Do not be ashamed to testify about our Lord, or ashamed of me his prisoner. But join with me in suffering for the gospel, by the power of God" (2 Tim. 1:8). Paul himself, as a "herald and an apostle and a teacher," is not ashamed of his suffering. He serves his Savior and radiates trust and confidence in him (2 Tim. 1:11–12).

This is apparent at the beginning of this period. At the first hearing before Festus Paul protests his innocence: "If . . . I am guilty of doing anything deserving death, I do not refuse to die. But if the charges brought against me by these Jews are not true, no one has the right to hand me over to them. I appeal to Caesar!" (Acts 25:11). Shortly thereafter, Festus himself acknowledges before Agrippa and Bernice and many prominent people from Caesarea that Paul is innocent of a capital crime, and thus there is a problem deciding what to write Caesar about Paul (Acts 25:25–27).

A further hearing by King Agrippa, who is the liaison with the Romans for Jewish concerns, leads to the same conclusion: "This man is not doing anything that deserves death or imprisonment. . . . [He] could have been set free if he had not appealed to Caesar" (Acts 26:31–32). This brief statement could be understood as implying that Paul's imprisonment was due to his own wrong tactic. What is not mentioned here is that the apostle had little choice but to appeal to Caesar because of Festus's unpredictability at the time when the Jews were trying to get Paul away from him. The real reason, as so often happens, is quickly forgotten. And Paul seems to go to Rome as a Don Quixote, as someone who has shot himself in the foot. But the apostle was already used to being a "spectacle to the whole universe" (1 Cor. 4:9). People in Caesarea may express pity, but Paul's innocence has been established!

Thus the apostle travels to Rome. Commander Julius treats him kindly, as an innocent man (Acts 27:3, 43). During a sea voyage full of danger and threat of shipwreck, Paul gains respect by his calmness and confidence. He becomes the moral leader of the 276 people on board the ship (Acts 27:33–37).[3]

When they finally drift ashore on Malta,[4] those around Paul witness another proof of his innocence. When a poisonous snake wraps itself around Paul's arm, the island's inhabitants view it as clear proof that "this man must be a murderer; for though he escaped from the sea, Justice has not allowed him to live" (Acts 28:4). But when Paul simply shakes off the animal and survives the poisonous bite, public opinion reverses itself—they even think he is a god (Acts 28:6).

Paul travels to Rome as an innocent man, and that is how he is received there. The leaders of the large Jewish community in Rome have not received letters about him from Judea, and none of his fellow-Jews has brought back a negative report about Paul (Acts 28:21). This is remarkable. Had the Jews in Jerusalem been able to draw up a legitimate charge against Paul, they would certainly have done so. But intrigues are difficult to document on paper. Paul arrives in Rome with a document from Festus (on Agrippa's authority) that exonerates him, and he finds that nothing adverse is known about him among the Jews.

Because of this general aura of innocence the attention of those he meets can focus on the question why the emissary of a world ruler must perform his task on earth in chains.

12.2 Preacher of the Gospel

During his years of imprisonment, Paul stays active as a preacher, both long-distance (through his letters) and in his immediate surroundings. He ministers directly as well as indirectly through his coworkers.

In Caesarea Paul was well known, and his imprisonment helped the cause of the gospel. Paul summarizes it thus: "Now I want you to know, brothers, that what has happened to me has really served to advance the gospel. As a result, it has become clear throughout the whole palace guard and to everyone else that I am in chains for Christ. Because of my chains, most of the brothers in the Lord have been encouraged to speak the word of God more courageously and fearlessly" (Phil. 1:12–14).

The years in prison are not viewed in a negative light. Paul asks the Christian communities to support him in his work. He may be bound, but he is not gagged: "God's word is not chained!" (2 Tim. 2:9). The apostle needs other people's intercession: "And pray for us, too, that God may open a door for our message, so that we may proclaim the mystery of Christ, for which I am in chains. Pray that I may proclaim it clearly, as I should" (Col. 4:3–4).

Familiarity with the book of Acts leads many Christians to the erroneous notion that Paul, after a fruitful period of ministry, was virtually immobilized for a long time. Granted, Luke does write much less about Paul's preaching from prison than about his preaching in the period that preceded it. But we must correct this distorted perspective with the help of Paul's letters. Paul remains a preacher of the gospel, albeit under different circumstances. He now becomes increasingly a messenger under the cross.

In the book of Acts, Luke nevertheless does give us an example of Paul's activities as preacher during his years of imprisonment. He tells how immediately after his arrival in Rome, the apostle invites the leaders of the Jewish community in order to speak with them about the gospel of Christ (Acts 28:17–27). Paul follows his usual pattern: first the Jew! There already was a Gentile-Christian community in Rome—the Greeks were here in fact the first Christians. But for Paul that is all the more reason to catch up. First and foremost, the Jews in Rome must now hear the good news about their own Messiah. Some respond, but many remain unbelieving. They harden their hearts. That is when Paul says, "Therefore I want you to know that God's salvation has been sent to the Gentiles, and they will listen!" (Acts 28:28). The apostle had said something similar many years before, in Pisidian Antioch, when the Jews there "talked abusively against what Paul was saying": "We had to speak the word of God to you first. Since you reject it and do not consider yourselves worthy of eternal life, we now turn to the Gentiles" (Acts 13:45–46). But there is a difference between that earlier period and the time in Rome. In Antioch the preaching to the Gentiles was just beginning. In Rome the gospel has already been sent to the Gentiles and has been widely disseminated among them, as the Jews in Rome know (Acts 28:22). Yet Paul does not view the synagogue in Rome as an unnecessary detour because there is already a Christian community in Rome: in every place and in every time the Jews are invited to accept the gospel for themselves. The fact that it has already reached many Gentiles is a warning. The last become the first, when the first allow the gospel to pass them by.

After his arrival in Rome as a prisoner of Christ Paul did turn first to the Jews, but he came also for the Greek—specifically for the emperor! He was not ashamed of the gospel and he had always been prepared to bring the gospel to Rome. Ultimately he arrived there in chains, but even now he was not ashamed and was ready to bear witness to the heavenly King before the greatest leader on earth, the emperor of the Roman world. That was his mission!

After his arrest in Jerusalem, the Lord Jesus had appeared to Paul. He stood by him in the night and said, "Take courage! As you have testified about me in Jerusalem, so you must also testify in Rome" (Acts 23:11). Because this appearance took place after the defense before the Sanhedrin, Paul may not have understood this charge to mean more than that he would be able to bring the gospel to the Jewish leaders in Rome. And that is what happened immediately after his arrival there.

But during the sea voyage to Rome it became apparent that Paul's charge to preach in Rome included not only the Jews, but also the Greeks and more specifically the emperor. During the storm that lasted for days, an angel of God appeared to Paul and said, "Do not be afraid, Paul. You must stand trial before Caesar" (Acts 27:24). For Paul this was a sure sign. Apparently his appeal to Caesar was a means used by God to carry Christ's name "before the Gentiles and their kings" (Acts 9:15).

Paul travels under guard, as a criminal. But under way he performs miracles and signs. He is viewed with awe as a servant of the Most High (Acts 27:21–26, 31–36; 28:6–10). In Rome he is under house arrest and has to stay in one place for at least two years. But during that time he "welcomed all who came to see him," and "boldly and without hindrance he preached the kingdom of God and taught about the Lord Jesus Christ" (Acts 28:30–31).

12.3 Christ's Image in Paul

It is striking that the Christian church remembers Paul more as a successful preacher than as a suffering prisoner. It would seem that the latter image has to some extent been suppressed, as if it would detract from the imposing figure of the preacher to the Gentiles.

It is a rather complex pattern. Paul would seem to be a Nelson Mandela in reverse. Mandela was first the prisoner on Robben Island and then, as president of South Africa, became a world traveler and chief witness against the politics of apartheid. But in Paul's case it is the other way around. He begins as traveling preacher and ambassador of a new kingdom and ends his life as a prisoner of foreign powers.

But this is the pattern that fits the kingdom of heaven. From the very beginning Paul preached everywhere that "we must go through many hardships to enter the kingdom of God" (Acts 14:22). That is why he later writes to one of the churches, "when we were with you, we kept telling you that we would be persecuted. And it turned out that way, as you well know" (1 Thess. 3:4).

This is why Paul does not act as if his chains are in any way thwarting the spread of the gospel. He holds to what his fellow-apostle Peter writes: "Do not be surprised at the painful trial you are suffering, as though something strange were happening to you. But rejoice that you participate in the sufferings of Christ, so that you may be overjoyed when his glory is revealed" (1 Peter 4:12–13). And the letter in which Paul writes most about the threat to his life is also the letter in which he speaks most extensively about the call to rejoice in the Lord (Philippians). There he equates suffering with "grace" (Phil. 1:7, 29), and he joyfully sees himself as "being poured out like a drink offering" (Phil. 2:17).

Suffering produces perseverance (Rom. 5:3; 2 Tim. 3:10–11). Christendom receives an apostle whose character has been molded and purified by suffering. And this is what makes Paul an example for all believers: "Persecutions, sufferings . . . the Lord rescued me from all of them. In fact, everyone who wants to live a godly life in Christ Jesus will be persecuted" (2 Tim. 3:11–12). Paul even dares to say, "I fill up in my flesh what is still lacking in regard to Christ's afflictions" (Col. 1:24). He refers here not to Christ's atoning death but to his sufferings.[5]

During his life on earth Christ experienced many afflictions for the sake of his calling and task: he was misunderstood, slandered, and hunted. All he did, he did for the sake of those who are his, whom he loved until the very end. And now Paul is the man who may take the gospel of the love of God farther into the world. And this cannot be done without a great deal of hostility and resistance. Not only the Master but also his servants must go through oppression for the sake of the salvation of many. Had Paul avoided the sufferings that came his way, he would have obscured the image of Christ and would have made it more difficult for people to see and grasp the kingdom of heaven. It is for the sake of the Christian community that Paul shares in the sufferings of Christ. He adds what is still necessary. Thus the messenger in chains becomes the complement of the Crucified One!

13

COWORKERS COMING AND GOING

During his years in prison Paul was, more than before, dependent on his coworkers to accomplish his long-distance work. He had gathered quite a number of coworkers around him, as is evident from the many names we encounter in his letters from this period. Paul had coworkers around him from the beginning of his work as an apostle, but their importance becomes most evident in the period of his imprisonment.[1]

13.1 The Brothers and Sisters at the Three Taverns

A notable moment is Paul's meeting with "the brothers" at the Forum of Appius and the Three Taverns (Acts 28:14–15). The apostle approaches Rome, where he has not been before. On the way to Rome he meets "brothers" in several places. The brothers in Puteoli extend hospitality to him and his fellow travelers for a week. But after that "*the* brothers" from Rome travel out to meet him and to escort him into the city. The definite article is striking, especially since the apostle did not know the recent converts from the Gentiles in Puteoli and Rome. Yet it is these brothers and sisters, who come from the city to meet him, who have a special significance for him. When he sees them he thanks God and is encouraged (Acts 28:15). It looks as if the apostle knows these people and sees them again with joy.

This is confirmed when we recall that Paul in his earlier letter to the church in Rome, where he had never been, nevertheless greets many acquaintances there by name. Paul had already met the people mentioned in Romans 16:3–15 in the east, beginning with the husband-and-wife team Priscilla and Aquila! It is likely that these are the brothers and sisters who travel from Rome to meet their apostle and friend, and that they are the acquaintances who meet and encourage him at the Three Taverns.

What kind of people are these? Are they merely casual acquaintances from among Christians in general? Most likely not. At least some of the people mentioned in the list in Romans 16 are coworkers of the apostle.

We already know that Priscilla and Aquila were coworkers of Paul's, but Paul also refers to them explicitly as "my fellow workers in Christ Jesus" in Romans 16:3. Also mentioned is one Epenetus, a "dear friend" of the apostle who was "the firstfruits of Achaia[2] for Christ" (Rom. 16:5 KJV).[3] We also read of Andronicus and Junia(s).[4] They are both well known among the apostles (Rom. 16:7).[5] They have been Paul's "fellow prisoners."[6] And they have outdistanced him in Christ.[7]

Then there are many names of people who are "beloved" or "dear friends" (Ampliatus, Stachys, Persis) or "fellow workers" and "tested and approved" (Urbanus, Apelles). Some women have spared no pains for Paul and the gospel (Maria, Tryphina and Tryphosa, Persis). The mother of Rufus, the "chosen in the Lord," is a mother also to Paul.

There are also individuals who are mentioned along with their family ("household"), such as Aristobulus and Narcissus, as well as the group of people around Asyncritus, Phlegon, Hermes, Patrobas, and Hermas. Finally there are people whom Paul simply mentions by name, but who are not forgotten by him: Herodion, Philologus, Julia, Nereus and his sister, and Olympas.

At least twenty-eight people and their acquaintances pass the review. This indicates that shortly before Paul's departure from Corinth for

Jerusalem, where he would be arrested, a large group of people whom Paul knew, and some of whom were his fellow workers, had already arrived in Rome.

It is not impossible that Aquila and Priscilla took the lead in spreading the gospel in Rome. Paul writes about them as "my fellow workers in Christ Jesus," and he states (according to many Bible versions) that "they risked their lives for me" (Rom. 16:3–4). But it is a bit of a puzzle what risk Aquila and Priscilla encountered in Rome and how their actions could have kept Paul safe from this risk.[8] Paul literally writes, "they have for my soul put their own neck under it." The apostle uses here the image of a draft animal that accepts a yoke on its neck. We would say, "they have put their shoulders to the wheel."[9] They did this in Paul's place; he could not come to Rome in person, so they took this task upon themselves.[10] Not only Paul is grateful for their efforts, but the Gentile-Christian communities are as well (Rom. 16:4).

Even as this couple did preliminary work for Paul in Ephesus (Acts 18:19, 26), so also are they pioneers who lay the groundwork for his coming to Rome. They were especially qualified for this task because they themselves came from Italy (Acts 18:2).

The majority of people who work with Aquila and Priscilla in Rome are of Jewish descent. Yet Paul addresses the church as if it were a Gentile Christian community. The people whom Paul knows occupy a special position in Rome: they are the coworkers who spread the gospel and who, as Jewish Christians, were apparently allowed to establish a predominantly Gentile Christian community.

This is also apparent from the special place the mention of these individuals occupies in the letter. It has frequently been noted that it is only after this long list of names that Paul adds his usual list of greetings from people in his immediate surroundings (Rom. 16:21–24). Why does Paul first conclude the long list with a warning against people who bring a different teaching (Rom. 16:17–20)? It is because the names from the long list belong to people who bring the true teaching—they are people Paul recommends to the Gentile Christians in Rome as exemplars. With these people they are safe: this is why all Gentile Christian communities are so grateful to the pioneers Priscilla and Aquila (Rom. 16:4)! Thus the warning that immediately follows, against people who may come with another doctrine, stands in contrast to the preceding commendation of trustworthy coworkers!

It has not always received adequate attention that Paul does not greet all these people personally, but that he instructs the readers to greet them. The wording (*aspasasthe*) is unusual and striking; its intent is to stimulate the readers to maintain fellowship with these brothers and sisters and to continue to assemble around them. We can compare this with what the apostle John writes: "If anyone comes to you and does not bring this teaching, do not take him into your house or welcome him. Anyone who welcomes him shares in his wicked work" (2 John 10–11). Fortunately Paul can say the opposite about the many acquaintances and coworkers who have already arrived in Rome: "Greet them!"

He can even add a new name to the list: Phoebe, who will arrive at the same time as the letter and who may have carried it to the church in Rome. She has helped many, including Paul himself. Let those in Rome welcome her as a sister and as a deaconess[11] of her home church in Cenchrea in Achaia (Rom. 16:1–2).[12]

At the Forum of Appius and the Three Taverns, Paul was allowed to see these people again after many years. Phoebe was probably there, and Priscilla and Aquila, as well as Epenetus and Rufus with his mother. No wonder Paul thanked his God and took courage!

At this crossroads where Paul and his friends meet, Paul sees the future of his coworkers before him: when he himself disappeared from the scene in Jerusalem, they were his advance team; and they now come, as it were, from the future to meet him and to take him with them. He is once again with them, but in the intervening years they have become independent. Yesterday's coworkers have become tomorrow's pioneers!

13.2 Coworkers Far and Wide

Coworkers were necessary not only for the actual work of preaching but also for a variety of support functions. As Jesus was served by many women, so there were also women who had great importance for Paul. And as Jesus could send out his disciples to prepare accommodations for him, so Paul can send out his coworkers to prepare journeys or deliver letters or solve problems. We see this involving of coworkers in a wide variety of tasks from the beginning of the first journey, when Paul and Barnabas have John Mark with them (at least for the first half of the journey). On the second journey Paul and Silas take young Timothy with them. Initially Timothy follows the two apostles, but after some time he is also sent out on independent "fact-finding missions" (1 Thess. 3:1–7). Beginning with the period in Corinth, Priscilla and Aquila also appear to be active: they bridge the time that Paul could not yet work in Ephesus (Acts 18:19, 26). Apparently Titus (possibly also since Corinth) travels with Paul during these months, since he is with him in Jerusalem (Gal. 2:1). During the third journey, Titus appears first to be working on Crete (Titus 1:5) and later makes a confidential mission to Corinth to mediate in the conflict of the Christian community there with Paul (2 Cor. 2:13; 7:5–7).

We do not have a comprehensive list of Paul's coworkers, but via the book of Acts we encounter in passing a whole series of names: Lydia in Philippi (Acts 16:14); Jason in Thessalonica (Acts 17:7); Aquila and Priscilla as well as Titius Justus in Corinth (Acts 18:1–4, 7); Timothy and Erastus (Acts 19:22); the Macedonians Gaius and Aristarchus (Acts 19:29); Sopater from Berea, and also Secundus from Thessalonica, and a Gaius from Derbe as well as Tychicus and Trophimus from Asia (Acts 20:4; cf. 21:29; 27:2).

Paul's letters from the period of the third journey not only provide a confirmation of this list, they also add considerably to it.

1. Timothy, Lucius, Jason, Sosipater, Tertius, Gaius, Erastus, and Quartus (Rom. 16:21–23).
2. Sosthenes, Apollos, Stephanas, Fortunatus, Achaicus (1 Cor. 1:1; 3:6; 4:6; 16:12, 15–19).
3. Artemas, Tychicus, Zenas the lawyer, Apollos (Titus 3:12–13).

Again and again we find new names side by side with familiar ones, and even so we can see only the tip of the iceberg. Everything points to the fact that the outpouring of the Holy Spirit moved not only many in Jerusalem to witnessing and charity, but that the same Spirit gave also elsewhere an abundance of believers who began to participate in the work of Christ.

13.3 A Prisoner and His Network

During the period of Paul's imprisonment, his coworkers gain in importance as liaisons with the established churches and as preachers in new regions.

From Philippi, Epaphroditus maintains contact with the apostle (Phil. 2:25–30; 4:18). In Colossae, Laodicea, and Hierapolis, Epaphras is Paul's active coworker (Col. 1:7–8; 4:12–13). Tychicus, together with Onesimus, will keep the Colossians informed about the welfare of the imprisoned apostle (Col. 4:7–9). In addition, while Paul is in Caesarea, he has Aristarchus, his fellow prisoner, nearby; Mark, Barnabas's cousin; Jesus Justus; and Demas (Col. 4:10–14), most of whom are also mentioned in the brief letter Paul sent to Philemon at the same time as his letter to the Colossians (Philemon 23–24).

Thanks to these coworkers Paul can, even as a prisoner, maintain a network of connections with the churches. During this period he not only stays active as a preacher, but he can also continue to care for the Christian communities to whom his heart goes out.

13.4 Testament for Coworkers (2 Timothy)

Not long before his death Paul wrote a letter to Timothy. We don't know where this coworker was at the time, but it is clear that the apostle saw the end of his race approaching (2 Tim. 4:6–8). Paul would appreciate it if his most intimate friend could visit him before winter with John Mark, another one of his coworkers from the early days of his ministry (2 Tim. 4:9, 11, 21).

The letter is written from Rome, where Onesiphorus once found the imprisoned apostle (2 Tim. 1:17). In the meantime, Onesiphorus as well as Aquila and Priscilla have left Rome again and are working in the same region where Timothy is currently active (2 Tim. 4:19). It is probably in the east, since Timothy, if he comes to visit Paul, will travel via Troas (2 Tim. 4:13).[13] Because the apostle does not allude anywhere to the persecution of Christians under Nero, the letter was probably written before A.D. 64, when that persecution began. This letter makes it apparent that in Rome (unlike Caesarea) Paul must prepare himself for a permanent imprisonment without much hope for release and with the possibility of death.[14]

In Rome Paul does not have many coworkers around him at this time; the only one, in fact, is Luke the physician (2 Tim. 4:11a). The other coworkers have left to go elsewhere. He does, however, have Eubulus, Pudens, Linus, Claudia, and others nearby (2 Tim. 4:21).

The apostle also suffers disappointment when it comes to his coworkers. Demas has left him (2 Tim. 4:10). Trophimus had to stay behind in Miletus due to illness and was no longer available for ministry.[15] More serious still is when we read that "everyone in the province of Asia has deserted me, including Phygelus and Hermogenes" (2 Tim. 1:15). These are probably coworkers, since in this same context Paul speaks positively of Onesiphorus from Ephesus. Apparently a whole group of coworkers from Asia have dropped out and have severed their ties with Paul. Not everyone shared with joy in Paul's sufferings!

It is understandable that especially in this last letter to his spiritual child Timothy, Paul writes much about the future of collaboration in the service of the gospel. Continuity of preaching and faith must be taken care of, which is why Paul gives this charge: "And the things you have heard me say in the presence of many witnesses entrust to reliable men who will also be qualified to teach others" (2 Tim. 2:2). The apostle also outlines the characteristics of the faithful laborer for Christ: sincere faith, a spirit of power, love, and self-discipline, willingness to suffer, continuing in what has been learned, and being thoroughly equipped for all good work (2 Tim. 1:5, 7–8; 3:14–17). And Paul warns (based at least in part on his personal experiences) against the coming of pride, false teaching, apostasy, worldliness (2 Tim. 2:14–3:13).

At the same time the apostle (who has almost run his course) encourages his younger friend Timothy with the assurance that there is a "crown of righteousness" awaiting the toiling and sometimes suffering servant, which "the Lord, the righteous Judge, will award to me on that day—and not only to me, but also to all who have longed for his appearing" (2 Tim. 4:8).

This second letter to Timothy is, perhaps unintentionally, the spiritual testament of an apostle who will die in chains. The testament is intended for his coworkers, who will in Christ's power continue the work without him (2 Tim. 4:1–5). Paul has learned that he cannot even always count on all coworkers. Yet he is optimistic: "God's solid foundation stands firm, sealed with this inscription: 'The Lord knows those who are his' " (2 Tim. 2:19).

As a pioneer among the nations for the Messiah of Israel, Paul was able to involve many people in God's work. Yet he did not form a party, nor did he found a school. He only strove to bind his coworkers to the gospel. Even if they ended up in a role different from that of the pioneer, they would nevertheless have to "share in suffering [i.e., with the others] like a good soldier of Christ Jesus" (2 Tim. 2:3 NRSV).

14

GIVEN UP AS MISSING

Suddenly Paul disappears from view, and we cannot find him again. We must give him up as missing. There is no official record of his martyrdom. And if he is buried somewhere, we do not know where to look for his grave. In Paul, Christianity has an apostle who has vanished without a trace.

14.1 Paul before the Emperor?

We would like to know whether Paul was allowed to plead his case before Emperor Nero. It remains an open question—but a meaningful one. The book of Acts sets up expectations. The hardships that Paul had been foretold through the Spirit on his final voyage to Jerusalem came in abundance (Acts 20:22–24). But later, on his voyage to Rome, the apostle received the assurance that he would appear before Caesar. This message was brought to him one night by none less than an angel of God. And because of Paul's destination, God even promised that he would save all passengers on the ship during the long and perilous sea voyage (Acts 27:22–25). Miraculously, all who were on the ship came ashore safely after the shipwreck (Acts 27:44). This is encouraging: now Paul will certainly have the opportunity to bear witness to Christ before the emperor![1]

The reader of Acts would like to keep on reading in Luke's book, but unfortunately it ends soon thereafter and leaves the ending of the story open. Luke tells how Paul for two years received all those who came to him in his rented house and preached unhindered the gospel of the kingdom of God to them. He taught concerning the Lord Jesus Christ in the city of the ruler of the world, "without hindrance" (Acts 28:30–31). Then the curtain falls, and from that point on, Paul is missing.

Some think that Luke planned to write a third book, in which he would report the meeting with the emperor.[2] Luke's Gospel ends with the ascension and thus prepares for a sequel; this comes in Acts, which begins with the ascension. Similarly, it is possible that Acts sets the stage for a third volume by broaching the theme "Paul and the emperor." Although this hypothesis is difficult to prove, there is reason for a conjecture in this direction. It would then be possible that Luke was unable to carry out his intention because he himself died in Nero's persecution shortly after the end of Acts. He was in any case in Rome when Paul wrote 2 Timothy toward the end of his life (2 Tim. 4:11), and it is possible that he became one of Nero's victims. In any case, such a book about "Paul and the emperor," whether or not it was planned, was never written. The book of Acts leaves us with an unanswered question.

According to others, the ending of Luke's second book is not open-ended but rather a triumphant conclusion. The ending of the book is then thought to suggest implicitly that after "two whole years" (i.e., after the full two-year term; Acts 28:30) Paul had to be released and that afterward he could continue his work in the world.[3] An image the ending then might suggest is that of a bird that is released after having been caged for a long time, pointing to the free flight the gospel now can continue to make under the heavens.

But this view is not very plausible. After all, Luke emphasizes precisely that in spite of Paul's imprisonment the gospel continues to be preached completely unhindered (Acts 28:31). Thus the spread of the gospel did not require Paul's release! It is possible that "two whole years" indicates a specific period of being in custody in expectation of the arrival of the accusers, but there is no guarantee that release was automatic at the end of that period, as is shown by Felix, who did not hesitate to continue holding Paul after a similar two-year period (Acts 24:27). Thus, when we read Acts 28 against the background of the story of Felix in Acts 24 and encounter the phrase "two years" again, we expect that the worst will happen next. Emperor Nero was at least as capricious and arbitrary as his governor Felix.

We cannot escape closing the book of Acts with gratitude for Paul's preaching in Rome during his detention there, but with complete uncertainty as to what happened next. He most likely appeared before Caesar, but how and with what results? History does not tell us.[4]

14.2 Decapitated

All we can say with a measure of certainty is that Paul was decapitated under Nero, as ancient tradition holds.[5] This manner of execution makes it less likely that Paul was one of the many Christians who were tortured and killed by Nero after the conflagration of Rome in A.D. 64. Tacitus tells how the Christians were thrown to the wild beasts or were burnt as garden torches. The historian Tacitus himself is very negative toward Jews and Christians. The reason why he regrets the vehemence of Nero's persecution of the Christians is that it elicited among the common people sympathy for the Christians who they felt were dealt with wrongfully and too severely.[6] The violence of Nero's action thus has a contrary effect on public opinion. From the way Tacitus describes the persecutions we don't get the impression that the Christians were given anything resembling due process. All that was required for being sent to die in the arena or to be burned at the stake was that it had to be determined that one was a "Christian."[7]

It is unlikely, however, that persons with Roman citizenship could be condemned to death so cavalierly. Nero went after the hated Christians, not after Roman citizens. Therefore Paul would have had a good chance to escape this persecution if at that time he was still alive and in Rome.

The manner of execution (decapitation) also points to Paul having been condemned to death after a legal process. Decapitation is the means by which Roman citizens were executed after being sentenced to death. This indicates that Paul may have stood trial before the emperor. The Jewish accusers had not shown up, but the emperor's arbitrariness may well have found another reason to try Paul and to condemn him to death—for example, the charge of stirring up unrest among the population by preaching a new Lord (see Acts 18:13; 19:26–27; 24:5; 28:22). Was it perhaps the process against Paul that drew Nero's attention to the Christians and gave him the idea to point to the Christians as those guilty of the fire that burned Rome? An emperor who considers himself to be god would be especially sensitive to the threat of those who, with Paul, worship another man as god and thereby weaken the emperor's prestige.

Because the historical record is silent about the period between Paul's unhindered preaching in his house in Rome and his decapitation by the Romans, there is room for many speculations but no basis for any certainty. We can say, however, that Paul's death matches his life. He fills up in his flesh "what is still lacking in regard to Christ's afflictions" (Col. 1:24). His decapitation makes the reality of the cross in this world even more apparent.

Christendom lives with a King who has been executed—and behold he lives! To his left and his right are two decapitated witnesses. One was a foreshadowing in Israel of Christ's execution on earth: John the Baptist. The other is a confirmation for future Christians from all nations of the gospel of the Crucified One: Paul.

Paul himself, in a personal note at the end of one of his letters, could write no more than "Remember my chains" (Col. 4:18). He mentions them as a foreshadowing of the narrow road that leads to the kingdom of heaven. After his disappearance we can rephrase this personal note in a way that he himself was no longer able to do: "Remember my decapitation!"

14.3 In Memoriam

When we look back on the life of the apostle who ended up missing, a striking pattern emerges. It is a pattern that is not readily discernable from close by. His life follows what seems to be an erratic course: plans are often canceled and unplanned activities force themselves into the foreground. It seems as if the apostle makes a number of well-organized missionary journeys, but that can be said only in retrospect. The missionary journeys are in fact the result of a long series of unexpected events. It is only in retrospect that we can connect the many points that seem scattered randomly across the map and see a pattern. But Paul himself did not see his life as being so streamlined.

The apostle experienced his life as uncertain, subject to many adversities and calamities (see the lists of sufferings in Paul's letters to the Christians in the rather proud city of Corinth: 1 Cor. 4:9–13; 2 Cor. 11:23–29). The word that is least appropriate here is the word "career." Paul's life is more a survival trip: in the end he does make it! This is why the apostle, when talking about his life, more than once uses images borrowed from sports: a race, a boxing match (1 Cor. 9:26–27; 2 Tim. 4:7).

But when we stand back, we can nevertheless discern a pattern. There are two intersecting lines. On the one hand, in the background is the silent guidance by Christ himself, which becomes apparent on occasion in encouraging appearances (Acts 22:17–21; 16:9–10; 18:9–10; 23:11; 27:23–24; 2 Cor. 12:1–5). On the other hand, in the foreground is a messenger of Satan who strikes Paul again and again and makes him a spectacle for the world (1 Cor. 4:9; 2 Cor. 12:7).

Paul himself had great difficulty with this. He could not see the connection between the two lines. They seemed to be at cross-purposes. He therefore prayed more than once to Christ that this messenger from Satan might be removed (2 Cor. 12:8). But he was commanded to stop praying this prayer. God himself had given Satan room to thwart the apostle. It is precisely here that it will become apparent how invincible the power of Christ is. Paul becomes living proof of the victory of the gospel. A satanic angel may knock him down, but Paul is not knocked out. A mysterious power keeps him going. It makes him endure floggings, stonings, imprisonment, and slander. This power protects him during a dangerous sea voyage to Rome, which ends in a shipwreck that no one should have survived. In the end the pattern becomes constant: in the foreground the chains of the Romans, in the background the strength to preach nonetheless. And then Paul's life on earth fades from view—but in later centuries this dual pattern has been enlarged on the screen of Christendom: a movement with a decapitated apostle and many martyrs, and yet at the same time a movement that continues in faith, hope, and love. This is the secret of Paul's life: "I can do everything through him who gives me strength" (2 Cor. 12:9–10; Phil. 4:13).

Although the historical record leaves us with a missing Paul, he pointed in his letters to his ultimate destination. Even though his grave cannot be found, his fellow believers know where he is. After choosing for a long time to remain with the Christian communities and to care for them, he has at last departed to "be with Christ" (Phil. 1:23–25). Paul is "at home with the Lord" (2 Cor. 5:8). That which is mortal has finally been swallowed up by life; the guarantee that this would one day happen was already implicit in the giving of the Spirit (2 Cor. 5:4–5). Thus the life of the oft-assailed apostle is finally crowned with the "crown of righteousness" (2 Tim. 4:7–8). It seems as if the apostle formulated his own epitaph when he wrote to his closest disciple, Timothy:

> At my first defense, no one came to my support, but everyone deserted me. May it not be held against them. But the Lord stood at my side and gave me strength, so that through me the message might be fully proclaimed and all the Gentiles might hear it. And I was delivered from the lion's mouth. The Lord will rescue me from every evil attack and will bring me safely to his heavenly kingdom. To him be glory for ever and ever. Amen. (2 Tim. 4:16–18)

14.4 Testament for Christendom (Ephesians)

Protestant Christendom after the Reformation often treated Paul's letter to the Romans as if this letter contained the central presentation of his gospel and as if this were his spiritual testament. Yet the letter to the Ephesians is the more likely candidate to be considered Paul's ecclesiastical and spiritual testament for Christendom.

The letter makes a somewhat timeless impression. It contains hardly any names, and there are few references or allusions to actual situations in the Christian community in Ephesus or elsewhere.

For some, this is reason to reject this letter as having been written by Paul. But it is not clear why some letters cannot be genuine simply because they do not exactly resemble other letters. Paul was a talented, very well educated man. There is no reason to think that he had only one way to express himself or that he could write only one kind of letter. When the situation calls for it, Paul can write very direct letters that deal with concrete problems (1 Corinthians), but he can equally well write a general and somewhat timeless letter when that is what different circumstances require.

It is true that there seems to be some dissonance between the content of the letter and its recipients. Nowhere did Paul work longer uninterruptedly than in Ephesus, and he knew many people there. Yet none of Paul's letters seems more impersonal than the one written to the Ephesians. Some conclude that if this letter was written by Paul, it was probably not addressed to Ephesus.[8]

At this point the text of Ephesians 1:1 is brought into the discussion. It is claimed that the words "in Ephesus" were not part of the original text.[9] Yet the authenticity of these words can be defended historically. The letter is indeed addressed to Ephesus.[10] But Ephesus had changed since Paul worked there. In a later letter we read that all coworkers in Asia have turned their back on the apostle, of whom he mentions Phygelus and Hermogenes by name (2 Tim. 1:15). Estrangement has sprung up. The apostle had foreseen this. In his farewell address to the elders at Ephesus he had predicted, "I know that after I leave, savage wolves will come in among you and will not spare the flock. Even from your own number men will arise and distort the truth in order to draw away disciples after them" (Acts 20:29–30). Apparently this prophecy was fulfilled after Paul's departure from the region. People gained prominence who tied the believers to themselves and fostered alienation from Paul.

Into this situation the apostle writes a letter that reminds the believers of his gospel. In the letter in which Paul writes that in Asia all have turned away from him, he also says that during that time he has sent Tychicus to Ephesus (2 Tim. 4:12). From the letter to the Ephesians we learn that Tychicus is the one who took Paul's letter to Ephesus (Eph. 6:21–22). Thus Paul writes to a Christian community with which he is very familiar, but he does so at a later time, when a distance has developed between this church and the apostle who at one time lived among them but who now as a "prisoner" is brushed aside.[11]

Paul must make clear that this imprisonment does not eliminate him and make him unimportant, but that to the contrary his imprisonment is for the sake of the Gentile Christians. They must not lose courage because Paul is suffering, since these sufferings "are your glory" (Eph. 3:1, 13).

It is due to the difficult relationship and the estrangement that have developed that Paul cannot discuss concrete situations. Perhaps he did not want to do so under the circumstances. But we do get the impression that he was aware of the attacks to which the Christian community was now exposed. The believers must grow together in Christ: "Then we will no longer be infants, tossed back and forth by the waves, and blown here and there by every wind of teaching and by the cunning and craftiness of men in their deceitful scheming" (Eph. 4:14)! He is also aware of the "bitterness, rage and anger, brawling and slander" they must get rid of (Eph. 4:31). The church is exposed to shepherds who lead them astray: "Let no one deceive you with empty words, for because of such things God's wrath comes on those who are disobedient. Therefore do not be partners with them" (Eph. 5:6–7).

It is not for nothing that the apostle presents, with detailed elaboration, the well-known image of the spiritual armor (see 1 Thess. 5:8) at the end of this letter. The Christian community in Ephesus must "put on the full armor of God so that you can take your stand against the devil's schemes" (Eph. 6:11). And it even seems that his handwritten greeting at the end is somewhat conditional and not very spontaneous. He does not write, as he usually does, "Grace be with you" or "Grace be with your spirit." He is more indirect and qualifying: "Grace to all who love our Lord Jesus Christ with an undying love" (Eph. 6:24).

Most striking in this last letter Paul wrote to a Christian community is the persistent way in which Paul reminds of his gospel and summarizes it.

1. To Paul has been revealed the mystery that the Gentiles are partakers of the grace that is in Christ. This mystery he has made known, and he continues to pray that the believers in Christ shall grow together into the fullness of God the Creator (Eph. 3).
2. Christ unites Jew and Greek by grace and builds them up on the foundation of apostles and prophets into a new, living temple for God Almighty (Eph. 2).
3. With Christ as their Head, the community of believers partakes of the Spirit of God, who is an earnest of the future (Eph. 1; 4:1–6).
4. The call to faith is also a call to break with the Gentile past and to be raised to a different kind of life (Eph. 4:17–6:9).
5. Because of the devil's opposition it is necessary to live vigilantly, wearing a defensive armor (Eph. 6:10–20).

In the letter to the Ephesians, the Christian community in that city, which Paul had already bid farewell, receives a spiritual testament. The situation in a church that seemed about to distance itself from Paul is the occasion for a letter that also in later times can focus Christendom's attention on the essence of its life. This is what motivated Paul! Saul the Jew was given the privilege of becoming the pioneer of this Christendom and the messenger of this Messiah: Paul was the "prisoner of Christ Jesus for the sake of you Gentiles" (Eph. 3:1)!

PAUL
THE APOSTLE

15

PAUL IN THE CONSTELLATION OF THE APOSTLES

The apostle Paul is often seen as a soloist, someone with his own ideas and with an individualistic approach to his work. Some appreciate him for this reason: to them Paul is the man who, far ahead of everyone else, carries the banner of Christendom. But this is also the reason why others reject him: to them, Paul with his stubborn ideas bears the responsibility for the break between Israel and the church. Whereas one group views Paul as the most outspoken apostle of grace and of justification by faith, the other views him as an apostate Jew who does not do justice to the teachings of Christ.

The development of church and theology in the past four centuries has greatly contributed to Paul's having been forced into this individualistic and controversial role. For Luther, the letter to the Romans was more or less the "gate to paradise." Compared to this Pauline teaching, the letter of James was for Luther less important: a "letter of straw." The Reformation has ranged itself behind the apostle Paul, more or less in contradistinction to the disputed "successor" of Peter in Rome. For many, Peter has become the central figure of the Roman Catholic Church, and Paul, of the Protestant churches.

In the nineteenth and twentieth centuries this tension was even projected back onto the New Testament era. Peter was thought to have been the leader of Jewish Christianity, and Paul then was seen as his antipode, as the leader of a Gentile Christianity that was free from the law. The book of Acts then was viewed as the first attempt at covering up this conflict, since in Acts both apostles are described in a manner that—contrary to the facts—suggests a great deal of agreement and symmetry.

Today, many people are surprised to learn that in the liturgical calendar Peter and Paul share the same feast day (June 29). This does not seem to fit with the idea one has of Paul: why does this solo performer not have his own feast day? The *St. Paul* oratorio of Mendelssohn-Bartholdy, in which the apostle ascends to solitary heights, would seem to fit this preacher better.

We must grant that Paul was not by any means an inconspicuous, off-the-shelf kind of apostle. Yet we do not do him justice when we see him as a solitary beacon that shines its light on deserted shores. It is better to compare Paul to a star that does not shine all by itself. He may be a conspicuously bright star, but he, together with the others, constitutes a constellation—the constellation of the apostles.

The apostle himself knows only the "foundation of the apostles and prophets," of which Christ himself is the cornerstone (Eph. 2:20). He does not view himself as a separate foundation or as a separate piece of the foundation. As an apostle he had the opportunity to start his own movement and to create a highly visible profile for himself that would have set him apart from people such as Peter or Apollos, but he firmly rejected doing so. From the beginning he reacted strongly against the tendency to make the personality of individual apostles the starting point:

> For when one says, "I follow Paul," and another, "I follow Apollos," are you not mere men? What, after all, is Apollos? And what is Paul? Only servants, through whom you came to believe—as the Lord has assigned to each his task. I planted the seed, Apollos watered it, but

> God made it grow. So neither he who plants nor he who waters is anything, but only God, who makes things grow. The man who plants and the man who waters have one purpose, and each will be rewarded according to his own labor. For we are God's fellow workers. (1 Cor. 3:4–9)

In part 1 the focus was on Paul's life. In part 2 we want to consider the place of Paul's gospel in its cultural and religious context. The first question, discussed in chapter 15, is whether Paul brings another (kind of) gospel that differs from that of the other apostles and how his preaching relates to the ministry and message of Jesus Christ.

Chapter 16 considers what characterizes Paul's gospel. He preaches to the Gentiles: how does he demarcate the position of these Gentile Christians, especially in relation to the Jewish Christians?

Chapter 17 goes into more depth on a specific point: Paul's attitude toward the law of Moses. How does he write about that law to Gentile Christians who do not live under the law?

Finally, chapter 18 discusses Paul's attitude toward his own people, Israel: how does he relate to his own past and to the non-Christian Jews who became his adversaries after he became a Christian?

15.1 Paul's Unique Place

15.1.1 Rabbi Saul and the Galilean Fishermen

Saul, the promising young Pharisee, was an intellectual from a socially prominent family. His parents could claim Roman citizenship and were also citizens of a well-known city, Tarsus. Saul himself stood out among his peers.

When he became a Christian and was allowed to serve as envoy, or apostle, of Christ, he ended up in the company of simple peasants from Galilee. None of the other apostles had studied with the rabbis, whereas Paul had graduated summa cum laude. A large percentage of the apostles were originally fishermen, tax collectors, or tradesmen, without impressive social status in city or empire. Saul stood with the rulers, elders, scribes, and high priests when the spokesmen of the apostles, Peter and John, were interrogated, and he shared the opinion these prominent Jews had of these simple souls: "they were unlearned and ignorant men" (Acts 4:13, KJV; NIV, "unschooled, ordinary men").

But not long thereafter, as a Christian, he associated with these men on a daily basis. The high priests and teachers of the law suddenly saw their promising rabbi in the circle of these "unlearned and ignorant men" from the common people: "Saul stayed with them and moved about freely in Jerusalem, speaking boldly in the name of the Lord" (Acts 9:28–29).

Did the social and cultural contrasts between Paul and the other apostles create a problem? Apparently not. After being called by Christ, Paul appears to be entirely willing to work with the simple folk. Nor does he act like a man who now will take over from the simple beginners. He honors those who are leaders in the circle of the apostles. Thus, after his journey to Arabia, Paul makes a special trip to Jerusalem, the city where he had for many years held a position of eminence in the circle around Gamaliel, to visit Cephas, the ex-fisherman from Galilee, whom he considered the most eminent apostle (Gal. 1:18). He takes his contact with his fellow-apostles seriously. He respects their position in Christ. And it goes without saying that during his visit he questions Cephas about the stories that had been handed down by those who had been eye- and ear-witnesses of Christ's life on earth (cf. 1 Cor. 11:2; 15:3–7).

Paul remained aware, of course, of the fact that his background was very different. Because others were also aware of it, Paul occasionally brought it up. After his first stay in Corinth he traveled to Jerusalem. There, he writes, he presented his gospel "privately to those who seemed to be leaders" (Gal. 2:2). A few verses later it looks as if Paul the intellectual uses this designation in a somewhat ironic vein, a bit condescendingly, when he writes about "those who seemed to be important" (*hoi dokountes einai ti*, Gal. 2:6a). But it is out of the question that it could be Paul's intention to be condescending, since he appears to think it very important that these leaders were willing to present a common front with him and Barnabas. He writes that they were "reputed to be pillars" (Gal. 2:9). Galatians 2:6a should therefore be translated without irony: "Those who are considered important."

This is a rather periphrastic way for Paul to express himself. The reason for this lies in the parenthetical statement that immediately follows: "whatever they were makes no difference to me; God does not judge by external appearance" (Gal. 2:6). Paul indicates that the unimportant fishermen and peasants are important within the Christian community, both because they were chosen by Jesus Christ and because of their experience as eyewitnesses and their having been given authority by the Master. Their present status does not derive from birth, social class, or education. In the past they were not held in high esteem, and for the intellectual rabbi Saul this could be a reason not to accord them respect—does a theologian such as Saul now have to defer to these people? Paul reacts with the comment that it is not one's past or background that is important. All that matters is whether a person has been accepted and chosen by God. God is no respecter of persons: he does not favor Saul the intellectual above the others. Because Saul is aware of his being chosen by God, he becomes part of this community and takes counsel from those whom the community considers important, without being hindered by pride in his own past or disdain for their background.[1]

It seems as if in 2 Corinthians Paul does speak with a measure of scorn about his fellow apostles. Twice he refers to them as "those 'super-apostles'" (*hoi hyperlian apostoloi*, 2 Cor. 11:5; 12:11). He does not think that he "is in the least inferior" to them. But in this context it is not Paul who initiates the measuring of himself against the others. Rather, there are those in Corinth who play the apostles in Jerusalem off against the (in their eyes) insignificant Paul. By doing this they try to undermine his authority. He is thus challenged to compare himself with the other apostles. This must have been an unpleasant situation for Rabbi Saul. The tone of his writing shows tension and emotion. He comments somewhat ironically that he can take on the so greatly respected "high" apostles. He does not outshine them, but he wants to stand side by side with them. Also, he preaches Jesus Christ and wants to bind the community to him (2 Cor. 11:1–6). Furthermore, he has performed the "signs, wonders and miracles" of the apostles, no more and no less (2 Cor. 12:11–12). The only difference Paul can think of is that he has refused financial support (2 Cor.

11:7–11; 12:13). The manner in which the apostle defends himself when others want to play the rest of the apostles off against him shows that he does not measure apostles on the basis of importance but of faithfulness. In service to the gospel he and the others stand together on equal footing. Saul the Christian does not think that this position is beneath him—but neither is he willing to be robbed of his rightful place.

15.1.2 Paul's Self-image

Paul the preacher was hated, feared, mistrusted, or brushed aside by his contemporaries. The non-Christian Jews hated him as an apostate (Acts 24:5–6). Initially he was feared by the Christian community, who did not trust his conversion (Acts 9:26). The Jewish Christians in Jerusalem mistrusted him as someone who—deliberately or unintentionally—would diminish the authority of the law among the Jews in the Diaspora (Acts 21:21–26). And later he was often brushed aside in the young Christian communities by preachers who brought a different gospel or who spread a different idea concerning the position of the Jews or of the Jewish Christians (Gal. 1:6; 2 Cor. 10:7–11; Acts 20:29–30; 2 Tim. 1:15).

How did Paul see himself? What self-image lay behind all the work he accomplished? More than once the apostle gives us hints. On the one hand he sees himself as the least of all the apostles, but on the other hand he knows his obligation to work to the utmost of his ability. It is as if Paul, as a latecomer, has to prove himself.

In a summary of the appearances of the risen Lord Jesus, Paul includes Jesus' appearance to himself. He then immediately adds a disclaimer: "last of all he appeared to me also, as to one abnormally born" (1 Cor. 15:8). He characterizes himself as *ektrōma*. This word does not refer to someone "born prematurely" or "born untimely" or even "born late," but to the afterbirth. Jesus' postresurrection appearances were completed when he appeared "to all the apostles" (1 Cor. 15:7). Then finally came the *afterbirth*. With this rather unflattering image Paul characterizes his place among the apostles. We might say somewhat more mildly that Paul was an "afterthought," a child born after the family was thought to be complete. Paul chose this humble image deliberately, because he continues, "For I [emphatic: *egō*] am the least of the apostles and do not even deserve to be called an apostle, because I persecuted the church of God" (1 Cor. 15:9).

At the same time Paul sees it as his obligation to exert himself more than the others, to compensate, as it were, for the time when he persecuted the church: "But by the grace of God I am what I am, and his grace to me was not without effect. No, I worked harder than all of them—yet not I, but the grace of God that was with me" (1 Cor. 15:10). Paul is aware of the special position he is privileged to have received as the most diligent and effective apostle. But he is not proud of it. Instead, he realizes that the grace extended to the persecutor of the church is great indeed!

Paul never suppressed his past as an opponent of Christ and of Christ's church; it is always in the background of his functioning as an envoy who had received a pardon. He mentions this more than once (Acts 22:4; 26:11; Gal. 1:13, 23; Phil. 3:6). The apostle sees his position in Christendom as determined by this past—a past that culminated in mercy being extended to a passionate enemy of Christ and of the Christians; he may for all later believers be an exemplar of grace extended to sinners (1 Tim. 1:15–16).

All his life, Paul's self-image is that of the prodigal son: "Father, I have sinned against heaven and against you. I am no longer worthy to be called your son" (Luke 15:21). In the background of his epistles that deal with justification by faith in Christ stands this deeply ingrained experience. This self-image has helped the apostle to take his place among the apostles whom he once looked down on because of their inferior status, and it has helped him to be prepared for great exertions for the sake of the gospel.

15.1.3 Not a Solo Performance

Although the apostle Paul operated very much independently, as an itinerant preacher, he did not fly solo through the world. We see him in contact with the rest of the apostles on a variety of occasions.

Shortly after his being called to faith, Paul already works together with the apostles in Jerusalem (Acts 9:28–29). When Barnabas asks Paul to come and help him in Antioch, Paul willingly goes with him, and he does not refuse when asked to take the proceeds of an offering to the brothers in Jerusalem, nor does he later hesitate to bring a conflict before the apostles and elders in the temple city (Acts 11:25–26, 30; 12:25; 13:1; 15:2–4).

During the travels to the west Paul works with Barnabas, a Levite from Cyprus, and later with Silas. Both these men were among the first Christians in Jerusalem, and they were counted among the apostles of Christ (Acts 4:36–37; 13:2; 14:3–4, 14; 15:22, 40; 1 Cor. 9:5–6; 1 Thess. 2:6). Even when Barnabas was no longer Paul's travel companion they maintained contact: Paul takes him along to Jerusalem for a consultation (Gal. 2:1), and he sees himself and Barnabas functioning within the circle of the apostles (1 Cor. 9:5–6).

The apostle is known for his outspoken positions in diverse situations. When necessary he even publicly challenges his travel companion Barnabas and the apostle Cephas in Antioch (Gal. 2:11–21). Yet he is also a man who can, when necessary, admit to being wrong. After refusing to take John Mark along again (Acts 15:37–39), Paul frankly admits several years later that he had misjudged this young man; he writes to Timothy, "Get Mark and bring him with you, because he is helpful to me in my ministry" (2 Tim. 4:11).

In his preaching of the gospel Paul shows himself more than once to be dependent on information he has received from other Christians, among whom we must primarily think of the apostles and elders—those who were eye- and ear-witnesses of Jesus' ministry. They had heard the gospel from Jesus himself and had been there. Their words deserve to be passed on. Those who preach don't have to invent their own message: they must transmit the tradition to others. Thus Paul the latecomer often writes humbly about "what I received." He was not a disciple during Jesus' life on earth. He leans here on the arms of his older colleagues in the circle of the apostles and elders, as if he were still the blind man from Damascus who had to allow himself to be led and taught (2 Thess. 2:15; 3:6; 1 Cor. 11:2, 23; 15:3). Paul the preacher is the dependent one among the apostles. When teaching what the Lord has said (1 Cor. 11:23), he must pass on to others the words of Jesus in the form of words that he himself had received from others (1 Cor.15:3 KJV, "I delivered unto you . . . that which I also received").

Saul the rabbi has learned to be more dependent on what is transmitted by the mouths of the simple, uneducated people in his own generation than on the tradition which he had studied so intensively as a young Pharisee (Gal. 1:14).

Respect for the apostles is especially evident in Paul's attitude toward James, the Lord's brother. During the later years of his apostleship, people from the circle of James caused (perhaps unintentionally) interference in the Gentile Christian communities (Gal. 2:12). Yet Paul does not interrupt his collection for the poor in Jerusalem; the Gentile Christians must show their gratitude for the spiritual gifts they have received from Jerusalem. This is not in the least affected by James's difficult attitude.

Paul is even prepared to follow the instructions of James and the elders when they ask him to bear the expense of a Nazirite offering in order to defuse the distrust the Jews felt toward him. It is surprising that at this point Paul does not object but complies and honors the request of Jesus' brother, even though it is to an extent motivated by fearfulness (Acts 21:18–26).

In the course of history, it is especially Paul's independence that has increasingly received attention; he, like Luther many centuries later, was the only one who dared openly confront Peter! This has led, incorrectly, to the image of a solo preacher. In reality there are many indications that point to Paul as someone who knew himself to be connected with the other apostles, who honored their traditions and consulted them (Gal. 2:1–10). Thus he did not create interference for the other apostles but rather enriched them, as Peter openly acknowledges in his second letter (2 Peter 3:15).

15.1.4 The Signature of a Tentmaker

Only when he speaks directly about himself does Paul present aspects that set him apart from most of the other apostles. He traveled without a wife and usually earned his own support as an artisan.

It is an open question whether Paul had always been single: a rabbi-in-training is supposed to get married! It is possible that Paul was a widower during his travels, in which case he did not remarry but denied himself the ministrations of a spouse on his journeys (1 Cor. 7:8–11). In this respect he differed from the other apostles and Peter (1 Cor. 9:5).[2]

It is especially striking that as a rule Paul did not make use of his right to receive financial support. In the Greek world it was considered humiliating for a philosopher or religious teacher to involve himself in manual labor and not to let himself be paid and served. Paul presents himself as one who serves: all that matters is Christ! He has made himself a servant to all in order to win as many as possible (1 Cor. 9:19).

Paul was a tentmaker, a trade he shared with Aquila (Acts 18:3). According to some, Paul was a leather-worker in the broader sense. In either case, it was an occupation that required handling rough and difficult-to-work-with material. Is this perhaps the reason why Paul wrote his personal postscript at the end of the epistles with large letters? Does he allude to his rough workman's hands in Galatians 6:11?

What we can say with certainty is that Paul's occupation, by which he supported himself, made him unique among the apostles. But he did not maintain this special position at the expense of collegiality. Paul nowhere suggests that he is in some way better than the others. He consistently emphasizes that the laborer is worthy of his hire, so that the other apostles are entirely correct when they accept the support of the Christian communities they visit. Paul's position as artisan is in line with his striving, as the least of the apostles, to put forth maximum effort. He exerts himself to make the gospel of Christ, who washed the feet of his disciples, as concretely visible as possible. Thus, at the end of his farewell speech to the elders at Ephesus, he says, "I have not coveted anyone's silver or gold or clothing. You yourselves know that these hands of mine have supplied my own needs and the needs of my companions. In everything I did, I showed you that by this kind of hard work we must help the weak, remembering the words the Lord Jesus himself said: 'It is more blessed to give than to receive'" (Acts 20:33–35).

15.2 The Unity in Preaching

15.2.1 This Is How We All Preach

In modern New Testament studies the view is dominant that Paul preached a gospel that was uniquely his and differed on essential points from the message brought by the other apostles. The number of publications on the theology of Paul increased sharply in the twentieth century. Paul is depicted as a theological trailblazer for a Gentile Christianity free from the law, or as the inspiration for mystical Christianity, or as the man who is supposed to have Hellenized Palestinian theology, and so forth. There is much discussion on the exact delineation of the unique element in Paul's theology, but there appears to be hardly any disagreement as to whether Paul did indeed have a message and a theology that were uniquely his. Even without the assumption of a partial contrast between Paul and the other apostles, many nevertheless look for the specific characteristics of his theology.[3]

Yet it appears to be very difficult to come to any agreement as to the content and perspective of this theology. Even attempts to portray it as a theology that is still under construction in his epistles do not lead to conclusions that all find equally convincing. As a result we have seen a growing pessimism in the last quarter of the twentieth century: according to Heikki Räisänen, Paul as thinker is not consistent, and it is therefore futile to try to reconstruct a Pauline theology.[4] Also, the growing conviction that Paul must be viewed as a Jewish apostle leads to the idea that he is dominated more by the actual tension between his Jewish background on the one hand and his work among the Gentiles on the other than by a clearly defined theological system.[5] Christiaan Beker's work *Paul the Apostle*, in which Paul's letters are seen as a cross between coherence and contingency, has become influential: although Paul's letters were written with specific incidents and historically delimited situations in view, they nevertheless are based on a measure of coherence, a foundational conviction that is the basis for the apostle's advice and arguments in varying situations.[6]

In the years 1986–1995 a number of New Testament scholars in the United States were intensively occupied with the problems surrounding a possible theology of Paul.[7] The end of this ten-year project, however, means that for the time being there is a pause in the discussion. It appears that if a theology of Paul can be formulated, it will be more the *product* of his struggle with the concrete aspects of the Christian communities than its *starting point*.[8] In writing his letters, Paul was moved more by general constants and realities (God, Christ, Israel, faith, law) than by his own thought system.[9]

In the present volume, then, there is no section on the theology of Paul. The apostle can be portrayed without a debatable reconstruction of a possible Pauline theology. In fact, it is very much open to question whether it is methodologically possible to speak of something like Paul's theology at all.

In order to compare the primary preaching and any ideas that may be specifically Pauline, we must, after all, have a thorough knowledge of the primary preaching as the background against which Paul can be delineated and brought into relief. At first glance this would not seem difficult. In Acts we have sermons or speeches by Peter and Stephen on the one hand, and by Paul on the other. It is a simple matter to compare these. But many reject this approach as too simple—the purpose of the book of Acts is, supposedly, to blur the contrasts in the early church, so it is no wonder that in Acts there are no remarkable differences between the speeches of Peter and of Paul![10]

In the twentieth century a different method was developed to make a comparison between Paul's message and the early apostolic preaching possible, consisting in distinguishing various layers of belief in the analysis of those letters that are accepted as genuinely Pauline. Paul is thought to have made use more than once of older creedal formulas, which he then proceeded to reinterpret in his own way.

Well-known examples are Romans 1:3–4, where Paul is thought to have used an older creedal formula about Jesus being adopted as the Son of God after his resurrection; and Philippians 2:1–11, where Paul is thought to have incorporated into his own Christology an older hymn about Christ as an example of reward for humility.

This method is open to challenge. The apostle himself writes on occasion passages that are more doxological or creedal in nature. Thus, when he does not explicitly quote, it is difficult to prove that passages with a more or less lofty or compact style cannot have been composed by Paul himself and must therefore be traced to older creedal formulas or hymns. Furthermore, the presumably older formulas can never be simply lifted from Paul's context. Rather, the idea is that Paul edited them slightly and that the Pauline elements must therefore first be removed from them. But methodologically this raises the question whether this may not be a case of creating a so-called older stratum by mutilating Paul.[11]

More significant, however, is the fact that Paul himself was not aware of such an idiosyncratic element in his preaching. He himself takes for granted the agreement between his gospel and that of the older apostles—he transmits their teaching. Thus he can write, "Whether, then, it was I or they, this is what we preach, and this is what you believed" (1 Cor. 15:11). In the preceding verses Paul had discussed primarily the bodily resurrection of Jesus, but his discussion stood in the framework of the whole of the gospel as handed down (1 Cor. 15:1–2). Paul was thus firmly convinced that he preached exactly the same gospel as all the other apostles. Is it not rather wrongheaded to want to know better than Paul himself—twenty centuries after the fact?

But it is not only Paul's understanding that argues against the modern reconstruction of various theologies within the circle of the oldest apostles. Peter, John, and James also were of the opinion that they and Paul brought the same message. This is apparent at the conference in Jerusalem held as a result of the unrest instigated by some Jewish Christians in the Gentile Christian communities. The report of this conference is contained in a letter that is considered authentic with virtual unanimity and that furthermore can legitimately be called a true "conflict" letter: the epistle to the Galatians. Yet it is precisely in this letter that we find strong proof for the agreement among the apostles. Peter, the foundation of the church, and John, the beloved disciple of Jesus, and James, the Lord's brother, extend at the end of the discussions the "right hand of fellowship" to Paul, the apostle among the Gentiles, and to Barnabas. There are differences among them as to their audience and sphere of work: the former go to the circumcision, the latter, to the uncircumcision. Whatever this may mean exactly, they bring in any case the same gospel that God entrusted to them.

> They saw that I had been entrusted with the task of preaching the gospel to the Gentiles, just as Peter had been to the Jews. For God, who was at work in the ministry of Peter as an apostle to the Jews, was also at

> work in my ministry as an apostle to the Gentiles. James, Peter and John, those reputed to be pillars, gave me and Barnabas the right hand of fellowship when they recognized the grace given to me. They agreed that we should go to the Gentiles, and they to the Jews. (Gal. 2:7–9)

In this mutual recognition, what is at issue is not the "preaching of *the* gospel" but only the division of the territory each will focus on and the audience each will primarily address. There is a deep awareness of the unity in preaching among the most influential leaders of the earliest church. Is it then not rather self-willed to want to know better, twenty centuries later, than Cephas, John, James, Barnabas, and Paul himself?

15.2.2 The General Pattern of Instruction

What do we know about the teaching that Paul had in common with the other disciples? It would be incorrect to read his epistles as a summary of the basic content of his gospel. They are, rather, occasional writings that presuppose this foundational content. For Paul's primary preaching we are better served if we analyze his speeches in Acts, but even then we must take into account that each of these speeches is aimed at a specific audience. There is no generally proclaimed gospel that is simply read to all people. After all, the gospel is not in the first place a theory but a Person who wants to bring people to himself and bind them to himself and who wants to care for them. When the apostles preach Christ, they call for conversion, for confession and baptism, and for repentance and a renewal of life.

It is the believers who later summarize the most important content of the preaching in creedal formulations. Even in Acts we do not find a written apostolic creed.

Nevertheless, such a creed is present in the background. It is presupposed.[12] We can trace it to some degree by noting those moments in Paul's letters when he reminds his readers of what he had taught them earlier (i.e., when he first preached to them).

In Romans 6:17 we read how the Christians in Rome "obeyed from the heart that form of doctrine which was delivered" to them (KJV; NIV:

"wholeheartedly obeyed the form of teaching to which you were entrusted"). Apparently there were not just miscellaneous traditions; they coalesced into a pattern of instruction. Paul writes about a *typos didachēs*: the teaching (*didachē*) has a recognizable form or a model (*typos*). The letter to the Romans is based on this model, but it is not simply a presentation of it. The letter is too specific for that and too much determined by the specific situation of both the author and his readers. The model itself stands in the background of these letters, is the measure for the speeches in Acts, and is formulated as accurately as possible in later creeds.

In Peter's speeches we find much argumentation aimed at his audience, but the message as such is relatively short. The God of the fathers has sent and has raised from the dead Messiah Jesus, who now pours out his Spirit on all who believe in him (Acts 2:36, 38; 3:13–16; 4:10–12; 5:30–32). Philip preaches in Samaria "the Christ" or "the good news of the kingdom of God and the name of Jesus Christ" (Acts 8:5, 12). Faith, baptism, forgiveness, the Spirit all are part of this (Acts 8:15–16, 22). To the Ethiopian eunuch this Philip preaches "Jesus" (Acts 8:35), and he moves the eunuch to be baptized in this name (Acts 8:36–38). After his conversion, Paul preaches that "Jesus is the Son of God, the Christ" (Acts 9:20, 22). A more detailed example of the preaching about Jesus is found in the report of Peter's words to Cornelius (Acts 10:34–48: the baptism of John, the miracles of Jesus, his death on the cross, his resurrection, the sending out of witnesses, the promise that Jesus is the Judge who grants amnesty to those who believe in him, baptism, the gift of the Spirit; see also Acts 17:3; 18:5; 28:23–28).

Outside Palestine's borders the same message resounds. In Antioch "the good news about the Lord Jesus" is brought (Acts 11:20). Barnabas and Paul speak to the Jews in Pisidia in exactly the same manner Peter spoke to the Jews in Jerusalem (Acts 13:17–41: the God of the fathers has sent the Messiah, Jesus, whose coming was prepared for by the Baptist; this Jesus was crucified and raised for the forgiveness of sins, and has been appointed Judge).

In the preaching to the Gentiles this gospel is preceded by the call to break with the idols and to acknowledge the God of Israel's forefathers as the one God and Creator (Acts 14:15–17; 17:22–31).

This pattern of instruction about the person of Jesus appears to constitute the background of Paul's letters as well. He mentions it briefly in the opening of the letter to the Romans. He describes the gospel there as "the gospel of God—the gospel he promised beforehand through his prophets in the Holy Scriptures regarding his Son, who as to his human nature was a descendant of David, and who through the Spirit of holiness was declared with power to be the Son of God by his resurrection from the dead: Jesus Christ our Lord" (Rom. 1:1–4). Paul then continues with the comment that he and others were given apostleship by this Christ "to bring about the obedience of faith among all the Gentiles, for His name's sake" (Rom. 1:5 NASB).

Paul states in Romans 1:4 that by his resurrection Jesus was declared to be "the Son of God" through the Spirit of holiness (*pneuma hagiōsynēs*). This latter phrase is often understood as being synonymous with "Holy Spirit" (*pneuma hagion*), but *hagiōsynē* means "sanctification" (cf. 2 Cor. 7:1; 1 Thess. 3:13). The genitive qualifies "the Spirit" as "the Spirit who sanctifies [humans]." Paul refers here to what has happened since Pentecost: the Spirit sanctifies a people for Christ from Jews and Greeks. This action shows that Jesus is truly the conquering Son of God. The triumph of the Spirit in this unholy world signals the divinity of Jesus Christ after his resurrection. There is thus a close connection between Romans 1:4 and 1:5 (the apostolate to "call people from among all the Gentiles to the obedience that comes from faith").

In all of Paul's letters the person of Jesus Christ, risen from the dead and expected to come as Savior, stands at the center. It is superfluous to provide references to support this. Even the short letter Paul gives to the escaped slave Onesimus to take back to his master Philemon mentions the name Christ or Jesus ten times. This small tableau of human relationships is framed in the relationship of master, slave, imprisoned apostle, and others with Jesus Christ who binds them together.

There are also instances where Paul makes his readers aware of the "pattern of instruction" that has the living Savior as its content. He describes the gospel not as a theory but as "the power of God for the salvation of everyone who believes" (Rom. 1:16). The "redemption which is in Christ Jesus" (NASB) consists in the fact that "God presented him as a sacrifice of atonement, through faith in his blood" (Rom. 3:24–25 NIV). Paul's preaching did not consist of a theory of wisdom; rather, he came "with a demonstration of the Spirit's power, so that your faith might not rest on men's wisdom, but on God's power" (1 Cor. 2:4–5). The foundation on which everyone builds is "Jesus Christ" (1 Cor. 3:11). This is not a theory: the reality of the new Lord is from the very beginning experienced through the powers that the Holy Spirit distributes (Gal. 3:2–5). In the first verses of the letter to the Galatians Paul characterizes the gospel in a few words: God raised from the dead Jesus, "who gave himself for our sins to rescue us from the present evil age" (Gal. 1:1–4). The good news can be characterized as "the glorious gospel of the blessed God" (1 Tim. 1:11): "Christ Jesus came into the world to save sinners" (1 Tim. 1:15). Paul has been appointed as proclaimer of this truth: "there is one God and one mediator between God and men, the man Christ Jesus, who gave himself as a ransom for all" (1 Tim. 2:5–7). In a later letter to Timothy, Paul gives a similar description: God "has saved us and called us to a holy life—not because of anything we have done but because of his own purpose and grace. This grace was given us in Christ Jesus before the beginning of time, but it has now been revealed through the appearing of our Savior, Christ Jesus, who has destroyed death and has brought life and immortality to light through the gospel" (2 Tim. 1:9–10).

Many more could be added to these few citations. Again and again it becomes apparent that the gospel or pattern of instruction is not a theory but a reality into which one can enter through faith. That is the good news: in this world a door is opened that leads to the kingdom of God. This reality is experienced through signs and wonders, through repentance and faith, by gifts and powers, by perseverance and through the Holy Spirit.

Peter and Paul shared this good news. For both of them it was also their personal pattern of instruction. Peter, who was unable to accept Jesus' suffering and denied him in the night in which he was betrayed, experienced how the Lord came to him after the resurrection and how he gave him power through his Spirit on the day of Pentecost. Paul, the persecutor of Christians, saw the light from heaven and heard the voice: "I am Jesus whom you are persecuting" (Acts 9:5). It is not for nothing that Paul returns more than once to this seismic shift in his life as he defends himself against the Jews (Acts 22:6–16; 26:12–18). The other reality broke through as good news in the lives of both Peter and Paul.

It is therefore not surprising that we do not find a Christian manifesto, a statement of principles, either in Acts or in the letters. Before the theory about Christ could be formulated, there was the word of Jesus to Cephas: "Simon son of John, do you [really] love me?" (John 21:17). And before Paul could think about Christian doctrine there was the light that blinded him for days and made him into a pray-er in darkness. They both speak from the reality which they experienced, together with the other apostles. As John states it, "That which . . . we have seen with our eyes, which we have looked at and our hands have touched—this we proclaim concerning the Word of life. . . . We proclaim to you what we have seen and heard, so that you also may have fellowship with us" (1 John 1:1–3). The reality of the gospel transcends the words; this is why formulations and dogmas are so slow in developing. Their development always comes after the facts.

15.2.3 Loyalty

The unity between Paul and the other apostles, then, is primarily a shared loyalty toward their common Lord and Savior Jesus Christ.

The apostle Peter is himself part of his gospel: he is "a witness of Christ's sufferings and one who also will share in the glory to be revealed" (1 Peter 5:1). He experienced on the Mount of Transfiguration how God the Father gave honor and glory to the Son: "So I will always remind you of these things. . . . And I will make every effort to see that after my departure you will always be able to remember these things" (2 Peter 1:12–17).

In Paul's writings we also read frequently about his efforts to be faithful. "So then, men ought to regard us as servants of Christ and as those entrusted with the secret things of God. Now it is required that those who have been given a trust must prove faithful" (1 Cor. 4:1–2).

Paul certainly does not say here merely that his preaching must conform to the truth. He means specifically personal loyalty to his Lord Christ. That is why people cannot render a final verdict: "It is the Lord who judges me" (1 Cor. 4:4–5). Paul views his faithfulness to Christ as a result of mercy: "I give a judgment as one who by the Lord's mercy is trustworthy" (1 Cor. 7:25). Christ Jesus has appointed Paul to his service because he considered him faithful (1 Tim. 1:12).

All believers must learn this same faithfulness. The new covenant is a covenant of the Spirit, not of the letter (2 Cor. 3:6). Therefore the first thing expected of the Christian community in Corinth is loyalty toward the faithful servant of Christ. They must be "a letter from Christ, the result of our ministry, written not with ink but with the Spirit of the living God, not on tablets of stone but on tablets of human hearts" (2 Cor. 3:3).

In Paul's letters to his coworkers Timothy and Titus we find several times the expression, "Here is a trustworthy saying." This is often understood as introducing or concluding a citation.[13] However, it is more natural to take it as an independent "amen exclamation": God's word is trustworthy![14] In what contexts does the apostle use these words? In every instance it is not only about theoretical doctrinal content but also about loyalty, faithfulness to the new Lord.

"Here is a trustworthy saying . . . Christ Jesus came into the world to save sinners—of whom I am the worst" (1 Tim. 1:15). This personal framing of the gospel ends in a statement of loyalty: "Now to the King eternal, immortal, invisible, the only God, be honor and glory for ever and ever. Amen" (1 Tim. 1:17).

In 1 Timothy 4:8–10 the exclamation "The Word is faithful" (*pistis ho logos*; NIV, "this is a trustworthy saying") stands at the center. This exclamation is occasioned by the statement that "godliness has value for all things, holding promise for both the present life and the life to come." And the exclamation is affirmed by Paul's own declaration of loyalty: "(and for this we labor and strive), that we have put our hope in the living God, who is the Savior of all men, and especially of those who believe."

In 1 Timothy 3:1 the exclamation about the trustworthy word is a reaction to an affirmation of salvation, focused in this case on Eve and her children—if they continue in faith, love, and sanctification (1 Tim. 2:15). And the exclamation is followed by the assurance that it is good to be an overseer of the Christian community "holding to the mystery of the faith with a clear conscience" (1 Tim. 3:9 NASB; NIV: "keep hold of the deep truths of the faith with a clear conscience").

In the letter to Titus the exclamation about the trustworthy word comes after a broad description of God's saving work through Jesus Christ and the Holy Spirit (Titus 3:3–7) and is followed by a call to be loyal and trustworthy, "so that those who have trusted in God may be careful to devote themselves to doing what is good" (Titus 3:8).

Finally we find this exclamation also in Paul's last letter to Timothy, written shortly before his death. There the expression also affirms a passage dealing with salvation: "Remember Jesus Christ, raised from the dead, descended from David. This is my gospel, for which I am suffering even to the point of being chained like a criminal. But God's word is not chained. Therefore I endure everything for the sake of the elect, that they too may obtain the salvation that is in Christ Jesus, with eternal glory" (2 Tim. 2:8–10). After Paul has affirmed his own gospel (which he briefly summarizes here) with this expression, he continues with a passage about the loyalty of the believers and of Christ himself: "If we died with him, we will also live with him; if we endure, we will also reign with him. If we disown him, he will also disown us; if we are faithless, he will remain faithful, for he cannot disown himself" (2 Tim. 2:11–13).

15.3 The Common Source

15.3.1 Paul and Jesus

It is the bond with Christ Jesus that links and unites the gifted Pharisee Saul and the older, unsophisticated apostles. All other apostles were eyewitnesses of the ministry of Jesus of Nazareth, as his disciples. But this is not true of Paul. Does this mean that there is a significant difference between Paul and the rest of the apostles? Many point to the fact that in Paul's letters Jesus' life on earth does not play a significant role and that Paul quotes hardly any of Jesus' words. Paul seems to write more about the spiritual Christ in heaven. Does this not mean that his perspective is essentially different from that of the four Gospels in which the recollections of the apostles have been recorded?

Some make a connection here with 2 Corinthians 5:16, where Paul writes that "though we have known Christ after the flesh, yet now henceforth know we him no more" (KJV).[15] Here the earthly Jesus does not seem important: "the old has gone" (2 Cor. 5:17). But this passage speaks of an "unadapted" knowing: Paul has left behind his earlier view of Jesus. He saw him before only as a human being (who was guilty of blaspheming by making himself equal with God). But now Paul has recognized that Jesus is the Messiah, the Son of God. He reminds his readers of the change in his understanding when he writes "we are convinced that one died for all" (2 Cor. 5:14). It is this insight that led him to view Christ no longer from an earthly perspective but rather in a heavenly light. Furthermore, Paul no longer views other people "after the flesh" (2 Cor. 5:16 KJV; NIV: "from a worldly point of view"): "henceforth know we no man after the flesh" (KJV). The apostle does not mean that his fellow human beings are no longer important to him as humans, but that he views them in a different manner than before. He sees them as people who need to be saved and to whom he may bring the gospel. He sees them in the light of heaven (2 Cor. 5:15, 20–21).[16]

Nevertheless, it remains strange to many that Paul hardly writes at all about the work and words of Jesus on earth. But this is not as strange as it may seem. The letters do not give us Paul's foundational teaching. The letters were written in later situations of building the communities and fending off attacks. The same is true of the letters of Peter and John, which also contain only incidental references to the words and work of Jesus.

It is therefore striking that in Paul's first preaching to Jews in Pisidia we do find a brief summary message about the earthly Jesus. Paul mentions not only the ministry of John the Baptist but also the earthly ministry of Jesus and his death in Jerusalem, followed by his resurrection (Acts 13:23–31).

In line with this is that the apostle in his letters refers back to Jesus' life on earth when he reminds his readers of the basic instruction and the traditions which he has passed on to them. The traditions Paul mentions in passing relate to the institution of the Lord's Supper (1 Cor. 11:23–26) and the details of Jesus' appearances after his resurrection (1 Cor. 15:3–8).

Besides these references there are not many citations of Jesus' words in the epistles, but now and then Paul does remind his readers of statements made by Jesus. The value Paul attaches to this tradition (which would ultimately be fixed in the Gospels) is apparent from these citations as such, not their number. Paul assumes that the tradition about Jesus' teaching is apparently known to his readers, and he considers it important to be able to refer back to it. Thus he reminds them of Jesus' unconventional teaching on divorce: "To the married I give this command (not I, but the Lord): A wife must not separate from her husband" (1 Cor. 7:10; cf. Mark 10:12). At his farewell to the elders at Ephesus he exhorts them to "remember the words of the Lord Jesus" and then quotes the words of the Lord Jesus (which we do not find in the four Gospels), "how he said, It is more blessed to give than to receive" (Acts 20:35 KJV). Commandments Jesus gave on earth are normative for Paul, as is apparent from 1 Corinthians 9:14: "the Lord has commanded that those who preach the gospel should receive their living from the gospel" (cf. Luke 10:7; Matt. 10:10). Paul also refers back indirectly to Jesus' teaching when he draws on that teaching for images he assumes to be known by his readers. Thus he writes to the Thessalonians that they "know very well" that the Lord will come "like a thief in the night" (1 Thess. 5:2; cf. Luke 12:39–40). And elsewhere the apostle uses more than once the striking phrase, which originated with Jesus, "inheriting the kingdom of God" (1 Cor. 6:9–10; 15:50; Gal. 5:21; cf. Matt. 25:34).

It is understandable that Paul in his letters only occasionally refers back to the deeds and words of Jesus during his life on earth: the story of Jesus' life is presupposed. But the church is not a historical society—it is a community of called saints who are being led toward a new life by the Spirit of the heavenly Savior. Paul's letters provide support along that road to the kingdom of God. And while under way, the community can occasionally glance back to the beginning of that road. But the foundation has been laid, and the letters are concerned with building on this foundation: "By the grace God has given me, I laid a foundation as an expert builder, and someone else is building on it. But each one should be careful how he builds. For no one can lay any foundation other than the one already laid, which is Jesus Christ" (1 Cor. 3:10–11). The foundation is not Christ as distinguished from Jesus: these two are one! Therefore the apostle also sees Jesus of Nazareth as present in the future: "We believe that Jesus died and rose again and so we believe that God will bring with Jesus those who have fallen asleep in him" (1 Thess. 4:14).

For Paul, as for the other apostles, the history of Jesus is the source, the spring from which Christendom must drink.[17]

15.3.2 Streams of Living Water

The history of Jesus is a beginning: he did not remain dead, but he lives on and continues to work. Paul has experienced this. The Jesus whom Paul persecuted so fiercely made himself known—alive—to Paul on the road to Damascus. And after that Jesus more than once helped Paul in critical moments (Acts 22:18; 18:9; 23:11).

Jesus Christ changed Saul by calling him: immediately after this experience Paul is a different man, full of the Holy Spirit while preaching the Messiah. He experiences Jesus' power to change him also in that he himself can from that time on perform many signs and wonders. The persecutor becomes a driven preacher and a remarkable miracle worker.

This is in line with what Jesus had proclaimed in the temple during the feast of tabernacles: "Whoever believes in me, . . . streams of living water will flow from within him. By this he meant the Spirit, whom those who believed in him were later to receive. Up to that time the Spirit had not been given, since Jesus had not yet been glorified" (John 7:38–39). When Paul is converted, Jesus has already been glorified, as Paul experiences near Damascus. By coming to faith, he now also experiences that through the Spirit "streams of living water . . . flow from within him."[18]

The apostle's letters were written in the age of Jesus' glorification. This is why the water of the gospel becomes in Paul and the other apostles a stream that slakes the spiritual thirst of their contemporaries. We must take this reality into account when we reflect on the question why the letters do not follow the phraseology or mention step by step the facts of the Gospels. Rabbi Saul had learned to stick with the letter of the law, but he is now driven by the fullness of the Spirit. He cannot pause to pass on traditions. He himself must build up and enrich the Christian communities. He himself must become a spring at which the communities can slake their thirst.

These streams that flow from Paul offer the same water that Jesus offered to those who thirst. But the Spirit refreshes and multiplies this water for many. The essential points of the gospel of God's Son illustrate this.[19]

John the Baptist taught Israel that she would not be able to stand at the coming of the Lord. He symbolically drowned the people in the Jordan and taught them repentance with the prayer for the Coming One who would bring amnesty. But Paul no longer has to write about the Coming One. He teaches as a trustworthy saying that Jesus Christ has come into the world to save sinners (1 Tim. 1:15). Nor does the apostle have to refer back to the baptism in the Jordan, but he works out its message for all Jews in his letter to the Romans. John told them that they should not say to themselves, "We have Abraham as our father" (Matt. 3:9). Paul writes along these same lines but with a broader application when he says to the Romans, "Circumcision has value if you observe the law, but if you break the law, you have become as though you had not been circumcised" (Rom. 2:25). Paul also points to the amnesty in Christ: "But now a righteousness from God, apart from law, has been made known, to which the Law and the Prophets testify. This righteousness from God comes through faith in Jesus Christ to all who believe. . . . God presented him as a sacrifice of atonement, through faith in his blood" (Rom. 3:21–25). Thus the stream of grace widens in Paul's writings. John the Baptist knew that God is able to raise up children for Abraham out of stones (Matt. 3:9), but Paul turns this into a positive statement: God makes out of uncircumcised Gentiles children of Abraham through faith (Rom. 4:11–12).

Jesus' ministry was characterized by many signs and wonders, by means of which God drew the attention of all Israel to him, the Son (Acts 2:22). Paul is given the ability to perform similar wonders. But he does not abuse this gift to draw attention to himself. He connects his own signs and wonders with the mystery of the gospel: Christ, who was and is the Power (Rom. 15:17–19). In the Gospels we read that Jesus' miracles are the signs of the kingdom of heaven (Matt. 12:28–29), and Paul speaks in the same vein when he writes that the kingdom of God does not consist in words but in power (1 Cor. 4:20). He knows that it was specifically Jesus' apostles who during their preaching received this gift to drive out many demons and to heal many people (Luke 9:2, 6; 10:17; Mark 16:17–18, 20). He therefore does not isolate himself from these apostles with his own gifts and powers; rather, Paul stands with them when he writes that he also was given "the things that mark an apostle" (2 Cor. 12:12; KJV: "signs of an apostle").

In Jesus' self-presentation his humanity appears to be essential: he is called the son of Joseph and Mary, and he is truly the Son of man. At the same time he claims to be infinitely more: God himself in the midst of Israel, with the authority to forgive sins and to transcend Moses. He is the Christ, the Son of the living God. Paul elaborates on this presentation when he refers to Jesus on the one hand as a descendant from the family of David (Rom. 1:3; 2 Tim. 2:8), as truly human (Rom. 5:15; Gal. 4:4), and as the definitive Adam (1 Cor. 15:45), while on the other hand he honors him as the Son of God (Rom. 1:3–4) in whom the fullness of God dwells bodily (Col. 1:19).

The Gospels show how Jesus' path through life became a path of suffering—to the vexation of his followers. But Rabbi Saul, like the other apostles, has learned that it had to be this way. His letters are permeated by the conviction that Jesus' death is decisive for the world. He exerts himself to persuade everyone of that fact. He can also state it more broadly than its expression in the Gospels, when Jesus was in the period of his humiliation. Thus he writes, "Jews demand miraculous signs and Greeks look for wisdom, but we preach Christ crucified: a stumbling block to Jews and foolishness to Gentiles, but to those whom God has called, both Jews and Greeks, [we preach] Christ the power of God and the wisdom of God" (1 Cor. 1:22–24). There is a connection here with a moment shortly before Jesus' suffering and death. Some Greeks wanted to see Jesus, but they were not received because Jesus had to die first and be put into the earth as a kernel of wheat before he could bear fruit (John 12:20–24). The Greeks who appear over the horizon at the last hour of Jesus' life stand for Paul at the center, and he now formulates explicitly the meaning of Jesus' death for them also.

The Gospels show that Jesus begins to gather the people of God around himself and around the twelve apostles. He establishes the baptism in his name as marking the boundary of faith within which this people is gathered. We find the same thought in Paul: Christ is the Head of a body (Eph. 1:22–23), and we are united with him by letting ourselves be baptized in him (Rom. 6:3–4). But the apostle works this out in more detail for the Gentiles. Because the basis for belonging to God's people is now faith in Christ, the boundary between Jews and Gentiles disappears. Paul writes, "For through him we both have access to the Father by one Spirit. Consequently, you are no longer foreigners and aliens, but fellow citizens with God's people and members of God's household, built on the foundation of the apostles and prophets, with Christ Jesus himself as the chief cornerstone" (Eph. 2:18–20). With the apostles, the water from the spring widens to a stream of living water from which all nations may drink.

Jesus' perspective on the future is his return, and before that, the giving of the Spirit, the preaching of the gospel, the persecution of the believers, and the oppression that comes over the Jewish people. It is clear from Paul's letters that he wants to prepare himself, together with his readers, for that return of Christ: "For we must all appear before the judgment seat of Christ, that each one may receive what is due him for the things done while in the body, whether good or bad" (2 Cor. 5:10). On the road to that judgment seat, the Spirit is the guide: the Christians' life began with the receiving of the Spirit (Gal. 3:2–5), and the fruit of the Spirit is manifest in their changed life (Gal. 5:22–26), as are the gifts of the Spirit in the Christian community (1 Cor. 12:4–11), while that same Spirit also bears witness in their hearts (Rom. 8:15–17, 26–27).

Paul sees the preaching of the gospel as a task for this age—he knows that it is his life's task to contribute to it with maximum effort (1 Cor. 9:16). In several letters he draws attention to the fact that the believers are called to suffering and oppression if they follow this path (e.g., 2 Thess. 1:5; 2 Tim. 3:12). The fact that the oppression of the

Jewish people as a whole is not mentioned explicitly is not particularly strange, because Paul lived before the beginning of that period. Yet this theme must have been part of his preaching, because he alludes to it in 2 Thessalonians. He reminds his readers of what he had told them: a time is coming when the temple of God will be desecrated by a Gentile who considers himself to be a god (2 Thess. 2:3–5). This profanation of the temple must not be confused with the coming of the Messiah (2 Thess. 2:8–12).

When we look at Paul's writings from the perspective of several main elements in Jesus' ministry and preaching, Paul appears not only to be in harmony with these core elements, but he also appears (along with the other apostles) to represent a widening of the stream relative to the Gospels. He does not copy their gospel but thinks it through, applies it, and presents it to the Christian communities of which the Spirit makes him the founder. At this point we leave out of consideration how his words are often entirely geared to the specific situations in the churches. It is this adaptation to specific situations that at times gives the impression that Paul's work constituted an entirely new departure—as if he were the founder of Christendom rather than its pioneer. But in reality Paul is full of that Christendom of which Jesus Christ is the founder. Paul never wanted to be more: "It is the Lord who judges me" (1 Cor. 4:4).

15.3.3 Paul and the Letter of James

The letter of James has been placed more than once in direct opposition to Paul. This letter, according to tradition, was written by Jesus' oldest brother. James was always close to the source. This is evidenced by his writing style: it is reminiscent of the Sermon on the Mount. There are many points of contact between what Jesus taught there and the letter of his brother James. Thus Jesus said, "Blessed are the poor in spirit, for theirs is the kingdom of heaven" (Matt. 5:3), which finds its echo in James: "Has not God chosen those who are poor in the eyes of the world to be rich in faith and to inherit the kingdom he promised those who love him?" (James 2:5).

At first glance there is a significant difference between Paul and this letter of James. According to some, the brother of Jesus even carries on a barely disguised polemic with Paul. After all, he writes, "You foolish man, do you want evidence that faith without deeds is useless? Was not our ancestor Abraham considered righteous for what he did when he offered his son Isaac on the altar? You see that his faith and his actions were working together. . . . You see that a person is justified by what he does and not by faith alone" (James 2:20–24). These statements would seem to be in tension with what Paul writes: "If, in fact, Abraham was justified by works, he had something to boast about—but not before God" (Rom. 4:2).

Does this discrepancy between James and Paul not point to the fact that Paul arrived at a partially new teaching? James would appear to be more in agreement with Jesus, who in the Sermon on the Mount teaches that our righteousness must exceed that of the scribes and Pharisees (Matt. 5:20). We must be able to show our "good deeds" to those around us (Matt. 5:16). If James seems to stay closer to Jesus, has Paul moved too far away from him?

At first glance this question seems inescapable. But the fact of the matter is that the sparks that seem to fly are the result of a short circuit of our own making: we simply connect the wrong wires. James argues against those who abuse the acceptance of the gospel as a cover for abandoning good works. But Paul also teaches that faith has to be accompanied by good works. Faith expresses itself through love (Gal. 5:6). Titus must set an example by doing what is good (Titus 2:7; cf. 3:8, 14). God will judge each one on the basis of his deeds (Rom. 2:6; 2 Cor. 5:10). It appears to be entirely possible to establish a direct connection between Paul and the letter of James without any short circuit!

Does Paul contradict himself? Sometimes he emphasizes that we are justified by faith, apart from works. But in that case he is speaking of the works of the law, not of the works that follow faith (Rom. 3:28). And when Abraham is the example for all who believe without works, these works are not the works of faith but works that are held in esteem as an alternative to faith (Rom. 4:13–17). We can establish a good connection between Paul's letters and the intent of James 2.[20]

Nevertheless, a question remains: Do the polemic tone and the way in which James formulates his statements not point in the direction of a confrontation with an unnamed person? And who could this nameless figure be other than Paul, who in a specific context does indeed say that human beings are not saved by works but by faith? Yet a hidden polemic against Paul is not likely.

In the first place, the letter of James appears to predate the earliest of Paul's letters.

Second, James does not address an absent opponent but the readers of his letter. In this passage he emphatically addresses them as "my brothers." It is these brothers who are at risk of claiming to have faith without having deeds (James 2:14). The concrete example of lack of love for the neighbor is applicable to "one of you" (James 2:16). This individual is shortly thereafter addressed as "vain man" (KJV; NIV "foolish man")—an empty man, a man without deeds (James 2:20). And in what follows, James also addresses people in the Christian community in the second person. The problem thus does not lie outside the circle to which James writes, but within it.

Third, the group James addresses is a community that still functions within the synagogue or has close connections with it. James was always the leader of the Jewish Christians. This is also evident in this passage. The "empty" or "foolish" man who has faith but does not evidence good works is a man who is proud of the fact that he believes that "God is One." This allusion to Israel's *Shema* (Deut. 6:4) shows that what is in view here is not a Gentile Christian but a Jewish Christian (James 2:19). Apparently there was a danger among Jewish Christians of viewing faith in Jesus as an alternative to works performed for God—as if accepting Jesus as Messiah would be reason to consider the good deeds of mercy, such as the Lord asks of his people, as being of lesser importance.

Whereas James moves within Judaism and speaks out for continued piety and love of neighbor, also on the part of those who have come to believe in Messiah Jesus, Paul is the apostle of the Gentiles, who must make it clear to them that faith in Jesus is enough and that it is no longer necessary to embrace Judaism to be reconciled with God. Gentiles who were used to acts of devotion for the gods in their temples must not think that they now must replace these idolatrous practices with works of the law to please the living God. James addresses the weak Christians among the Jews and discusses the ethics of good works, while Paul writes to Christians from the Gentiles and discusses the religious issue of the relationship between works and reconciliation with the gods. The two discussions meet, not at a level crossing but at an overpass!

When we take into account the very different perspectives of Paul and James, it becomes clear that both draw from the same well. When we read what Paul writes at the end of Galatians about the works of the flesh and the fruit of the Spirit, we can almost see it as a table of contents for the letter of James (Gal. 5:19–21, 22–23). In the background of both documents stands Jesus' teaching about a life without divorce, quarrels, and disobedience, but full of love for God and neighbor.

11

GOD'S ENVOY TO THE NATIONS

This chapter deals with the specific task Paul has within the circle of the apostles: he is the apostle to the nations.

Paul is not the only Christian Jew who preached among the Gentiles, although he is the most prominent one. Others are Barnabas, Silas, and Apollos. Paul is well aware of the fact that he is not the only one who works among the Gentiles. He uses the plural when he writes to the Romans about this work: "Through him and for his name's sake, we received grace and apostleship to call people from among all the Gentiles to the obedience that comes from faith" (Rom. 1:5). These apostles for the nations, among whom Paul was a leader, clearly distinguished themselves through their work from other apostles or elders such as Peter, John, and James (who, with Jude, are the authors of the so-called general or catholic epistles).

Why is Paul, who always began his preaching in the synagogues, known especially as the preacher to the Gentiles? Did the other apostles not have a responsibility to preach to the nations?

In recent decades these questions have been asked with greater emphasis than before.[1] There was a time when the spread of the gospel among the nations was considered normal, a matter of course. After all, the time of the Jews had passed and the era of the world church had begun! Paul is then viewed as a man who did what could be expected of all the apostles. Someone like James, who maintained strong ties with Jerusalem, seems to have been a straggler. Who wants to continue to value the law and Israel after the universal gospel has come? This perspective was dominant for a long time, but it is increasingly being exchanged for a different vision. Judaism is no longer judged negatively (i.e., as being legalistic and a religion of works), and the ministry of Jesus and the apostles is interpreted more within the framework of Israel. With this shift in perspective James's lagging behind is no longer problematic, but Paul's moving ahead of the others is. How did Paul get involved in mission to the Gentiles? Did that not make him a traitor to God's people, Israel? What moved him to set himself apart from the other apostles? And did this not give Paul, the disciple of Gamaliel, an ambivalent attitude toward the law and toward Israel? This chapter discusses the question of the historical place of the mission to the nations as it relates to the spread of the gospel concerning Messiah Jesus among the Jews. The two chapters that follow focus on two related topics: Paul's attitude toward the law (chapter 17) and toward Israel (chapter 18).

16.1 Paul's Mission to the Uncircumcised

More than once Paul emphasizes his special task for the nations. From Israel's perspective they are the *goyim*, the Gentiles, all those who do not belong to the nation of Israel, God's chosen nation from of old. It is they to whom Paul, together with others, turns to fulfill the apostolate "to call people from among all the Gentiles to the obedience that comes from faith" (Rom. 1:5; cf. 15:18; 16:26). He strives for results among all these nations, including the population of Rome (Rom. 1:13). He can call himself simply "the apostle to the Gentiles" (Rom. 11:13) or "a minister of Christ Jesus to the Gentiles" (Rom. 15:16) or "a teacher of the true faith to the Gentiles" (1 Tim. 2:7). For

God has revealed his Son in Paul "so that I might preach him to the Gentiles" (Gal. 1:16), and that is where he is the herald of this good news (Gal. 2:2; cf. 2:8–9). Even after his arrest Paul remains the prisoner of Christ "for the sake of [the] Gentiles" (Eph. 3:1). The gift of grace he had received was "to preach to the Gentiles the unsearchable riches of Christ" (Eph. 3:8).

It is striking that Paul does not mention this ministry to the Gentiles in all his letters, but that he does mention it explicitly in his letters to Ephesus (Ephesians and 1 Timothy) and to Rome, two highly cosmopolitan cities. In the letter to the Galatians he mentions his special task in a historical retrospective: how was he called to this task and how was his task acknowledged by others? Apparently Paul does not casually call himself an apostle to the Gentiles, but he does mention the specific nature of his work very consciously at times when this carries special weight.

His calling to preach to the Gentiles has been discussed above (chapter 3). As stated there, Paul's conversion to Christ near Damascus did not immediately coincide with the insight that he had to preach this Christ unconditionally to the Gentiles. This became clear to him only later, not through growing personal insight,[2] nor through conflict with others. He received a special revelation from God that made it clear to him that he was to preach Christ directly to the Gentiles. The unexpected and surprising turn in the life of this fanatical Pharisee, who was converted to Christ and became a preacher to the uncircumcised, is of supernatural origin.

How this special calling to preach to the Gentiles received recognition on the part of Peter and others was discussed in chapter 7. But one question remains: What was the content of the amicable agreement Peter and others reached with Paul and Barnabas? And why was this mutual recognition necessary? Why didn't all apostles participate in the work among the Gentiles?

At first glance the agreement between Peter and the other apostles on the one hand, and Paul and Barnabas on the other, looks very straightforward: "They agreed that we should go to the Gentiles, and they to the Jews" (Gal. 2:9). The statement is brief, but it appears to divide up the spheres of activity. What is, however, in view here: preaching or the building up of the Christian communities? Questions such as this that ask for more specificity are probably out of order. The direction of the work has been established, and that direction will be the determining factor in new missionary activities as well as in care for existing communities.[3]

Furthermore, it appears impossible to understand the agreement as a division of responsibilities, as if some apostles would be responsible only for the preaching to the Gentiles and others only for preaching to the Jews. The fact that a joint agreement is reached indicates that they all share a sense of responsibility for the task of preaching as a whole. Also, the reason for the division of labor is pragmatic rather than a matter of principle. The leaders in Jerusalem noted that Paul was entrusted with "the task of preaching the gospel to the Gentiles just as Peter had been to the Jews" (Gal. 2:7). They reached this conclusion because they saw that God was at work in Peter's ministry "as an apostle to the Jews" as he was in Paul's "ministry as an apostle to the Gentiles" (Gal. 2:8). Thus it apparently evolved, but this bifurcation in two separate directions stems from a later date.

When we read Acts 10, it appears that Peter (who was the first preacher to the Jews on the Day of Pentecost) was also the first to receive the apostleship to the Gentiles when through a vision he was given the freedom to enter the house of Cornelius, a Gentile. And Paul began by preaching to the Jews in Damascus and Jerusalem. We must apparently conclude that in practice Paul's work became much more effective among the Gentiles, while the work of Peter remained more effective among the Jews.[4] Thus the agreement does not involve an absolute separation of responsibilities, but rather a division of labor within the joint sphere of responsibility for the gospel in the entire world, among both circumcised and uncircumcised. The course of events makes clear where each person's strength and task lie.

It is more difficult to determine the precise content of the principle of division. Many are of the opinion that the key is (ethnic-)geographic.[5] The Gentiles then are the nations who live outside Palestine, specifically west of Palestine, while the circumcised live in the land of promise, in Palestine, and in large numbers also in Syria and to the east. The fact that during this period many non-Jews lived in Palestine does not negate the fact that this region continued to be considered in principle the Jewish homeland. Conversely, the fact that many Jews lived in the western Diaspora does not take away that they lived as strangers among the *goyim*. It therefore seems simple: Paul and Barnabas outside Palestine (westward), and Peter with John and James inside Palestine (and perhaps also eastward). In this territorial division one problem is relatively easily solved. In the Diaspora Paul always emphatically turns to the circumcised first, while on the other hand the Christians in Palestine do not avoid the Gentiles, as, for example, is apparent in the case of Cornelius. If the agreement is indeed geographical, then the task of all preachers is apparently to bring the gospel to all those living in their assigned territory, and not only to the Jews or only to the Gentiles.

But this (ethnic-)geographic view does not answer all questions. In later years, Paul takes the liberty of defending the gospel in Palestine; he even gives account of himself before the Sanhedrin in Jerusalem. And Peter does not stay within the boundaries of Palestine. In Corinth he is as well known as Paul and Apollos (1 Cor. 1:12), and he also writes letters to Gentile Christian communities (1 and 2 Peter). Apparently the apostles are not confined to specific territories after all. A purely (ethnic-) geographic explanation is therefore not satisfactory.

This then argues for thinking of a purely ethnic division rather than an (ethnic-)geographic one.[6] Paul's most important sphere of work was the non-Jews, while Peter's most successful work was done among Jews. There is a bond of fellowship between these two work spheres: Paul and Peter give each other the right hand "of fellowship" or "of cooperation." There is no division: it is one gospel, one God who empowers, and therefore also one community they labor to build, Paul among the Gentiles, Peter among the Jews.[7] This meant that Peter, John, and James could in principle also work outside Palestine, in areas where there were Jews or Jewish Christians. Peter did indeed preach in Babylon, an area where since the Babylonian Captivity a great number of Jews lived (1 Peter 5:13).[8]

But what happened in the case of a city where many Gentiles lived as well as many Jews? An example of this is Antioch. Here we find both Paul and Peter after the agreement about work spheres. At this point Peter appears to be more the apostle to the Jewish Christians in Antioch, and Paul the apostle to the Gentile Christians. But initially there is genuine fellowship between the two groups and the two apostles, as indicated by the fact that Peter also ate with the Gentiles (Gal. 2:12). But the way this is stated is rather striking. It gives the impression that Peter's presence in Antioch was not strictly among the Gentile Christians but that he did communicate openly with them. The fact that he "used to eat with" them would not be mentioned specifically if he had been entirely absorbed into their community and worked among them. The phraseology makes more sense if Peter was especially active as preacher and pastor among the Jews and the Jewish Christians in Antioch, but had an open and communicative attitude toward the Gentile Christians by eating with them (we should think here of communal meals). But when some individuals come from James, Peter begins to withdraw and separate himself, and "the other Jews joined him" (Gal. 2:13). The Jews in question are Jewish *Christians*. But what is striking is that Peter here is referred to as a "Jew," as is implied in the reference to "the other Jews." Apparently Jewish and Gentile Christians were groups that communicated with one another; Paul moved primarily among the Gentile Christians, Peter among the Jewish Christians. This did not constitute a problem—until the moment when Peter with his Jewish contingent closed off the bridge connecting them with the Gentile group. At that point the fellowship that had been sealed with a handshake in Jerusalem was suddenly threatened. It was precisely because of this handshake, the "right hand of fellowship," that Paul reacted vehemently against this disruption in communication and this separation.

Unfortunately we know little about the organization of the earliest Christian communities. From the incident in Antioch we might infer that Jewish and Gentile Christians, socially speaking, were not one unified whole. This is not altogether surprising, since there were many cultural differences between those who had grown up under the law and those who came to faith apart from the law. We must also realize that Jews who became followers of Messiah Jesus did not automatically leave their families and businesses which often entirely encapsulated them in a Jewish community! And the same holds true for the

Gentiles who came to confess the Messiah of Israel. The critical aspect was the openness toward each other in Christ Jesus and the communal meal. It is then entirely possible that the house churches or the gatherings in specific homes were in some places more or less grouped as "circumcised" and "uncircumcised," without necessarily representing two parties or opposing groups. The Jews in Jerusalem were already used to various synagogues existing side by side for groups of divergent backgrounds and ethnic origin. In Acts 6:9 Luke mentions "the synagogue of the Libertines, and Cyrenians, and Alexandrians, and of them of Cilicia and of Asia" (KJV). These Greek-speaking Jews had their own synagogue within an undivided Judaism.

The agreement reached in Jerusalem ("we to the Gentiles, they to the Jews") is then in principle an ethnic agreement, with at its core the agreement of fellowship. In practice this agreement will have led to a partial geographical division, because Jews did not live everywhere. This also explains why tensions in the fellowship between Jewish and Gentile Christians could arise rather quickly in places and regions where both groups were heavily represented (as, e.g., in Antioch), and why these tensions could later arise in regions where initially Gentile Christians were in the majority but where later also Jewish Christians came (see the letter to the Galatians, which speaks of an unexpected problem that surfaced there, and 2 Corinthians 10–13, which shows an increasing influence of Jewish Christians).[9]

But is it not strange that Paul and others are especially delegated to go "to the Gentiles," and others "to the circumcision," even though the first apostles had already before the ascension received the commission to "go and make disciples of all nations" (Matt. 28:19)? Viewed from a distance this is striking indeed: why do the twelve apostles after their Master's commission go for the time being only to the Jews and not to the Gentiles? It is possible that they initially understood this to mean a preaching of the gospel that would result in Gentiles being incorporated through circumcision into the nation in which Messiah Jesus had appeared. Only gradually did they come to realize what it meant that the Holy Spirit was also poured out on uncircumcised Gentiles. The vision Cephas received (Acts 10) then helped not only him but also the rest of the Christians in Jerusalem (Acts 11) to understand with increasing clarity that salvation is intended, without respect of persons, for both the circumcised and the uncircumcised. That is also when it became clear why, when Jesus commanded the apostles to baptize believers from among the nations, he made no mention of their being circumcised. At the time when this understanding began to dawn, God called especially Rabbi Saul for this work, and later also Barnabas, Silas, and Apollos. The fellowship agreement now means that, within the universal charge of Christ, the apostles have divided their tasks on the basis of the guidance of the Spirit in each of their lives. Peter, James, and John thus do not keep themselves aloof from the command to make disciples of all nations, and they also accept that circumcision no longer plays a decisive role. But they implement the command via work agreements and via the acknowledgment of the special task among the Gentiles that was assigned to Paul and others.

For the apostle Paul, preaching the gospel to the uncircumcised (primarily the work of himself, Barnabas, and Apollos) is of one piece with the preaching of that same gospel to the circumcised (primarily the work of Peter and others). This is apparent in his zeal for the collection that was agreed on, intended for poor Christians in Jerusalem.[10] In this act of sharing (Rom. 15:25–27; 2 Cor. 9:12–15) the fellowship between the converted Gentiles and the oldest Jewish Christians is apparent.[11]

Thus Paul is able to see his work especially as a work among the *goyim*. And he can write about a period during which he had often begun his preaching in the synagogues, "I will not venture to speak of anything except what Christ has accomplished through me in leading the Gentiles to obey God by what I have said and done—by the power of signs and miracles, through the power of the Spirit. So from Jerusalem all the way around to Illyricum, I have fully proclaimed the gospel of Christ" (Rom. 15:18–19).[12]

16.2 "My Gospel"

Did Paul, as preacher to the Gentiles, have his own gospel? Several times he speaks of "*my* gospel." But it seems improbable that his gospel would have had a content different from that of the other apostles, for he continues in that which has been transmitted to him, and he speaks almost incessantly of "the gospel of God" (or "the gospel of Christ"). Furthermore, he speaks about the gospel preached by Silas, Timothy, and himself as "our gospel."[13] The expression "my gospel" does not refer to a different gospel. Paul's gospel is *the* gospel (Gal. 1:7–9).

Yet the apostle can also speak of his gospel; in Jerusalem he explains "the gospel that I preach among the Gentiles" (Gal. 2:2). Such an exposition would make little sense if Paul's preaching of the gospel was not characterized in some way by something unique that needed explaining.

Paul uses the expression "my gospel" when he speaks of the fact that "God will judge men's secrets through Jesus Christ" (Rom. 2:16). From what follows in Romans 2 it appears that he means something specific by this: God will not judge on the basis of circumcision of the body but rather of circumcision of the heart (Rom. 2:28–29).

We find the same expression in the doxology in the letter to the Romans: "Now to him who is able to establish you by *my gospel* and the proclamation of Jesus Christ, according to the revelation of the mystery hidden for long ages past, but now revealed and made known through the prophetic writings by the command of the eternal God, so that all nations might believe and obey him . . ." (Rom. 16:25–26). Here also Paul refers to the strengthening of the Gentiles by faith apart from circumcision.

For the apostle, this is the implication of the grace in Christ Jesus. He writes to Timothy: "Remember Jesus Christ, raised from the dead, descended from David. This is my gospel, for which I am suffering even to the point of being chained like a criminal" (2 Tim. 2:8–9). Although the acceptance of the Gentiles by Jesus Christ is not specifically mentioned here, it is nevertheless implicit in Paul's reference to his being chained: he is not in chains because he believes in the resurrection, but because he, as a Jew, preaches the resurrection of Jesus Christ to uncircumcised Gentiles and wants to expand Israel by the inclusion of uncircumcised fellow-citizens.

The phrase "my gospel" is essentially the same as "the gospel [preached] to the Gentiles" (Gal. 2:7).[14] The apostle Paul has received (through revelation, see chapter 3.4) insight into the mystery that the

Gentiles are fellow-heirs in Christ. This is probably why he speaks occasionally of "my gospel": it is the gospel as he personally received it from God (Gal. 1:12, 15–16; Eph. 3:3). It is not a private gospel, but it is a gospel that Paul may in a sense call his very personal possession. It has been entrusted to him—God took him into his confidence (1 Tim. 1:11; Titus 1:3)!

When we read Paul's address in the synagogue in Pisidian Antioch (Acts 13:16–41), it is not representative of the specific aspect of his gospel—he speaks to Jews about the Christ, and the topic of circumcision does not enter in. Nor is his address in Athens representative, because the apostle never gets beyond the topic of the resurrection (Acts 17:22–31). In both speeches the universal offer of grace is present, but they are not focused on the acceptance of the uncircumcised through faith in Jesus Christ.

Paul gives us more information about his gospel in the letter to the Ephesians, where he explains the "mystery" he has received. The first part of the letter is a summary: "In reading this [i.e., the first part of the letter], then, you will be able to understand my insight into the mystery of Christ" (Eph. 3:4). The first two chapters deal with the grace in Christ, also for the Gentiles, and with the unity between Jew and Gentile this grace brings: "For through him we both have access to the Father by one Spirit. Consequently, you are no longer foreigners and aliens, but fellow citizens with God's people and members of God's household, built on the foundation of the apostles and prophets, with Christ Jesus himself as the chief cornerstone" (Eph. 2:18–20). It is the unity in Christ that is central: the Spirit builds from both Jews and Gentiles "a dwelling in which God lives by his Spirit" (Eph. 2:22).

Although Paul preaches primarily to the Gentiles, his gospel is a gospel of fellowship, and that is why it is so important that Peter, John, and James gave him and Barnabas the "right hand of fellowship." The gospel without circumcision is brought to the Gentiles who remain uncircumcised. The gospel with circumcision is brought to the Jews who do not have to abolish circumcision when they accept Messiah Jesus. But there are not two gospels—one with and one without circumcision. There is only one gospel that spreads in two directions: "first the Jew and also the Greek"! Because of the unity of this gospel of the Christ, Paul is very concerned that his gospel stand in the service of the building up of the one body of Christ. There may be various social groupings (Jewish-Christian and Gentile-Christian groups), but they eat the one bread of grace. As soon as this table fellowship in Christ is sacrificed to the fear of the non-Christian fellow Jews, Paul's ire is stirred—even against Cephas (Gal. 2:11–14). Paul's gospel is also *the* gospel!

16.3 Moses and Those on the Outside

In the wake of Paul's preaching to the nations follow problems concerning law and circumcision, which erupt in the encounter with the synagogue and in living together with Jewish fellow-Christians. These problems do not play a large role in Paul's gospel, since the heart of the gospel is faith in Christ and the Spirit who is poured out. God himself bypasses law and circumcision when he reaches out to the Gentiles!

Thus the curse of the law bypasses the Gentiles ("Cursed is everyone who does not continue to do everything written in the Book of the law," Gal. 3:10). God has redeemed from that curse those who lived under the law, and from that moment on it is not the (curse of) the law that confronts the Gentiles, but the blessing of Abraham. If it can be said at all that the Gentiles also have been redeemed from the curse of the law, then it happened before that curse could reach them. Thus it more or less bypasses them (Gal. 3:10–14). They skip the law and go directly to the blessing!

Nevertheless, in Galatians Paul writes much about the law, which may create the impression that the law as such was an important topic for Christians from the Gentiles. However, it *was* not important—it *became* important. It became important because the Gentiles who turned to God and became Christians were confronted in more than one way with the influence of the ancient (circumcised) people of God, specifically in the encounter with their fellow-Christians among those Jews. For the non-Christian Jews the uncircumcised Christians are of no relevance; they are simply unconcerned about these *goyim*. The Sanhedrin does not concern itself with non-Jews; uncircumcised Gentiles are outsiders who do not fall under their jurisdiction. But it is different for the Christians among the Jews. On the one hand they fall under the jurisdiction of the law and of the Sanhedrin, but on the other hand they now encounter "fellow-citizens" who are uncircumcised. When it comes to circumcision, the Gentiles are not brothers or fellow-citizens—but "in Christ" they are. The Jewish Christians are thus faced with an enormous dilemma: how can one remain a Jew while at the same time communicating with brothers and sisters from the Gentiles? The problem these Jewish Christians faced cast a long shadow over the young Christian community from the Gentiles. It is about this shadow that Paul must occasionally write.

The difficulty with the letters to the Romans and Galatians, however, is that Paul writes about a Jewish problem from a non-Jewish perspective. This makes it complicated, but the reality of early Christendom was complex and overwhelming due to the rapid spread of the Spirit among Jews and Greeks. We might view letters such as those to the Romans and the Galatians as reflections on the implications of what was happening at the time.

The fact that Paul does not write about the law in all his letters to Gentile Christians indicates that circumcision and law became topics for discussion only when there was an external stimulus to do so. Thus the topic is discussed at length in only two letters—Galatians and Romans. On the basis of these two letters the incorrect impression later emerged that liberation from the curse of the law is at the center of Paul's gospel. But we must realize that the law was for the readers of these letters a topic they looked at from some distance. They had never lived under the law and were at most familiar with the special traditions the Jews observed on the basis of their Holy Scriptures. But Jewish traditions were not their traditions!

It was radically different for the Jews: for them living according to the law was the natural expression of belonging to God's people. This people was characterized by a number of customs, of which circumcision, Sabbath observance, and dietary laws are best known. When we read Josephus we do not get the impression that these customs were viewed as a means to justification; rather, they were understood as the hallmark and virtues of the people. Whoever wanted to belong to the God of Israel had to live as a fellow-citizen of Moses and the prophets.

It is important to note that the law looks very different from the Jewish than from the Gentile perspective. What for the Jews is self-evident tradition, handed down from the forefathers, would be a new duty for Gentiles when they become Jews. In a sense the law of Moses is for outsiders primarily a law, for the Jews themselves a custom, a way of life. The law as obligation is not a theme because the law is so demanding and coercive, but rather because to every non-Jew the law looks like a precondition.

At issue were not the monotheistic faith and its moral and ethical values that many God-fearing people admired and adopted. Rather, it was about the law as a closed system that included rites of passage, sacrificial customs, and dietary laws that often made it difficult for God-fearing non-Jews to become Jews. Viewed from the outside, it was possible to make a distinction between, on the one hand, beliefs and values that could easily be adopted and, on the other hand, specific customs that permeated daily life. From the inside no such distinction existed—the whole system of laws and customs was of one piece. That is why only the circumcised Gentile can be considered a believer, since the requirement of circumcision cannot be separated from the law as a whole.[15]

In the letters to the Galatians and Romans Paul is forced to go into detail about the law as a whole because of the presence of the synagogue (in Rome) and the arrival of Jewish Christians (in Galatia). Thus the immediate cause for dealing with the topic is Jewish, but he does not write from a Jewish perspective. Rather, he writes from the context of those outside Judaism!

16.4 Obedience of Faith among the Gentiles

The Gentile Christians do not become Jews, but they are converted to the God of Israel. Jesus is the Son of the Father; in him the Lord appears to his people, Israel. Gentiles cannot accept Jesus without turning at the same time to the God of Abraham, Isaac, and Jacob. The apostolic decree (Acts 15) did in fact ask this of them. They did not have to join the Jewish nation through circumcision, but they had to leave their idols to turn to the true God.

The underlying assumption is that this God has a claim on all peoples. He is not the national God of one people, but he is the Creator of all humanity. Therefore it must be seen as sin that the nations have not worshiped him for a long time and have exchanged him for various idols and images. Paul says to the worshipers of Zeus and Hermes that they must "turn from these worthless things to the living God, who made heaven and earth and sea and everything in them" (Acts 14:15). The citizens of Athens (a city full of idols) hear that "the God who made the world and everything in it is the Lord of heaven and earth and does not live in temples built by hands" (Acts 17:24). To the Romans Paul writes that the wrath of God is upon the nations because "they neither glorified him as God nor gave thanks to him"; they "exchanged the glory of the immortal God for images made to look like mortal man" (Rom. 1:21–23). The first step, therefore, that the Gentiles are asked to take is to turn "to God from idols to serve the living and true God" (1 Thess. 1:9).[16] Only after that conversion can they "wait for his Son from heaven, whom he raised from the dead" (1 Thess. 1:10).[17]

In a sense, idolaters must first become God-fearers before they can come to the Christ of God. This conversion to the Creator has always been the fundamental message of the Jews toward all Gentiles.[18] Paul's argumentation and choice of words thus are easily recognizable as a continuation of a long tradition of Jewish mission in the Gentile world.

The apostle sees himself as having been called to bring about the "obedience of faith" among the Gentiles. He uses this striking phrase several times to characterize his apostolate. In the introduction of his letter to the Christians in Rome he calls his own apostolate and that of others an apostolate "to call people from among all the Gentiles to the obedience of faith" (Rom. 1:5). Not only at the beginning of the letter to the Romans but also at the end we find the phrase "obedience of faith," again in connection with the conversion of the Gentiles. It is in the doxology at the end of chapter 16, where Paul speaks of the revelation of the mystery that had long been hidden; it has now been "made known to all nations for the obedience of faith" (Rom. 16:26 KJV).[19] We read about this same topic in abbreviated form in

Romans 15:18: Christ works in Paul, which results in "the obedience of the Gentiles by word and deed" (NASB).

What sets the phrase "obedience of faith" apart is that it refers especially to the obedience of the nations and that "obedience" elsewhere is not further qualified by the word "faith."[20] Paul does use the verb "obey" (*hypakouein*) more than once in connection with "the gospel." In Romans 10:16 he says that "not all obeyed the gospel" (KJV; cf. NRSV).[21] On the other hand he can write with joy about the Christians in Rome, "Everyone has heard about your obedience" (Rom. 16:19). They "wholeheartedly obeyed the form of teaching" to which they were entrusted (Rom. 6:17). Not only in the letter to the Romans, but also in other letters Paul uses this obedience terminology to characterize the attitude of the Christians.[22] Within this broader application of the terms "obey the gospel" and "obedience" stands the specific phrase "obedience of faith among the nations."

How should we understand and translate this phrase?[23] The difficulty here, as is so often the case, lies in the word that is added ("of faith"), as a glance at various versions of Romans 1:5 shows: "obedient faith" (NACB); "obedience to the faith" (KJV); "the obedience of faith" (NASB, NRSV); "the obedience that comes from faith" (NIV).[24] There is a clear distinction between those who see "of faith" as an objective genitive ("obedience to the faith") and those who do not. The (often Roman Catholic) proponents of the objective genitive view "faith" as the content of faith (the *fides quae*) that is obediently accepted. An interesting parallel is found in Romans 6:17 ("ye have obeyed from the heart that form of doctrine which was delivered you," KJV). The (often Protestant) opponents of this exegesis, however, point to the fact that in Paul "faith" always refers to the act of believing (*fides qua*). These exegetes represent a continuum of interpretations. Obedience *consists in* faith,[25] *flows from* faith,[26] is *characterized* by faith,[27] *implies* both the faith through which one becomes obedient and the obedience to God that flows from this faith,[28] or, stated differently, it is an obedience that is characterized by a continuing commitment to a person.[29]

These differences of opinion as to whether "of faith" is an objective genitive are intersected by a wholly other difference of opinion, namely, whether we are dealing here with a polemic formulation. Those who see "of faith" as the content of faith (objective genitive) do not see a polemic here, but among those who hold that "of faith" refers to the act of faith we often find the suggestion that this phrase represents a deliberate antithesis to legalistic Judaism.

Thus, according to Garlington and others, the expression "obedience of faith" is the opposite of "obedience of the law," so that this phrase then expresses that which divides Paul's gospel and the non-Christian Jews.[30] Mark Nanos, on the other hand, sees here significant agreement with the Jews: Paul also insists on obedience! The believing Christian is obligated to keep the stipulations of the apostolic decree, and according to Nanos this implies taking into account a number of aspects of the Jewish way of life.[31] By this obedience to parts of the law, uncircumcised Christians could maintain a place within the Jewish synagogue.

There are reasons for understanding the phrase "obedience of faith" as referring not primarily to faith in Jesus Christ. Paul says concerning justification by faith in Jesus that it is first for the Jew and also for the Greek. But when he uses the phrase "obedience of faith" he thinks, not of the Jews, but especially of the nations, since it is these nations (the Gentiles) who are disobedient (Rom. 1:18–32). They do not glorify God and fall into the foolishness of idolatry (Rom. 1:22–23) because they do "not think it worthwhile to retain the knowledge of God" (Rom. 1:28).

What is special about Paul's work is that Gentiles, through faith in Jesus and the reception of the Spirit, are changed from disobedient Gentiles into obedient nations. They once again acknowledge God the Creator. The "Hear, O Israel: The LORD our God, the LORD is one" (Deut. 6:4) separated the Jews and the idolatrous Gentiles. Now that the Gentiles are baptized in Jesus' name and receive the Spirit of sanctification, they also break immediately with the idols. They subject themselves to the Father of Jesus Christ, "the Creator—who is forever praised. Amen" (Rom. 1:25)! Thus Paul can write to the Roman Gentile Christians, "you who were at one time disobedient to God have now received mercy" (Rom. 11:30). Here the apostle speaks of their disobedience before the gospel reached them and thus thinks of their lack of faith in the true God and Creator. The mercy of this God in Christ Jesus has healed them of that disobedience and thus brought them to faith in the true God. It is therefore for Paul an honor to be a minister of Christ Jesus to the nations "so that the Gentiles might become an offering acceptable to God, sanctified by the Holy Spirit" (Rom. 15:16). The converted Gentiles are now themselves the offering that for a long time was withheld from God by the unbelieving nations! A sentence later Paul writes about Christ who worked through him, "resulting in the obedience of the Gentiles" (Rom. 15:18 NASB).

We encounter various negative characterizations of the *ethnē* in Paul. They do not have the law (Rom. 2:14); they do not pursue righteousness (Rom. 9:30); they are led astray to mute idols (*eidōla*, 1 Cor. 12:2); they live in the futility of their thinking (Eph. 4:17); they do not know God (1 Thess. 4:5). The entire pericope Ephesians 4:17–5:8 presents a broad characterization. Ephesians 5:5 is interesting: "For of this you can be sure: No immoral, impure or greedy person—such a man is an idolater (*eidōlolatrēs*)—has any inheritance in the kingdom of Christ and of God." Those who are called from the Gentiles know (also via the apostolic decree) that the entry into the kingdom of heaven through Jesus Christ involves by implication breaking with the idols and with idolatrous practices to turn to the living God.

In Romans 1:5 Paul does not write that the Gentiles have come to the obedience of faith in the name of Jesus but "for his name's sake" (*hyper tou onomatos autou*). Thanks to their faith in Jesus' gospel they have come back to the obedience of faith in God. This obedience of faith does not stand in contrast to the obedience to the law—rather, it stands in contrast to the disobedience of those who worship idols instead of the one God.

The apostle Paul never switches to a different religion.[32] He continues to serve the God who had set him apart from his mother's womb. Through his ministry Christ brings the prodigal sons back home and reunites them with the eternal Father! They who had abandoned this God return, together with Israel, to obedience to him by believing in him!

16.5 The Circumcision of Izates

Do we encounter in Paul's life as the envoy to the nations an irreconcilable bifurcation? On the one hand Paul, as a good Jew, calls the Gentiles to convert to Israel's God. On the other hand he teaches that as Gentiles they have the freedom to not let themselves be circumcised and thus to remain outside the Jewish nation. Is it possible to serve Israel's God without circumcision? Was it not unavoidable that many Jews hated this Paul and held him in contempt as being a traitor to his own nation?[33]

The combination of these two aspects of Paul's preaching—faith in Israel's God and freedom from the law of circumcision—makes sense only if we accept that Jesus is the Messiah and that he apparently gives his Spirit also to uncircumcised people on the basis of faith alone. Only thus could the apostles and elders come to the formulation of the apostolic decree, in which they exempt Christian Gentiles from the obligation to live according to Jewish customs. And it was only through revelation that Paul learned to understand the mystery that the Gentiles are coheirs.

The apostles received from God a justification for the gospel of the uncircumcised. Doesn't God thereby contradict himself? Were the Jews at all able to comprehend this new revelation? At first glance faith in God was unthinkable apart from circumcision, but a closer look shows that there were indeed in Judaism contexts in which this new perspective could fit.

Important here is the position of the God-fearers: although they were not Jews because they were not circumcised, they were nevertheless honored as servants of the Most High! Thus we read the following testimony concerning the uncircumcised Roman Cornelius: "He is a righteous and God-fearing man, who is respected by all the Jewish people" (Acts 10:22). From the words of the angel we can also deduce how much this centurion meant for the Jews: "Your prayers and gifts to the poor have come up as a memorial offering before God" (Acts 10:4). Something comparable is true of the centurion in Capernaum. The Jews commend him to Jesus with the words "he loves our nation and has built our synagogue" (Luke 7:5). The fact that the God-fearers were uncircumcised did not keep them from being valued and recognized. The absence of circumcision did, however, create a practical problem in communication (such as entering a home, eating together, etc.). But this was a problem only on the part of the Jews, since they were not allowed to enter the home of a non-Jew (Acts 10:28) or to eat with a non-Jew (Gal. 2:12). Such actions could lead to a transgression of the laws on ceremonial cleanness and of the dietary laws.

When about a century before Christ the Hasmonean high priests conquered the area of Idumea and later Iturea, they gave the population a choice: deportation or circumcision! This demand to be circumcised was in fact a demand for nationalization: the Jewish lifestyle had to be adopted. This was the only way in which the Jews could communicate without restrictions in the conquered regions. Josephus describes the requirement on the native population as follows: "Hyrcanus . . . permitted them to remain in their country so long as they had themselves circumcised and were willing to observe the laws of the Jews,"[34] so "they submitted to circumcision and to making their manner of life conform in all aspects to that of the Jews."[35] Circumcision and "becoming Jews" are identical; we read about a Roman, Metilius, who escapes death by promising "to turn Jew and even to be circumcised."[36]

Is it possible to serve God without becoming a Jew, and thus without circumcision? Is the necessary sign of national identity also religiously essential? This was apparently an issue on which there was a difference of opinion among the rabbis, as is evident from the interesting story, related by Josephus, about the circumcision of Izates.

The story takes place in the days of Paul, in an eastern kingdom ruled by Monobazus. The kingdom, called Adiabene, was located in the region of the Armenians. One of Monobazus's wives was his (half) sister Helena. She bore him Izates, who was the king's favorite and was raised elsewhere for reasons of safety. In the meantime, the wives of King Monobazus came under the influence of a Jewish merchant named Ananias, who convinced the women "to worship God after the manner of the Jewish tradition."[37]

These God-fearing women then put Ananias in touch with Izates, who lives elsewhere, and Izates is also won to faith in Israel's God. This leads to his refusal, after his father dies, to have all the other princes, who are potential rivals, put to death, as was customary. He considers this to be in conflict with respect for God. He does expel them and their families from the country, and sends them to Rome and Parthia. As the new king he feels himself compelled to accept circumcision because otherwise "he would not be genuinely (*bebaiōs*) a Jew."[38] But his mother counsels against this, because his people will "not tolerate the rule of a Jew over them."[39] As Izates hesitates, his spiritual guide, the Jew Ananias, gives him the same advice as Helena. He tells Izates that he could "worship God even without being circumcised if indeed he had fully decided to be a devoted adherent of Judaism, for it was this that counted more than circumcision."[40]

This is the more flexible position. But then another Jew enters the picture, Eleazar from Galilee. When during a visit Eleazar notices that Izates is reading the Torah, he severely reprimands him: One must not only read, but also keep the law! He is of the opinion that Izates is committing a serious sin of omission by not having himself circumcised. If Izates has not yet read the law on circumcision, he should do so forthwith.[41] Izates immediately has himself circumcised in another room. Only after the fact does he inform his mother and Ananias, who are very fearful of the reaction of the people. Nevertheless, the king stays in power, in spite of several threats.

Josephus concludes from this happy ending that the benefit of godliness befalls those who look to God and focus their faith entirely on him.[42] Josephus is apparently grateful for Izates' circumcision and for the fact that in that time a believing Jewish king reigned in Adiabene, who (thanks in part to the support of his mother) did much for the needy in Jerusalem and thus could be considered a role model for a converted king.[43]

It is incorrect to assume from Josephus that a convert to Judaism could decide for himself whether or not he should have himself circumcised.[44] Josephus nevertheless shows that the question of circumcision can be viewed from different perspectives within Judaism. He characterizes Eleazar as someone with the "reputation for being extremely strict when it came to the ancestral laws."[45] Thus, Eleazar does not represent Judaism as a whole, but rather its strict wing.[46] His approach, based on the law, is correct, but Ananias has a different perspective. Ananias also sees circumcision as a duty, but he takes into consideration that one duty can be greater than another, and that there may be important reasons to leave a lesser duty unfulfilled.[47] For Ananias tells Izates that "God himself would pardon him if, constrained thus by necessity [*di' anankēn*] and by fear of his subjects, he failed to perform this rite."[48] Ananias considers Izates' responsibilities as king to outweigh the duty to be circumcised. He thinks that God himself would approve of this weighing of priorities.[49]

Josephus's story does not indicate whether he favors Ananias's or Eleazar's position. As a historian who knows what happened next he is grateful for Eleazar's courage of faith. He presents the opinions of Ananias and Eleazar as an internal difference of perspective between the radical Galilean and the more cautious merchant.[50]

The story about circumcision takes place in the same border region where not much later a certain Titus accompanies Paul on a visit to Jerusalem. Titus, though a Greek, is not forced by Peter and the others to undergo circumcision. Josephus's report shows that it was possible to have a discussion within Judaism about the circumcision of God-fearing Gentiles. But this discussion is possible only when there are important reasons for considering not being circumcised. For Ananias it was in this case a political consideration.

For the apostles it is very different. They have a religious reason for not asking God-fearing Gentile Christians to be circumcised. The outpouring of the Holy Spirit without prior circumcision and on the basis of faith in Christ makes it clear that for God faith in Christ among Gentiles is more important than circumcision and incorporation into the Jewish nation. Whereas Ananias makes a humanly well-founded consideration, Peter asks, "who was I to think that I could oppose God?" (Acts 11:17).

We now come back to the question as to whether Paul and the other apostles did not ask the impossible of the Jews when they wanted to give Gentile Christians without circumcision equal standing in and with God's people. For the strict Eleazar, Ananias's consideration was inadequate grounds for exempting Izates from a commandment. Josephus also is of the opinion that fear of his subjects was not an adequate religious basis for Izates' not being circumcised. But no one denies that it is in principle possible to weigh commandments. And this is what the apostles also do, when they consider the fact that "God, who knows the heart, showed that he accepted [the Gentile Christians] by giving the Holy Spirit to them" (Acts 15:8) is an adequate reason "not to burden you with anything beyond the following requirements," stated in the apostolic decree (Acts 15:28).

The key question for the Jews is therefore not how binding the law on circumcision is, but how unbinding the works of Messiah Jesus and of the Spirit are when what is at issue are the uncircumcised Gentiles who come to faith in him.

16.6 Jointly with the Gospel of the Circumcision

In later Christendom the Pauline gospel of noncircumcision has become dominant. The gospel of the circumcision hardly plays a role and is frequently still a matter of controversy. This can easily lead to a false perspective and to a misinterpretation of Paul in light of the later development, namely, that the gospel without circumcision was the only gospel and, in any event, the norm.

But in Paul's own day, many preached the gospel of circumcision among the Jews side by side with Paul's gospel of noncircumcision. The Gentile Christians are exempted by Christ from the requirement of circumcision, but for the Jews it remains a custom established by the forefathers that has not been abrogated or forbidden by Christ.

Paul and Barnabas themselves offered the right hand of fellowship to Cephas, James, and John—three apostles who were to work with the gospel of circumcision! This means that Paul most definitely did not work for an abrogation of the law of circumcision. On the contrary! There is no change in lifestyle for the Jews. The law is not binding for Gentile Christians—but that does not mean that it has been abolished for the Jews. After all, Jesus himself had said to them that he had not "come to abolish the Law or the Prophets" (Matt. 5:17–18), and he commended to the people the teaching of the legal experts concerning Moses (Matt. 23:2–3). But he did make it very clear that he himself had the authority to make the law of Moses more stringent (marriage laws) or to declare certain commandments subordinate to higher laws (Sabbath and ceremonial cleanness).

Paul himself continued to keep the Jewish customs. Thus he could make a vow that had to be concluded with an offering in Jerusalem (Acts 18:18; 21:23–26). Events such as the feast of unleavened bread and fasting retain their significance (Acts 20:6; 27:9). Paul goes to Jerusalem to worship God (Acts 24:11), and he brings offerings to the inner temple court (Acts 24:17–18). He circumcises Timothy because as the son of a believing Jewish mother he should be circumcised (Acts 16:3; cf. 2 Tim. 1:5). Paul wants to avoid the impression that he considers circumcision to be unimportant for a Jewish boy simply because the boy's father is a Greek.

It was utter slander when people said of Paul that he taught "all the Jews who live among the Gentiles to turn away from Moses, telling them not to circumcise their children or live according to our customs" (Acts 21:21). It was especially Paul who strictly kept to the terms of the agreement of fellowship between the gospel with circumcision for the Jews and without circumcision for the Gentiles. As he puts it himself, "To the Jews I became like a Jew, to win the Jews" (1 Cor. 9:20), and he urges the believers in Corinth, "Do not cause anyone to stumble, whether Jews, Greeks or the church of God" (1 Cor. 10:32).

Paul cannot be characterized as a traitor to his own people or to his own religious past. The only thing he fought for was the fellowship between Jewish and Gentile Christians in the Lord Jesus Christ. His efforts in Jerusalem to prove that he was not against the Jewish way of life cost him years of imprisonment!

As God's emissary to the nations, the apostle Paul was subject to ever-varying dynamics and tensions. To understand his place it will be useful to give a brief sketch by way of summary of the various reactions his gospel of noncircumcision encountered. Paul had friends and enemies of different kinds. He alternately dealt with persecution, misunderstanding, support, avoidance, undermining, and acceptance.

Persecution. The non-Christian Jews (among them Paul's former fellow-students) condemn Jesus as a blasphemer of God. They are therefore unable to see faith in Jesus as a basis for exempting God-fearing Jews from circumcision. In their eyes, Paul fails to adequately respect God's law, and he is therefore a threat to the adherence to that law among the Jews. They therefore persecute Paul as an apostate.

Misapprehension. Christian Jews (especially Christians from the party of the Pharisees) acknowledge Messiah Jesus and the gift of the Spirit to uncircumcised believers, but they are of the opinion that these Gentile Christians are not exempt from the requirement to be incorporated into Israel through circumcision (Acts 15:1–2, 5).

Support. The apostles and the elders in Jerusalem uphold Moses for the synagogues, but on the basis of the work of the Spirit they no longer expect that Gentile Christians will let themselves be circumcised, as long as they refrain from idolatry and from an unholy life (Acts 15:19–29; 21:25).

Avoidance. Christian Jews from the circle of James allow Gentile Christians their freedom from the law, but they refuse to have any contact with them. They want to avoid the appearance that they are no longer good Jews because they eat with uncircumcised Gentiles in the meetings of the Christian community (Gal. 2:12).

Undermining. Some Christian Jews urge (directly or indirectly) the Gentile Christians to let themselves be circumcised to keep their Jewish fellow-believers from being persecuted because of their contact with them, uncircumcised non-Jews (Gal. 6:12–13). The work of the Spirit of Christ is acknowledged, but it is undermined by a pragmatic compromise-proposal concerning becoming Jewish.

Acceptance. Paul and Barnabas on the one hand, and the leaders of the church in Jerusalem on the other, accept that the uncircumcised Christians from the nations and the circumcised Christians from the Jews constitute one community. This means that living as a Jew is circumscribed by this new fellowship in Christ: Jewish customs may not be used to keep the door between Jewish and Gentile groups closed. The command of Jesus to be one through the Spirit transcends certain commandments of the Torah of Moses.

17

GOSPEL WITHOUT LAW FOR GENTILE CHRISTIANS

Paul preached the gospel to the uncircumcised Gentiles, and his gospel did not require circumcision. This quickly raised fundamental questions on the part of Jewish Christians (Acts 15), and it later caused practical problems that affected the experience of unity within the Christian community (Gal. 2:1–14). This chapter looks in more depth at the place of the law of Moses in the work of the apostle Paul.

This it is a topic that did not occupy a central place in the preaching to the nations. Themes such as "law" and "circumcision" were not part of the core of the gospel about the one God, about his Christ, and about the gift of the Spirit. But these themes unavoidably intruded later, specifically in the encounter with the Jews in general and with some Jewish Christians in particular. Can uncircumcised persons (in Christ) be servants of Israel's God? Or is the position of Gentile Christians comparable to that of illegal aliens in modern society? In two letters (Romans and Galatians) Paul had to address this issue at length. The topic of the law may not be central in his gospel, and it does not play a crucial role in the origin of the Gentile Christian communities, but sooner or later Paul's gospel for the uncircumcised evokes discussion of this topic.

At the same time the law is a topic with which the apostle was existentially involved from the very beginning of his life. He was a fiery champion of living in accordance with the law as a requirement for all people. But through Christ he was made into a preacher of the gospel of noncircumcision. Before he could preach a gospel without circumcision to Gentiles, he himself had to undergo a change. He goes so far as to describe this change with these words: "I died to the law" (Gal. 2:19).

This combination of, on the one hand, existential involvement on Paul's part and, on the other hand, only a secondary interest on the part of the Gentile Christians, makes the way in which the apostle writes on this theme rather complicated. Furthermore, because in later centuries a great deal of theology was woven around the topics "law" and "grace," and around the corpus of Paul's letters, it is impossible to deal with this subject in a few words. This chapter, which deals with the historical context in which we must place Paul's explanations about the law, incorporates the extensive recent discussions on this topic. (For more on the place of the law in Judaism see appendix 3.)

17.1 Current Views on the Problem

17.1.1 Set Free from the Law?

The first theory on Paul and the law holds that Paul grew up with a law that appealed to human merit. In his letters he is then thought to distance himself from the law as a soteriological guidebook. He came to understand that not the law but faith is the means to come to God, to be saved, and to be able to be righteous. His letters then are written against the background of a law that was in fact a dead end.

This theory leans heavily on the fact that when Paul speaks of the (works of the) law it is often in contradistinction to words such as "faith" and "grace." This leads to the overwhelming impression that Paul on principle sets himself over against "the (works of the) law." Those works would as such be of no value and contrary to the God of grace. Before he could become the apostle of faith and grace to the uncircumcised, he would have to distance himself from the law that is aimed at merit and at salvation by one's own power.

But the question that comes immediately to mind is, Did God then perhaps give a wrong law? How do Paul's negative statements relate to the positive Old Testament revelation? And what foundation for a religious ethic is the apostle left with? Furthermore, if this view is correct, how do we explain that Paul nowhere disavows his past as a bad and shameful period in his life? He knows himself to be a sinner because he persecuted the church of Christ, but nowhere does he say that he was a sinner because he was zealous for the law. He continues to speak positively about that zeal for the law, even after he has learned to be zealous for more than the law—for Christ Jesus (see Gal. 1:14; Phil. 3:4–11).

This cluster of questions invites us again and again to delve more deeply into what it is that Paul wanted to say about faith and law, and about law and works. For Paul, the law was not something that was simply to be crossed out.

17.1.2 Converted from Legalism?

According to some, Paul does not really turn against the law but rather against the Jewish misunderstanding of this law. The Jew Saul learned through his calling to Christ how wrongheaded the religious system was to which he had devoted his entire life up to that point. His conversion to Christ then involves a break with the legalistic system of works and merit. The works of the law could, in and of themselves, have a positive function in religion, but in the practice of Judaism they functioned entirely in a perverted manner. Paul then views "the works of the law" in the light of this structural abuse of the law by the Jewish community.

But is it correct to characterize the Jewish religion as a religion of (works of) the law and as a religion of merit? This question was not much discussed a century and more ago. Back then it was for many a foregone conclusion that the Jewish religion, as it had developed after the exile, can be characterized as a legalistic religion. Later Judaism differed in this respect from the primary Israelite religion. The latter was more prophetic, while later Judaism shifted the emphasis toward legalism and casuistry, so that the doctrine of merit stood at the heart of soteriology. Not only Jesus, then, protested against this degeneration of the religion, but Paul also learned finally to distance himself from this debased form of religion. Christianity, then, is in a sense a return to the more prophetic aspect of Israel's original religion.[1]

In the course of the twentieth century the basic assumption of this viewpoint came increasingly under criticism. Already in the first half of the century, the work of Solomon Schechter and George Foot Moore made clear that, to the contrary, Judaism remained a religion in which God's electing grace is central and in which mankind is called to acceptance, love, and faith.[2] In the second half of the twentieth century this perspective gained broader acceptance thanks to the work of E. P. Sanders and others.[3] Sanders introduced the term "covenantal nomism" to characterize Judaism: On the basis of God's electing love for Israel as his covenant people, the believer knows him- or herself invited to a life of mercy. Living "according to the law" is not at all legalistic; rather, it expresses the believer's joy in the grace of the Lord. The Jews are not concerned with getting into the covenant with God but rather with staying in the covenant. The law does not function within soteriology (within the doctrine of justification) but rather in the context of ethics. There it shows the chosen people the way to live out their election. Whoever is born a Jew or is allowed to become a Jew learns in the law how one may live "Jewishly." The law demarcates the style, the mores, the customs of the fathers.

In the light of this view on Judaism, Paul would appear to picture his own past in negative terms. His somber vision on the requirements of the law (over against faith and grace) is, then, according to some a product of a deliberately drawn contrast: Paul draws the law too black in order to let the light fall on the grace of Christ.

Sanders himself is not of the opinion that there is a true conflict between Paul and this more recent image of Judaism. According to Sanders, Paul does not accuse the Jews of legalism. All he reproaches them for is that they are not Christians. Paul is not anti-legalist but pro-Christian. He simply prefers another faith without thereby putting the previous faith in a negative light.

James D. G. Dunn looks for a solution in a different direction.[4] He also does not think that Paul fought legalism. But where Sanders sees a radical break develop between Paul and Judaism, Dunn sees more points of agreement between the two. According to him, Paul condemns Judaism only to the extent that it makes certain "identity markers" obligatory for Jewish Christians (the so-called works of the law).

Dunn sees only a partial separation between Paul and Judaism that involves only the limited area of a number of specific "works of the law." According to Dunn the expression "works of the law" has a restricted meaning. It does not refer to the law as a whole but rather only to the social "identity markers" that set a Jew apart from the Gentiles: circumcision, Sabbath, dietary laws. After his conversion Paul does not, therefore, differ from Judaism as such (as Sanders claims); rather, he fights against the false confidence that the Jews of that time had in their privileges as God's covenant people, and he fights against their exclusivism toward everyone else. In this way Dunn seeks to harmonize Paul's polemic with Sanders's more positive view of Judaism. Paul seems to detach himself from the Judaism Sanders describes, but this actually is not the case. Paul looks at the law only from a specific angle. He does not address the essence of religion but rather the Jews' attitude toward others (their "ghetto mentality"). In his commentary on Romans (1988)[5] Dunn applies what he had written earlier about *erga tou nomou* in Galatians (1983, 1985).[6] The upshot according to him is that the curse of the law that is removed consisted in the separation between Jew and Gentile. Confining the Torah to Israel is a curse for the Gentiles; Jesus removes this boundary and thus extends the blessing of God's covenant and election also to the Gentiles.[7]

By establishing specific requirements for external behavior (Sabbath, circumcision, dietary laws), the Jews made grace and election particular, whereas Paul wanted to make them universal. The Jews wanted to keep "being elect" too much to themselves. After his conversion, therefore, Paul was not an anti-legalist but rather an antinationalist.[8]

Whatever can be said about Judaism in the first century, it is certainly incorrect to generalize and characterize it as a religion with a soteriology of merit (see also appendix 3). This means that Paul's statements concerning the law can in any case not be viewed as pronouncements against a Jewish misapprehension of the law. It also means that Paul himself cannot be perceived as someone who was converted from a legalistic understanding of the law to a more spiritual understanding of that same law.

17.1.3 Is It Really about the Law of Moses?

If the background of Paul's writing about the law must be sought neither in the law itself nor in a misapprehension of the law, is there perhaps a misapprehension on our part? Do we perhaps think erroneously that Paul is speaking of the law of Moses while he is actually referring to another (kind of) law? When Paul uses *nomos* ("law"), should we in fact think of the Jewish law at all?

This question is raised in articles by Michael Winger and Harm W. Hollander.[9] Both argue that we must not immediately equate *nomos* with Torah. The meaning "Jewish law" emerges from the context rather than from the dictionary. Thus Hollander tries to show for 1 Corinthians that Paul uses *nomos* in this letter for the generally valid law(s) in the Greco-Roman world. By means of this nuanced description of the meaning of *nomos*, these authors implicitly argue against the view that Paul uses this term as a technical term in a massive theological vision on "*the* law," that is, the Jewish or Old Testament law.

It would certainly simplify things if we did not have to establish a connection between (part of) Paul's statements about the law and the Mosaic law. However, it is not quite so easy to get rid of the problem. The apostle has at least one series of statements about "the law" that refer unquestionably to the Old Testament revelation and that are cause for further inquiry. Even if he was not a "theologian of the (Jewish) law," he nevertheless did write on the topic a number of times!

Furthermore, the readers of his epistles knew Paul as a Jew. Even though the word *nomos* in Greek does not refer exclusively to the Jewish law, it is natural to think in Paul's case immediately of that law—all the more because he speaks of "*the* law," apparently with a specific law in mind. The context indicates that Paul does in fact write about the Jewish law (1 Cor. 15:56).[10]

Important as it may be to realize that for non-Jewish readers the word *nomos* has broader connotations than, for example, the designation "Moses," the decisive factor nevertheless is that Paul's non-Jewish readers were aware that they were reading letters from a Jew, which made it natural to read "the law" as referring to "the Jewish law." This is all the more true because Paul in the context of his usage of "law" often explicitly uses data from Moses.

17.1.4 Plea for Part of the Law?

But assuming that Paul does write about the Jewish law, could it be that he intends it in a less comprehensive sense than would seem to be the case? Recent publications increasingly argue that Paul should not be viewed as a writer against the law as such, nor as someone converted from legalism. The truth is thought to be more nuanced. The apostle Paul wanted to bring the Gentile Christians partially under the law, for the sake of a harmonious coexistence of Jewish Christians and Gentile Christians in a single community: expanded Israel. Paul then does not fight against the law but rather against imposing too much of the law on the Gentile Christians.

Thus Alan F. Segal sees the apostle as a convert within Judaism: he turned away from Pharisaism and became an adherent of the more mystical and apocalyptic wing of Judaism.[11] This also made him more open toward the uncircumcised. And because mystical experience is more important among apocalyptic Jews than is the legalistic aspect of the law, the accents have shifted for Paul as well. But he remains a Jew, and his gospel seeks to incorporate the Gentile Christians into a particular kind of Judaism. He thought that he could establish a connection with the ideas within Judaism concerning the "righteous Gentiles." Paradoxically, this approach led, in spite of his intentions, to a distancing from first-century Judaism.[12]

Mark D. Nanos also views the apostle Paul as living within the framework of Judaism.[13] Over against the exclusivism of certain Gentile Christians in Rome, the apostle emphasizes the necessity of obedience to God, in agreement with the minimum requirements set forth in the apostolic decree of Acts 15. Paul wants to keep the uncircumcised Gentile Christians within the walls of the synagogue, and he fights against a model in which Israel is replaced by the church.[14]

According to Peter J. Tomson, Paul drew heavily on Jewish ethics (the *halakah*) in his letters.[15] This is possible because the apostle was of the opinion that the Gentile Christian was bound by the universal elements of the law, as they were formulated in later Judaism as the "Noachide Commandments."

Similarly Karin Finsterbusch, in her study on Paul's ethics,[16] also defends the idea that Paul combats a total applicability of the law to Gentile Christians, although he does seem to argue for a partial validity of the Torah for them.

By way of comparison we should also mention the work of Matthias Klinghardt and Jacob Jervell.[17] On the basis of the book of Acts, both are of the opinion that the Christian church remained a Jewish-Christian community for much longer than is often thought. The new element was that the God-fearing Gentiles who were willing to submit to a series of Torah provisions concerning aliens, now received through faith in Christ a legitimate place and full membership in the Jewish-Christian synagogue.

The contributions of these authors can help our nuanced reflection on the symbiosis of Jewish and Gentile Christians in a single community, but they do not resolve the problem of Paul's attitude toward the law. The apostle often writes without qualifications and in absolute terms about the freedom from the law for Jewish Christians. If what Paul was in fact aiming at was a partial freedom from the law, combined with a partial submission to that same law, would he not have expressed himself differently?

17.1.5 Was Paul Inconsistent?

The multiplicity of Pauline interpretations led the Finnish New Testament scholar Heikki Räisänen to conclude that the apostle was simply not consistent in his writing about the law, creating all kinds of misunderstandings by doing so.[18] If we are to understand Paul, we must be prepared to accept that his arguments are frequently ad hoc, created for the occasion. His letters are not theologically consistent but, rather, aim at convincing readers in diverse situations.

Paul indeed appears to show a somewhat ambivalent attitude toward the law. On the one hand it is not difficult to find a series of passages in his letters in which the apostle speaks in praise of the law and of his own past under the law. The commandment of the law is intended to lead to life (Rom. 7:10) and is "holy, righteous and good" (Rom. 7:10–12). Paul boasts of the fact that he was "as to the righteousness which is in the Law, found blameless" (Phil. 3:6 NASB).

On the other hand, however, there are also many apparently negative statements about "(the works of) the law." "By the works of the Law shall no flesh be justified" (Gal. 2:16 NASB), and "Christ redeemed us from the curse of the law" (Gal. 3:13).

Even though the above may not be sufficient reason to speak immediately of inconsistency in Paul's letters, there is at least cause to raise questions about the negative series. Should these statements not be taken as rhetorical when viewed in light of the positive place the law has always enjoyed in Israel, and also in later Judaism? And is this not all the more true when we take into consideration that the law remained fully the climate in which the Jewish Christians lived?

Thus, after an overview of the theories[19] of the historical background of Paul's statements about the law, the core question remains unanswered: Does Paul do justice to what is good in the law of the Lord? Does he not speak evil of a good gift? Does he not play off Golgotha against Sinai?

17.2 The Parameters of the Problem

The problem of Paul's statements about the law can easily expand into a broad and general theological problem. To prevent this, the problem must be well defined from the outset. It is, after all, a rather specific problem that involves only a few of Paul's letters, and to solve the problem requires that we be aware of the special circumstances in which Paul wrote his negative passages about the law.

17.2.1 Only Two Letters: Romans and Galatians

In the first place, Paul's discussions about the law and the works of the law are not central in all his thinking and in all his letters. It is striking that the negative statements about "(the works of) the law" are actually found in only a few of his letters.

The expression "works of the law" (*erga tou nomou*) is found only in Romans (e.g., Rom. 3:20, 27–28; without the addition of *tou nomou* in 4:6; 9:12) and in Galatians (2:16; 3:2, 5, 10). In a few other letters we find only the term "works" (*erga*), in contradistinction to "gift" (*dōron*, Eph. 2:9), "purpose" (*prothesis*, 2 Tim. 1:9), or "mercy" (*eleos*, Titus 3:5).

Negative statements about the law are found with some regularity only in Romans and Galatians; elsewhere such statements are found only incidentally (1 Cor. 15:56; Eph. 2:15; Phil. 3:9). The negative statements are not represented at all in 2 Corinthians, Colossians, 1 and 2 Thessalonians, 1 Timothy, and Philemon.

This leads to the conclusion that the negative terminology about the law is probably linked to the concrete situation of only a few of the Christian communities to which Paul wrote letters.

17.2.2 Gentile Readers

Are we to assume that what is involved here is a group of Jewish readers and that Paul presents an alternative perspective on the law only in letters to them? The opposite appears to be true. The letter to the Romans is written to non-Jews, as is the letter to the Galatians.

Did the apostle then present a too facile, and in fact wrong, image of the law to readers who did not know Judaism from the inside, in order to keep them from listening to those who perhaps wanted to convince them to be circumcised? In the letter to the Galatians this could indeed have played a role, but not in the letter to the Romans, where there is no hint of pressure to be circumcised.

It seems more plausible that Paul, in these letters to Gentile Christians, puts himself in the position of his readers and that he formulates his thoughts, as it were, from the outside, from their perspective on Judaism and the Old Testament. There were special circumstances in Rome and Galatia that led to Paul's doing this. The Galatians looked from the perspective of outsiders at Jewish Christians who invited them directly or indirectly to participate in their lifestyle based on conformity to the law. The Christians in Rome lived in the shadow of a large and influential Jewish community that could impress the young Christian community with their history and special lifestyle. When the Gentile Christians come under the spell of Jewish life lived in conformity with the law, Paul sees this as a reason to engage them in discussion about the value that that life under the law might or might not have for them. But it is incorrect to derive a general theology of the law from these two letters.

17.2.3 The Sacred Scriptures: Israel's Law

What exactly does Paul mean when he uses *nomos* in these letters? Is he thinking of a special system of commandments and rules (i.e., "law") or of the teachings of God in general (the Torah)? Is he focusing on the Mosaic legislation ("Moses") or is he thinking of the totality of the writings that Christians call "the Old Testament" and the Jews call "the Law and the Prophets" or "the Law, Prophets, and Writings" (the *Tanakh*)?

Later history has a profound impact on the way this question is formulated. In theology, "law" has acquired a meaning of its own that is contrasted with "grace." And the addition of the Gospels and the rest of the apostolic writings to the books of Genesis through Malachi puts the latter writings in a different light: they become the Old Testament. Furthermore, because in Christendom the Bible is no longer linked to a national religion, the Old Testament is now viewed differently. It is for most Christians no longer the sacred book of Israel but the first part of the Christian Bible.

Lest we take the words Paul used and imprison them in distinctions he himself did not know, we should understand the position the writings of Moses and the prophets occupied in first-century Judaism. At Sinai, Israel received the books of Moses. Even if one is of the opinion that these books as a whole are from a later date, the fact remains that they were viewed among the Jews simply as the Torah, given by Moses. It is true that these books contain much about the history of creation, of Abraham, and of the patriarchs, but this history is embedded in a complex aggregate of writings that has functioned since the time in the wilderness as Moses' legacy. Because these writings form in fact the constitution undergirding Israel's formation and existence, it is understandable that designations such as *graphai* (writings) and *Mōysēs* (Moses) and *nomos* (law) are used almost interchangeably. In fact, each of these refers to the same foundational documents of Israel, but each views them from a different perspective (more as sacred literature, as foundational history, or as constitution respectively).

The people of Israel lived as a nation under this constitution. Portions of it were read each Sabbath in the synagogues in the whole world (Acts 15:21), which is why the Jews can be designated "the people under the *nomos*" (Rom. 6:14–15; 1 Cor. 9:20). This does not mean that they are burdened by the law and that they can with great effort earn life by keeping the law. It means that as Jews they hear these divine words, including commandments and wisdom. The law addresses this people to whom it was given (Rom. 3:19). Jews have the law by birth! The nations do not have the law (Rom. 2:14), in spite of the fact that the Law and the Prophets (*Tanakh*) were translated into Greek. It remains, even in that translation and in the hands of the Greeks, fully the book of the Jewish people.

Thus the apostle Paul sees the whole of the "Words of God" as a gift entrusted to Israel. This is the most important privilege that distinguishes them as circumcised Jews from all other nations (Rom. 3:2; cf. also Stephen's words in Acts 7:38). To the Israelites belongs the "receiving of the law" (*nomothesia*; Rom. 9:4). The Jews feel secure through the possession of their *nomos* ("law"); through this they are the "instructed nation" on earth and through this they can be a guide for the blind Gentiles (Rom. 2:17–19). In this connection Paul also indicates why this law is such a rich possession for Israel: it gives them the "embodiment of knowledge and the truth" (Rom. 2:20).[20]

The apostle is well aware that this *nomos* as revelation from God dates back to Sinai; it is more recent than the prehistory of the creation and the patriarchs (also described in the Torah) and has been added later (Rom. 5:20; Gal. 3:19).

It is striking that Paul, whenever he makes a direct and positive appeal to the *Tanakh* in his letters to the Romans and the Galatians, always uses *hai graphai* or *hē graphē* ("the Scriptures" or "Scripture"), not *nomos* (see Rom. 1:2; 4:3; 9:17; 10:11; 11:2; 15:4; Gal. 3:8, 22; 4:30; cf. 1 Cor. 15:3; 1 Tim. 5:18; 3:16). In 1 Corinthians

Paul does use *nomos* when referring to the Scriptures in a positive sense (1 Cor. 9:8–9; 14:34), but Hollander has pointed out that Paul can do this against the background of the general use of *nomos* in the sense of "[general] rule" (as distinct from a specific regulation). Thus the apostle occasionally refers here to "the rule" of Moses. In general we can conclude that the apostle Paul uses *nomos* only by exception when referring to the *Tanakh* in a positive sense. In such cases he prefers to use *graphai*, *graphē*, or *hiera grammata* ("sacred scriptures," 2 Tim. 3:15). It seems as if in his correspondence with Christians from the Gentiles he no longer wants to see the Law and the Prophets as the constitution for the nation of Israel, but rather as the divine Scriptures that give wisdom to everyone who wants to serve God (2 Tim. 3:15–17).

The conclusion we can draw appears to be that Paul uses *nomos* both in a more restricted sense (the commandments of the law) and in a broader sense (the entire revelation given to Moses and the prophets). However, in both cases *nomos* refers to the "law" of Israel. This "law" as law cannot be divorced from the national existence of Israel. Discussions about the validity of the law are by definition discussions about the necessity of becoming a Jew, being circumcised, and gaining a share in the law and the fathers by becoming a member of this people of God. As a law for Jews the law has no significance for the Christians from the nations; they belong to the people of the Spirit of Christ, who make use of the earlier sacred Scriptures but for whom these Scriptures are not a national constitution.

17.3 Human Works and Works of the Law

When we read words such as "work" or "do" in Paul's letters, we almost immediately think of the problem of the Jewish law. But this narrowing of the historical background to include only Judaism is incorrect. The "works" do not come from Judaism into a Gentile world without "works." The reverse is true: from a Gentile world full of "works," life under the law also looks like a life of "works" (in this case the works of the law). Paul uses phrases that carry connotations derived from the religious world of his Gentile readers!

In the phrase "works of the law," the words "of the law" (*tou nomou*) are most often understood as explaining "works" (explicative genitive). In that case, the phrase would refer to works on which the law insists. The law of Moses is then seen as aimed at actions. And those actions then are characteristic of the law. Thus Judaism is characterized as a "religion of doing." Whoever says "law" says "works," and when "works" are mentioned, many immediately conclude that it is the Jewish law that is being discussed.[21]

At this point it is worth looking at those negative statements in which only "works" are mentioned, without the addition of "of the law." Are these shorthand expressions that mean the same as "works of the law"?[22]

In Ephesians 2:8–9 we read, "For it is by grace you have been saved, through faith—and this not from yourselves, it is the gift of God—not by works, so that no one can boast." The expression *ouk ex ergōn* is parallel with *ouk ex hymōn*. Here it is especially the Gentiles who are addressed (see Eph. 2:1–5, 11–13). Obviously these people have not been saved through "[Jewish] works of the law." If that is what Paul had in mind, his comment would, at the time this letter was written, have had only theoretical value and been unrelated to the reality of the life of the Ephesians.[23] It is more natural to think here of "works, achievements" in general.

In the Gentile world, works were definitely also known—efforts to put the gods in a more charitable mood and to implore their mercy. This was the purpose of the sacrifices as well as of days of repentance and of a variety of acts motivated by piety or superstition. The gospel, however, is not in any way an answer to the achievements of paganism in its efforts to please the gods. The God of Israel was ignored among the Gentiles, but he mercifully now turned toward them with the gospel of Jesus. They had not been able to add anything to this gospel with their religious activities (Acts 14:15–17; Rom. 1:16–23).

Furthermore, Paul writes in 2 Timothy 1:9, "[God] has saved us and called us to a holy life—not because of anything we have done but because of his own purpose and grace. This grace was given us in Christ Jesus before the beginning of time." The basis for God's redemptive calling was his purpose and his favor, not *ta erga hēmōn* ("our works").

Paul here writes as a Jew to a man with a Jewish mother (Timothy), and he thus has most likely in view here also the works that are part of the Jewish faith: works of the law. Nevertheless, Paul's statement does not imply a negative judgment of that law. Paul simply says that religio-ethical achievements (whether Jewish or non-Jewish) are not the basis of God's redemptive calling. In fact, what Paul says here to Timothy (who grew up uncircumcised, as the son of a Greek father) is comparable to that which he wrote in Ephesians 2:8–9.

The same is true of Titus 3:5. Here also Paul speaks as a Jew with an uncircumcised coworker about the fact that works are not the basis for salvation, which we owe entirely to God's love for humanity and to his kindness. Not "because of righteous things we had done" (*ex ergōn tōn en dikaiosynē ha epoiēsamen hēmeis*). In view here are righteous and good deeds such as those performed by Jews and Gentiles. Nevertheless, these are not what God's salvation is based on; the reason for salvation is to be found in his mercy.

In these three quotes from Paul's letters, the reason for speaking in negative terms about "the works" does not lie in a negative character of the law, or of those works, or of religion in general. The negative assessment holds true only in the context of the ground of God's calling and salvation. Because human achievements are placed over against God's initiative, this comparison can also be made when Paul writes to people with a pagan past. It is precisely through sending his Son that God proves that he bypasses the religious and ethical actions of Jews and Greeks. He himself paves a way, a bypass from himself to humanity. The works of Jews and Gentiles (no matter how wonderful they may be) appear to be irrelevant when it comes to the definitive work of salvation of God through Jesus Christ.

Against this background we should consider the possibility that the genitive *tou nomou* ("of the law") in the phrase "works of the law" (*erga tou nomou*) should not be understood as explaining (explicative genitive) but rather as specifying. There are all kinds of actions and it is possible to speak in a more restrictive sense about the achievements that flow from "the (Jewish) law." In this case the word "works" does not give a specific characterization of the law, but the word "law" indicates that what is in view here are not pagan religious works but rather works connected with the Jewish religion. "Works" are found in all religions, including the Israelite one. For the latter, the Torah (the book of the law) is the defining source of inspiration. Even as a Gentile can perform the works of his or her idols without these gods becoming legalistic gods, so the Jew can perform the works of the Torah without the Torah leading to a religion that can be characterized as legalistic.

It is striking that the word "works" does not play a central role in the written sources of Judaism itself, whereas in Paul's case it does appear to be a key term. But the perspective shifts when the apostle uses the word "works," not because it would be characteristic of Judaism, but rather because the Gentile world in general paid much attention to religious efforts and religious acts in order to appease and mollify the gods. It is from their perspective that the word "works" enters the discussion, and from their perspective Israel also has its own works (in this case the works of the Torah). It is then not Paul's idea of a too-legalistic Judaism that makes him write about "works" as if this were the most concise characterization of this particular religion. Rather, it is the pagan world in which he travels and the pagan view of religion and Judaism that invite him to explain certain things with the help of the "works" terminology. Viewed from the perspective of paganism, with its many religious activities in temples and in cemeteries, and with its superstitious concerns about favorable and unfavorable days, life under the law of Moses equally appears to be about "works for the gods." In this case the concern is (in contrast to the Gentile works) the works of the (Jewish) religious law.

17.4 No Works of the Torah!

When Paul in his letters to the Romans and Galatians uses the phrase "works of the law," he teaches the Gentiles, who were used to works in the worship of their gods, that they should not fall again under the spell of that kind of (pagan) works. Judaism could have an appeal to non-Jews precisely as a religion of pious works. Circumcision and Sabbath seem to the Gentile Christians acceptable as safe works, suitable to the God of the new Savior Jesus! The works of the (Jewish) law seem to be a good alternative to the works of the pagan temples, with which they now have broken.

17.4.1 Galatians: Remain in Grace!

In the letter to the Galatians, the apostle Paul raises the issue of the works of the law in his recounting of a dialogue with Peter. Jews are privileged: they are not sinners like the Gentiles. They have the law, the revelation of God! Nevertheless, the Christians among the Jews have come to realize that they have not been accepted by God on the basis of the works that go with the Torah, but by faith in Jesus Christ.

Paul's premise is not that the Torah is evil—to the contrary: it is through the Torah that Jews are no longer sinners like the Gentiles. The premise is that God in Christ and through the Spirit offers a definitive redemption. He does this out of grace (see Gal. 1:3–4). Nothing can or should be added. Peter must live out of this reality, also in his contact with Gentile Christians. If, when he is with other Jewish Christians, he rather disingenuously tries to keep up the works that belong to the Torah (in this case the dietary laws) and by doing so isolates himself from the Gentile Christians, he gives the impression that God's calling is not based on grace but on achievement, in this case the accomplishments of the Torah. This is especially confusing for the Gentile Christians. They were since childhood used to viewing religion in the framework of works, duties, efforts, and it is they who are inclined to interpret Jewish life as a system of religious accomplishments. For them the question arises whether they should perhaps move from the duties they performed for the idols and have abandoned to the imposing and very ancient works of the Jewish people to whom their Jewish-Christian brothers and sisters belong and from whom their new King, Christ, has come.

In Galatians 3:2, 5, 10 Paul writes further about the basis for God's mercy. The Galatians have not received the Spirit through works of the law but through faith in Jesus Christ. From a historical standpoint it does not make much sense to claim that the Galatians did not receive the Spirit through works of the law. After all, as Gentiles they lived entirely outside the law and had no connection with it whatsoever. The apostle nevertheless uses this hypothetical construction to set up what follows: in Galatia, some push for circumcision of the Gentile Christians, and now it becomes meaningful to point out that they became Christians before they could even consider living like Jews. Religious acts (connected with the Galatian religion) did not matter. The Galatians back then were not asked to move from their Galatian works to Torah works. This is why the Galatians must not allow themselves now to be caught in a net of actions "to win God." Such a transition to Judaism would—now that they are already Christians—be in fact a return to what they had viewed from old as a system of achievements.[24]

The apostle looks here at "the law" from the perspective of the Gentile Galatians. If they were to let themselves be circumcised because of their Jewish-Christian brethren (in order to spare these Jewish Christians persecution), they would have to *do* something. This looks similar to the performance-religion to which they had been accustomed as Gentiles: "do something for the gods so that they will do something for you." Paul does not suggest that the Jewish religion is a works-religion; rather, he derives the works-language from paganism. And he uses that language to make clear that Christians who have already been baptized by the Holy Spirit without circumcision would in fact be returning to their old system of extra works if they let themselves be circumcised. The custom of the Jewish people would then become a "work" for them.

17.4.2 Romans: Reward or Grace?

In his letter to the Gentile Christians in Rome, Paul also speaks of "the works of the Torah": no one will be justified by them (3:20). Only through faith in Christ is there salvation, without "the works of the Torah" (3:27–28).

Is the expression "works of the Torah" a specific instance of the more general term "(religious) works," focused on the religion of the people of Israel, or does Paul use the term "works" as shorthand for the law ("works of the Torah")? In other words, are the "works" specific to the Torah, or are the "works of the Torah" a specific instance of religious works in general?

The latter appears to be the case, for the following reasons.

1. In chapter 4 Paul speaks of the fact that Abraham was not justified "by works" (4:2). Because the law of Moses did not yet exist in Abraham's time (4:13), the works of the law cannot be in view here. Rather, 4:4–5 shows that what Paul writes about here are works, actions, accomplishments in general, since in those verses Paul speaks in general about "when a man works" and receives wages for his work, whereas grace is for the person "who does not work but trusts God." When Paul later quotes David (Ps. 32) he also speaks in very general terms about a righteousness "apart from works" in the sense of "without any contribution on the part of the person."

2. In chapters 1–3 Paul continuously focuses his attention on humanity as a whole (Jew and Greek). All are under the wrath of God, and this is due to an actual shortcoming. God wants to reward anyone who does good (2:6–11); we could call this the universal law or rule. In the final analysis it is about human virtues as they are expressed in the law of Moses, but as they can also be found in people apart from that law. What matters ultimately is not the possession of the Torah but doing "the work of the Torah" (2:14–16, 26–29 NASB). And the doing of this work of the Torah can be found also among the Gentiles, specifically the God-fearing Gentiles. They are not circumcised, and thus not Jews, but they are merciful and God-fearing. Nevertheless it appears that the Greeks have no excuse—but neither do the Jews (3:1–20). Thus 3:20 is the conclusion drawn from 3:9–19: "By the works of the Law no flesh will be justified in His sight; for through the Law comes the knowledge of sin" (NASB). What is generally valid for humans is even valid for the Jews!

But now God has opened a way of reconciliation in Christ through faith (3:21–26). There is now no reason to boast. But why not? What law precludes it? "The law of works" (3:27 NASB)? Here we suddenly encounter an unusual expression: "the law of works." This expression stands in contrast to "the law of faith." In this particular phrase the word *nomos* cannot refer to the law of Moses specifically; rather, we must think here of a general law or rule. The "rule of works" was formulated in 2:6–11. According to that rule some people might perhaps be able to boast in their virtues, but God follows the rule of faith, and then human virtues suddenly don't matter. And if people are saved by faith, then it is also apart from the works of the Torah (3:28). Paul says this by way of particularization. It is true in general that the performance rule does not work, but this then also applies to its special formulation in the law of Moses. God is not only a God of Jews (3:29)!

3. In chapters 9 and 11 we encounter several times the expression "by works." In 9:12 "works" stands over against the purpose of God who calls. Before their birth Jacob and Esau had not yet done anything good or bad, yet God's purpose was already apparent. Therefore it is not based on works in general—in this case certainly not the works of the Torah, since the law of Moses did not yet exist. In 9:31–32 Paul says that Israel pursued a law of righteousness but did not attain it "because they pursued it not by faith but as if it were by works." The majority text reads here *hoti ouk ek pisteōs, all' hōs ex ergōn nomou* ("not by faith, but as it were by the works of the law" [KJV]). Other versions follow a few older manuscripts in which *nomou* ("of the law") is missing. The sentence then is simpler: over against faith stand works. But if we do include *nomou*, the connection becomes more complicated. It is then also possible to understand the sentence as follows: *hoti ouk ek pisteōs (nomou), all' hōs ex ergōn nomou* ("not by the law of faith but as if it were by the law of works"; cf. 3:27 for these phrases). Why does Israel not attain to the law of righteousness? Because in their pursuit of that law they are motivated by the rule of doing and not by the rule of believing.

Paul is not writing about the Jewish people as a whole but about the Jewish people insofar as they are negative toward faith in Christ. Paul writes after Pentecost, and most Jews at that moment had already made the decision not to accept Jesus as the Messiah of God. Over against the grace of Jesus they latch on to the law and their Jewish identity. They refuse to surrender to faith in Jesus and the grace of God through Christ. In this negation of grace and of faith in the Messiah, life under the law now becomes a work they are not willing to give up. Hardening against the gospel changes the character of life under the law: it rigidifies from faith to self-confidence, from living out of grace to confidence in sacrifices and good works in the face of God's grace! The divine shelter of the law becomes for the Jews who continue to reject Jesus a bunker, a fortification in which they close themselves off from the light.

Finally we find in 11:6 the contrast "grace vs. works." The verse reads, "And if by grace, then it is no longer by works; if it were, grace would no longer be grace."[25] Here "works" is not a specific characterization of the law of Moses; rather, Paul makes a general distinction between grace and merit.

17.4.3 Retrospective

When we look back at the preceding paragraphs we can conclude that the expression "works of the law" must not be understood primarily from the perspective of Judaism. Rather, Paul uses the phrase from the viewpoint of the Gentile Christians. Accustomed as they were to the performance of religious works and the value of human virtues, they could easily perceive the Jewish religious way of life as a special form of works. This is then not intended to be understood as an a priori negative characterization. The apostle Paul reminds his readers again and again that the Spirit of Christ came over Jews and Gentiles, without respect of persons and not on the basis of their virtues. Christians, from the Jews as well as from the Greeks, are born through grace and live by faith. Because God in this era approaches humanity in this way, human virtues (including Jewish virtues) appear not to determine the future of the world. Not because works are "toxic," but because now Christ is distributed as food for all eternity. This is why works are now subordinate to grace. In the light of the gospel the limitations of human works and virtues (including the Jewish ones) become visible! Whoever closes him- or herself off from the glorious light that rises in Christ is condemned to his own works and will without this Savior end up the loser.

17.5 Does Paul Speak Negatively about the Law?

Up to this point we have come to the conclusion that when Paul uses the expression "(works of) the law," he does not intend to place the law or the Jewish religion in a negative light. The context of his terminology is God's dealing with humanity in general. God's grace in

Christ teaches us to take distance from our own religious achievements. It would then be wrong for Gentile Christians to turn the Jewish tradition into a new set of works.

But there is a second topic. Paul does not judge the performance of the works of the law on the part of Jewish Christians negatively (assuming that they do not give the impression that they trust in the works of the law more than in Jesus Christ by being afraid to have contact with Gentile Christians). The apostle himself still lives to a large extent as a Jew. And yet he seems to judge that law as such negatively, for whatever reason. Although these negative comments are limited to the letters to the Romans and the Galatians, they emphatically are an integral part of the letters. We must therefore look more closely at the reason why Paul includes these comments. Are they occasioned by the circumstances of his readers? If so, how are Paul's statements about the law connected with developments in Galatia and Rome?

But before looking at these two key letters, we must first look at a few phrases from other letters. These phrases occur in incidental passages that seem to convey an attitude toward the law that is as negative as some phrases in Romans and Galatians.

17.5.1 Incidental Statements

In 1 Corinthians 15:56 Paul says that "the sting of death is sin" and that the law (*nomos*) is the power or driving force of that sin (*dynamis tēs hamartias*). This statement is actually not negative about the law, but rather about the effect of the law in a situation of transgression. Why is sin in the end lethal? How can it have such a great effect? Because there is a law that condemns sin. Whoever is guilty is condemned to death. If there were no law (with a penalty for sin), sin would not be so disastrous. But the law brings both the sin and the penalty for that sin to light. That does not mean that the law is the cause of death. Paul does not say that the law should be discarded, but rather that sin (which is so detrimental because of the just and retributive law) will ultimately disappear, and with it also the law. Paul actually uses the word *nomos* here in a neutral rather than a negative sense.

The same is true of Ephesians 2:15, where Paul writes of "the law with its commandments and regulations" (*ton nomon tōn entolōn en dogmasin*). This law separated Jews and Greeks, but Christ has broken down the wall that divided. Thus the Gentile Christians are no longer "foreigners and aliens" (2:19). A negative effect of the law (the separation) was lifted when the law was fulfilled by Christ. The law itself is not viewed as negative. All Paul points out is that this was for many centuries an impenetrable dividing wall between Jews and Greeks.

Finally we must consider Philippians 3:9, where Paul contrasts "a righteousness of my own that comes from the law" and "the righteousness that comes from God and is by faith." But his statement is neither cynical nor deprecating. His righteousness that came from the law was indeed a form of righteousness (3:4–6), but in the light of the greater and better righteousness that comes from faith in Christ, the Crucified One, he has left the lesser behind in favor of that which is better (3:8–11).

We now can return to the list in section 17.2.1, which, as we saw, shows that it is primarily in the letters to Rome and Galatia that negative statements about the law play a role. We have shown that Paul does not condemn the law because it should have been a "law of works." Furthermore, we have seen that the various incidental statements in other letters are not significant for our inquiry. But when we focus solely on Romans and Galatians, we must all the more keep in mind that the theme of the law is not a priori a central theme of Paul's preaching, and that he addresses this theme probably because of the specific circumstances of the readers of these two epistles.

17.5.2 The Law in Galatians

It is striking that the law is not mentioned at all in Galatians 1:1–2:15. Paul describes salvation through Christ not as a salvation from the law, but as a rescue from "the present evil age" (1:4). He describes his past as dominated by zeal for Judaism and for the traditions of the fathers (1:14); the statements here parallel the zeal the Galatians might have for their nation and tradition. Nor is the law mentioned in 2:1–10 in connection with the consultation in Jerusalem:

the starting point in the discussion there is God's work among Jews and Gentiles. In Christ there is freedom (2:4); the Gentiles do not have to become circumcised Jews (2:8–9).

The law is not mentioned until Peter distances himself from his Gentile Christian brothers by reverting unconditionally to the Jewish lifestyle, specifically in terms of eating and drinking. At this point Paul must construct an argument that shows that this is not a good thing. But Paul's argument does not deal with the law in general; rather, Paul takes on his Jewish brethren who within Christendom assign greater weight to the Torah of Moses than to their fellowship with uncircumcised fellow-Christians.[26] At this point the presumed surplus value of the law in relation to the gospel must be considered. It appears that Peter and the other Jews became Christians precisely because they had come to recognize the surplus value of the gospel. Christ is greater than Moses. Moses could take Israel only so far, but Christ finished the work! Without the Messiah one can't make it as a Jew. Choosing Jesus Christ implies a negative judgment on the adequacy of living life according to the Torah. Once this choice is made, it becomes impossible to reintroduce the law to the Gentiles as a precondition for the Christian life. That would mean switching from the greater to the lesser.

Galatians 2:16 is sometimes translated as if there were an absolute contrast between faith and law: "knowing that a man is not justified by the works of the Law but through faith in Christ Jesus" (NASB). The Greek, however, does not have "but" (*alla*) but "if not" (*ean mē*). Life according to the law leads nowhere if it is not combined with the decisive faith in Messiah Jesus: "knowing that a man is not justified by the works of the Law *without* faith in Christ Jesus."

That Paul speaks about the law from the vantage point of Christ and with the Gentiles in view is clear from 2:19–20: "For through the law I died to the law so that I might live for God. I have been crucified with Christ and I no longer live, but Christ lives in me." Jesus was not murdered by bandits. He was condemned in the name of the Jewish constitution ("through the law"). Through his sentencing and death he no longer lives under the Jewish constitution (the constitution under which he was also circumcised). In its place now comes his life in heaven, at the right hand of his Father. Whoever in Israel chooses Messiah Jesus chooses to be an excommunicated person who has gone over to a different, higher order of being! Paul himself was led to this choice (as a Jew). How dare some people claim that the Gentile Christians still must be brought under the Jewish law—a law under which they never lived in the first place?

Paul's statements in 2:11–12 are closely linked with the course of his own life. He was pre-eminently a Jew (1:13–14). Being a devoted Pharisee made him sensitive to the fact that the Crucified One stood outside the law. It was precisely because Paul saw Jesus as having become an outcast that he persecuted the Christians, the followers of this Nazarene. But when near Damascus Paul was called to order by this dead man (who turned out to be alive after all!), his world was turned upside down. Jesus the Outcast thus turns out to be Life itself, taken up into the highest heaven! But then faith in him also means a relativizing of the Jewish national law. For Paul, the revelation of Christ transcends his own nation and his own "flesh and blood" (1:16b KJV). The conclusion that the law does not justify is an after-the-fact conclusion, reached on the basis of the facts of Christ.[27] Israel could find a way out of all its misery only through the hands of the Healer who appeared—yet it was he who was condemned in the name of the law. This made the law (which is good) subordinate to the higher life of the risen Messiah. The law is no longer the decisive line of demarcation between God's people and the Gentile nations.

In 2:21 we also see how Paul writes about the law from the perspective of Christ: "I do not set aside the grace of God, for if righteousness could be gained through the law, Christ died for nothing!" Paul is not giving a general reflection on the extent to which the Torah brings righteousness. Rather, in the light of Easter he is speaking about the new situation that has come about. *Now* we do receive righteousness, not through the national law that condemned Jesus, but through the death of God's Son. The fact of the coming of the Son of God and his death causes a shift in perspective. We can no longer simply retain the law as the line of demarcation between faith and unbelief without at the same time saying no to the grace of Golgotha!

In 3:10 Paul says that those who are *ex ergōn nomou* (lit., "from the works of the law") are under a curse, because it is written that anyone is cursed who does not "continue to do everything written in the Book of the Law" (cf. Deut. 27:26). It looks as if Paul here ends up with a negative characterization of Judaism in general. But if we consider this passage as a whole, we see Paul's comment in a different light. Paul addresses a specific situation at a particular point in time. His writing is located in *time*: in 3:13–14 he presupposes that Christ has been crucified and that he now lets the blessing of Abraham come to all nations through faith. Paul also writes to a specific *situation*: Gentiles who have already received the Spirit through faith are now in danger of being pulled away from Christ by the undertow of circumcision and the law of Judaism.[28] This means that Paul in 3:10 is not writing about the Jews of all preceding centuries, but rather about those who now choose law over grace (*hosoi* are those Jews who reject Jesus, who choose life under the law rather than faith in the Messiah). They must realize that the curse of the law now rests on them. Whoever continues to reject the Resurrected Lord, and continues to treat him as an accursed crucified individual, no longer has any shelter left while trying to fulfill the law. Now the curse will come upon him: whoever chooses the law over Christ no longer has any protection.

In 3:15–18 Paul speaks in neutral terms about "the law" as a historical entity that came later than the promises. Abraham's inheritance is received through faith, not through the law. This raises the question what the function of the law is in this world. This is the burning question for the Gentiles who are tempted to join the ancient people of God, Israel. This is the question Paul deals with in 3:19–25.

The law in this world constitutes a narrowing of the road, a temporary measure on the way to the promised seed (Christ). In all this the law is not in competition with the promise (3:21), but rather in support of it. The law was added "because of transgressions" (3:19). In the midst of the Gentile world, one nation was, as it were, preserved. It was kept within the framework of divine redemption. This one nation became the narrow gate for all nations that led to the worship of the Creator. Yet this was a temporary measure. The law was like a "tutor" (a *paidagōgos*, 3:24 NASB) that led "to Christ" (*eis Christon*). In 3:22 Paul gives his most substantive statement about the law in this context: it "has shut up all men under sin" (NASB). He does not use *pantes* ("all people") but *panta* ("everything"). Israel was surrounded by a large number of taboos; many things were labeled forbidden, and many things became sin. Because all these things were sealed and closed off, Israel remained restricted and was kept in check. At the same time, anyone who did not join this nation was excluded!

We can compare this with children for whom cupboards and drawers are locked and off-limits. In the concrete situation that gave rise to Paul's argument, Peter and the other Jewish Christians in Antioch let it be known clearly that a variety of foods were sin for them, or non-Jewish, forbidden. And thus they broke fellowship with the Gentile Christians. The law, their master, did not allow them! And their actions suggested that the Gentile Christians were in fact still outsiders. But the law never was God's first word for humanity. The promise to the nations preceded the law, and the law of Moses kept only the nation of Abraham temporarily in check and kept it together as a people to be the gateway to God. But everything has changed now that "(faith in) Christ" has come. The law is not abrogated for the Jewish people, but it loses its function as a narrowing of the road in the world of the nations.

Paul makes the point again in 4:1–5. Through his coming Christ brought, from the inside, an end to the period of the law as an isolating factor. Foster children became adult sons, and those who were lost came back home. The road that leads through Israel is not closed, but the road is no longer the constricted road through which all nations have to come to God. Since the main road, Christ, has been opened, the Gentiles as well as Israel can come to God directly, through the Spirit.

The extent to which Paul is motivated by the acute danger that the Galatians may go over to Judaism is evident in 4:21–5:1. The apostle writes, "Tell me, you who want to be under the law, are you not aware of what the law says?" (4:21), which is followed by a reference to Hagar and Sarah. This seems odd, since this example comes from the time before the giving of the law of Moses (see 3:17). But the apostle uses the expression "to be under the law" (*hypo nomon einai*), and this points to being a Jew and to being connected with the whole revelation in the law. The Galatians apparently want to be Jews, under the law. This "under" does not mean that they then will be dominated by the law, but that the law appeals to them. In the synagogue the law is read, and then the Jew sits under the hearing of the law and under the power of expression of the law, which is, after all, the book of the Jews. Apparently the Christian Galatians want to become people of the Torah, as did many proselytes in that century (and in earlier centuries).

But then the Galatians had better listen carefully to the law. After all, the law of Moses is not a separate law code, divorced from the story of Abraham; rather, that story is the preface to the law and an integral part of it. "Listening to the law" here is thus broadened to include listening to the law of Moses as it comes to us in the Pentateuch. Whoever listens to Moses must also read about Abraham! This elaboration is a bit ironic but nevertheless significant because "want[ing] to be under the law" is ultimately motivated by a desire to belong to "Abraham's seed" (to become a Jew). If circumcision and the decision to live under the law lead to belonging to Abraham, then are these people not forgetting that Abraham and the law are not the same, but that at Abraham there still is a fork in the road? The two options are the option of the free woman and that of the slave woman (4:22)!

Paul then goes on to work this out in a humorous but also somewhat cynical manner. He projects the fork in the road where one must choose between non-Christian Jew and free Christian back onto Sarah and Hagar (and their respective offspring, Isaac and Ishmael, 4:28). The Gentiles are immediately (through the Spirit) placed in the freedom of the true children of God. The gospel sets them free from the slavery of pagan works (idols and superstition). Why then would they let themselves be placed under a different yoke—but a yoke nonetheless? Why go from being Gentile to Jew, from a pagan astrological calendar to the calendar of the Jews, and so on? If the Gentile Christians want to belong to Abraham, they must remain with Sarah, the free woman, and not join Hagar, the unfree slave woman!

In 5:3 Paul says that someone who as a Gentile Christian has himself circumcised thereby obligates himself to keep the whole law. He opposes a circumcision that is done for the sake of peace. It is either Christ or honoring the whole law.

Whoever wants to be justified by the law is alienated from Christ (5:4). Is this the kind of justification the Galatians wanted? Did they really think in terms of justification at all? It is unlikely. It is more likely that they wanted to become Jews for a very different reason: as a safety net under their Christian faith or as a solution to the communication problem with many Jewish Christians. Nevertheless, they would let themselves be circumcised for God's sake, as if it were necessary or better for God. And then Paul says: you look for your identity in circumcision and the law. Apparently Christ has insufficient power without these identity markers in you.

In 5:13–15 Paul suddenly and adroitly uses the law against those who want to force the law on the Gentiles as being valid also for them. Those Jewish Christian defenders of the law split the Christian community and cause strife and criticism, as was the case in Antioch. Is that good? Those who are so concerned with the taboos of the law should begin with the heart of the law: love for one's neighbor. Again there is a measure of irony: it is some kind of defense of the law when someone for the sake of that law in fact repels and menaces his brothers in Christ!

In 5:23 we find a brief comment that shows that Paul is not arguing against the law but rather against the way in which the law is handled by some Jewish Christians, to the detriment of the fellowship that Jewish Christians now have with Gentile Christians. He says almost parenthetically, "Against such things there is no law." He is referring to people who show the fruit of the Spirit in their lives. The law does not stand as an enemy over against these (Gentile) Christians. On the contrary, they fulfill the intent of the law through the power of the Spirit. How can Jewish Christians separate themselves from these spiritual Christians as if the law placed them under a taboo because they have not been circumcised? This is not in accordance with the law. The purpose of the law was—within a strict legal framework—nothing else than the sanctification of life before God!

In 6:13 the law is mentioned one more time: "Not even those who are circumcised obey the law, yet they want you to be circumcised that they may boast about your flesh." Here surfaces the fact that the core of the conflict is not a rigid nomism or perfectionism but rather a nationalistic championing of the Jewish people as the one community of God. The law (circumcision) is then a hallmark of the true children of God. In chapter 2 Paul has already said that Peter himself had begun to transcend some of the requirements of the law in his own life—before he began to act as an observant Jew again. Apparently the Jewish Christians (the party of James) were not primarily concerned with sanctity or obedience to the law, but rather with solidarity with the people of Abraham. They wanted to gain the respect of their fellow-Jews by bringing Gentiles into the Jewish fold. Thus they would be able to avoid the persecution that threatened them as Nazarenes in a period of growing nationalism.

In summary we can say that the Galatians are pressured by Jewish Christians who (in part out of fear of their non-Christian fellow-Jews) want to remain fully Jewish and who want to convince the Gentile Christians, directly or indirectly, to join them by means of circumcision. Only thus can one be not only a Christian who has received the Spirit but also a child of Abraham and thus an heir. This is the context in which Paul speaks several times about the law. For him the law is in principle the entire Torah (the whole Old Testament), but especially the law of Moses as the focal point of the Old Testament. Paul makes clear that the Gentiles are in danger of being put under the law of Moses, the "narrowing of the road," as if the widening of the road to God in Christ had never occurred. Insofar as Paul's statements about the law seem to be negative, it is because the discussion takes place after, and in the light of, Pentecost. Paul is not combating formal legalism but rather an incorrect understanding of the grace that has now been revealed. In other words, the dispute is about salvation-historical facts and their implications.[29] In its own time and in its proper function the law was a good gift from God for the well-being of Israel. After Pentecost, however, life under the law has become a lonely venture for those who continue to reject Christ, the protector against the curse of the law. And for the Gentile Christians, the law is no longer a fenced-in enclosure into which they must be brought.

For the Jewish Christians under the law this means that they must not use their life under the law to create a barrier that prevents them from eating with their uncircumcised fellow-Christians from the Gentile nations. On certain points the works of the law become for Jewish Christians subordinate to the work of love for the fellow-Christians from the nations. Jewish Christians don't have to break with a life lived in conformity with the law, but they must realize that living according to the law is meaningful only thanks to Messiah Jesus. At the same time they will then realize how some of the works of the law (specifically dietary laws and laws concerning ceremonial cleanness) now must be subordinate to the reality that the Messiah accepts not only Jews under the law but also Gentiles without the law as belonging to his people by giving them his Spirit solely on the basis of faith.

In the letter to the Galatians Paul sometimes gives the impression that he condemns the law or dismisses it as no longer of importance for the Jews. He could easily have avoided this misunderstanding were it not for the challenge posed by Peter's attitude in Antioch and the threat of the Judaization of the Galatian Christians. This forced him to react vehemently and to emphasize again in no uncertain terms in a hastily written (and seemingly one-sided) letter that the national law of God's people Israel should be understood in light of the international Spirit of the Messiah.

17.5.3 The Law in Romans

The letter to the Romans was written in a much quieter climate than the letter to the Galatians. There was no aggressive Judaism of any kind in Rome. The readers of the letter came from the Gentiles, and only at the end of the letter are they warned against people who would come into the Christian community with a different message (Rom. 16:17–19). Although the reality of this intrusion is on the horizon, it is not yet an actuality in this Christian community.

The passages about the "strong" and the "weak" in Romans 14–15 have to do with the accepting of differences within a Gentile-Christian community. When Paul also mentions the question as to whether to eat certain foods or observe certain days, he seems to point to the problems surrounding the Jewish dietary laws and Sabbath days (as was true in Galatia). But here it is not the case. At issue here are differences concerning dietary habits and the routines of daily life among Christians from the Gentiles. These are specifically differences between vegetarians and nonvegetarians, between proponents and opponents of teetotalism (Rom. 14:2–3, 21), and between those who do and those who do not pay attention to the distinction (so important in Rome) between "favorable and unfavorable days" (*dies fasti et nefasti*, Rom. 14:5).

Paul's statements about the law in this letter are more reflective than those in Galatians.[30] They are less aggressive. It is, for example, striking that he speaks in Romans 2:6–11 about "the works" without limiting himself to the Jews; he addresses Jews and Gentiles. The issue here is doing what is good in general. Such works are not self-seeking (2:8). They are done in obedience to the truth. The word "truth" refers—after 1:18!—to the reality of God's existence and of his claim on us (2:8). The result of this respect for the reality of God is that we do not engage in injustice toward our neighbor (see 1:29–31), but that we love our neighbor instead (2:8). Jew as well as Greek can do evil (2:9) or good (2:10). The works in view here consist in fact in respect for God and love for neighbor. That is why the absence of such works is not limited to those who are under the law of Moses. On these points both Jew and Gentile can stand guilty before God the Creator: the one as Jew, with the Torah, the other without the Torah (2:12).

We could ask why they who sinned without the law nevertheless perish. Don't they stand outside the law? Yes—but not outside God. For this sole Creator can be known from the works of his creation, and when we deny him and distort him to fit anthropomorphic images we must confess this as guilt over which God's anger is active in the human world (1:18–32). This God calls all people to account, without regard of persons (2:11).

But neither are the Jews given preferential treatment in God's judgment. We could ask why people who sin under the law can be condemned in spite of the protection of the law. Are they not protected and elected? Yes—but not in order to sin against God! In 2:13 Paul says that it is not the "hearers of the law" as such who are righteous. "Hearing" points to being a Jew and sitting in the synagogue. But belonging to the Torah is not decisive. For what matters is not *having* the Torah but being obedient to the Creator, who for Israel is the God of the Torah.

For Gentiles the reverse is true. They are not under the law and do not belong to the Torah, but that does not mean that they get off scot-free before God. Not having the Torah does not put a person out of range of God's judgment. Even those who are outsiders with respect to the law are expected to be obedient to the God of the Torah because this God is the Creator of all. Such obedience can be found among some Greeks, persons of noble character, and God-fearers (2:14–16). The "work of the law" is written on their hearts. Granted, they do not join the Jewish people (through circumcision and keeping the dietary laws), but they nevertheless take very seriously the requirements of a God-fearing life and of mercy and love for the neighbor. Well-known examples are the centurion in Capernaum and Cornelius and his friends in Caesarea.

Paul speaks very positively about having the law as such in 2:17–20, especially in verse 20, where he calls the law "the embodiment of knowledge and truth." But he says this in the context, not of "identity markers" (circumcision or Sabbath) that set the nation of Israel apart from all other groups, but of general moral issues such as faithfulness in marriage, fairness in the administration of justice, and worship of the one, true God.

In 2:25–29 it appears that everyone must obey the commandments of the law. Whether or not we have the law, what it contains is important for the hidden heart! When God and his works have a place there, there is honor from God's side. He does not reject the individual. We therefore do not do wrong at all when we want to do something that is in accordance with the law.

In 3:2 Paul also writes positively about the law as the gift of "the very words of God."

It looks as if Paul turns negative in 3:20b (the law makes us conscious of sin). However, this statement does not refer to an essential characteristic of the law, but rather to the effect of the law in our reality. The light of the law reveals the darkness. The love and mercy demanded by the law put into sharper relief the hate and cruelty of the world. The statement "no one will be declared righteous in his sight by observing the law" (3:20a) is not limited to those who possess the Torah (the Jews), but also includes those who do not have the

Torah but could have "works of the law" (see 2:15). This is precisely why the wording is broad: "works of the law" rather than "law."

The argument of 3:1–20 then is as follows. The Gentiles (Gentile Christians) can easily think that the Jews have an advantage because they possess the law (3:1–4). In 3:1 Paul addresses non-Jews with the question what the advantage is of being a Jew or what the value of circumcision is. In the eyes of the Gentiles these things give the Jews a very great advantage indeed. While enemies disdained the Jewish religion because of its exotic dietary laws and the curious Sabbath taboo, sympathetic Gentiles in those days were deeply impressed by Jewish monotheism and its humane ethic. The Christians in Rome probably looked up to the synagogue and the large Jewish community in Rome. Didn't the new Christian community seem a bit meager by comparison?

Paul acknowledges that many great things can be said about the privileges of the Jews, even if only because the "very words of God" were entrusted to them. True, many of them became unfaithful to God by rejecting Christ Jesus, but this does not negate God's faithfulness (for a broader discussion of this point, see Romans 9–11). More than that: here it appears that "every man [is] a liar"—even the privileged Jews. Thus it is "our unrighteousness," which includes the Jews as well as the Greeks, that demonstrates God's righteousness (3:5). Even the Jews were in dire need of the redemption that came through faith in Jesus; it is therefore good that God gave his Son (see 1:16–17).

But what about the wrath of God about which Paul has been speaking from 1:18 on: is it a just wrath (3:5)? How can God both be wrathful and send the gospel? After all, the intent is not for us to sin in order to achieve something good (3:5–8). Then follows in 3:9 the repeated question, What about the privileges of the Jews? If they have the very words of God, do they have an advantage? No, not for themselves, because not only the Greeks but also the Jews fall short in righteousness. That is what the law itself told them (3:10–19b). Thus the whole world—not only the Greeks—become culpable before God. No one, not even the Jew, can manage to save himself with works as they are extolled in the law (morality, love, faith in God). The law, which formulates quite clearly what moral and ethical actions are, causes this world to discover its shortcomings—first the Jew and also the Greek.

However, the righteousness of God (1:16–17) has now come as the fulfillment of the law and the prophets (!) "apart from the law" (*chōris nomou*), that is, not as a Jewish affair (3:21). Jesus is the Savior for all people, for sinners and tax collectors in Palestine and for Greeks and "barbarians" after Pentecost (see 3:22–26)! Jesus Christ came to the Gentiles, not with the national law of the Jews and the requirement of circumcision, but with the gift of the Spirit.

Human (specifically Jewish) boasting is now excluded. "By what kind of law?" (3:27 NASB). This abrupt question shows that Paul here is not thinking exclusively of the Torah. Rather, he is thinking of an option: this law or that law. He then states what the options are: is boasting precluded because of the law of works? This is a striking expression. Paul here points to a "rule" (*nomos*) that focuses on works. He had stated that rule himself in 2:6–11: "God 'will give to each person according to what he has done.' . . . There will be trouble and distress for every human being who does evil: first for the Jew, then for the Gentile; but glory, honor and peace for everyone who does good: first for the Jew, then for the Gentile. For God does not show favoritism."

This rule excludes any human boasting. No one is sufficiently virtuous to stand up before God, as will become apparent in the judgment, when God brings to light the hidden things of each person. When human boasting is thus excluded, by applying the rule of works, it is a moment of total honesty, but it is also fatal. At that very moment the individual would perish under God's wrath. The rule of works crushes in the end the individual who failed!

But God has chosen a very different way to teach us not to boast, a way that saves us! We are shamed because God comes to us with the means of atonement—with Christ. The way in which we as humans become modest is the way of mercy and of the power of God for salvation. In the gospel the manner in which both Jews and Gentiles are condemned is not depressing but uplifting! It is the way of faith: only believe and you will be saved! This applies to both Jews and Greeks. That is why Paul in 3:29 once again poses the question whether God is only a God of the Jews or also of the Gentiles. His readers have come to the "obedience of faith" in God, and they will concur that God is the God of all nations. This one God now justifies Jews and Greeks through the power of faith: since Pentecost the reality of the gospel is manifest in the workings of the Spirit! This gospel does not ask that we first exchange the works of idols for the works of the law before the Spirit of Christ can be poured out. And that is significant for the Christians from the Gentiles.

In 3:31 the question comes up whether the Torah has been nullified by faith. The answer is negative: to the contrary! The proof for this we find in chapter 4: faith is as old as Abraham—before he was circumcised (Rom. 4:1–12)!—and does not begin with the law, which came later (Rom. 4:13–16). In this connection Paul says that the law "brings wrath," because "where there is no law there is no transgression" (4:15). The law points out the transgression, makes it visible. That is why it is a law. Because under the law transgressions become visible (see 3:9–19), the law as such (apart from promise and faith) would be only an instrument to justify God's wrath (since we are incapable of keeping the law). But now that the law is added to the promise, it is very useful indeed. It proves effectively how valuable it is that already Abraham received a promise and was justified by faith. Faith is not an emergency exit from the law, but the law confirms the safety of faith.

In 5:12–21 Paul emphasizes again (as he did in chapter 4) that sin is universal and that justification is also universal. The perspective cannot be limited to the line that runs from Moses to Christ; it is broader and connects Adam with Christ. In the interim Moses makes clear how dark the world is: people appear not to do the works of God (as the law shows). With this, Moses supports the significance of the road of salvation that runs from Adam to Christ.

In 6:14 Paul says that sin shall not be our master, because we are not under law but under grace. This statement is a promise: sin will lose its control over us. It makes sense to rebel against this sin; the call to rebellion was voiced in 6:12: "do not let sin reign in your mortal body"! Sin will not have the victory over us. Under the law (which shows crystal clear what sin is) we are stuck with that sin, but under grace sin, as guilt, is expelled and powerless.

Chapter 7 as a whole makes clear that the law of God brings knowledge of sin. The law, therefore, is not a showpiece that a Jew could put on display on the mantelshelf; especially for the Jew, the law (as a good and spiritual law) is an indictment. This is thus certainly not about the dietary laws or other, ceremonial laws, but most definitely about the moral law of God.

In 8:2 Paul speaks of "the law of sin and death." In the light of chapter 7 this means that the law (because of my weakness, cf. 8:3) leads to my demise. This way of looking at the law (from Christ's perspective) is very different from the way it was viewed by the Pharisees (who made it into Israel's glory).

Modern text editions and versions read in 9:31, "Israel, who pursued a law of righteousness, has not attained it" (NIV, or "that law," NASB, NRSV). The Majority Text is more explicit: "Israel . . . hath not attained to the law of righteousness" (KJV). Gentiles who made no particular effort to pursue *dikaiosynē* (righteousness) are justified by faith, but Israel has lost the race with the law of righteousness. The whole history of the nation reflects the fiasco, and now, in Paul's time, the hardening sets in because they continue to hang on to the accomplishments of the law in the face of Messiah Jesus.

In 10:4 Christ is called the "end" or "purpose" (*telos*) of the Torah. This is substantiated in 10:5–13: "For (*gar*) Moses writes . . ." (KJV, NASB; NIV omits "for"). Moses writes, Paul says, that those who do righteousness according to the law will live. Then the "righteousness that is by faith" is introduced as the speaker in verse 6. It seems as if the writing Moses is placed in juxtaposition with the speaking righteousness that is by faith. But this cannot be the intent. The statement made by "the righteousness that is by faith" is supported in 10:6–8 by quotations from Moses himself! Paul therefore most likely means that Moses writes two things: (1) the righteousness that is by the law requires doing in order to live; (2) we don't have to reach the word of God (the law) by works to bring it either down from heaven or up from hell—it is simply brought to us. In other words, already in Moses we see that the ultimate goal of the law is not that we get righteousness ourselves, but that it is brought to us through faith. Thus the goal of the Torah is reached when Christ comes, whom we may confess with mouth and heart unto salvation (10:9–13).

Finally the law is referred to as the law of love (13:8, 10). Love does not harm its neighbor (see 1:18–32, where Paul describes how much evil flows from the absence of love for God, and 2:1–16, where the positive capabilities of mankind are also discussed). Love is the work of the law that can also be written in the hearts of Gentiles. This law remains valid, but in Christ. That is, it remains valid but not as a law of works, as unfortunately it does for the Jews who reject Jesus and do not love him. The law does remain valid as the norm for the behavior of the believers who have been justified in Christ.

In summary, it appears that Paul clarifies for the Gentile Christians in Rome what their own position is. They are a small, new group in the shadow of an ancient, venerable synagogue (which remains aloof from Messiah Jesus). But the Christian community owes its identity to God the Creator. Liberated from idolatry, the Romans now arrive at the obedience of the faith in Israel's God. Thus they are grafted into the Israel of the Messiah.

17.6 Conclusions

1. In the letter to the Romans, the law (of Moses) does not relate primarily to circumcision and other laws that give shape to the external life of the nation of the Jews, but rather to the written demand of being God-fearing and loving one's neighbor. This is why Paul, through God's grace, brings about "obedience of faith" among the Gentiles. And this is why he continues to honor love as the fulfillment of the law!

2. In the concrete reality of punished and doomed humanity, the written law is an extra floodlight that shows how dark the human world is and how deservedly it lies under the wrath of God.

3. In the concrete situation of Rome there is a large synagogue where Messiah Jesus is not acknowledged, and elsewhere also there is a largely unbelieving Israel (see Rom. 9–11). What should the attitude toward the synagogue be? Does the synagogue without Jesus yet have privileges? From this perspective the Torah easily becomes something that

can be used to give others the sense that they stand outside of God. Paul challenges this perspective. It is, in fact, the non-Christian Jews who fall short of keeping the law, since the law is a supplement to faith in God that is required of all, and the end (*telos*) of this law is Christ.

4. Paul's perspective on the law is not negative, and it does not have to come into conflict with Judaism, as Sanders thinks. To the contrary, the Torah is also for Paul the embodiment of morality and religious faith.

5. According to Dunn, Paul does not have a problem with the law but rather with the "identity markers"—the commandments the Jews cut out of the law and used as badges to mark themselves as the chosen people. But it cannot be shown that the Jews themselves made such a distinction between the law and the identity markers. Besides, we cannot reduce the term *nomos* in Paul (and certainly not in the letter to Rome) to "a portion of the law," that is, identity markers. For Paul (as for all Jews) "the law" is ultimately the revelation of the living God in this world. Not until the unbelieving Jews close themselves off from Christ Jesus does their identity become significantly more important—which is precisely what Paul fights against in this specific period after Pentecost. He thus does not fight against a warped Judaism but rather for an acceptance of Messiah Jesus through a true faith. If a Jew thinks that he can ignore Messiah Jesus while under the law, he isolates that law from its true role in salvation history and gives it an inflated value.

6. In the letter to the Romans (unlike the letter to the Galatians) the requirement to become a Jew and to be circumcised is not in view. For this reason the law as discussed in Romans is much more a general Decalogue: valid also for Gentiles (in Christ), but not something to boast in as Jews.

7. The Holy Scriptures of God remain normative for the Gentile Christians, but no longer as a national constitution for the set-apart nation of Israel. This means that it is precisely the more external laws, those that are tied to a place or institution, that are rendered inoperative, laws such as those on circumcision, sacrifices and ceremonies in the temple, and political and civil laws—in short, all works of the law that can be performed only after circumcision and as a member of the Jewish nation. To the extent that the Torah is a model for a religious

nation, it is overtaken by the Spirit who created a new model for that nation. To the extent that in the Torah the embodiment of the knowledge of the Creator and the wisdom of God can be found, the Scriptures remain relevant for the Gentile Christians.

8. The decisive turning point for Paul lies in the crucifixion and resurrection of Jesus; there the road widens toward the nations (without circumcision, without Jewish national law). We could also say that there we reach the end of the narrowing of the road, which accommodated only one nation under one Mosaic law. The era of the national law is past, the era of the Scriptures of the Most High continues. Rabbi Saul did not become an opponent of the law but a follower of Jesus Christ, the Crucified One. He remained a Jew and became a Christian.

18

IN PRAYER FOR ISRAEL

Paul is not a solo performer: he stands with his gospel in the circle of all the apostles and on the foundation of Jesus Christ (see chap. 15). At the same time he has a very special task as envoy to the Gentiles (see chap. 16). His task with regard to Gentile Christian communities brought with it that he had to write several letters from their vantage point about the significance of the Jewish law and of the people of Israel. The accent in these writings fell on the freedom from this law for uncircumcised Christians (see chap. 17).

But what was Paul's attitude toward his own people? As a Pharisee he belonged to the nucleus of Israel, but the persecutor of Christians became a pioneer for Christendom (Gal. 1:23). Does this mean that he became anti-Jewish? Or did he remain true to the faith in Israel's God and not want to alienate the Jews from either their roots or their traditions?

In this concluding chapter we will view Paul first through the eyes of the non-Christian Jews (18.1). Then we turn around and look through Paul's eyes at the non-Christian Jews (18.2 and 18.3). And finally we draw a conclusion concerning the place of Christendom in the history of Israel (18.4).

18.1 Judaism and Paul

What does the apostle Paul look like in the eyes of non-Christian Jews, both in his own time and in the centuries that followed? Generally the opinions of him are quite negative, although there is much diversity in how the essence of his work and his personal intentions are viewed.

18.1.1 Anti-Semite?

The most serious charge against Paul is that he presumably became an anti-Semite. The term "anti-Semitism," which in its broader form can encompass anyone of Semitic descent, is often used in a narrower sense to mean specifically hatred of Jews, and this is what Paul is accused of. The champion of the Jewish tradition is supposed to have changed into a man with an aversion toward Judaism, who in fact came to hate it. Paul is then thought to have moved to its polar opposite: the world of Hellenistic culture and thought.[1]

This negative image certainly does not square with the facts (unless acknowledging Jesus as Messiah is considered ipso facto un-Jewish!). We do find in Paul many signs of his undiminished love for his own people.

When mentioning his coworkers, Paul often notes with gratitude that they are fellow Jews, and he mourns the fact that at one point only a few fellow Jews remain in his immediate circle (Rom. 16:7, 11, 21; Col. 4:11).

During his arrest and imprisonment Paul maintains solidarity with his own people, even when standing before governors and kings (Acts 22:3, 18–20; 23:5–6; 24:14–17; 26:6–7, 22–23).

In his letters the apostle continues to speak of the privileges of the Jewish people, and he lets Gentile Christians know that he has a warm heart for his unbelieving fellow Jews (Rom. 2:20; 3:1–2; 9:1–5).

Nowhere does Paul say or write that the law has been abrogated for the Jewish people or that the law has been a bad thing.

It is in this light that we must read a passage that has quite often been pointed to as being negative and anti-Jewish. In his first letter to the Thessalonians Paul notes that they are being persecuted by their own fellow townsmen. He then draws a comparison between what they are experiencing on the one hand and the suffering the Jewish Christians experienced at the hands of their fellow Jews on the other. The Jews, "killed the Lord Jesus and the prophets and also drove us out. They displease God and are hostile to all men in their effort to keep us from speaking to the Gentiles so that they may be saved. In this way they always heap up their sins to the limit. The wrath of God has come upon them at last" (1 Thess. 2:15–16).

This is a striking passage. Paul himself had been the point man in this kind of persecution, yet here he writes about it as if he had nothing to do with it whatsoever. Yet it is difficult to blame this on a desire on Paul's part to suppress his own past; in other letters he openly and with shame speaks about his activities as a persecutor of Christians. But in 1 Thessalonians it is not his own past but rather the shared present that he is writing about. Today the Thessalonians are being persecuted. And today they are also touched by the persecution non-Christian Jews have initiated against the apostles to the Gentiles. Because of the Jews, Paul and Silas had to flee Thessalonica and later also Berea—it was made impossible for them to stay in Macedonia (Acts 17:5–10, 13–14). In this second chapter the apostle does not write a retrospective on his own life, but he alludes to this present situation. People such as Silas are also involved, but Silas never persecuted the Christians. In a discussion of the actual persecution of the Jewish apostles to the Gentiles in general, Paul's personal history has no place.

The Jews who hindered Paul and others from addressing the Gentiles "are hostile to all men." They are not motivated by love for people; if they were, they would let Paul and Silas preach the gospel of salvation among all people. But now that they, to the contrary, want to silence Paul and Silas, they have become enemies of the human race (later this accusation is often wrongly leveled against Christians).

By doing this they "always heap up their sins to the limit." Paul observes that the killing of Jesus and of the prophets now is completed by keeping the preachers of Jesus among the Gentiles from carrying out their task. The persecution of Paul, Silas, and others is the most extreme consequence of this Jewish aversion to Jesus. As the apostle fills up in his life what is still missing in the persecutions of Jesus, so also do his persecutors finish up what is still lacking in their sins against Jesus and the prophets.

Because they have done this, the wrath of God "has come upon them to the utmost" (NASB). This last statement seems to refer to a definitive rejection of the Jews by God. If this were true, it would be in conflict with Paul's prayer and hope for unbelieving Israel in Romans 9–11. Various interpreters call the statement in 1 Thessalonians 2:16b anti-Jewish and think that it cannot be harmonized with what the apostle writes elsewhere.[2]

Some see here a clear example of the inconsistencies in Paul's letters that result from his rather rhetorical form of argument.[3] Others deny the authenticity of 1 Thessalonians 2:15–16 and view it as a later interpolation.[4] Still others think that this passage should not be taken too literally, since Paul uses emotional language here.[5] Attempts are also made to soften the statement somewhat.[6]

However, many interpreters correctly point out that in 1 Thessalonians 2 Paul does not speak of the final judgment of God. That is "the coming wrath" (1 Thess. 1:10). Here Paul writes about the anger or wrath of God as it finds expression in history today. We also find this distinction in Romans 3:5–6, where Paul asks whether "God is unjust in bringing his wrath on us." The answer there is, "Certainly not! If that were so, how could God judge the world?" Apparently there is a difference between the wrath as it finds expression already in this age and the future, definitive judgment. The expressions of wrath in this age are, as is apparent in the prophets, always still aimed at the conversion of the people and at preventing the future wrath. In this way there is no conflict between on the one hand Paul's words about the anger or wrath of God, which when Paul writes is focused in full force on the unbelieving Jews, and on the other hand Paul's intercession and hope for these unbelieving fellow-Jews in Romans 9–11. Did Paul not write in Romans 1:18 that "the wrath of God is being revealed from heaven against all the godlessness and wickedness of men who suppress the truth by their wickedness," and does not this reality apply to the Jew as well as the Greek?[7]

In Romans 1 it appears that God's wrath in the present age can find expression in God's giving people over to their own evil will and letting them get lost in their own idolatry and debauchery (Rom. 1:24–32). This is what 1 Thessalonians 2 is about. The Jews who rejected Jesus and the prophets now even reach the point where they begrudge all people in the world the good news. God allows them to lose their way in this antihuman attitude, since the law called them to the opposite: love for their neighbor. This totally wrong attitude is as such a manifestation of God's utmost wrath; he no longer restrains his renegade people and allows many Jews to rage against Paul, Silas, and others.

Others think here of temporal judgments that struck the Jews, such as the expulsion of the Jews from Rome or the destruction of the temple.[8] But in 1 Thessalonians 2:16b the final sentence about God's wrath does not refer to all Jews (to the extent that as a whole nation they suffer temporal disasters), but rather only to the Jews who are hostile toward the gospel. The passage about God's wrath is preceded by comments about the serious straying within the Jewish people. It is then more plausible to see the manifestation of wrath in these internal developments that are to the detriment of the Jewish people. When Jews don't hesitate to kill prophets, to crucify Jesus, and to hinder apostles from speaking to the Gentiles, it is a manifestation of God's full and extreme wrath on their lack of faith in the prophets and the Messiah. God now lets them wander, lost in their unbelief. Paul can very well combine this reality with hope and expectation. The wrath that comes on the unbelieving Jews "to the utmost" (NASB) should be equated with the "hardening in part" that has come over Israel (Rom. 11:25). This "hardening in part" does not keep the apostle from writing at the same time that "all Israel will be saved" (Rom. 11:26), because "as far as the gospel is concerned, they [the Jews] are enemies on your account" (Rom. 11:28a; cf. 1 Thess. 2:15–16a); but "as far as election is concerned, they are loved on account of the patriarchs" (Rom. 11:28b).

Paul's statement about the wrath that rests on the non-Christian and hostile Jews is in contrast to the sympathetic attitude of the Christian Jews toward the Gentile Christians. Immediately after the statement about the wrath coming "to the utmost" follows a passage about the attitude of other Jews during this time, such as Paul and Silas: "But, brothers, when we were torn away from you for a short time (in person, not in thought), out of our intense longing we made every effort to see you" (1 Thess. 2:17). Over against the fury with which the non-Christian Jews seek at this point to keep the gospel of Jesus from the Gentiles stands the affection of the apostles, who by contrast are longing to make them share in the love of Christ. The passage about the wrath on the Jews (1 Thess. 2:14–16) is also preceded by declarations of Paul's love for the Thessalonians: "But we were gentle among you, like a mother caring for her little children. We loved you so much that we were delighted to share with you not only the gospel of God but our lives as well, because you had become so dear to us" (1 Thess. 2:7–8). The raging Saul became a loving Paul! God's wrath "to the utmost" on Saul turned into grace!

In summary we can say the following. In 1 Thessalonians 2 Paul describes the reality of Jews who (like Paul himself in time past) angrily agitate against Jesus and his apostles. He sees in this attitude of the unbelieving Jews the coming of God's wrath "to the utmost": God gives these Jews over to the hardening of their hearts. This is wrath to the utmost, without holding back. But this statement about the Jews who hostilely persecute the gospel is not a statement about the nation of Israel as a whole. The apostle does not say in this passage that the utmost wrath of God has already written off the nation of Israel. He does not even write that it is impossible that some may yet repent and be saved from this utmost wrath before the irrevocable future wrath comes on the Last Day.

There is therefore no reason to accuse Paul of anti-Semitism or to view him as an apostle who has taken leave of his people now that many of his fellow-Jews persecute him and rage against him and against other Jews because of their preaching of Messiah Jesus among the nations. But the seriousness of his words cannot be evaded. To the extent that, and as long as, the Jews continue to harden their hearts against the gospel and continue to persecute it, God's wrath has come on them "to the utmost."

18.1.2 Apostate Jew?

The accusation that Paul wanted to tear down Judaism from within is an ancient one that already circulated in Jerusalem during the apostle's lifetime (Acts 21:21) and motivated people to want to kill him if at all possible, as they had killed Stephen for the same reason (Acts 21:28; 23:29–30; 24:5–6; cf. 7:54).

Paul refuted this accusation in all kinds of ways. In Jerusalem he was even prepared to give a demonstration of his respect for the law. At the request of James and the elders Paul took upon himself the expenses of purification rites connected with a vow, in order to suppress the false rumors (Acts 21:22–26). In his speeches in his own defense he also points out that he is faithful to his own people (Acts 25:8), that he still believes fully in the resurrection of the dead (Acts 23:6; 24:14–15; 26:6–8), and that he came to Jerusalem to bring gifts to the poor (Acts 24:17–18).

The letters present the same image. The apostle says, "To the Jews I became like a Jew, to win the Jews [i.e., for Christ]. To those under the law I became like one under the law (though I myself am not under the law), so as to win those under the law" (1 Cor. 9:20). In addition he calls upon his readers to "not cause anyone to stumble, whether Jews, Greeks or the church of God" (1 Cor. 10:32).

The apostle to the Gentiles is not on an anti-Jewish mission. He even cooperates fully with the apostles "of the circumcision," even though his own charge takes him to the nations (Gal. 2:8–9).

18.1.3 Defected Pharisee?

In *Paul the Convert*, Alan Segal has argued that within Judaism Saul merely went from the Pharisaic type of spirituality to a more apocalyptic type.[9] All we see in Paul is thus a transition from one branch of Judaism to another. It is then easier to understand that as a Jewish Christian, Paul can have a somewhat broader view of circumcision than the strict position of the Pharisees. For apocalyptic Judaism other values were of greater importance. This means that Paul never truly became an apostle to the Gentiles. What he had in mind was a synagogue in which there was also room for uncircumcised God-fearers who believed in Messiah Jesus.[10]

It is difficult to imagine that the radical turn in Saul's life was limited to such an intra-Jewish shift. We can agree with Segal that Paul's ideal consisted in the formation of one people composed of Christian Jews into whom are grafted uncircumcised Christians from the nations.

But it is difficult to explain his openness toward uncircumcised Christians on the basis of what is supposed to be merely a shift within Judaism on Paul's part. The requirement of circumcision was universal for all Jews. Nowhere do we read that some Jews considered it of minor importance if circumcision was omitted. This is (according to some Jews) at best possible by way of exception and then only if there are urgent and approved reasons for such an exception.[11] The idea that Christian Gentiles could en masse get out of the requirement of circumcision can hardly be understood as an extension of the perhaps broader standpoint of apocalyptic circles within Judaism.

Also, after becoming a Christian, Paul continues to appeal to his past as a Pharisee. He is not ashamed of it and continues to speak positively about it (Phil. 3:5). When he stands before the Sanhedrin he again closes ranks with his own party on the subject of the resurrection: "My brothers, I am a Pharisee, the son of a Pharisee. I stand on trial because of my hope in the resurrection of the dead" (Acts 23:6). Paul was a Pharisee and never switched to another party or movement within Judaism.

Though Paul did in fact strive for a relaxation of the Jewish laws when it came to contact with uncircumcised Christians, this fit in with his Pharisaism, which held that the lesser commandments of the law always make way for the more important ones. But the application of this rule presupposes a choosing for Jesus as the Son of God, who is greater than Moses and Solomon. If Paul switched allegiance, it was not a switch from the Pharisees to another movement, but rather from Hillel to Jesus Christ, the fulfillment of all that the Pharisaic Jews also expected (Acts 24:14–16; 26:22–23).

18.2 Paul and Israel

Many non-Christian Jews mistakenly view Saul of Tarsus as an apostate, an opponent. It is worth letting him speak for himself about his Christian vision on his own people and on the future of Israel. This will show that this apostle to the Gentiles neither forgot nor left his own people. To the contrary!

18.2.1 An Unchanged and Enriched Vision

Our critical discussion of the negative images of Paul has shown that he continued to see Israel as the chosen people of God, with many privileges, and continued to maintain a positive attitude toward his fellow Jews (see above, 18.1.1–3). To this we must add that he speaks even more highly of the privileges of the Jewish people than his non-Christian fellow-Jews do. Besides the ancient privileges of revelation, wisdom, and law Paul sees a new privilege of more recent origin: Israel now has also received the Messiah and the gift of the Spirit of God on all who believe. For Paul the one is an extension of the other. Thus he writes to the Gentile Christians in Rome about "my brothers, those of my own race, the people of Israel": "Theirs is the adoption as sons; theirs the divine glory, the covenants, the receiving of the law, the temple worship and the promises. Theirs are the patriarchs, and from them is traced the human ancestry of Christ, who is God over all, forever praised! Amen" (Rom. 9:3–5).

The apostle Paul believes that only now, in this age, can Israel be a source of spiritual riches and abundance for all nations. Until now God-fearers could take part in the expectation the Jews were given of their God. But now, beginning from Jerusalem, the fulfillment of that expectation may be shared with all nations. Thus Paul says to the Jewish king Agrippa: "I am saying nothing beyond what the prophets and Moses said would happen—that the Christ would suffer and, as the first to rise from the dead, would proclaim light to his own people and to the Gentiles" (Acts 26:22–23).

Because the spiritual blessing of God in this age reaches the nations from Jerusalem, the Gentile Christians are obliged to acknowledge the central place of Israel. Therefore Paul zealously organizes a collection among the Gentile Christians on behalf of the poor in Jerusalem (Gal. 2:10; 1 Cor. 16:1–4; 2 Cor. 8–9). This collection is more than humanitarian help: it is an acknowledgment of the place God has granted the people of Abraham from whom Jesus was born. Thus Paul writes to the Gentile Christians in Rome that this collection is a duty: "For if the Gentiles have shared in the Jews' spiritual blessings, they owe it to the Jews to share with them their material blessings" (Rom. 15:27).

In addressing the Jews Paul emphasizes that Jesus Christ is given in the first place to them. Thus he says in the synagogue in Pisidian Antioch, "We tell you the good news: What God promised our fathers he has fulfilled for us, their children, by raising up Jesus. As it is written in the second Psalm: 'You are my Son; today I have become your Father'" (Acts 13:32–33).[12] It is therefore not for nothing that Paul in his letter to the Gentile Christians in Rome states repeatedly that God's revelation is intended "first for the Jew, then for the Gentile" (Rom. 1:16; 2:9–10). For God there is no distinction between Jew and Greek (Rom. 9–11). God is the God of the nations (Rom. 2:29)! And Jews as well as Greeks deserve God's wrath (Rom. 3:9). But all of this cannot negate the historical reality that God gave his promises to the people of Abraham and that the Messiah was sent in the first place to them (cf. Peter's statement in Acts 3:26).

The apostle to the Gentiles has actually an even more positive image of Israel after his conversion to faith in Messiah Jesus than he had before. But those who reject this Messiah will not want to accept this more positive understanding. What separates Paul and his persecutors is not his view on Israel but his view of Jesus of Nazareth!

18.2.2 Expanding the People of God

Does the apostle to the Gentiles found a new religion to stand beside the Jewish religion? Does he create a second people of God and, by doing so, harm the one nation of Israel?

For Paul himself the reverse is true. He acknowledges only one people of God. The Gentiles who come to faith in Christ are viewed as being grafted into Israel. In one of his final letters the apostle describes at some length his confession concerning Israel. It is the letter to the Ephesians, in which he states that the Gentiles have been "brought near" through Jesus Christ (Eph. 2:13). They were "excluded from citizenship in Israel and foreigners to the covenants of the promise, without hope and without God in the world" (Eph. 2:12). But Christ united the two into one: the law, which had been a wall around Israel, no longer divides (Eph. 2:14–15). The reconciliation on the cross and the pouring out of the Holy Spirit create a new situation: they who were near and they who were far off are now united in one faith in the Father of Jesus Christ (Eph. 2:16–18). But this change in situation does not imply a negation or deconstruction of the past. The kingdom of Israel is not replaced by a republic of the new Christians. The converted Gentiles may now through the Spirit (not through circumcision and the law) belong to Israel and to the King from Israel, Jesus of Nazareth. Instead of foreigners and aliens they have become "fellow citizens with God's people and members of God's household" (Eph. 2:19). Because God brought about changes in Israel and allows the Gentiles to participate in these changes, it has become possible for Gentiles to share in the ancient rights of citizens of Israel.[13]

This is manifested also in the "obedience of faith" that now springs up among the Gentile Christians.[14] Christians among the nations are converted to monotheism and to the God of Abraham, Isaac, and Jacob. In those centuries it was recognized more easily than it is today that this was a becoming connected with the religion of Israel. The course of history has established three religions that see themselves as being linked to Abraham: Judaism, Christianity, and Islam. All three are monotheistic, but they stand side by side. Faith in one God does not make one recognizably a Jew or Christian or Muslim. This was not true at the beginning of the Christian Era. Among philosophers there existed an abstract notion of one deity behind the many gods, but only the Jews practiced worship of the one God. The Jewish people were known for the peculiarity that they acknowledged only one God and worshiped him fanatically but without any images. When the Gentiles were impressed by the gospel of Christ and his Spirit, they had to convert to the God of this Jesus Christ. And that was, in those days, the God of the Jews. Active worship of only one God was unknown outside Judaism. Christianity and Islam did not exist. It was therefore for the Gentile Christians who converted to the one God and Creator of all things a matter of course that they thereby belonged to the religion of the Jews, albeit without circumcision.

This is also true of another point. Faith in the resurrection from the dead did not exist in the world of that day, except among the Jews. For the Greeks the idea of a resurrection is foolishness, as is evident in Athens (Acts 17:18, 31–32). Even in the Christian community in Corinth it is still difficult for many to really believe in the resurrection of the dead (1 Cor. 15:12). Already during Paul's lifetime there are Christians, such as Hymenaeus and Philetus, who view the resurrection as a spiritual reality and preach that the resurrection has already taken place (2 Tim. 2:18). Belief in the resurrection is a hallmark of the Jewish religion. Paul appeals to this belief when he stands before the Sanhedrin and again, when he addresses Governor Felix and later Governor Festus and King Agrippa (Acts 23:6; 24:15; 26:8, 23). Festus considers what Paul says gibberish (Acts 26:24–25). His reaction symbolizes the attitude of every Greek toward the idea of the resurrection from the dead. It is a peculiar idea that is found only among orthodox Jews (in Paul's day even the Sadducees had already abandoned the idea). Even as today the notion of reincarnation is strongly associated with India, so in the same way the idea of a physical resurrection was considered Jewish. A Gentile who came to faith in Christ had to accept that a Jew had risen from the dead and that the Jewish idea of a resurrection is therefore true. Gentiles in the first century A.D. who worshiped a resurrected Jewish Christ, created in their environment the impression that they had joined the Jews.

Paul, the apostle to the Gentiles, sees in his day an expansion of Israel through the Spirit of Messiah Jesus. Paul does not turn away from God's people when he no longer dares to ask believing Gentiles to be circumcised because the Spirit has been poured out on all through faith.

The nation of Israel does not fade away in the age in which the gospel is preached. It is expanded, but it is also tested. John the Baptist had already made it clear to the whole nation of Israel that no one among the Jews can exist before God simply on the basis of being a descendant of Abraham (a message that, incidentally, we also find in the Old Testament prophets!). This pointed message we find again in Paul: "not all who are descended from Israel are Israel. Nor because they are his descendants are they all Abraham's children" (Rom. 9:6–7). Not all Jews responded to the gospel of their God (Rom. 10:16). But there was a believing segment, to which Paul himself belonged (Rom. 11:1), with many, many thousands in Jerusalem (Acts 21:20) and outside that city (Acts 13:43; 14:1; 17:10–12; 18:8, 24; 28:24). There was a "remnant chosen by grace," even as in the days of Elijah there had been seven thousand people who did not bow down before Baal (Rom. 11:2–5).

Elsewhere Paul calls this remnant "the Israel of God" (Gal. 6:16) and says that being circumcised does not mean anything. The question is whether one is a new creation. Paul urges his Gentile Christian readers in this way not to let themselves be circumcised. If they observe the rule of the new creation (through the Spirit of Christ), peace and mercy will come upon them. They will as uncircumcised people participate in the grace of God. And this blessing also continues to rest on the Israel of God. This is circumcised Israel, to the extent that it does not resist the Messiah sent from God. On the one hand Paul fights for the rights of the uncircumcised Christians in Galatia, but on the other hand he does not allow them to isolate themselves from Israel. Believing Israel remains the Israel of God in the full sense of the term! They may now belong to God's Israel through faith in him and his Son.

18.2.3 Appeal to Israel

The apostle Paul must have given a great deal of thought to the meaning of his work. Why are Gentiles now accepted by God, without circumcision, as fellow citizens of the saints? For Christians living in later centuries this appears to be normal and a matter of course. But for the Jewish Rabbi Saul it must have been strange indeed. He follows the Master, but the path is startlingly unexpected. How does his success among the Gentiles benefit his own people?

Paul discusses this question in his letter to the Gentile Christians in Rome. He has come to the conclusion that his work can be meaningful as an incentive for and a challenge to Israel: "I am talking to you Gentiles. Inasmuch as I am the apostle to the Gentiles, I make much of my ministry in the hope that I may somehow arouse my own people to envy and save some of them" (Rom. 11:13–14). Paul wants to make his fellow Jews envious (Rom. 11:11). He hopes that the partial hardening that has come over the Jewish people will melt when they see how many Gentiles in this period have come to faith in and obedience to the one God and Creator.

The passion of Saul the Jew is manifest in his actions. Untiringly he renders account of himself during his imprisonment, and when he arrives in Rome he immediately invites the leaders of the Jewish community for a conversation. The apostle to the Gentiles does not have his back to his people. As apostle to the Gentiles he wants to become indirectly an apostle to the Jews!

We can also see this in the manner in which Paul approaches the Gentiles. Whenever possible he preaches first to the Jews in the synagogue. Only when the Jews make it impossible for him to preach in the synagogue does Paul devote himself to true mission to the Gentiles. It looks as if preaching to the Gentiles is his second choice—as if Paul has become apostle to the Gentiles, not by calling but from necessity, and as if he is actually a failed missionary among the Jews. This is not the case: preaching to the nations has become his primary calling. But the way in which he begins that preaching in each city makes it clear that he has not come to build on virgin soil, but rather that he comes to the Gentiles via Israel. Thus his work in the Greek cities becomes automatically an appeal to the Jews who remain behind by their rejection of Messiah Jesus in their synagogue. And to all Greeks it is from the very beginning clear that salvation comes from Zion!

18.2.4 A New Dispensation

For Paul, a new period in Israel's existence has dawned. Because it has long been customary in Bible translations, we generally refer to this period as the "New Testament" (= "new covenant"). But this phrase suggests something Paul did not intend, namely, that the so-called Old Testament or old covenant (which God made with the nation of Israel) is entirely in the past—as if the age of the people of Abraham has come to a close and as if one relationship (the old covenant with Israel) was dissolved to bring into existence a new relationship (the new covenant with the nations, including, if so desired, Israel).

But this conception of an old covenant with a Jewish nation that is now abrogated in favor of a non-Jewish covenant does not find support in much of what the apostle Paul writes about the people of Israel (see above, 18.2.1–3). Furthermore, the Greek word for covenant (*diathēkē*) does not refer to an all-encompassing pact that regulates an exclusive relationship between two parties and that allows for only one pact to be in force at a time, so that any change always results in a change in partners. The word *diathēkē* means "testament," "covenant," "decree." Thus Paul can write in the plural about the covenants of God in which the people of Israel could rejoice ("theirs [are] the covenants [i.e., the decrees of God], the receiving of the law," Rom. 9:4). Paul speaks here of the decrees that the Lord gives within his relationship with Israel. God has not only given his own people the law, but he also made many other arrangements for them, for example, that Canaan would be the inheritance of the Jews and that the house of David would rule and that Solomon would build the temple.

Thus God also promised Israel that in the future he would make an arrangement by which he would remove the sins of his people altogether. Paul reminds his readers of this in Romans 11:26–27:

> And so all Israel will be saved, as it is written:
>
> "The deliverer will come from Zion;
> he will turn godlessness away from Jacob.
> And this is my covenant with them
> when I take away their sins."

This certainly is not about a covenant that would bring the special relationship of the Lord with Israel to an end. After all, this covenant is "with them" also; it remains a covenant with the same people! And this covenant is aimed at the salvation of "all Israel" (Rom. 11:26a, 28–32). In addition, Paul incorporates Isaiah 59:20–21 here (italics indicate where Paul quotes verbatim from the Septuagint; note the change from "to [or 'for the sake of'] Zion" to "from Zion").[15]

Isaiah 59:20–21	**Romans 11:26–27**
	And so all Israel will be saved, as it is written:
"*The Redeemer will come* to Zion,	"*The deliverer will come* from Zion;
to those in Jacob who repent of their sins," . . .	*he will turn godlessness away from Jacob.*
"*As for me, this is my covenant with them* . . .	*And this is my covenant with them*
My Spirit, who is on you, and my words that I have put in your mouth will not depart from your mouth, or from the mouths of your children, or from the mouths of their descendants from this time on and forever."	when I take away their sins."

In this prophecy God makes (within his covenant with Israel) a new arrangement: he sends a Redeemer, takes away sins, and teaches the people a new life in which sins have disappeared and must make room for a life through the Spirit.[16] The apostle Paul quotes these words from Isaiah in a passage in which he focuses on God's enduring faithfulness to his people Israel (Rom. 11:25–32). It is therefore impossible that Paul would discuss a change of covenants here and a replacement of the covenant people.

The chapter that appears to make the strongest case for such a switch in covenants is 2 Corinthians 3. We read there about Paul and others as "ministers of a new covenant" and about the reading of "the old covenant" among the Jews (2 Cor. 3:6, 14). This gives the impression that in the place of the old covenant (with Moses) something new has come: the new covenant of the Spirit. But there are several objections to the idea of the termination of an old relationship and the start of something else.

For later Christian readers the "reading of the old covenant" is very misleading. We have become so used to calling the books from Genesis to Malachi the Old Testament that we immediately understand "reading of the old covenant" in 2 Corinthians 3:14 to refer to the reading of the *Tanakh* (the Hebrew Bible consisting of Law, Prophets, and Writings).[17] But at the time of Paul's writing it was not yet possible to refer to the books from Genesis to Daniel (in the order of the books in the *Tanakh*, Daniel comes last) as the Old Testament, since there was not yet a book called the New Testament. When Paul wants to use a direct object with "reading," he chooses the designation "Moses": "Even to this day when Moses is read" (2 Cor. 3:15). But the expression "reading of the old covenant" refers not so much to what is read as to reading as such, reading as a hallmark of the dispensation of the law. The old arrangement God made for his people was the dispensation of the law. A law must be read: that is the "reading of the old covenant," the reading that belongs to the dispensation of the law. But for Paul this is now, in the light of Christ, an old, superseded arrangement. It is therefore intended in a qualifying sense when he says "to this day the same veil remains when [the law of the now outdated dispensation] is read." We must understand "to this day" from the perspective of the first century.

The leaders of the Jews crucified Jesus. Then came the gospel of Pentecost. But the conversion of all Israel did not happen. And more than twenty years later that is still true. Paul had hoped that by now the eyes of all Israel would have been opened, as had happened to him, but the preceding twenty years had shown instead a hardening against the gospel. Sadly enough, though the light has been shining for some time, the people continue to read in the twilight without realizing that the dispensation of reading (in a book that is hung as a curtain before the true glory) has been rendered obsolete by the sunlight of Pentecost.

After all, the dispensation by which God bound his people to the reading of the law has been replaced by a dispensation in which he fills them with the Spirit of Christ. In Corinth, God had written with his Spirit on the tablets of the heart. Even as Moses came down from Sinai with the two tablets of stone that were to be read, so Paul may, as a letter of commendation from God, show the Christian community in Corinth where God has written through the Spirit on their hearts. This happened without these Gentiles first having been circumcised in accordance with the law or having adopted a Jewish lifestyle.

Paul's words in 2 Corinthians are polemically charged. Jews read the Torah—that is their glory! They boast of it to the Gentiles. And it is indeed a great gift! But they don't realize that that same Torah is a veil that hangs in front of the radiance of the Shekinah, the Glory of God. At Sinai the people did not get to see the Almighty in person. Moses did see the Almighty, but afterward the radiance of his face was too bright for the Israelites to look at. Moses had to wear a veil after he had talked with the Lord. In the same way, the law is for Israel the veil of the Shekinah. God shrouds his glory with a veil of paper and letters. Whoever looks at Moses looks, while reading, at that veil. But whoever looks at Christ sees the veil disappear. Jesus radiates the glory of God in such a way that we can look at it. In his humiliation he did the works of God. Thus they came very close to us. And thus the veil has been lifted. Through the Spirit we have fellowship with Christ and God.

The new arrangement thus does not mean a break with the Jewish past but an apotheosis of Israel's history! Now that Christ, who is the glory of the invisible God, has appeared on earth, Paul is no longer the minister of the veil but of the manifestation. The dispensation of the veil was merely temporary. But the covenant of God with his people remains—and now in greater glory, through the dispensation of the Spirit.

The contrast between the letter and the Spirit is this: "the letter kills, but the Spirit gives life" (2 Cor. 3:6). Here also Paul writes from the perspective of the Gentile Christians. The law represents "the ministry that condemns" (2 Cor. 3:9): whoever is not under the law does not belong to Israel's God. And although the law was the shelter above Israel's head, it was at the same time the great excluder and executioner for the uncircumcised Gentiles and for all those who did not really belong to Israel through an inward faith. Over against this stands the ministry of Paul and others. God now justifies through the Spirit of Christ all those among the nations who believe, and he renews the Corinthians so that they become a letter of commendation for Paul. The apostle draws the comparison between law and Spirit to make clear that the present "ministry that brings righteousness" is a glorious ministry that asks for total commitment.

As Gentiles we can pass negative judgment on the phase in which Israel and the law meant in fact a condemnation of the entire world outside of Israel. And yet that phase already had its own splendor and glory, which could be seen reflected in Moses' face! How much more is the ministry of justification full of glory; the Spirit of God comes to live in us and we are allowed to change "from glory to glory" (2 Cor. 3:17–18 KJV).

Thus the letter of the law in Israel requires circumcision of the body (as a sign of the circumcision of the heart), but in Paul's days the Spirit gives the Gentiles the circumcision of the heart directly through the Spirit (Rom. 2:27, 29). Now that the new, fresh wind of the Spirit has come, the letter of the law can be characterized as old and worn-out.

Paul does not view the dispensation of the letter (reading, the law) negatively. But it passes away and becomes obsolete now that the intended reality has appeared. A new period dawns for Israel. Israel's imperfect dispensation is replaced by a better and definitive one.

18.3 In Prayer for Israel

We discover Paul's deep personal intention when we take a separate look at what he expects and hopes for Israel.

18.3.1 The Future of the Jewish People

Paul's letters are addressed to Christian communities within his own sphere of responsibility, communities of uncircumcised Christians. Their relationship to the circumcised people of God is naturally a point of particular interest in several letters. But the future of Israel is of less interest to the Gentile Christians, and it is understandable that in most letters the apostle does not pay attention to this point. It is at first glance surprising that he does bring up the topic in his letter to the Gentile Christians in Rome, yet not so on further reflection. The Christian community in Rome had begun as a community of Gentile Christians and had therefore come into being outside the synagogue. Thus, unlike most other congregations elsewhere, it had never gone through a conflict caused by some Jews becoming Christians while others closed themselves off from the gospel. There are as a result no individuals in the Christian community in Rome who pressure the new believers to be circumcised. This community, therefore, seems to be entirely separate from the Jewish people. Nevertheless they know that salvation comes from the Jews. What, then, is the position of the Jewish people in this age of Christ? Do they stay behind permanently, or is there still a relationship between Christians and Jews? And what is the eschatological perspective for the nation that was represented in the city of Rome by a large Jewish community? In a sense the Christian community in Rome finds itself in the position in which the later church will also find itself when Judaism and Christianity appear to be (or to have become) two separate entities.

In Romans 9:6–10:21 Paul first describes the current perspective. A partial hardening has come over Israel; some accept Messiah Jesus, but others close themselves off from him. This situation is, sadly, not a new one. It has always been true that "not all who have descended from Israel are Israel." Through the centuries the Israel that was related to God inwardly, through faith, had always been smaller than the nation as a whole (Rom. 9:6–29). Jews who in the present close themselves off from Messiah Jesus thereby close themselves off from the intent of the law. In the age when God pours out his Spirit on all flesh they continue to hold up the works of the law before the Gentiles. Thus they wrap themselves in those works as if by doing so they could screen out the light of the gospel among the nations (Rom. 9:30–10:21).

Does the present situation mean that God has rejected his people? That is the opening question in Romans 11. Paul immediately answers in the negative: "By no means!" (Rom. 11:1), and proceeds to make several points to support his answer.

There remains in the Jewish nation a segment that does believe. As there were still many who did not worship Baal even in Elijah's day, so there are in Paul's day many who do not reject the Messiah of God but worship him (Rom. 11:1–12). God continues to choose the remnant of Israel!

Furthermore, Israel is enriched because many Gentiles are accepting faith in the one Creator by being incorporated into Christ Jesus. They are grafted into the olive tree (Rom. 11:13–24). These Christians from the Gentiles enter Israel according to God's plan. He has determined "the full number" of believers. When that full number has come in, all Israel shall be saved (Rom. 11:25–27). The road to Israel's salvation goes through the entering of many believers from the nations—thus (*houtōs*) and in no other way (Rom. 11:26). Paul here quotes Isaiah 59:20–21: when the Deliverer comes, he will come to Zion, and he will take away Jacob's sins. All nations must be incorporated into Jacob or Israel so that they may participate in the absolution and cleansing Israel will receive.

There remains hope for the future of the unbelieving Jews. Even as God has had mercy on the disobedient Gentiles, so he can have mercy on the Jews who at present reject the Messiah. In Paul's day the obstinacy of many Jews resulted in the gospel being pushed out of the synagogue—thereby helping it reach the world. And so the entry of the Gentiles into Israel can bring about that at God's time the unwilling Jews also will partake of his mercy (Rom. 11:28–32).

Paul teaches the Gentile Christian community that they are only a recent branch on the tree of Israel. So Gentile Christians should not boast

(Rom. 11:18–21). They are not God's final destination; the mystery of salvation lies beyond the Christian community in Rome (Rom. 11:25)!

18.3.2 Intercession

The apostle Paul includes very personal statements in his emotional passages about Israel's unbelief and future. As apostle to the Gentiles he yet has strong emotional ties with his people, the Jews. Paul shows his tears: "I have great sorrow and unceasing anguish in my heart. For I could wish that I myself were cursed and cut off from Christ for the sake of my brothers, those of my own race" (Rom. 9:2–3).

Nor is the apostle ashamed to share with an unknown Christian community from the Gentiles an insight into his personal prayer life: "Brothers, my heart's desire and prayer to God for the Israelites is that they may be saved" (Rom. 10:1).

The apostle shows here how the modesty of the Gentile Christian community can find expression. The church in Rome can, with Paul, stand before the closed door of the synagogue, weeping yet trusting God. "For God has bound all men over to disobedience so that he may have mercy on them all" (Rom. 11:32)!

18.4 Pioneer for the Messiah of Israel

As apostle to the Gentiles, Paul was a pioneer for the people of God. He was given the task of going to uncultivated areas and making them fruitful for the Creator. For his part, Paul wanted to cooperate in the growth of a Jewish-Christian synagogue that embraced both circumcised and uncircumcised Christians. Paul emphatically did not want to start from scratch. He wanted to expand Israel and open the synagogue for all believing children of Abraham from the nations.

In practice, Paul's project is still unfinished. Because of the many centuries that have elapsed since, it has become normal to refer to non-Christian children of Abraham as "Israel" or "synagogue" and to Christian children of Abraham as "church" or "Christendom." Because Paul's task lay among the uncircumcised, it seems as if he was the founder of a new religion, separate from the Jewish religion. But the history of his life, and his attitude toward the law and Israel make it clear that the apostle saw Christendom as a new phase in Israel's existence. The appearances of the Son of God, Jesus of Nazareth, to him made Paul a visionary, prepared to sacrifice himself for an ideal that became a promise: one nation that lives in the peace of Israel's God through Christ's sacrifice.

Many Jews held—and hold—the door of the synagogue closed to their fellow Jew, Messiah Jesus, and thereby also for his disciples, first the Greek but then also the Jew. Thus a Christian community developed, so to speak, in the forecourt of the synagogue, a community that bears the imprint or image of the apostle Paul. When his image (which is the image of Christ) continues to be honored, the church will, in that forecourt, continue to pray for Israel.

The figure of Paul became increasingly vague, already during his life. The suffering of Christ led to his disappearing from the picture. Also, in later Christianity, Paul all too often has remained offstage, out of sight, or has been distorted. But his final words continue to resound, unchanged, from prison:

> For God did not give us a spirit of timidity, but a spirit of power, of love and of self-discipline.
>
> So do not be ashamed to testify about our Lord, or ashamed of me his prisoner. But join with me in suffering for the gospel, by the power of God, who has saved us and called us to a holy life—not because of anything we have done but because of his own purpose and grace. This grace was given us in Christ Jesus before the beginning of time, but it has now been revealed through the appearing of our Savior, Christ Jesus, who has destroyed death and has brought life and immortality to light through the gospel. And of this gospel I was appointed a herald and an apostle and a teacher. That is why I am suffering as I am. Yet I am not ashamed, because I know whom I have believed, and am convinced that he is able to guard what I have entrusted to him for that day.
>
> What you heard from me, keep as the pattern of sound teaching, with faith and love in Christ Jesus. Guard the good deposit that was entrusted to you—guard it with the help of the Holy Spirit who lives in us. (2 Tim. 1:7–14)

Appendix 1

THE CHRONOLOGY OF PAUL'S LIFE

Conquerors create their own calendar, prophets are given a place on the calendar only after the fact. The apostle Paul did not institute a new calendar, nor was his career recorded in the annals of the consuls in Rome. He was neither a general nor a revolutionary. His life was spent in the service of the kingdom of heaven, which is why here on earth the apostle has no dates of his own.

On the basis of preserved documents we can try to reconstruct a chronology long after the fact. We can approach this task from two angles: (1) borrowed dates, and (2) the rhythm of the apostle's life.

Paul was a chosen vessel through whom Christ presented his name to governors and kings (Acts 9:15). When Paul the prisoner appears before rulers, we can assign him dates for those appearances on the basis of their dates, which he thus "borrows" from them. The tenure of governors such as Gallio, Felix, and Festus, and the reigns of kings and emperors such as Aretas, Claudius, and Nero provide boundaries for the periods within which Paul came into contact with them, and they give us some fixed chronological points for his biography.

Second, we have the rhythm of the life of the apostle himself. We know something of the successive journeys of the apostle and the minimum time these required. We can also determine the sequence of many events, so that we know what came first and what later. This, combined with the borrowed dates, allows us to reconstruct a chronological pattern for his life, albeit an incomplete, summary one.

1. Sources and Method

This reconstruction calls for a measure of modesty. There is much that we do not know. In the first place, the book of Acts was not written to provide a complete biography with dates, and Paul's letters are undated, occasional writings. Second, many documents from the first century that could have added to or changed our picture have been lost. When we try to imagine what a reconstruction of the chronology of Paul's life would look like without the letter to the Galatians, we can suspect that the lost letter to Laodicea or the letters to Corinth that have not been preserved might well force us to adjust our image of Paul's life. As is so often true in the discipline of history, we cannot hope to go beyond a knowledge "to the best of our abilities."

It is nevertheless useful to put together a chronological sketch of Paul's life, even if it will have to remain incomplete and tentative. Such a reconstruction can help us to arrange, date, and collate the materials we still have into a somewhat orderly whole.

Because the available material is incomplete and heterogeneous, it can easily lead to unnecessary confusion and apparent contradiction. This then can lead to a simple setting aside of part of the material—either from desperation or from overconfidence—and using the remaining selections from the material to create entirely new and novel reconstructions of Paul's life. Many examples of this can be found in the history of New Testament scholarship in the last centuries.

1. Letters are branded inauthentic because they do not seem to fit easily into the pattern of the rest of the material. This criticism of the authenticity of Paul's letters began with historical criticism of 1 Timothy (a letter that does not seem to fit into the travels of Paul as

described in Acts).[1] Soon other letters came under similar criticism (e.g., 2 Timothy, Titus, Ephesians, and Colossians).[2]

2. On the other hand, the book of Acts is thought to be of lesser value because it does not seem to fit with the data from some of the letters. Thus the reports of the apostolic convention (Acts 15) and of Paul's arrival in Rome (Acts 28) are judged unhistorical on the basis of comparison with, respectively, Galatians 2 and the letter to the Romans.

The methodological drawback of this approach is that parts of the historical material are pushed aside without any consistent standpoint with regard to the sources as a whole. Acts and Paul's letters frequently take turns being the accused and being witness for the prosecution. This methodological inconsistency can be avoided only by means of radical criticism of the sources as a whole or as a group.

Thus the Dutch Radical School in the nineteenth century considered all of Paul's letters to be inauthentic.[3] Because this school also viewed Acts in a negative light, there were no sources left for a reconstruction of Paul's life. It is understandable that this radical approach held little appeal for New Testament scholars who wanted to know at least something about this apostle.

In the twentieth century a new form of radical criticism was launched, the so-called new chronology of Paul's life. Here the starting point is that only the letters can serve as source material and that Acts should be left out of consideration altogether. Given the limited number of historical comments in the epistles and the incidental nature of those that do occur, it is understandable that it now becomes a simple matter to come up with entirely new reconstructions of Paul's life. When the reins of Acts are cast off, there is little left to bridle the imagination.

The starting point of this new chronology is found in a few publications from the middle of the twentieth century; of these, *Chapters in a Life of Paul* by John Knox has become best known.[4] The chronology is based on the assumption that Galatians 2 is equivalent to the Jerusalem visit of Acts 18:22.[5] This visit is, on the basis of Galatians 1:18 and 2:1, viewed as the second visit after Paul's conversion. Consequently the narrative of the apostolic conference (Acts 15) is considered unhistorical. This in turn leads to the elimination of the partition between the first and second missionary journeys, so that Paul made only one long trip before the visit of Galatians 2 (=Acts 18:22). Luke's narrative about the first journey is thus either fiction or represents only the first part of a much longer journey that led relatively quickly to Macedonia.

One of the cornerstones of the new chronology is Paul's comment that the Philippians already supported him with gifts "in the beginning of the gospel" (Phil. 4:15, *en archēi tou euangeliou*). The word "beginning" is taken as referring, not to the beginning of the gospel in Macedonia (the NIV reads, "in the early days of your acquaintance with the gospel"), but rather to the beginning of the preaching of the gospel in general. This would mean that Paul must have advanced into Greece relatively soon after his calling.

The following sketch of Paul's life could be the result of a consistent handling of his letters only, without connecting them in any way with the data from the book of Acts.

1. Paul's conversion (Gal. 1:15–17).
2. First visit to Jerusalem, after three years (Gal. 1:18).
3. Preaching in Syria and Cilicia (Gal. 1:21) and into Macedonia (Phil. 4:15). Acts contains memories of this journey through (Pisidia, Lycaonia, Phrygia?) Galatia, Macedonia, Achaia, and Asia.
4. Second visit to Jerusalem, after fourteen years (Gal. 2:1).
5. Work in Asia and Greece down to Illyricum; gathering of the collection for Jerusalem (Rom. 15:19–29).
6. Last visit to Jerusalem: the collection is handed over and Paul is arrested.

For a number of years it seemed that this chronology would be left behind among the curiosities of New Testament scholarship. But the last two decades of the twentieth century witnessed a surprising revival of this new chronology, beginning with Jewett's study.[6] In Germany Gerd Lüdemann's book occupies center stage.[7] In the English-speaking world the book by Jerome Murphy-O'Connor is a detailed representative of this movement.[8] Via these publications we see the theory take on new life, and it is now applied in an increasing number of theological studies. Thus Karl P. Donfried uses this chronology to date 1 Thessalonians exceptionally early (A.D. 41!), and this then becomes the foundation for his thesis that the letters to Thessalonica reflect the theology of the early Paul.[9]

The new chronology flourishes in times when confidence in the historical reliability of Acts is on the wane. It is, in fact, a variation on concepts championed by earlier authors with a critical attitude toward Acts.[10]

Yet this new theory cannot do entirely without data from Acts. Those data are, as it were, salvaged from a condemned building, but doing so proves clearly that a chronology of Paul's life is impossible to reconstruct without using sources outside the letters. For example, when the visit of Galatians 2 is identified with Acts 18:22, an external point of comparison is sought in *Acts*! It is also unclear why Paul would not have traveled from Syria and Cilicia (Gal. 1:21) directly by ship to Philippi (Phil. 4:15). The idea that he traveled over land through Turkey is based solely on Luke's book!

Not only is it methodologically objectionable to take the historical data from Acts selectively, there is every reason to adopt as point of departure the view that this second book of Luke's is as a whole historically reliable. Since Ramsay[11] it has been concluded more than once that Luke deals very carefully with various historical and geographical details.[12] He also makes the claim to be writing with the conscience of a serious Greek historian, as is apparent from the prologue to his Gospel (Luke 1:1–4) and from the fact that in Acts he distinguishes carefully between the sections in which he himself traveled with Paul and those in which he did not.[13] Even though Luke has a specific purpose in writing his book, on the basis of which he selects, condenses, or omits material, this does not mean that he would have distorted the historical data gratuitously—if only because distorting the data would have detracted from the credibility of the message the author wanted to pass on. No one can point convincingly to any kind of pattern or systematic approach behind the alleged historical distortion.[14] The aim of his book did not require Luke to be unfaithful to the self-imposed demands of a good historian—even in those days—for the proper handling of names of people, of times, and of places. And it is the latter two around which chronology primarily revolves.

2. "Borrowed" Dates

There are four periods in Paul's life that can be anchored chronologically on the basis of known dates of governors and kings.

1. *The period in which Paul became a Christian.* His call to Christ must be dated after Jesus' death, resurrection, and ascension, and after the feast of Pentecost. Jesus was brought before the high priests Annas and Caiaphas and before Herod the tetrarch, and finally before the Roman governor Pontius Pilate. Their dates mark indirectly (via the chronology of Jesus) the terminus a quo, the earliest moment after which Saul can have gone into action as a persecutor of Christians.
2. *The period during which Saul no longer persecuted Christians but preached the gospel.* We know that this period began during the reign of the Nabatean king Aretas, so that the date of this ruler's death marks a date before which Paul began to preach among the nations.
3. *The period of the three great journeys described in Acts.* The end of the second journey (the departure from Corinth) can be dated with relative accuracy on the basis of points of contact with the expulsion of the Jews from Rome by Emperor Claudius and with the tenure of Gallio as governor of Corinth.
4. *The long period of imprisonment in Jerusalem, Caesarea, and Rome.* Within this period we can date the transfer from Caesarea to Rome on the basis of the succession of Felix and Festus as governors of Palestine.

2.1 Conversion after Jesus' Ascension

Jesus appears to Saul in heaven's light on the road to Damascus. In what year did Jesus ascend to the Father? The final date in Jesus' earthly biography is of importance for establishing the first date in the biography of Saul.

We cannot determine the date of the crucifixion and resurrection, and of the ascension and Pentecost, without going into the overall chronology of Jesus' life. Here we can mention only the conclusion of that investigation, which is that Jesus' ascension must be dated A.D. 33—not earlier and at most one year later.[15]

Saul's work as persecutor of Christians and Jesus' appearance to him near Damascus thus must be dated after the summer of A.D. 33. It is difficult to estimate how much time elapsed between Pentecost and Paul's conversion. During this time there were confrontations in Jerusalem that culminated in the stoning of Stephen (Acts 2–7). After this the systematic persecution under Saul's leadership began, as well as the spread of the gospel in Samaria and other places (Acts 8). These were special times, after the outpouring of the Holy Spirit, and the tempo of events was also abnormal, as illustrated by the conversion of thousands of Jews in a single day. Nevertheless, we must allow for at least a year between Jesus' ascension and his appearance to Saul, and probably even longer, since the persecution in Jerusalem and in the synagogues in Judea must have taken considerable time. We can only conclude that Paul did not become a Christian any earlier than A.D. 34.

2.2 Apostle to the Gentiles during Aretas's Reign

Paul's first work among the nations took place in Arabia, where he went immediately after God had revealed his Son in him to send him to preach to the nations (Gal. 1:16–17). He stayed in Arabia (also called Nabatea) for at most three years, after which the king of the Nabateans had him pursued all the way to Damascus (2 Cor. 11:32–33). Before this king died, three years had already passed since Paul's being called to be apostle to the Gentiles.[16]

The king who was irritated by the actions of the Christian preacher was Aretas IV Philodemos, who ruled over Nabatea for many years. George Ogg writes, "The most probable date of his accession appears to be 9 B.C. From two well-preserved inscriptions and also from coins it is known that he reigned for forty-and-eight years. Consequently

Paul's flight from Damascus cannot be put later than A.D. 40."[17] While it is true that Aretas ruled for at least forty-eight years, how do we know that he did not rule longer than that? It is, after all, possible that by sheer coincidence no coins have been found from the last years of his reign. Establishing Aretas's death date requires rather complicated calculations, working back from the dates of the reigns of Aretas's successors. These calculations show that his immediate successor, Malichos II, came to the throne at the latest some time between the fall of A.D. 37 and the early spring of A.D. 40. This is then also the window for Aretas's death. Ogg's conclusion can thus be formulated with more certainty and can even be narrowed somewhat. Because Aretas ruled for forty-eight years, he cannot have died before the end of A.D. 38. Because of his successor's tenure as king, however, Aretas's death cannot be dated any later than early A.D. 40. We can thus say with virtual certainty that Aretas died in A.D. 39 (at most a month or so earlier or later).[18]

It is not clear how Paul counted his three years' preaching in Arabia. He probably refers to three full years (Gal. 1:18, *meta etē tria*). Paul thus received the vision that sent him to the Gentiles no later than A.D. 36 (or early 37). His calling to faith in Christ took place some time before that (see section 2.1 above).

2.3 In Corinth until the Arrival of Gallio

During his so-called second journey, Paul was allowed to work in Corinth and Achaia without any opposition (Acts 18:11). But this changed at the end of a period of a year and a half. Luke writes, "[But (*de*)] while Gallio was proconsul of Achaia, the Jews made a united attack on Paul and brought him into court" (Acts 18:12). The sequence of verses 11 and 12 suggests a connection between the action of the Jews and the beginning of Gallio's proconsulship.

An inscription found in Delphi[19] indicates that Gallio was proconsul in Corinth during the twenty-sixth *acclamatio* of Emperor Claudius as *imperator*. This twenty-sixth *acclamatio* took place during A.D. 51 or in the first half of A.D. 52. We do not know for sure, however, whether at the time of the edict mentioned in the Delphi inscription Gallio had just arrived in Corinth or had been governor for some time.[20] We can therefore not deduce much more from this inscription than that Paul was brought before Gallio not any later than early A.D. 52.

But how much earlier? Here a date borrowed from a different context comes to our aid. From Acts 18:2 we can infer that Claudius had expelled the Jews from Rome some time before Paul arrived in Corinth, since Aquila and Priscilla had recently come from Italy with a report about the expulsion of the Jews from the city of Rome. This act on the part of Claudius can be dated in the ninth year of his rule,[21] that is, between January 25 of A.D. 49 and January 25 of A.D. 50. If we take into account that Aquila and Priscilla came by sea to Corinth, the report of the expulsion reached the apostle Paul during the shipping season of A.D. 49, or at the latest during the shipping season of A.D. 50.[22]

The somewhat indeterminate data about Gallio and Claudius now become mutually delimiting. Between the moment when the report of Claudius's action reaches Corinth and the beginning of Gallio's governorship lies the one-and-a-half-year period during which Paul works quietly in Corinth.

Furthermore we know that Paul, some time after the incident before Gallio, travels to Palestine by sea—which is possible only during the shipping season, that is, between March 10 and November 11.[23] Paul thus left Corinth no later than approximately September 1 (he had to sail to Ephesus, stay there for a short time, and sail on to Caesarea, all before November 11). He most likely did not leave much earlier than approximately March 1 (the sea route from Cenchrea to Ephesus had to be open again).

Governors always arrived at the location of their new assignment shortly after the beginning of the shipping season, and Emperor Claudius made the rules for a speedy departure of newly appointed governors even more stringent.[24] There is no long period separating the incident before Gallio and Paul's departure. Acts 18:18 says that Paul remained (lit.) "many *days* longer" (NASB). Thus it is unlikely that Paul would not have left Corinth until a year after the arrival of Gallio. The sequence therefore must be (a) arrival of Gallio (around

May 1); (b) the demonstration of the Jews against Paul (around June1); (c) Paul's departure from Corinth (no later than September 1).

This sequence of events cannot have taken place any later than A.D. 52. Paul arrived in Corinth in A.D. 49 or in early A.D. 50. He worked there for one-and-a-half years before the incident with Gallio, which took place around June 1. Paul's arrival, then, fell a year-and-a-half earlier, around the month of December. But this cannot have been December of A.D. 48 (at that time the Jews had not yet been expelled from Rome), nor can it have been December of A.D. 50 (when this expulsion was no longer news in Corinth). This leaves December of A.D. 49. In light of the above we conclude that Gallio's governorship began in A.D. 51.

This combination of data makes it possible to assign dates to a small portion of one of Paul's travels.

1. Arrival in Macedonia after the sea journey (!) from Troas: no later than the spring of A.D. 49. There must be time for Paul's work in Philippi, Thessalonica, Berea, and Athens after Paul's departure from Troas and before his arrival in Corinth, around December of A.D. 49.
2. Arrival in Corinth (from Macedonia via Athens): late A.D. 49.
3. Departure from Corinth: July-August A.D. 51.
4. Visit to Jerusalem and Antioch (Acts 18:22; Gal. 2:1–14): September-November A.D. 51. The feast the apostle wanted to attend then was the feast of tabernacles.
5. Beginning of the three-year period of work in Ephesus: no earlier than the spring of A.D. 53, perhaps even later. Paul leaves Antioch no earlier than the first part of A.D. 52 for a journey through Galatia and Phrygia that lasted at least half a year. But he does not arrive in Ephesus until the early spring. It appears from 1 Corinthians 16:8 that Paul left Ephesus around the feast of Pentecost for this interim journey. By that time he had already worked in Ephesus for two years (or two years and three months; Acts 19:8–10). He must therefore have arrived around the feast of Pentecost or three months earlier—that is, in the first two to five months of A.D. 53.

2.4 Prisoner from Felix to Festus

The apostle Paul was prisoner in Caesarea during the time when Festus succeeded Felix as governor. Governors came and went, but the apostle stayed in chains (Acts 24:27). When the change in governor took place, the second anniversary of Paul's imprisonment was already past!

Can we borrow a date for Paul's stay in Caesarea from these governors? The dating of this transfer of power is useful for the chronology of Paul, but it is not as simple as it might seem. In the first part of the twentieth century, a relatively early date was given for Felix's departure from Palestine. This was due to the influence of von Harnack's work: he moved the *Chronicon* of Eusebius up and inferred from that that Felix had already left Judea in A.D. 54 (according to the Armenian translation of the *Chronicon*) or in A.D. 56 (according to Jerome's edition of the *Chronicon*). All this then led to early dates in Paul's chronology.[25]

This narrowing to more precise, early dates does not do justice, however, to the rather global manner in which the data in Eusebius's *Chronicon* are placed side by side. In fact, we cannot conclude much more from the Armenian version than that Felix left Judea shortly before or at the time of the murder of Nero's mother Agrippina in A.D. 59, while Jerome's edition leads only to the conclusion that Felix did not end his tour of duty as governor before Nero's accession to the imperial throne.[26]

We can bypass here the details of the *Chronicon*, since in the course of the twentieth century it became clear that the date of Gallio precludes the early dates suggested by von Harnack. Paul cannot stand before Gallio in A.D. 51 in Corinth and begin his period of imprisonment in Caesarea already in A.D. 54—this does not leave enough time for a journey from Corinth to Ephesus, Jerusalem, Antioch (Acts 18:18–23a: at least half a year), the journey from Antioch to Ephesus through Turkey (Acts 18:23b: at least half a year); the stay in Ephesus (Acts 19:1–40; 20:31: at least three years); and the trip through Macedonia to Corinth and back via Macedonia to Jerusalem (Acts 20:1–21:16: at least half a year). Even when we keep our calculations as low as possible, we find that if Paul stood before Gallio in mid–A.D. 51, he could not have begun his imprisonment under Felix before early A.D. 56. Because Felix was governor for at least two years after that, his departure from Judea cannot be dated earlier than A.D. 58.

The beginning of Felix's tenure as governor must be dated in A.D. 52.[27] He was thus governor for at least six years. Paul knew what he was saying in his defense speech: "I know that for a number of years [lit., for many years] you have been a judge over this nation" (Acts 24:10).

Is the earliest possible date for Felix's departure also the definitive one? Or were the "many years" during which he was judge over the Jews in fact more than the six years we have calculated? The answer is affirmative: Felix was indeed governor for more than six years.

In his autobiography, Josephus tells that he was sent to Rome to plead for the release of priests who had been sent by Felix to Rome as prisoners.[28] We may assume that the Jews would not have let many years pass before trying to effect the release of these priests. They may have observed a cooling-off period, or their efforts at intervention may have been delayed by disagreements among the priests themselves during this time, but it would have been strange if the delegation to Rome did not get under way until five or six years later. All this means that Felix must have been in charge in Palestine for at least some time before Josephus's trip to Rome. We can date this trip in A.D. 64.[29] This means that Felix must have left Caesarea later than A.D. 58.

But if Felix did not leave until A.D. 59, 60, or 61, is there enough time left for his successor, Festus? We do know with certainty that Festus was already dead by the time of the feast of tabernacles in (the fall of) A.D. 62.[30] Does this mean that he was governor for only one or two (or at most three) years? When we consider how much Josephus has to say about Felix and how little about Festus, we get the distinct impression that Festus's tenure was short.[31] Furthermore, Josephus sketches a specific development that took place during Felix's years: the disturbances in Palestine continued to escalate and in the end also caused a division among the priests, and finally even tensions between Jews and Gentiles in Caesarea. Josephus cannot tell more about Festus than that he intervened in a number of incidents. All this would seem to point to a brief and rather insignificant administration under

Festus as opposed to a long and influential one under Felix. If Felix left after A.D. 58, and in A.D. 61 at the latest, the years A.D. 60 or A.D. 61 seem more likely than A.D. 59 as the year in which the transition of power took place. This is not only because of the significance of Felix's tenure and the relative brevity of Festus's governorship, but also because of the connection between Felix's actions against the priests and Josephus's journey to Rome in A.D. 64.[32]

The date of Felix's departure has an impact on the chronology of Paul. In the first place, this date determines the time span between Paul's stay in Corinth on the one hand and the beginning of his imprisonment in Caesarea on the other. How much time was available for the so-called third missionary journey and all that went with it? Paul had already been in prison for at least two years before Felix left Judea (Acts 24:27). His custody then did not begin before the period A.D. 57–59, and most likely in A.D. 58 or A.D. 59. This means that between his departure from Gallio (A.D. 51) and his arrival before Felix (A.D. 58/59) a period of some seven or eight years elapsed. Many recent works present this period as having been shorter. However, the information that Paul spent three years in Ephesus is merely a small piece of all that happened in those years. Earlier in this section we already concluded that we must allow at least four-and-a-half years for the events that took place between Corinth (Gallio) and Caesarea (Felix). But now it appears that a period is available that is two to three years longer. This means that the journey through Galatia and Phrygia probably lasted longer and that Paul did more traveling from his home base in Ephesus than is generally thought. Even though we cannot fill in any more of the blank spots on the map of Paul's life, nevertheless there is room for what Paul writes to the Romans at the end of the so-called third journey: "So from Jerusalem all the way around to Illyricum, I have fully proclaimed the gospel of Christ" (Rom. 15:19). Paul's travels even took him to the southern reaches of the Balkans! He can legitimately say, "There is no more place for me to work in these regions" (Rom. 15:23).

Second, the date of Felix's departure determines the amount of time in Paul's life between his arrival in Rome and his death. Paul then does not arrive in Rome until A.D. 61 or 62 (Acts 27:1–28:16: after a sea journey and a shipwreck that led to a winter on Malta). He was imprisoned in Rome for at least two years (Acts 28:30) and died there in A.D. 68 at the latest. His death as a martyr either marked the end of his many years of imprisonment, or was the end of a new period in prison, after a short period of freedom during which Paul perhaps visited Spain. If Paul was released from prison, he could have worked at most three or four years outside Rome. For chronological reasons alone it is then not very likely that in addition to his possible trip to Spain he also made lengthy journeys in the east again.

3. Distinct Periods

In the preceding discussion of the borrowed dates it appeared that these few dates are useful as fixed points for the periods in Paul's life that are directly connected with these dates. But these dates anchor only unconnected parts of the apostle's life. How can we arrive at a linking of the various parts so that a pattern emerges?

In Galatians 1:18 and 2:1 we find two unusual pieces of information about the length of time that elapsed between a number of events. Three years after a certain point in time Paul went to Jerusalem (Gal. 1:18), and he visited that same city also fourteen years after a specific point in his life. Which points and which visits are referred to here?

3.1 The Visit to Cephas "After Three Years"

The three-year period begins with the moment when God revealed his Son in Paul so that the apostle might preach him as good news to the nations (Gal. 1:16) and with the departure for Arabia that followed immediately thereafter (Gal. 1:17). In chapter 3.4 we noted that this revelation must be distinguished from the appearance of Jesus near Damascus (cf. section 2.2 above). It thus involves an event that took place at least half a year later than Paul's call to faith. After this initial call he preached for some time in Damascus, Jerusalem, and Judea, and then had to flee to Tarsus. There he received the revelation that sent him to the nations. If Paul's conversion took place in A.D. 34 at the earliest, we may assume that the revelation referred to in Galatians

1:16 and the departure for Arabia took place no earlier than A.D. 35 and probably somewhat later.

Paul's work in Arabia and the renewed visit to Damascus that followed cover a period of three years. At the end of these three years Paul goes to Jerusalem to visit Cephas (Gal. 1:18). This visit thus cannot be dated before A.D. 38. Nor can the visit have taken place any later than A.D. 39 or early A.D. 40. The terminus ad quem is the death of King Aretas, who, immediately before Paul's departure for Jerusalem, had set an ambush to kill Paul. Thus when Paul escaped from Damascus over the wall and traveled to Cephas, Aretas was still alive.

Luke does not mention this visit to Cephas in Acts; it falls within the period of Paul's life that Luke does not cover (from his flight to Tarsus to Barnabas's coming to get him for the work in Antioch).[33]

3.2 The Visit to Jerusalem "Fourteen Years Later"

When did the period of fourteen years begin that ended with another visit to Jerusalem (Gal. 2:1)? Many seek the answer via a comparison of the dates of the two journeys to Jerusalem (Gal. 1:18; 2:1). First we will discuss the problems inherent in a direct comparison, then the comparison as such.

According to some, the terminus a quo for calculating the fourteen years (Gal. 2:1) is the same as that for the three years (Gal. 1:18). This is the so-called inclusive approach: Paul visited Jerusalem three years after he received the revelation, and again fourteen years after the revelation.

Others follow an exclusive approach: Paul visited Jerusalem after three years, and then again fourteen years after this first visit. The second visit then takes place some seventeen years after the revelation. In favor of the exclusive approach is Paul's statement "Fourteen years later I went up again to Jerusalem." The word "again" (*palin*) suggests that Paul uses the earlier-mentioned visit as the beginning point for calculating the length of the period between the two visits. The rhetorical effect of this comment then is that Paul could not only confer with Peter peacefully back then, but could still do so fourteen years later.

As for Paul's journey to Jerusalem mentioned in Galatians 2:1, we now can say that (via the more likely exclusive approach) it cannot have taken place earlier than in the seventeenth year after the revelation, that is, in A.D. 51. According to the (less likely) inclusive approach, we arrive at the fourteenth year after the revelation (which took place in A.D. 35 or later), which is then A.D. 48 at the earliest.

Which visit mentioned in Acts is in view here? The exclusive approach has the visit to Cephas as its starting point (A.D. 38–39). The phrase "fourteen years later" (*dia dekatessarōn etōn*) is broad enough to allow for counting the beginning as the first year ("in the fourteenth year"). In that case the exclusive approach leads to a date of A.D. 51 or 52. This date forces us to locate the visit of Galatians 2 after Paul's contact with Gallio in Corinth (which took place around the middle of A.D. 51) and thus after the so-called second missionary journey. The trip to Jerusalem of Galatians 2:1 then coincides with the visit that is mentioned briefly in Acts 18:22.

Does the (less likely) inclusive approach make it possible to see the visit of Galatians 2:1 as coinciding chronologically with the apostolic convention mentioned in Acts 15? The answer to this question hinges on when we date the apostolic convention. This took place some time before the beginning of the so-called second journey. Paul arrived in Corinth in A.D. 49 and was therefore already in Macedonia before or in the spring of A.D. 49 (see section 2.3 above). Prior to this he had visited the Christian communities in Syria and Cilicia (Acts 15:41), preached in Phrygia and Galatia (Acts 16:6), was ill there for some time (Gal. 4:13–14), and wandered in a westerly and northerly direction (Acts 16:6–8) until he finally arrived in Troas for the crossing to Macedonia (Acts 16:8–10). We must allow at least one year for these many activities. It is then theoretically possible that the apostolic convention took place at the very beginning of A.D. 48, before Paul began his so-called second journey. But since this approach involves a sequence of minimum times, it is more likely that we should accept A.D. 47 as the date. But this does not fit in well with the earliest date found on the basis of the inclusive approach (A.D. 48). The conclusion must be that identifying Galatians 2:1 with Acts 15 is unlikely for chronological reasons, but not altogether impossible.

After this comparison of the inclusive and exclusive approaches, we must now raise the question as to whether the dilemma they present is not in fact too narrowly focused. Because of the modern interest in Paul's journeys to Jerusalem, people are readily inclined to view the two Jerusalem journeys in Galatians 1 and 2 in relation to one another, and to take the "fourteen years later" in Galatians 2:1 as referring back to the visit to the same city mentioned a few verses earlier. But in Galatians 1–2 Paul is not particularly interested in counting journeys to Jerusalem. What is important to him here is the divine origin of his gospel and the recognition of that gospel by the other apostles. Paul therefore does not organize the events around visits to Jerusalem; he simply presents a few brief statements about the sequence of events. He does this by using *epeita* three times in a brief sequence ("*then* . . . I went," 1:18; "*later* I went," 1:21 and 2:1). The events Paul mentions successively are

(1) the departure for Arabia after receiving the revelation (Gal. 1:17);
(2) ("thereafter") a journey to Jerusalem after three years (Gal. 1:18);
(3) ("thereafter") a departure for the region of Syria and Cilicia fifteen days later (Gal. 1:18–21);
(4) ("thereafter") a departure for Jerusalem fourteen years later (Gal. 2:1).

The visit of Galatians 2:1 (event 4) is formally related to the departure for Syria and Cilicia (event 3): *epeita* ("thereafter") in both 1:21 and 2:1 connects the contents of both verses. The date of this departure does coincide with the Jerusalem visit mentioned in Galatians 1:18 (event 2), but there is no direct linking of the visit after fourteen years (event 4) to the short visit of fifteen days (event 2). It is therefore logical to count the fourteen years in Galatians 2:1 (event 4) from Paul's departure for Syria and Cilicia (event 3). This eliminates the problem as to whether the fourteen years should be considered exclusive or inclusive of the three years mentioned earlier. Even though the dating via the successive sequence of four events leads in fact to the same chronological result as the exclusive approach to the dating of the

Jerusalem visits, the method that leads to this result fits in better with the text of Paul himself and is therefore less uncertain.

In chapter 7.1 we had to conclude that because of the collection agreement (Gal. 2:10) the consultation in Jerusalem "fourteen years later" must be dated after the so-called second missionary journey, since this collection was not organized until after the third journey. This conclusion now appears to be confirmed by the chronological data. A date for the Jerusalem consultation (Gal. 2:1–10) after the second journey appears to fit in well with the fixed points and intervals in the chronology.

3.3 Looking Back on a Disputed Dating

The questions surrounding the identification of the apostolic convention (Acts 15) and Paul's visit to Jerusalem (Gal. 2) led to vehement discussions in the last two centuries. At stake was the reliability of the book of Acts. The result of identifying Acts 15 with Galatians 2 is that we are forced to see many discrepancies between Luke's and Paul's descriptions of the convention, discrepancies that according to many amount to irreconcilable differences.

What is surprising is that these contradictions were also seen in the past, when Acts was still considered to be of equal standing with Paul's letters as historical documents. The difference is that the conclusion back then was that Galatians 2 should not be identified with Acts 15 and instead should be identified with another visit to Jerusalem.

Although this issue did not play a significant role in the early church, Chrysostom already argued for identifying Galatians 2 with Acts 18:22 (the visit after the so-called second missionary journey).[34] Luther followed in his footsteps in his 1535 commentary on Galatians.[35] Calvin and Beza were well aware of the issue, and defended the identification of Galatians 2 with a visit prior to Acts 15. They considered the differences between Galatians 2 and Acts 15 as too great to consider the two passages synchronous.

His chronological studies led Iacobus Cappellus (professor at Sedan, France, at the beginning of the seventeenth century) to identify Galatians 2 with Acts 18:22.[36] His brother, Ludovicus Capellus, professor at Saumur, France, did not adopt Iacobus's view but did mention it in his *Historia Apostolica*. Ludovicus defended the identification of Acts 15 with Galatians 2 on historical grounds, but he proposed a rather drastic solution to the chronological problem that had occupied his brother: he emended the text of Galatians 2:1 to read "four years later" rather than "fourteen years later."[37] Readers of his work felt uneasy about his equating Galatians 2 with Acts 15, since it involved a textual emendation. This is clear in Witsius's work who, with a sigh of relief, observes that Spanheim has in the meantime found a way to defend Ludovicus's solution—without any textual changes. But Salomo van Til, a colleague of Witsius in Leiden at the beginning of the eighteenth century, was less convinced by Spanheim.[38] Like Iacobus Cappellus he argued for the identification with Acts 18:22.

At the beginning of the nineteenth century we find the same identification by Jakob Hesz, I. F. Köhler, Karl Schrader, and others.[39] It was therefore not a move of desperation when in the middle of the nineteenth century Karl Wieseler, faced with Baur's critical view of Acts 15 (on the basis of Gal. 2), made the case for an identification of the consultation of Galatians 2 with the Jerusalem visit mentioned in Acts 18:22. The choice between an identification of Galatians 2 with either Acts 15 or Acts 18:22 had been left open as late as 1833 in Rückert's commentary on Galatians.[40] Originally Wieseler himself leaned toward Acts 15, but further chronological study caused him to change his mind.[41] Baur's ideas on the evolution of the early church had, however, a major impact on the majority of scholars at that time, and chronological details were generally not much appreciated. Wieseler's position was discussed but met with little approval. Nevertheless, we see with some regularity the appearance of publications by individuals who, like Wieseler, arrived at a comparison of Galatians 2:1 with Acts 18:22b (not 15:1–29) on the basis of chronological considerations. At the same time, however, they viewed this visit (contrary to Acts) not as at least Paul's third visit to Jerusalem after his conversion, but as his second.[42]

The identification of Acts 18:22 with Galatians 2 similarly surfaces again in the middle of the twentieth century, in the so-called new chronology of Paul (discussed earlier in this appendix). In this new chronology, Baur's perspective on Acts becomes dominant. This is not surprising, since once we question, on the basis of Galatians 2, the description of the apostolic convention in Acts 15, we will sooner or later have to deal with the question as to why Luke should be taken seriously when it comes to the historicity of the event. But if there was no apostolic convention at all after the first missionary journey, why would Galatians 2 (which chronologically fits better after the second journey) not be the first and only time when there was a consultation in Jerusalem? This unique event then fell in the time of Acts 18:22!

But how can we explain that after Wieseler the identification of Galatians 2 with Acts 18:22 is rarely found among the defenders of the historicity of Acts? This is undoubtedly due to the work of Ramsay, whose studies in the beginning of the twentieth century became very influential due to his growing appreciation for Acts as an accurate historical book. But Ramsay referred Galatians 2 (without paying much attention to the chronological implications) to the visit to Jerusalem from Antioch described in Acts 11–12. Due to Ramsay the debate has, in apologetically oriented circles, narrowed to the dilemma "Acts 11 or Acts 15" while Acts 18:22 as an option has dropped below the horizon.

The identification of Galatians 2 with the visit of Acts 11:29–30 (and 12:25) has a measure of appeal.[43] It allows for a simple explanation as to why in Galatians Paul does not appeal to the apostolic decree: the visit mentioned in Galatians took place before the meeting of the apostolic convention (Acts 15).[44] But the removal of this major problem comes at too high a price—which not everyone is aware of.

1. The letter Paul writes to the Galatians then must also have been written before Acts 15, since otherwise we have not found a real solution to the question as to why Paul does not mention the apostolic decree in the letter.

2. Such an early date requires in turn that the letter be viewed as addressed to the Christian communities of the so-called first missionary journey (Paul's first visit to Galatia comes after the apostolic convention). Ramsay considered this to be entirely possible, since (part of) the Christian communities of the first journey belonged to the Roman province of Galatia (which included much more territory than the original kingdom of Galatia, or Galatia proper). There remain,

however, decisive arguments against the letter to the Galatians being addressed to churches in a region outside Galatia proper. The inhabitants of Galatia proper had their own ethnic identity (they were in all probability Celts), and it is highly doubtful that Paul would have addressed inhabitants of the larger province of Galatia as "Galatians"—let alone as "foolish Galatians" (Gal. 3:1).

3. The visit of Acts 11 takes place before the death of Herod Agrippa I (Acts 12). He died in A.D. 44, before the Passover. This means that the visit of Paul and Barnabas (around the time of the feast of unleavened bread; Acts 12:3) took place in A.D. 43. But even if we calculate the fourteen years that had already passed after Paul's revelation in such a way that we compress them into as short a time as possible, we still collide with the chronology of Jesus' life. Even if we accept an early date for Jesus' death (A.D. 30 is often suggested),[45] too little time remains for the events of Acts 2–9 and the fourteen years that follow. We can gain enough time only if we put Jesus' death in A.D. 27, a date that is possible only if various other historical data are left out of consideration.

4. Sometimes attempts are made to solve these problems by assigning a later date to the visit of Acts 11. It is then believed to have been a visit during the famine that had been predicted by Agabus in Antioch. This famine is thought to have occurred in conjunction with a Sabbath year, and thus we get a reconstruction that ends up with the year A.D. 48.[46] But in Acts 11:27–30 two things stand side by side. On the one hand the arrival of the prophets *from Jerusalem*, among them Agabus who prophesied concerning a famine that indeed came over the entire world under Claudius (Acts 11:28). On the other hand, the decision to send financial support to the *mother church* of these prophets. What connects the two elements are Jerusalem and the exchange of spiritual and material gifts respectively, not the time when the famine occurs.

The identification of the consultation in Galatians 2 with Acts 11 is tenable only to a limited degree. That this view nevertheless gained wide acceptance in the twentieth century (more so in the Anglo-Saxon world than in continental Europe) can be explained historically by the need to find shelter against the sharp criticism that since Baur has been leveled against Acts 15 from the perspective of Galatians 2.

In conclusion, the preceding brief comments on the history of the issue show that the identification of Galatians 2 with Acts 18:22 is not new but has a long history and has been defended through the centuries. These comments also explain why in the last century and a half—thanks to Baur on one side and Ramsay on the other—most attention has been given to identifications other than with Acts 18:22. On the other hand, also during the last hundred years the identification with Acts 18:22 has found defenders again and again, but (unlike earlier centuries) their defense was strongly marked in this period by a hypercritical attitude toward Acts. From a historical perspective, however, there is every reason to take the chronological data (including those from Acts) seriously in this whole debate. They support the decisive argument that is taken from the dating of the collection for Jerusalem. This argument from the collection, strengthened by these chronological data, can begin to have an impact, however, only when it is combined with a perspective that does justice to the differences between the problems at the time of Acts 15 and those at the time of Galatians 2 (see chap. 7.2–7.4).

4. Chronological Synopsis

Tables with dates are a simple aid to get a quick overview of the outline of a biography. The problem is that such tables often do not indicate the degree of certainty or the margin of uncertainty for a given date. This may suggest a greater degree of certainty than is actually possible. The systems by which years were counted in Paul's day differed from our calendar, and these systems differed among themselves as to when the year began (January, spring, fall). It is also not always certain whether or not an author such as Paul or Luke included the first, partial year of a series of years in the count. And finally, the dates for emperors and kings are in turn deductions from historical sources whose interpretation is not always beyond dispute.

In order to show as clearly as possible the degree of certainty of the date(s) of a given event, the following table frequently includes more than one year for an event (all dates are A.D.). The dates in parentheses are less likely, but not impossible. Dates connected by a dash (–) indicate a period during which an event took place. A minus sign (-) before a date indicates that the event cannot have taken place *after* (and probably occurred somewhat earlier than) that date. A plus sign (+) before a date indicates that the event cannot be dated earlier (and perhaps occurred somewhat later) than that date. A slash (/) between two dates indicates that the date is not quite certain. (The slash is used sometimes for both the starting and ending dates of a period of preaching or travel.) The absence of a sign indicates that the date or series of dates may be considered virtually certain.

Paul's year of birth is uncertain; nevertheless, a date has been inserted, based on Philemon 9, in which Paul calls himself an old man (*presbytēs*). In Paul's day it was customary to refer to a person sixty or over as old. The letter to Philemon was written shortly before A.D. 60, which leads us to surmise that Saul was born in Tarsus around the beginning of the Christian Era.[47]

FIG. 6
CHRONOLOGY OF THE LIFE OF THE APOSTLE PAUL

Date (All dates are A.D.)	**History**	**Reference**
ca. 1	Saul born in Tarsus	
33 (-34)	Ascension of Jesus	appendix 2.1
34 -36	Jesus appears to Paul near Damascus	appendix 2.1
35 -early 37	Revelation to preach to the nations	appendix 2.2
35/38–early 37/40	Preaching in Arabia	chapter 3.2
38 -early 40	Visit to Cephas in Jerusalem (Gal. 1:18)	appendix 3.1
38/early 40–42/43	Preaching in Syria and Cilicia (Gal. 1:21)	chapter 3.5 (#7)
-early 43	Collection from Antioch to Jerusalem	appendix 3.3
43/44–46/47	With Barnabas through southern Turkey (so-called first journey)	chapter 4
-47 (early 48)	Apostolic convention	appendix 3.2
(47) 48–49	Via Phrygia and Galatia to Troas and Macedonia	appendix 2.3
late 49	Arrival in Corinth	appendix 2.3

Date	History	Reference
July -August 51	Departure from Corinth	appendix 2.3
fall 51	Consultation in Jerusalem (Gal. 2:1)	appendix 2.3; 3.2
spring 53	Arrival in Ephesus for a stay of more than two years; possible visit to Crete (?)	appendix 2.3
Pentecost 55	Beginning of journey (Macedonia, Corinth, and elsewhere)	chapter 8.1
fall 55–spring 56	Back in Ephesus; beginning of third year there	chapter 8.1
fall 56–spring 57	Departure from Ephesus to Macedonia (as far as Illyricum?)	appendix 2.4
+winter 57	Corinth	appendix 2.4
+58	To Jerusalem	appendix 2.4
+58	Before Felix	appendix 2.4
+58ff.	In prison in Caesarea	chapter 11
+61	Arrival in Rome	appendix 2.4
+61ff.	In prison in Rome	chapter 12
63 -early 68	Died	

Appendix 2

BIBLIOGRAPHY OF THE APOSTLE PAUL

In Part 1 of this book, "Paul the Pioneer," the letters of the apostle are discussed in the context of his life story. This appendix provides a summary overview of the basic information for each letter (addressees, date, sender[s], circumstances of writing, character). The sequence is not that of the canon (where both the length of the letters and their nature played a major role in their order), but the chronological sequence as reconstructed in this book. In cases where an alternative view of the date or the addressees is currently widely accepted, this is mentioned separately.

A preliminary question is whether the letter to the Hebrews should also be counted among Paul's correspondence as was usually done in the early church. This letter does not mention its author, and others besides Paul could easily, and perhaps more appropriately, qualify as the author. Hebrews is therefore left out of consideration in this bibliography.

1 Thessalonians

The earliest letter of Paul still in existence.

Addressees
The Christian community in Thessalonica, capital of Macedonia. Paul had founded this community during his second journey.

Date
Written from Achaia (probably Corinth), not earlier than mid–A.D. 50 and not later than the end of A.D. 50 (about halfway into Paul's stay in Corinth).

Senders
Paul, Silvanus, and Timothy.

Circumstances
Timothy has traveled from Athens to Thessalonica on behalf of Paul and Silas. He has returned with good news about the Christian community he has visited there.

Character
Strengthening a still young community.

Alternatives
Rather widely held is a date that places this letter about half a year earlier (immediately after Paul's arrival in Achaia).

Further Information
Chapter 6.5.

2 Thessalonians

Addressees
The Christian congregation in Thessalonica, capital city of Macedonia. Paul had founded this community during his second missionary journey and had sent it a letter about half a year later (1 Thessalonians).

Date
Written from Achaia (probably Corinth), not long before the departure from Corinth for Ephesus and Jerusalem, in late A.D. 50 or early A.D. 51.

Senders
Paul, Silvanus, and Timothy (the same three who sent 1 Thessalonians).

Circumstances
Renewed occasion for encouragement and warning because of temptations the Christian community faced from its own non-Christian surroundings.

Character
Strengthening of a still young but embattled community.

Alternatives
It is rather widely held that the occasion for this letter should be sought in overwrought eschatological expectations, which made it necessary for Paul to present a more nuanced explanation concerning Jesus' return.

Further Information
Chapter 6.5.

1 Corinthians

Addressees
The community of God in Corinth, the capital city of Achaia.

Date
Written from Ephesus toward the end of the first two years Paul worked there, shortly before his departure on a journey to Macedonia and Corinth (also Crete?) in the spring of A.D. 55.

Senders
Paul and Sosthenes "our brother."

Circumstances
Paul had received information via relatives of Chloe and Stephanas and others. The church in Corinth had sent him a letter with questions. Paul plans to travel to Corinth, not directly but via Macedonia, and now writes this letter.

Character
A letter that, because of Paul's familiarity with details from long-term proximity to Corinth, stands close to the daily life of the Christian

community. Paul had already written at least one letter to them, which no longer exists (see 1 Cor. 5:9–11).

Alternatives
Since the nineteenth century many see this letter as written to a large group of Christians that had in fact been divided and disintegrated into various parties (Peter vs. Paul, etc.).

Further Information
Chapter 9.2.

1 Timothy

Addressees
Timothy, Paul's closest coworker, who stayed behind in Ephesus during the time when Paul made a circular tour from Ephesus (initial destination: Macedonia). Indirectly the letter also addresses the Christian community in Ephesus, whose care had been entrusted to Timothy for the period of Paul's absence.

Date
Written en route (probably from Macedonia) in the summer of A.D. 55.

Sender
Paul.

Circumstances
Concern for the deputy who stayed behind and for the church in Ephesus.

Character
This, like 1 Corinthians, is a letter that stands close to the daily life of the community. Paul instructs his deputy how to carry on the battle for building up the community without their falling victim to syncretism between the new faith and their old pagan way of thinking and acting (or Jewish speculations about genealogies and Haggadah).

Alternatives
In the last two centuries two dates have been defended most strongly. (1) During the period of travel after Paul's (alleged) release from prison in Rome (ca. A.D. 63/64). (2) After Paul's death, in which case

1 Timothy is considered a pseudepigraph produced by the school of the apostle.

Further Information
Chapter 8.3.

Titus

Addressee
Titus, a trusted coworker who stayed in Crete and whom Paul did not take along on his journey. Not until later was Titus allowed to rejoin the apostle (during his planned winter stay in Nicopolis).

Date
During the third missionary journey, probably after the first period of working in Ephesus, which lasted two years, and in any case in the summer or fall of A.D. 55, 56, or 57.

Sender
Paul.

Circumstances
Titus has been sent or left behind for missionary work on Crete. He was instructed to appoint elders everywhere. Since this has not been done, Paul does not yet recall him but leaves him at his post.

Character
The letter gives insight into the kinds of topics that were already discussed immediately after the founding of the Christian communities.

Alternatives
In the last two centuries two dates have been defended most strongly. (1) During the period of travel after Paul's (alleged) release from prison in Rome (ca. A.D. 63/64). (2) After Paul's death, in which case 1 Timothy is considered a pseudepigraph produced by the school of the apostle. (These are the same alternatives as those suggested for 1 Timothy.)

Further Information
Chapter 9.1.

2 Corinthians

Addressees

The congregation of God in Corinth, and all the saints in Achaia (the province of which Corinth was the capital).

Date

Written from Macedonia, where Paul is now for at least the second time during the third missionary journey. The first time he was there during the interim visit from Ephesus (see 1 Timothy). He is here this second time after having left Ephesus permanently, and he visits the congregation in this region for the last time (perhaps he even traveled on to Illyricum). Around the middle of A.D. 57 or a year later.

Senders

Paul and Timothy.

Circumstances

By way of clarification an overview of the previous contacts between Paul and Corinth will be helpful:

- Mid–A.D. 55: Paul visits Corinth during his great interim journey, but the visit does not go as Paul had hoped it would, and in this letter we still hear echoes of this disappointment. He had left Corinth earlier than planned, but he promised to return soon.
- Fall A.D. 56/spring A.D. 57: The reports from Corinth continue to be unfavorable. Paul decides to change his itinerary for the final farewell journey. He sends a so-called tearful letter (which is lost; see 2 Cor. 2:2–4) and has it delivered by his trusted coworker Titus (see 2 Cor. 7).
- A.D. 57: Titus arrives in Macedonia with better news. A relieved Paul writes 2 Corinthians.

Character

Paul's person had become the focus of controversy, and the gospel of grace was at stake. Thus 2 Corinthians becomes in effect a letter that is almost entirely devoted to the person of the preacher of the gospel.

Alternatives

The seemingly abrupt transition from a quiet tone to the fiercely emotional section in chapters 10–13 has led many to detach this last part from the letter and to consider it the so-called tearful letter.

Further Information
Chapter 9.3.

Galatians

Addressees
The Christian congregations in the region of Galatia (central Turkey) that were visited by Paul on the second and third journeys.

Date
Written, after the second visit, from an unknown location somewhere on the Ephesus-Macedonia-Corinth circuit. During the third journey, probably toward the end, ca. A.D. 57/58.

Senders
Paul and all the brothers who are with him (at the end of the third journey).

Circumstances
Paul has heard that an acute danger has developed and writes with deep concern. Christians in the Galatian churches have accepted a measure of Judaization for the sake of the Jewish Christians who are anxious to avoid persecution because of their contacts with Gentiles.

Character
This, like Romans, is a letter with many foundational reflections on the gospel. Romans, in a somewhat less emotional manner, describes the fundamental relationship between the Christian church and unbelieving Israel. Galatians is more emotional because here, under the guise of a pragmatic "solution," the very nature of the divine gospel threatens to erode in the praxis of the church.

Alternatives
The so-called South Galatian hypothesis views the letter as addressed to the churches in southern Turkey, located not in Galatia proper but in the Roman province called Galatia. If this hypothesis is carried to its logical conclusion, the letter must be dated around A.D. 47 (before the apostolic council).

Further Information
Chapter 7 and appendix 1, sections 3.2 and 3.3.

Romans

Addressees

Those who are called to be saints in Rome. The Christians mentioned in Romans 16:1–16 were probably the active cells in the spread of the gospel among the Gentile inhabitants in Rome. There is then an indirect connection with the apostle Paul, whose helpers and friends already work in Rome.

Date

Written from Corinth (Cenchrea?) or Macedonia at the end of the third journey, when Paul sets out for Jerusalem with the collection, planning to go from there via Rome to Spain (Rom. 15:14–33). End of A.D. 57 or beginning of A.D. 58.

Sender

Paul.

Circumstances

Paul had wanted to bring the gospel to Rome himself (Rom. 1:13–15), and now that it has already arrived he looks for mutual encouragement (Rom. 1:8–12). His letter lays the groundwork for this, and Paul uses the occasion to help prepare this "offering of the Gentiles" in Rome for God (Rom. 15:14–19).

Character

Because Paul knew the circumstances of the congregation in Rome only second-hand, the letter is less personal. It looks more like a general exposition of his gospel in which he may be using material he had used before on various occasions in his disputations with the Jews (the discursive style in chapters 2–3) or in catechetical sessions with Christians (the question-and-answer style in chapters 9–11). But the entire exposition is determined by the fact that the Christian community in Rome had not come into being, via a split, "out of" the synagogue, but had grown more or less "side by side" with the synagogue in a city where there were many Jews.

Alternatives

The unusual character of Romans 16 has led some to view this chapter as having been addressed to Ephesus or to view the whole book as a general circular letter of which we still have the "Rome edition" of chapters 1–15, whereas chapter 16 is the afterword to Ephesus.

Further Information
Chapter 10 and chapter 13.1.

Colossians

Addressees
Addressed to the saints and believing brothers in Colosse, a city in Phrygia. Paul visited this region on the second and third missionary journeys. It is assumed that not Paul, but Epaphras at a later date, brought the gospel to the Hierapolis-Laodicea-Colosse region, although it is open to question whether this follows of necessity from 1:4, 7; 2:1; 4:13.

Date
Written from prison in Caesarea, around A.D. 59.

Senders
Paul and Timothy.

Circumstances
Paul has received reports via Epaphras. A development in the direction of (Greek/Jewish?) syncretism threatens. Paul warns and teaches from a distance.

There are connections with the letter to Philemon, which was sent at the same time (Col. 4:9, 17; cf. Philemon 2, 11–12).

Character
Because the (Greek/Jewish?) syncretism devoted itself to cosmic speculations, known both from Greek syncretism (magic/astrology) and from Jewish esoteric circles (apocalyptic), Paul emphasizes the cosmic significance of Christ and its consequences for faith and life. In a letter to Ephesus he will write similarly about Christ as the Head of his church.

Alternatives
Written from prison in Rome rather than in Caesarea; according to others during an earlier imprisonment in Ephesus.

Further Information
Chapter 11.6.

Philemon

Addressees

Addressed to the beloved Philemon, Apphia "our sister," Archippus "our fellow soldier," and to the church in their house, with a special message for the master of the house. Philemon belongs to the congregation in Colosse (Col. 4:9, 17).

Date

See under Colossians (the letters were sent at the same time).

Senders

Paul and Timothy.

Circumstances

Onesimus, Philemon's slave, ran away and visited Paul. He came to repentance during this visit and became a useful helper. Paul now sends him back with the request that Philemon accept him again with kindness and with the silent suggestion that he be released for service in the gospel as a free man.

Character

A private letter that shows how private life also can be sanctified by Christian love and humor (this letter shows something of the wit and humor of the apostle).

Alternatives

See under Colossians.

Further Information

Chapter 11.7.

Philippians

Addressees

Addressed to the saints in Christ Jesus who are in Philippi (together with their overseers and deacons). Philippi in Macedonia is a place where many Roman citizens lived (veterans); a colonia (*politeuma*; cf. the allusion in Phil. 3:20). Paul brought the gospel here on his second journey (after coming over from Troas).

Date
Written from prison, at the end of the period of imprisonment in Caesarea, A.D. 59–60.

Senders
Paul and Timothy.

Circumstances
Epaphroditus, who had been sent by the congregation in Philippi to Paul with material support, helped the apostle, became very ill, then regained his health, and now returns to Philippi, carrying a letter.

Character
An emotional appeal, from life-threatening captivity, that the Philippians persevere in the faith without letting themselves be impressed by the Jews or frightened by unbelieving fellow-citizens.

Alternatives
See under Colossians.

Further Information
Chapter 11.6.

Ephesians

Addressees
Addressed to the saints and believers in Christ Jesus who are in Ephesus, the place in Asia where Paul spent three full years during his third missionary journey.

Date
Written from captivity in Rome, in a later period of that captivity: A.D. 63–64.

Sender
Paul.

Circumstances
Tychicus is sent to Ephesus (Eph. 6:21–22). It seems plausible that the general and impersonal nature of the letter (written to a community Paul knew very well) flows from the circumstance that many in Asia had turned away from Paul (2 Tim. 1:15).

Character
Paul wants to arm the community (Eph. 6:10–20) in the battle against the temptation as Christians to once again start living a worldly life (Eph. 4:17–6:9), and for this reason points to the foundations of the church. The letter gets the (unintended) opportunity to function as the ecclesiastical testament of the apostle. Where the cosmic significance of Christ was central in the epistle to the Colossians, here the central thought is that Christ is the Head of his church.

Alternatives
Some consider the letter spurious. Others view it as a circular letter.

Further Information
Chapter 14.4.

2 Timothy

Addressee
Timothy, who is somewhere away from Rome. He probably is coming from the east (2 Tim. 4:13) to Rome (4:9) for the winter (4:21). Is he working in the regions of Pontus and Cappadocia (cf. 1 Peter 1:1; 2 Peter 3:15–16)?

Date
Written from captivity in Rome, facing the prospect of death, around A.D. 63/64. A later date is not likely because by then the apostle would have taken into consideration that Rome had become too dangerous for his coworker because of the persecution of Christians by Emperor Nero.

Sender
Paul.

Circumstances
The coworkers have left for different locations (4:10–12) or are absent (4:20). Of the known coworkers only Luke is with Paul (4:11). And there are Paul's new friends in Rome (4:21b).

Character
Paul's last letter that we have is a spiritual testament for Timothy. Its theme is to follow Paul's example of perseverance in the spreading of the gospel against the pressure of false doctrine and oppression.

Alternatives

Some consider this letter to be spurious.

Further Information

Chapter 13.4.

Fig. 7
Chronology of the Letters of the Apostle Paul

Date (A.D.)	Historical Setting	Letter
33 (-34)	Ascension of Jesus	
34 -36	Jesus appears to Paul near Damascus	
35 -early 37	Revelation to preach to the nations	
35/38–early 37/40	Preaching in Arabia	
38 -early 40	Visit to Cephas in Jerusalem (Gal. 1:18)	
38/early 40–42/43	Preaching in Syria and Cilicia (Gal. 1:21)	
-early 43	Collection from Antioch to Jerusalem	
43/44–46/47	With Barnabas through southern Turkey (so-called first journey)	
-47 (early 48)	Apostolic convention	
(47) 48–49	Via Phrygia and Galatia to Troas and Macodonia	
late 49	Arrival in Corinth	
mid -late 50		1 Thessalonians
late 50 -early 51		2 Thessalonians
July -August 51	Departure from Corinth	
fall 51	Consultation in Jerusalem (Gal. 2:1)	
spring 53	Arrival in Ephesus for a stay of more than two years	
spring 55		1 Corinthians
Pentecost 55	Beginning of journey (to, among others, Macedonia, Corinth; perhaps Crete)	
summer/fall 55		1 Timothy
fall 55 (?)		Titus
fall 55–spring 56	Back in Ephesus; beginning of third year there	
fall 56–spring 57	Departure from Ephesus for Macedonia (as far as Illyricum?)	

Date (A.D.)	Historical Setting	Letter
57		2 Corinthians
57/58		Galatians
+winter 57	Corinth	Romans
+58	To Jerusalem	
+58	Before Felix	
+58ff.	In prison in Caesarea	Colossians, Philemon, Philippians
+61	Arrival in Rome	
+61ff.	In prison in Rome	Ephesians 2 Timothy
63 -early 68	Died	

Appendix 3

JEWISH RELIGION AND THE LAW

What was the place of the law in the religion and spirituality of Judaism? The answers to this question vary. Traditionally the idea is that the law did in fact function as the way to salvation: by living in accordance with the law one earned God's salvation. It is, then, against this doctrine of merit that Paul's letters agitate. But in newer publications on Judaism this traditional vision has come under attack. God's election of Israel is thought to be the basis of salvation in Judaism. Life in accordance with the law, then, is the manner in which believers live in the light. Fulfilling the demands of the law has no place in soteriology but only in ethics. It is no longer possible to read Paul's letters against the background of a Judaism that is supposed to have viewed the works of the law as the means to salvation.

Because the perspective from which Paul is viewed is to a large extent determined by one's answer to the question of the place of the law in the Jewish religion, it will be useful to devote a short appendix to it. One of the more recent studies on the topic is *Tora und Leben* by Friedrich Avemarie (1996).[1] Avemarie presents a summary of earlier publications that dealt with the place of merit in Judaism[2] and concludes that these studies are often hindered by a priori ideas that the authors brought to their studies.[3] Avemarie correctly argues that the rabbinic data should be allowed to speak for themselves. In line with this he presents a meticulous discussion of many citations from the older Jewish sources.

Avemarie's conclusions are twofold. On the one hand he is in line with the trend of many recent studies: Judaism cannot be characterized one-sidedly as legalistic.[4] On the other hand, Avemarie is of the opinion that within Judaism the doing of good works was accorded a measure of merit. It would be distorting to lose sight of this aspect when emphasizing the other aspects of Judaism (election, grace, faith).[5] This second conclusion is important for our perspective on Paul: if Avemarie is correct, may we once again read Paul's letters as a reaction against the too-dominant place of merit in Jewish soteriology?

Because of the importance of this topic for the study of Paul, we will in section 1 discuss briefly a few passages from the rabbinic literature that are of relevance. Section 2 looks at the significance of the pseudepigraphical book of 4 Ezra for an understanding of the nature of Jewish soteriology. Section 3 looks at what Josephus at the end of the first century writes about the significance of the law for the Jews. Finally, in section 4, the results of the discussion are briefly compared with the non-Pauline portions of the New Testament.

1. More Law, More Merit!

There are a few rabbinic pronouncements that create the impression that the law had to be observed in order to gain merit. These involve pronouncements that speak of an increase in merit when the law increases. Thus we read:[6]

> R. Hananiah b. Aqashia says, "The Holy One, blessed be he, wanted to give merit to Israel. Therefore he gave them abundant Torah and numerous commandments, as it is said, It pleased the Lord for his righteousness' sake to magnify the Torah and give honour to it (Is. 42:21)." (M. Makkot 3.16)

Avemarie resists Moore's idea[7] that this passage does not speak of reward for specific meritorious deeds, but speaks only about the benefits of the multifaceted nature of the law in general. Even if Moore were correct, it nevertheless remains true, according to Avemarie, that this passage teaches that the multifaceted law provides more merit and is thus a means to earn merit before God.

The quote we are considering comes from the end of the tractate Makkot, a somber tractate that deals with punishment. In this conclusion the positive side of the law is pointed out: it is not in the first place a penal code, but rather (for the righteous) a law that shows how to earn God's favor by means of earning merit.[8] But the question this raises—and Avemarie does not address—is what the nature of this merit is. The tractate here deals with the increasing meritoriousness of the nation. But this meritoriousness should not be understood soteriologically, as if individual members of the nation owed their right to exist before God to the law. At issue is rather the quality the nation of Israel shall exhibit among the nations by means of living according to the law. An example of this is King Solomon. Even the queen of Sheba exclaims, "Because of the LORD's eternal love for Israel, he has made you king, to maintain justice and righteousness" (1 Kings 10:9).

It is not accidental that the Mishna here quotes Isaiah 42:21: "It pleased the LORD for the sake of his righteousness to make his law great and glorious." According to this word of Isaiah the law is not given for the sake of the righteousness of people, but for the sake of the Lord's own righteousness. The rabbis also make a connection between this verse and the fact that Abraham was not circumcised until he was ninety-nine years old, in order that this might create room for proselytes who also were circumcised when they were older.[9] The greatness of the law benefits Israel's welfare, the welfare of the nations, and the expansion of the people of God!

The significance of Israel in this world increases because the nation has many good laws. More law leads to more merit, more blessing, and a greater future on this earth. The discussion of this Mishna passage in the Talmud also points in this direction. First is explained how the many commandments are summarized by Amos in a single commandment: "Seek me and live" (5:4). Then follow several citations from Rabbi Akiba (second century A.D.) in which he encourages Jews who mourn the destruction of the temple and the prosperity of their enemies: if the ungodly fare so well, how well will God's people fare, and if the prophecy of the destruction of the temple was fulfilled, how surely then will also the promise of restoration be fulfilled! These words of Akiba illustrate the blessing of the abundance of Torah. Because the Torah contains many pronouncements, there is not only sorrow but also hope! It is worth staying with the Torah, even though the Romans seem to be winning the world.

A comparable Mishna text is found in the familiar collection of sayings of the fathers (*'Avot* 2.7):

> (A) Lots of meat, lots of worms; lots of property, lots of worries; lots of women, lots of witchcraft; lots of slave girls, lots of lust; lots of slave boys, lots of robbery.
>
> Lots of Torah, lots of life [lots of discipleship, lots of wisdom; lots of counsel, lots of understanding; lots of righteousness, lots of peace].
>
> (B) [If] one has gotten a good name, he has gotten it for himself.
>
> [If] he has gotten teachings of the Torah, he has gotten himself life eternal.

According to Avemarie, (A) involves a crescendo, from little to much and from nonliving to living. At the end (Avemarie omits the rest of the sentence in square brackets) "the Torah" refers to the studied law (more study of the Torah brings more life). (B) then complements this with an eye to the world to come. Here again the studied law is in view, which is why the verb "get" can be used.[10]

The series of five negative examples in (A), however, is not primarily a series that leads from the lesser to the greater. It is rather (with the exception of the sixth example) a series that shows how the increase in something can turn into a disadvantage. All the things listed are good things (meat, property, women, slave girls, slave boys), but their increase will usually lead to an increase in misfortune (worms, worries, witchcraft, lust, robbery). There is, however, one exception to this cycle: the more Torah, the more life. The law of God is the only thing here on earth that does not contain the seed of destruction. This direction of the Mishna is also apparent in the phrases that in various manuscripts are added after the words "lots of Torah, lots of life." Avemarie does not include these additional phrases in his quotation,[11] but they elaborate the idea that the law has a beneficial effect: "lots of discipleship, lots of wisdom; lots of counsel, lots of understanding; lots of righteousness, lots of peace."

The unexpected turn after a negative series is an invitation to use a second, positive series by way of medicine against the preceding misfortune. The Torah of God goes against the negative, downward flow. Where the Torah is observed, immorality, theft, sorrow, and suffering decrease. Property, slave girls, women, and slave boys are blessed: this is a law that leads *to life*! Even the negative sequence "more meat, more worms" is halted—on this earth by means of the dietary laws and the laws on ceremonial cleanness, and in the world to come through the promise that the righteous shall see no destruction (the worms in the grave are not the end for the believers).

It is therefore doubtful that (B) deals with the studied law and its benefits for eternal life. There is a parallelism between "a good name" and "teachings of the Torah." Both are acquired. In the first case an individual manages to gain other people's recognition by means of his or her own deeds. In the other case he or she is known as someone who "is (has become) a Jew." One is successful for oneself, but one is an Israelite for eternity![12]

This saying does not deal with the manner in which one becomes a Jew and acquires the words of the Torah. The acquisition of the words of the Torah could never be a merit; rather, this "property" is received through election, birth, faith. But once one lives under the law, one has as a (reviled) Jew an advantage over the (successful) Gentile, since one has joined the people of the Lord and may be assured of his favor and of life in the world to come.[13] This Mishna text encourages people who under the name "Jew" are often persecuted whereas the Gentiles prosper under their own successful, important names.

Conclusion: When the rabbis speak of "more law, more merit," they do not do so in a soteriological framework. Rather, they address the earthly reality in which life in accordance with the law is healthy, restoring, and blessed. The more the better! This life under the law (within Israel) offers as such (not through merit) perspective on eternal life. The idea of eternal life as an extension of life under the law is an expansion of the promise that there is life under the law. Because this promise is not always fulfilled in this earthly life, there must be more than only this mortal life on earth.[14] It is typical of Avemarie's Protestant outlook that in his own formulation he uses exactly the reverse order: "not only eternal life but also life in this world."[15] Living in accordance with the commandments is worth the effort! But that does not at all imply that eternal salvation can be earned by keeping a series of commandments. There is no life outside the Torah of the Creator, but this is very different from saying that we owe this life to living according to the Torah.

2. Israel's Downfall through Its Own Failing

It is not easy to find traces of a legalistic soteriology in the literature from the intertestamental period. This is remarkable. If Paul spoke out against a Judaism that focused on earning salvation through good works, we should be able to find proofs for this view precisely in the intertestamental literature. But these proofs are absent. The supporting material is in fact limited to quotations from the apocalyptic book 4 Ezra. This book from the end of the first century A.D. is believed to reflect a legalistic soteriology and is, according to some, representative of first-century Judaism. In 4 Ezra we find many citations that prove that Israel's demise was due to its own failing. The counterpart to this thesis is, then, that Israel should have earned its preservation by not falling short in good works.

E. P. Sanders has defended the thesis that 4 Ezra was an exception to then-current Judaism, but this idea is controversial.[16] At this point we can leave the question undecided as to whether 4 Ezra is representative of contemporary Judaism. More important is the question whether 4 Ezra proves the existence of a (whether or not widely held) doctrine of merit in Judaism.

This impression of a legalistic soteriology of merit in 4 Ezra ignores the context in which this book is presented. It is a (fictional) work, written from the context of the exile that is supposed to still continue during Ezra's time (!). The book views sin as an aversion to God. At issue is the continued existence of Israel as the people of the Most High God. Because the people distance themselves from this God, the situation is hopeless. The presumed historical context of the book can be compared with the situation in the days of Elijah, when the people of the ten tribes followed Baal and were in fact no longer God's people at that time.[17] The theme that runs through 4 Ezra is what will happen to the world when there is no longer an Israel. The book's underlying perspective is not individual soteriology but rather cosmic soteriology.

1. The commandments are kept because of faith in God as the Creator and Redeemer. And the failure to obey the law is due to forgetting the one God.[18] Few people are saved; the many who perish are all people who did not want to have anything to do with the Lord and his commandments.[19] In 7:116–31 we find the famous reproach to Adam ("O Adam, what have you done?"). But here also salvation is not the result of the performance of an adequate number of good works, and perishing is the result of lack of respect for the Creator and a rejection of the commandment to love him and believe in him.[20] The nation of Israel owes its existence to the election of Abraham. The exodus from Egypt was the salvation of the people as a whole—it preceded the giving of the commandments.[21]

2. When Israel ceases to believe in one God and descends into idolatry and sin, the name of God is lost among the nations. At issue is the salvation of the nation (as is clearly indicated in 8:4–36): Why can those who fail to serve God not be accepted for the sake of those who are faithful? Why would God not be merciful to the nation (8:45)? This mercy then involves overlooking unbelief in a nation where there is also faith. In this connection we read that "the righteous . . . shall receive their reward in consequence of their own deeds" (8:33).[22] The accent falls on the fact that the individual must him- or herself have faith, and that the faith of others cannot be imputed to unbelievers.

3. Life in accordance with the law proves faith in God. His salvific acts come first, and the elect of Israel then follow these acts in faith and works. "It shall be that all who will be saved and will be able to escape on account of their works, or on account of the faith by which

they have believed, will survive the dangers that have been predicted, and will see my salvation in my land and within my borders, which I have sanctified for myself from the beginning" (9:7–8). This promise is tied to perseverance in faith. It is anachronistic to read a later contrast between "faith and law" back into 4 Ezra.

Conclusion: The book of 4 Ezra does not deal with the question to what extent believers establish credit with God by means of doing the works of the law, but rather with the question of what is left in this world without faith in the God of Israel. The work consists in what Paul calls "the obedience of faith" (in contrast to the disobedience of the idolaters). Without this work (faith in God and love for the law of this God) Israel will not remain and God's name will be lost among the nations. The problem in 4 Ezra is not how believers earn eternal salvation but how they lose it![23]

3. Josephus on the Significance of the Law for the Jews

At the end of the first century A.D., Josephus wrote a small book in which he combats the slander against the Jews and describes what the significance of the law is for this nation. This work later came to be called *Contra Apionem*, but it is in fact a general treatise against the Greeks, of which the refutation of Apion is only a part.[24]

When Josephus describes the significance of the law, he addresses a non-Jewish audience, which has undoubtedly some influence on the way he states things. But it is striking that he nowhere draws a parallel between the obligations of the Jewish law and the religious duties of the Greeks (offerings, prayers). Rather, he compares the Jewish law with the ethics of the Gentiles: their civil law, their social organization, and their personal lives.[25]

> From this, I think, it will be apparent that we possess a code excellently designed to promote piety, friendly relations with each other, and humanity toward the world at large, besides justice, hardihood, and contempt of death. (2.146)

Josephus coins the term "theocracy" for Israel (2.165). Moses placed control of all things with God:

> To Him he persuaded all to look, as the author of all blessings, both those which are common to all mankind, and those which they had won for themselves by prayer in the crises of their history. (2.166)

The heart of the law is that its aim is to develop piety and reverence toward God (2.170–71, 181):

> [R]eligion is the end and aim of the training of the entire community, the priests are entrusted with the special charge of it, and the whole administration of the state resembles some sacred ceremony. (2.188)

God-fearing, mild, and humane behavior is stimulated by means of punishments and reward. If one is willing, for the sake of the law, to give up his or her life, then life in accordance with the law is not a dead-end road. For God has promised those who keep his laws that they will be born anew and will partake of a better life (2.218). The promise of a future life serves to increase the commitment to the laws that have been given to teach reverence toward God and to make society humane. Josephus concludes his overview as follows:

> I would therefore boldly maintain that we have introduced to the rest of the world a very large number of very beautiful ideas. What greater beauty than inviolable piety? What higher justice than obedience to the laws? What more beneficial than to be in harmony with one another, to be a prey neither to disunion in adversity, nor to arrogance and faction in prosperity; in war to despise death, in peace to devote oneself to crafts or agriculture; and to be convinced that everything in the whole universe is under the eye and direction of God? (2.293–94)

This testimony of the Jew Josephus about the law makes it clear that the Jews in the first century A.D. did not describe their law in soteriological terms (as a means to being accepted by the deity) but in ethical terms (as a means of honoring God in all things).

4. New Testament Writings and Judaism

What impression of Judaism do we get from the New Testament writings? We exclude Paul's letters here, both because their interpretation is at issue here and because his standpoint with respect to the law has already been discussed at length in chapter 17.

4.1 The Gospels

In the Gospels Jesus does not appear primarily as someone who is in active opposition to the existing religion. He preaches the kingdom of heaven, and he is not actively opposed to the teachers of the law and the Pharisees. It is only when these groups turn against him that a conflict situation develops. The core of the conflict is not what religion should be like, but who Jesus is. Even at the end of his earthly ministry, Jesus tells the people to obey the teachers of the law and the Pharisees and to "do everything they tell you" (Matt. 23:2–3). What Jesus criticizes is what these leaders actually do. They sometimes use ethics to their own advantage (Matt. 15:1–9); and whatever else they may do, they misuse their traditions to slander and persecute the Son of God. This is how their good works become in fact stumbling blocks (Matt. 23). The conflict is ultimately not a difference of opinion about religion. Rather, these spiritual leaders in the final analysis stumble over their human feelings of pride and self-confidence (Matt. 9:13; 23:28; Luke 18:9). Because of their self-confidence they cannot imagine how they as healthy people would have to be healed by a simple Galilean (Matt. 9:11–13; 23:28).

The Gospels are often read from the perspective of a negative prejudice against the Pharisees. But a careful analysis of the data about the Pharisees in Josephus and in Paul's letters makes it clear that this party as such was the best party in Israel, humane, zealous for the faith in the one God, and careful in maintaining a lifestyle that suited this faith.[26] Of course, this group also had members who were not a credit to their party, and belonging to this party could lead to spiritual deformation (pride). But this is not sufficient reason for not taking Paul seriously when even as a Christian he still takes pride in and speaks positively about the fact that he was and is a Pharisee (Phil. 3:6; Acts 23:6; 26:5).

4.2 Acts

In Acts we read how the Jews, when the gospel of the Crucified One is preached to them, sometimes close themselves off as if this gospel could endanger their nation and their law (Acts 17:13–15; 21:21). But the apostles do not attack the Jews for holding to a soteriological legalism, but rather for rejecting God's Messiah. Their battle is not against the Jewish religion of those days as such (see Acts 21:23–24; 24:11–18).

Those Pharisees who became Christians still keep the law (Acts 21:20); only Gentile Christians are not obligated to do so (Acts 15:1, 28–29). Moreover, Paul has no trouble bringing a Nazirite offering to avoid the impression that he teaches defection from the law to the Jews in the Diaspora (Acts 21:26).

4.3 The Epistles and the Book of Revelation

In the epistles of John, Peter, James, and Jude we find no criticism of the Jewish religion as such. In Revelation we do find a sharp contrast with the synagogue (Rev. 2:9; 3:9), but this contrast reflects the fact that the Jews in the synagogue reject the love of Jesus Christ (Rev. 3:9–12). It is not the law that separates; rather, it is the gospel that is in dispute.

5. Conclusion

In our Christian Era there are two (since Muhammad three) forms of worship of the one Creator-God: Judaism and Christianity (and later also Islam). Because there are two (three) ways in which the One God is worshiped, there is a mutual questioning as to the specific way in which one may belong to God. We have, respectively, the Halakah (the Jewish way of life), faith (in God and his Son through the Spirit), and the Five Pillars (the unifying pattern in Islam). Any one of these three ways is rejected by the other two. They take on the function of distinctive criteria, as if Christianity does not know about living in accordance with a law, or Judaism knows nothing of faith, or as if Islam has only an ahistorical conception of God. But these distorted images of the other two religions do not do justice to their reality. They not only hinder us in our descriptions of the other religions, but also in the understanding of our own.

For Judaism we must go back to the time of Israel before the Christian Era. Back then there was only one nation that believed in one God. This nation coincided with the religion of monotheism. There was no alternative (at most the related Samaritans, who as separatists were hated most by the Jews). One was either under the law, or one was a Gentile. Whoever despised the law, despised the one God.

It is therefore impossible to view the Halakah within Israel as the reason for salvation. The Halakah is the yoke under which one places one's shoulders by way of confessing that one believes in the God of this law (Israel's God); it is the yoke with which one is harnessed for faith in the one God.

When there is a difference within Israel in degrees of obedience, it involves the greater reward that is intrinsic to a good life (obedience leads to a blessed life), and it involves the intensity of faith (with heart and soul). Over against this gain stands, not a being lost through too few good works, but only a being lost through unbelief and disdain for the law (by living with the nations).

Therefore there are many formulations for people who do not have part in the world to come. And there are many benedictions concerning Israel under the law. But what is conspicuously absent are statements about Israelites who bear the yoke of the law but have too low a percentage of good works.[27] This shows that good works do not occupy a decisive place in the soteriology.[28]

NOTES

Introduction

1. Rudolf Hoppe ("Aufgabenstellung und Konzeption einer 'Einleitung in das Neue Testament': Eine Standortbestimmung, *Biblische Zeitschrift* 43 [1999]: 204–11) is of the opinion that the field of New Testament introduction must pay more attention to the connections between the literature of the New Testament and first-century non-Christian literature. This relationship is indeed of importance. *Literary* connections, however, play a role especially in the *exegesis* of the content of the various documents. The field of New Testament *introduction*, on the other hand, must focus primarily on the historical context in which the documents originated.

Chapter 1: Gone from Tarsus

1. Jerome Murphy-O'Connor, *Paul: A Critical Life* (Oxford: Clarendon Press, 1996), 33–35; Sherman E. Johnson, *Paul the Apostle and His Cities* (Wilmington, Del.: Michael Glazier, 1987), 25–43; F. F. Bruce, *Paul: Apostle of the Heart Set Free* (Grand Rapids: Eerdmans, 1977; U.K. title, *Paul: Apostle of the Free Spirit*), 33–36.

2. Thus, for example, C. J. den Heyer, *Paul: A Man of Two Worlds* (Harrisburg: Trinity Press International, 2000), 40.

3. Van Unnik appeals to Greek usage, which distinguishes between the terms *anatethrammenos* and *pepaideumenos* as meaning respectively "parental upbringing" and "[school] education." He thus feels that the phrase "at the feet of Gamaliel" cannot be connected with *anatethrammenos*, and the translation should be "I am a Jewish man, (a) born in Tarsus in Cilicia; (b) brought up (by my parents) in *this* city; (c) carefully schooled in the law of the fathers at the feet of Gamaliel" (W. C. van Unnik, *Tarsus or Jerusalem: The City of Paul's Youth* [London: Epworth Press, 1962; Dutch ed., 1952]). Although his view received criticism, it is still finding much acceptance. See Klaus Haacker, *Paulus: Der Werdegang eines Apostels* (Stuttgart: Verlag Katholisches Bibelwerk, 1997), 50–53. A balanced, critical discussion is presented by Andrie B. Du Toit, "A Tale of Two Cities: 'Tarsus or Jerusalem' Revisited" (*New Testament Studies* 46 [2000]: 375–402).

4. Martin Hengel points this out in *The Pre-Christian Paul* (London: SCM Press, 1991), 18–39, 54–62. See also Seyoon Kim, *The Origin of Paul's Gospel* (Tübingen: Mohr, 1981), 36–39.

5. See also Jürgen Becker, *Paul: Apostle to the Gentiles* (Louisville: Westminster/John Knox, 1993), 53–59; Joachim Gnilka, *Paulus von Tarsus: Apostel und Zeuge* (Freiburg: Herder, 1996), 27–31.

6. See Richard Wallace and Wynne Williams, *The Three Worlds of Paul of Tarsus* (London and New York: Routledge, 1998), 3–92.

7. See also Brad H. Young, *Paul the Jewish Theologian: A Pharisee among Christians, Jews, and Gentiles* (Peabody, Mass.: Hendrickson, 1997), 12–16.

8. Most manuscripts read *en tōi ethnei mou, en Hierosolymois* (within my people/among my people, in Jerusalem); some manuscripts read *en tōi ethnei mou en te Hierosolymois* (among my people *and* in Jerusalem).

9. Ben Witherington III (*The Paul Quest: The Renewed Search for the Jew of Tarsus* [Downers Grove, Ill.: InterVarsity, 1998], 72) draws attention to the fact that Paul never uses the triple name he must have had as a Roman citizen (*praenomen, nomen, cognomen*; cf. Gaius Julius Caesar).

10. See Karl-Wilhelm Niebuhr, *Heidenapostel aus Israel: Die jüdische Identität des Paulus nach ihrer Darstellung in seinen Briefen* (Tübingen: Mohr, 1992), for a discussion of the manner in which Paul in his letters speaks of his Jewish identity.

11. His descent from the tribe of Benjamin had great significance for Saul. See Haacker, *Paulus*, 18–21.

12. Most manuscripts read *huios Pharisaiou* ("son of a Pharisee [father]") in Acts 23:6. Some manuscripts, however, have a plural: *huios Pharisaiōn* ("son or member of the [sect of the] Pharisees"). But the latter reading would mean that Paul says the same thing twice, since he had already stated that he was "a Pharisee."

The plural reading has led to a discussion as to whether we can speak of a Diaspora Pharisaism (Becker, *Paul*, 42–53) or whether Pharisaism remained confined to Palestine, in which case we would have to accept that "Luke's claim that Paul was a 'son of Pharisees' (Acts 23:6) must be dismissed as a rhetorical flourish without historical value" (Murphy-O'Connor, *Paul*, 56–59).

However, the reading of the majority of the manuscripts (*son of a Pharisee*) makes this discussion superfluous: it is always possible that an individual Pharisee from Jerusalem (with his convictions) moved out into the Diaspora.

13. Haacker (*Paulus*, 26) describes Paul's family as prosperous but believes that his family suffered economic reverses, so that Paul later had to learn a trade. Justin J. Meggitt (*Paul, Poverty and Survival* [Edinburgh: Clark, 1998], 75–96) offers many arguments against the rather widely held notion that the family's social status, reflected in their citizenships, would also have meant that Paul enjoyed a prosperous economic environment in his youth.

Chapter 2: From Persecutor to Deserter

1. Karl-Wilhelm Niebuhr writes about a general "calling into question of the Torah" (*Heidenapostel aus Israel: Die jüdische Identität des Paulus nach ihrer Darstellung in seinen Briefen* [Tübingen: Mohr, 1992], 10).

2. Jerome Murphy-O'Connor (*Paul: A Critical Life* [Oxford: Clarendon Press, 1996], 62–65) suspects that Saul's wife and children perished in a catastrophe (earthquake, fire, epidemic?). As a religious person he could not direct his anger at God. His suppressed emotions (he never writes about his wife or children!) then found an outlet in his aggression against the Christians in Jerusalem!

3. C. J. den Heyer (*Paul: A Man of Two Worlds* [London: SCM Press, 2000], 56–60) follows Heinrich Kraft (*Die Entstehung des Christentums* [Darmstadt: Wissenschaftliche Buchgesellschaft, 1981], 240) in the opinion that the book of Acts as well as Paul himself grossly exaggerate his part in the persecution. Den Heyer judges this rather mildly: "Paul 'may be forgiven' " (p. 59). But it is questionable whether Paul would have appreciated mildness on the part of those who do not take him seriously. In Galatians 1, where he specifically writes about his role as persecutor, he says, "I assure you before God that what I am writing you is no lie" (Gal. 1:20).

4. There is no reason whatsoever to draw from the remark that the apostles escaped this persecution the conclusion that the persecution was aimed at one group within the Christian communities, namely, the group that distanced itself most from the observance of the law. This group, according to many, would then be the Greek-speaking Christians around Stephen (Kraft, *Die Entstehung des Christentums*; Martin Hengel with Ronald Deines, *The Pre-Christian Paul*, trans. John Bowden [London: SCM Press, 1991]; den Heyer, *Paul: A Man of Two Worlds* [London: SCM Press, 2000], 51–56). This hypothesis is presented in detail by Heinz-Werner Neudorfer, *Der Stephanuskreis in der Forschungsgeschichte seit F. C. Baur* (Giessen: Brunnen Verlag, 1983). However, it is not supported by the data in Paul's letters and is in conflict with the data in Acts.

5. See J. Duncan M. Derret, "Cursing Jesus (1 Cor XII.3): The Jews as Religious Persecutors," *New Testament Studies* 21 (1975): 244–54.

6. For an overview, see David Wenham, *Paul: Follower of Jesus or Founder of Christianity?* (Grand Rapids: Eerdmans, 1995).

7. In 2 Corinthians 5:16 (KJV) Paul writes that he once knew Christ "after the flesh" (not through the Spirit). For a discussion of this passage, see chapter 15 (15.3.1).

8. Graetz sees a connection between Paul's conversion and the coming of Helena, the queen mother, from Adiabene to Jerusalem. She had been converted to Judaism and used the wealth of her non-Jewish people to assuage the famine in Jerusalem. Her presence in Jerusalem is then thought to have brought the young enthusiast Saul to believing that the messianic era was near and that means had to be found to convert the Gentiles on a large scale. Paul's conversion then cannot have taken place until the period A.D. 41–44. This hypothesis is unfounded and contradicts all data known to us. See H. Graetz, "Zeit der Anwesenheit der adiabenischen Königin in Jerusalem und

der Apostel Paulus," *Monatsschrift für Geschichte und Wissenschaft des Judenthums* 26 (1877): 241–52, 289–306.

9. Precisely because in the New Testament the verb "to call" (*kalein*) is applied to all Christians, it does not appear to be correct to view Paul's *calling* to Christ on the road to Damascus in the narrower sense of the calling to be an apostle or prophet. For a discussion of the question whether Paul is here called to be an apostle or prophet see Hans-Martin Storm, *Die Paulusberufung nach Lukas und das Erbe der Propheten: Berufen zu Gottes Dienst* (Frankfurt am Main: Peter Lang, 1995).

10. Alan F. Segal, *Paul the Convert: The Apostolate and Apostasy of Saul the Pharisee* (New Haven: Yale University Press, 1990), 25–30, 34–38.

11. Den Heyer, *Paul*, 68–69.

12. For this and other models of Paul's conversion, see James D. G. Dunn, "Paul's Conversion—A Light to Twentieth Century Disputes," in *Evangelium, Schriftauslegung, Kirche*, ed. Jostein Adna et al. (Göttingen: Vandenhoeck & Ruprecht, 1997), 77–93. Dunn himself is of the opinion that Paul was converted from a particular type of Judaism (not from Judaism as such). He is thought to have converted from Pharisaic Judaism, which was characterized by fanaticism, to a preparedness to turn to the Gentiles.

13. See also Brad H. Young, *Paul the Jewish Theologian: A Pharisee among Christians, Jews, and Gentiles* (Peabody, Mass.: Hendrickson, 1997).

Chapter 3: Gone to Arabia

1. See Martin Hengel and Anna Maria Schwemer, *Paul between Damascus and Antioch: The Unknown Years* (Louisville: Westminster/John Knox, 1997), 11–15. They view as decisive the period between A.D. 33 (when they date Paul's call) and A.D. 49 (when the apostolic council marks the end of Paul's preaching with Antioch as his base). "This obscure period of time, which is twice as long as the 'seven years of harvest,' is particularly worth thorough investigation, for it is precisely these unknown years between Damascus and the end of the Syrian-Antiochene period which must be regarded as the decisive era in which Paul gained that towering missionary (and theological) profile which we meet in the same way in his letters during the missionary work around the Aegean" (p. 12).

2. See Josephus, *Jewish Wars* 5.159–60; *Antiquities* 5.82.

3. King Aretas IV Philodemos reigned for a long time over this country—almost half a century (from ca. 10 B.C. until ca. A.D. 39). For details see Jakob van Bruggen, *"Na veertien jaren": De datering van het in Galaten 2 genoemde overleg te Jeruzalem* (Kampen: Kok, 1973), 12ff.

4. Documents dating from the second century A.D. indicate that some Jews in Arabia could write Aramaic as well as Greek and Nabatean (Arabic Aramaic). There was a Jewish community in Petra, the capital. For these data, see Hengel and Schwemer, *Paul between Damascus and Antioch*, 112–13.

5. In Galatians 1:17 Paul says that after receiving the revelation that sent him with the gospel to the nations, he did not go to Jerusalem, but rather to Arabia. In Galatians 1:18 we read that "after three years" he did go to the temple city. Paul spent these three years in Arabia (except for the period when he hid in Damascus after his flight from Arabia). We do not know whether the apostle refers to three full years or three calendar years. In any case he was active in Arabia for about one to two years.

6. The historicity of this statement is defended in detail by L. L. Welborn, "Primum tirocinium Pauli (2 Cor 11,32–33)," *Biblische Zeitschrift* 43 (1999): 49–71.

7. Jerome Murphy-O'Connor (*Paul: A Critical Life* [Oxford: Clarendon Press, 1996], 5–7) agrees with the view that after the death of Tiberius, Damascus was allotted to Aretas for a period of time.

8. Rainer Riesner provides in-depth argumentation in *Paul's Early Period: Chronology, Mission Strategy, Theology* (Grand Rapids: Eerdmans, 1998), 84–89.

9. Welborn ("Primum tirocinium Pauli," 49–71) is of the opinion that the ethnarch of Aretas held power in Damascus, because it is said of him that he had the city guarded (*ephrourei*). According to Welborn this verb is always used for "controlling" a bridge, a road, or a city. But this phraseology is strange if the city was simply part of Aretas's territory. Welborn's line of reasoning could lead to the conclusion that Aretas's men lay in ambush on the inside of the gate and thus had sufficient control of the city to prevent Paul from leaving Damascus.

10. Paul had used this escape route on an earlier occasion, shortly after his call near Damascus (Acts 9:25).

11. See also Hengel and Schwemer, *Paul between Damascus and Antioch*, 110–11.

12. Riesner (*Paul's Early Period*, 235–37) is of the opinion that for Paul the mission to the Gentiles flowed directly from the Christ-revelation ("aus der Christus-Offenbarung"). For a more detailed description of the traditional viewpoints, see Terence L. Donaldson, *Paul and the Gentiles: Remapping the Apostle's Convictional World* (Minneapolis: Fortress, 1997), 4–8; idem, "Israelite, Convert, Apostle to the Gentiles: The Origin of Paul's Gentile Mission," in *The Road from Damascus: The Impact of Paul's Conversion on His Life, Thought, and Ministry*, ed. Richard N. Longenecker (Grand Rapids: Eerdmans, 1997), 62–84.

13. Alan F. Segal (*Paul the Convert: The Apostolate and Apostasy of Saul the Pharisee* [New Haven: Yale University Press, 1990], 8) characterizes the event near Damascus as a "revelation" and the sending to the Gentiles as a "commissioning." With respect to Luke he then writes, "Only in Luke's third version (26:16–17), a shortened narrative, is Paul's commissioning made part of the revelation itself." And about Paul he writes, "In Paul's own writing, however, the connection is more ambiguous."

14. Seyoon Kim sees on the one hand the "apostolic commission" included entirely in the appearance of Christ to Paul on the road to Damascus. On the other hand he judges that Paul needed a longer period of time to reach an awareness of the implications of this appearance, so that it is not surprising that Paul limits himself for quite some time to the preaching to the Jews. The problem, is, however, that Paul himself

indicates in Galatians 1:15–17 that immediately after the revelation of God's Son he departed for Arabia and then to Syria and Cilicia to preach the gospel to the Gentiles. This direct connection argues against equating this "revelation" and the earlier call to the Christian faith near Damascus. See Seyoon Kim, *The Origin of Paul's Gospel* (Tübingen: Mohr, 1981), 55–62.

15. The construction of the sentence makes it clear that the main sentence begins as follows: "When it pleased God . . . to reveal his Son in me" (*hote de eudokēsen [ho theos] . . . apokalypsai ton huion en emoi*). A subordinate clause is added: *ho aphorisas me ek koilias mētros mou kai kalesas dia tēs charitos autou*. The events in the subordinate clause ([1] set apart; [2] called) are not identical with the main clause and must be distinguished from (3) the revelation of the Son in Paul.

16. For a description of the visions from a history-of-religions perspective see Bernhard Heininger, *Paulus als Visionär: Eine religionsgeschichtliche Studie* (Freiburg: Herder, 1996). Heininger takes note of the fact that the vocabulary Paul uses to describe the revelation in Galatians 1:16 differs significantly from that in the narrative of his calling in Acts. However, because he sees the two as being historically the same, Heininger has to resort to complicated explanations for these differences: for the sake of opponents who boast in having received a revelation of the Son, Paul now describes the *appearance* near Damascus as an *inner* revelation (p. 200).

17. See, e.g., Paul Barnett, *Jesus and the Rise of Early Christianity: A History of New Testament Times* (Downers Grove, Ill.: InterVarsity Press, 1999), 250–58.

18. N. T. Wright ("Paul, Arabia, and Elijah [Galatians 1:17]," *Journal of Biblical Literature* 115 [1996]: 683–92) is of the opinion that Paul did not go to preach in Arabia but that, like the prophet Elijah, he returned to Mount Sinai in the desert that was part of Arabia. Ben Witherington III presents arguments against such a Sinai journey (*The Paul Quest: The Renewed Search for the Jew of Tarsus* [Downers Grove, Ill.: InterVarsity Press, 1998], 307–9).

19. Riesner, *Paul's Early Period*, 241–63.

20. S. Greijdanus is of the opinion that Paul, before he began to preach in the synagogues in Damascus, spent a brief period of retreat and reflection in Arabia, but did not preach there (*Is Handelingen 9 [met 22 en 26] en 15 in tegenspraak met Galaten 1 en 2? Een vergelijkende, exegetische studie* [Kampen: Kok, 1935], 43–44).

21. Joachim Gnilka (*Paulus von Tarsus: Apostel und Zeuge* [Freiburg: Herder, 1996], 49–50) assumes that Paul, if he preached in Arabia, would have addressed only the Jews and the proselytes. The preaching in Arabia then fits in better with the events of Acts 9 (at least with respect to his audience), but in Galatians 1:16–17 it is clear that Paul went to Arabia specifically "to preach [Christ] among the Gentiles."

22. George Ogg (*The Chronology of the Life of Paul* [London: Epworth Press, 1968], 14) views it as impossible to fit the trip to Arabia into Luke's report of the period immediately after Paul's calling: "To insert it between Acts 9:19a and 9:19b is to make a gap in a verse the two parts of which are obviously very closely connected—Paul stayed some time with the disciples in Damascus, not after returning

from Arabia, but after his strength had returned; and to insert it between verses 22 and 23 is to ignore the word 'immediately' (*euthеōs*) in Galatians 1:16."

23. It is noteworthy that A. N. Wilson (*Paul: The Mind of the Apostle* [New York: Norton, 1997], 75–92) gives his chapter about the "silent years" the title "Paul in Arabia," even though he sees the stay in Arabia as preceding the actual period of the "silent years."

Chapter 4: Wandering through Southern Turkey

1. Martin Hengel and Anna Maria Schwemer (*Paul between Damascus and Antioch: The Unknown Years* [Louisville: Westminster/John Knox, 1997]) present the following sequence of events: (1) Paul preaches to Japheth (the nations) in Syria and Cilicia (pp. 174–77); (2) Barnabas brings him to Antioch, and thus Paul returns to Shem (p. 180); (3) together with Barnabas Paul makes a number of missionary journeys from Antioch, of which Luke mentions only two (the journey with the collection for the famine in Jerusalem and the journey to Cyprus, Pamphilia, Pisidia, and Lycaonia (p. 261). The final journey then brings both of them into the territory of Japheth.

2. Jürgen Becker (*Paul: Apostle to the Gentiles* [Louisville: Westminster/John Knox, 1993], 87–131) devotes a separate chapter to "Paul as Antiochian Missionary and Theologian." Entirely devoted to this topic is Nicholas Taylor, *Paul, Antioch and Jerusalem: A Study in Relationships and Authority in Earliest Christianity* (Sheffield: Sheffield Academic Press, 1992). Anna Maria Schwemer ("Paulus in Antiochien," *Biblische Zeitschrift* 42 [1998]: 161–80) challenges the widely held idea that Paul's theological development was determined by (1) a period of formation in Antioch, and (2) a break with Antioch at the beginning of the second journey. She suggests that Paul already before his time in Antioch was active as an independent preacher among the Gentiles and that he did not have a significant conflict at Antioch until after the second journey (see also Hengel and Schwemer, *Paul between Damascus and Antioch*). Anton Dauer (*Paulus und die christliche Gemeinde im syrischen Antiochia: Kritische Bestandsaufnahme der modernen Forschung mit einigen weiterführenden Überlegungen* [Weinheim: Beltz, 1996], 127–28) views Antioch, because of the conflict that developed, as Paul's trauma in a later period! See also A. Suhl, "Der Beginn der selbständigen Mission des Paulus," *New Testament Studies* 38 (1992): 430–47.

3. See Jakob Van Bruggen, *Jesus the Son of God: The Gospel Narratives as Message* (Grand Rapids: Baker, 1999), 91–92.

4. See also Romans 1:4, 16; 1 Corinthians 1:18, 24; 4:20; 12:10. (Some also refer to 1 Thess. 1:5.)

5. James M. Scott (*Paul and the Nations: The Old Testament and Jewish Background of Paul's Mission to the Nations with Special Reference to the Destination of Galatians* [Tübingen: Mohr, 1995]) thinks that Paul developed his strategy on the basis of the table of nations in Genesis 10 (cf. 1 Chron. 1:1–2:2) and that he personally decided to turn to the nations that are descended from Japheth. The idea of territorial-strategic travel plans is not sufficiently convincing: (1) Paul lets himself be led

by the Spirit and is frequently faced with surprises; (2) the regions Paul visited and the territory of Japheth as described by Josephus (*Antiquities* 1.123–26) coincide only in part. Rainer Riesner (*Paul's Early Period: Chronology, Mission Strategy, Theology* [Grand Rapids: Eerdmans, 1998], 207–25) is of the opinion that in determining the routes he would travel, Paul let himself be guided by, among other things, the territorial descriptions in Isaiah 66:18–21 (LXX). For a critical discussion of this theory, see Paul Barnett, *Jesus and the Rise of Early Christianity: A History of New Testament Times* (Downers Grove, Ill.: InterVarsity Press, 1999), 267–69.

6. For this so-called new chronology, see appendix 1. S. Dockx even denies that Paul made this journey at all and asserts that Acts 13–14 describes, in fact, a journey made by Barnabas and Mark ("The First Missionary Voyage of Paul: Historical Reality or Literary Creation of Luke?" in *Chronos, Kairos, Christos*, ed. J. Vardaman and E. M. Yamauchi [Winona Lake, Ind.: Eisenbrauns, 1989], 215–16).

7. Cilliers Breytenbach, *Paulus und Barnabas in der Provinz Galatien: Studien zu Apostelgeschichte 13f.; 16,6; 18,23 und den Adressaten des Galaterbriefes* (Leiden: Brill, 1996), 3–97.

Chapter 5: Called to Account

1. Galatians 2:1–10 is left out of consideration in this chapter because the identification of Acts 15 with Galatians 2:1–10 is problematic. For the dating of the consultation described in Galatians 2:1–10, see chapter 7 and appendix 1.

2. M.-É. Boismard and A. Lamouille (*Les Actes des deux apôtres* [Paris: Gabalda, 1990], 3:195–205) view Acts 15 as a later narrative, composed from two sources. One of their main arguments is that when Paul and Barnabas relate what God has done through them (vv. 3–4) the dispute is not mentioned. Paul and Barnabas played no role in the oldest version of the narrative. Thus also Justin Taylor, *Les Actes des deux apôtres: Commentaire historique (Act. 9,1–18,22)* (Paris: Gabalda, 1994), 197–225. This problem is virtual rather than real, however. In Acts 15:3–4 Paul and Barnabas tell of their work. After this (15:5) some individuals from the party of the Pharisees attack their work because they do not require circumcision of converted Gentiles. It is logical to assume that these protesters are primarily individuals who had been sent from Antioch—the men who opposed Paul in Antioch hailed from Jerusalem (vv. 1–2)! The community in Jerusalem listens to both sides, after which the apostles and elders convene (15:6) to discuss among themselves the question that both sides, each from their own perspective, have presented on behalf of the church in Antioch. The coherence of the narrative in Acts 15 is demonstrated by Alex T. M. Cheung, "A Narrative Analysis of Acts 14:27–15:35: Literary Shaping in Luke's Account of the Jerusalem Council," *Westminster Theological Journal* 55 (1993): 137–54.

3. F. F. Bruce ("The Apostolic Decree of Acts 15," in *Studien zum Text und zur Ethik des Neuen Testaments*, ed. W. Schrage [Berlin: De Gruyter, 1986], 115–24) thinks that the original decree dealt only with circumcision; in a later version (supported by Peter but not by Paul) the second part (with the four points) was added.

Peter saw in this addition the potential for bringing together Jewish and Gentile Christians, whereas Paul viewed the collection for the famine in Jerusalem as a means to bridging the gap. But the texts do not provide any reason for this splitting up of the apostolic decree.

4. In this manuscript (D) the negative "golden rule"—"What you do not want to happen to you, do not do it to others"—is inserted in two places. Several exegetes think that this addition twists the apostolic decree from a specific compromise pronouncement to a general ethical rule. Matthias Klinghardt (*Gesetz und Volk Gottes: Das lukanische Verständnis des Gesetzes nach Herkunft, Funktion und seinem Ort in der Geschichte des Urchristentums* [Tübingen: Mohr, 1988], 176–77) has shown that this variant cannot be forced into the framework. Besides, it is also possible that the insertion in D was made to include in addition to the apostolic decree concerning love for God (no idols) the command to love one's neighbor.

5. Thus Maertens Philip, "Quelques notes sur *pniktos*," *New Testament Studies* 45 (1999): 593–96.

6. See also E. A. de Boer, "Ethiek in de Acta van Jerusalem: Een exegetisch onderzoek naar de betekenis van het besluit van Handelingen XV," in *Almanak Fides Quadrat Intellectum* (Kampen: Zalsman, 1980), 139–68.

7. Bruce, "Apostolic Decree of Acts 15," 115–24. Eduard Lohse (*Paulus: Eine Biographie* [Munich: Beck, 1996], 90–91) is of the opinion that this compromise statement was soon forgotten, which is why we do not find any traces of it in Paul's letters. According to Joachim Gnilka (*Paulus von Tarsus: Apostel und Zeuge* [Freiburg: Herder, 1996], 100–101) this absence of any echoes in the letters proves that the compromise statement is of a much later date and has incorrectly been linked to the earlier apostolic council by Luke. Nicholas Taylor (*Paul, Antioch and Jerusalem: A Study in Relationships and Authority in Earliest Christianity* [Sheffield: Sheffield Academic Press, 1992], 140–42) considers the apostolic decree to be an internal agreement between Jerusalem and Antioch, of which Paul did not become aware until much later (probably at the time of Acts 21) and therefore did not use it in his letters. Otto Böcher ("Das sogenannte Aposteldekret," in *Vom Urchristentum zu Jesus*, ed. Hubert Frankemölle and Karl Kertelge [Freiburg: Herder, 1989], 329–33) thinks that the decisions were so self-evident that Paul did not have to mention them separately in his letters.

8. Jacob Jervell, *Die Apostelgeschichte* (Göttingen: Vandenhoeck & Ruprecht, 1998), 396–99.

9. Taylor, *Paul, Antioch and Jerusalem*, 140–42, evades this argument by positing that the prohibition on pork was so generally known that it did not need to be mentioned separately in a decision concerning the relationship between Jewish and Gentile Christians.

10. For a more extensive discussion of "the obedience of faith," see chapter 16.4.

11. Markus Bockmuehl ("The Noachide Commandments and New Testament Ethics, with Special Reference to Acts 15 and Pauline Halakha," *Revue Biblique* 102 [1995]: 93–99) thinks that the intent of Acts 15 is to exempt the Gentile Christians

from the obligation to become proselytes if they are willing to submit to the Noachide commandments.

12. Acts 15 is supposed to treat the Gentile Christians as the "aliens in the gates of Israel"; see Terrance Callan, "The Background of the Apostolic Decree (Acts 15:20, 29; 21:25)," *Catholic Biblical Quarterly* 55 (1993): 284–97. Matthias Klinghardt (*Gesetz und Volk Gottes*, 181–206) focuses on the commandments in Leviticus 17–18 that include the threat that whoever does not keep these commandments will be "cut off from the people." See also Jürgen Wehnert, *Die Reinheit des "christlichen Gottesvolkes" aus Juden und Heiden: Studien zum historischen und theologischen Hintergrund des sogenannten Aposteldekrets* (Göttingen: Vandenhoeck & Ruprecht, 1997), 396–99.

13. Alan F. Segal (*Paul the Convert: The Apostolate and Apostasy of Saul the Pharisee* [New Haven: Yale University Press, 1990], 195) links the development of the Noachide commandments with the laws for the aliens in Leviticus 17–26: "These two passages are associated because they point to the origin of the laws for the legal treatment of resident aliens."

14. The connection between the apostolic decree and the Jewish rules for living for Gentiles was increasingly emphasized in Jewish as well as Christian studies in the second half of the twentieth century. See Peter J. Tomson, *Paul and the Jewish Law: Halakha in the Letters of the Apostle to the Gentiles* (Assen/Minneapolis: Van Gorcum/Fortress, 1990); and Stefan Meissner, *Die Heimholung des Ketzers: Studien zur jüdischen Auseinandersetzung mit Paulus* (Tübingen: Mohr, 1996), 257–80.

15. (1) There are seven Noachide commandments, at the heart of which stands the requirement of a good administration of justice and the condemnation of theft; both of these are missing from the apostolic decree. See Klinghardt, *Gesetz und Volk Gottes*, 177–80. (2) Even if only those commandments for aliens that carry an explicit penalty are counted in the list of Leviticus 17–18, the total still does not come to the four of Acts 15 (the term *pnikton* ["strangled"] is missing in Lev. 17–18).

16. Peder Borgen, *Early Christianity and Hellenistic Judaism* (Edinburgh: T & T Clark, 1996), 243–51.

Chapter 6: Vanished in Greece

1. For some suggestions as to an itinerary, see chapter 4, notes 1 and 5.

2. Many equate the consultation in Jerusalem, described in Galatians 2, with the apostolic conference in Jerusalem (Acts 15). As a result, the conflict between Paul and Peter (and Barnabas) in Antioch over eating with the Gentile Christians (Gal. 2:11–21) is then dated before the second missionary journey. It is then logical to equate this conflict with that which is described in Acts about taking John Mark along. However, these two narratives do not fit together at all. The hypothesis that Luke covers up the seriousness of the conflict by giving it a trivial cause does not do justice to the character of Acts. Furthermore, there are decisive reasons to date the consultation described in Galatians 2:1–10 after the second missionary journey and thus in a later

period than the apostolic conference (see chapter 7 and appendix 1, sections 3.2 and 3.3). This means that the conflict between Paul and Peter (Gal. 2:11–21) also took place in a later period, a number of years after the incident involving John Mark.

3. In the twentieth century, the translation "Phrygio-Galatian land" in Acts 16:6 gained currency in connection with the plea for the south-Galatian hypothesis. For supporting arguments, see Colin J. Hemer, *The Book of Acts in the Setting of Hellenistic History*, ed. Conrad H. Gempf (Tübingen: Mohr, 1989), 282–85. Although this more recent translation is not impossible philologically, the older understanding remains philologically well defensible (see Cilliers Breytenbach, *Paulus und Barnabas in der Provinz Galatien: Studien zu Apostelgeschichte 13f.; 16,6; 18,23 und den Adressaten des Galaterbriefes* [Leiden: Brill, 1996], 113–15). Decisive here is that the newer view does not appear to fit in Acts. Luke clearly distinguishes between two separate regions in 18:23 (they traveled through "the Galatian region *and* Phrygia"). Luke's comment that they traveled there, "strengthening all the disciples," suggests that Paul had been in these regions before. Luke indirectly points back to the only place in his book where the same geographical names occur: Acts 16:6. There mention is made of preaching in exactly these regions. In 16:6 Luke must have had the same two regions in mind as in 18:23, and apparently he intended to indicate two regions (even though it is philologically possible to understand the phrase as referring to one region). One cannot escape the force of this argument by claiming that a single "region" is defined in 16:6. In his Gospel (3:1) Luke writes in the same way about "the region of Ituraea and Trachonitis" (NASB) (*tēs Itouraias kai Trachōnitidos chōras*), clearly referring to two separate regions. He can mention them, as he does in Acts 16:6, in one breath because the regions are contiguous.

4. See Jakob van Bruggen, *De oorsprong van de kerk te Rome* (Groningen: De Vuurbaak, 1967).

5. See appendix 1 for a discussion of the dating of the expulsion of the Jews from Rome by Emperor Claudius.

6. F. F. Bruce, *1 and 2 Thessalonians* (Waco, Tex.: Word, 1982), xxxv; Leon Morris, *The First and Second Epistles to the Thessalonians* (Grand Rapids: Eerdmans, 1991), 92–93.

7. Charles A. Wanamaker (*Commentary on 1 & 2 Thessalonians: A Commentary on the Greek Text* [Grand Rapids: Eerdmans, 1990], 127) rightly considers Acts 17:15 with 18:5 to be incompatible with 1 Thessalonians 3:1–5 and draws the conclusion that Acts is therefore inadequately informed. Curiously enough, Wanamaker derives the idea that 1 Thessalonians 3:1–5 took place immediately after the first arrival in Athens from Acts 17:15!

8. Earl J. Richard (*First and Second Thessalonians* [Collegeville, Minn.: Glazier, 1995], 143–44) says, "There is a contrast intended between verses 1–2 and 5. The former expresses the group's motivation, the second focuses on Paul's reason. While he may have similar concerns ('able to bear it no longer') he nonetheless contrasts his own motive for agreeing to the embassy." Although a number of exegetes consider

the plural in verse 1 ("*we* thought it best") to be an epistolary plural with which the author refers only to himself, they nevertheless must acknowledge that this kind of epistolary plural is not part of Paul's usual style and occurs here only by way of exception. Furthermore, verse 5 (in which Paul repeats the content of verse 1 but now in the singular) would be entirely pointless if verse 1 already had the *meaning* of a singular! This is all the more true because Paul in verse 5 confirms that what he has written before also applies to him personally (*kagō*). For Paul's use of the first person plural, see also C. E. B. Cranfield, "Changes of Person and Number in Paul's Epistles," in *Paul and Paulinism: Essays in Honour of C. K. Barrett*, ed. M. D. Hooker and S. G. Wilson (London: SPCK, 1982), 280–89.

9. E. E. Ellis (*The Making of the New Testament Documents* [Leiden: Brill, 1999], 111) calculated that 37 percent of 1 Thessalonians consists of "traditional" material.

10. Glenn S. Holland (*The Tradition That You Received from Us: 2 Thessalonians in the Pauline Tradition* [Tübingen: Mohr, 1988]) views 2 Thessalonians as a letter, not written by Paul, in which the views of 1 Thessalonians are supplemented and a specific interpretation of those views is promoted.

11. This was perhaps made possible in part by gifts from Philippi. This Christian community was the only one that "at the first preaching of the gospel, after I departed from Macedonia" (Phil. 4:15 NASB), supported Paul financially. They already did this even when he was still in Thessalonica (before his departure from Macedonia).

12. See also chapter 15.1.4.

Chapter 7: Reappearance in Jerusalem

1. Thus, from the perspective of Jerusalem, *Syria* can be used to indicate "Syria without Palestine" (Acts 15:23, 41; Gal. 1:21).

2. Among the Greeks it was customary to describe what we today refer to as Palestine as a part of the extensive region of Syria (*hē Palaistinē Syria*). In Acts 20:3, a later journey Paul makes from Greece to Jerusalem is referred to as a departure for Syria (Acts 20:3; cf. 19:21). There is therefore no reason to assume that Paul wanted to travel only to Antioch in Syria but ended up by accident (due to a strong northeasterly wind) in Caesarea, the harbor of Palestine. (See, among others, George Ogg, *The Odyssey of Paul* [Old Tappan, N.J.: Revell, 1968], 128.)

3. Ogg, *Odyssey*, 127–32. Anton Dauer (*Paulus und die christliche Gemeinde im syrischen Antiochia* [Weinheim: Beltz, 1996]) discusses various recent hypotheses concerning Acts 18:18–23.

4. It appears from 1 Corinthians 16:1–4 that Paul had already made arrangements for this collection in Galatia, just as he now advises Corinth on the organization of the collection. Apparently the collection is something that was not organized until the time of 1 Corinthians (that is, during the third missionary journey). The completion of the collection comes up in the next letter to the Corinthians, which dates from the end of the third journey (see 2 Cor. 8–9). From Romans 15:25–28 it appears that the third journey ends with the transfer of the gifts from Macedonia and Achaia to Jerusalem.

5. See appendix 1 (section 3.2) for a more chronological discussion of this topic.

6. Anna Maria Schwemer, even though she equates Galatians 2:1–10 with Acts 15, argues for a dating of the Antiochian conflict (Gal. 2:11–21) after the second journey: "Wenn wir diesen Zusammenstoss in Antiochien nicht direkt nach dem Apostelkonzil ansetzen, sondern mit der Apg 18,21–23 geschilderten Reise des Paulus von Ephesus auf dem Seeweg nach Caesarea, dann nach Jerusalem und schliesslich nach Antiochien verbinden, werden die Zusammenhänge verständlicher. Diesen Vorschlag haben schon Bernhard Weisz u.a. vertreten" ("If we do not fix the time of this conflict in Antioch immediately after the apostolic council, but rather link it with the journey of Paul from Ephesus by sea to Caesarea, then to Jerusalem, and finally to Antioch, the connections become more understandable. This suggestion was already made by Bernhard Weisz et al.") ("Paulus in Antiochien," *Biblische Zeitschrift* 42 [1998]: 161–80). Considering the close connection between Galatians 2:1–10 and 2:11–21 it seems advisable to not identify Galatians 2:1–10 with Acts 15 but rather to date it after the second journey, shortly before the incident in Antioch.

7 Jerome Murphy-O'Connor does not take Paul seriously on the subject of his "fear of the Jews," as is apparent in his comment "Some exegetes take him seriously"! (*Paul: A Critical Life* [Oxford: Clarendon Press, 1996], 152 n. 110).

8. The NIV is somewhat misleading when it renders *tous ek peritomēs* as "the circumcision group," implying that it is a group within the church.

9. J. Munck, *Paulus und die Heilsgeschichte* (Aarhus: Universitetsforlaget, 1954), 98–99.

Chapter 8: Embattled in Ephesus

1. Various authors minimize the importance of Acts 18:19–21 by denying its historicity or by assuming that Paul did not have any lasting contacts from this first, brief visit. The actual founder of the Christian community here is then thought to be Apollos, and thus there would have been various currents among the Christians in Ephesus. See, among others, Werner Thiessen, *Christen in Ephesus* (Tübingen: Francke Verlag, 1995), 28–86; Rick Strelan, *Paul, Artemis and the Jews in Ephesus* (Berlin: Walter de Gruyter, 1996), 204–29; Helmut Koester, "Ephesus in Early Christian Literature," in *Ephesos, Metropolis of Asia* (Valley Forge, Pa.: Trinity Press International, 1995). For a defense of the historicity and significance of Acts 18:19–20, see Eckhard J. Schnabel, "Die ersten Christen in Ephesus: Neuerscheinungen zur frühchristlichen Missionsgeschichte," *Novum Testamentum* 41 (1999): 349–82.

2. Thus Gerhard Schneider, *Die Apostelgeschichte* (Freiburg: Herder, 1982), 2:263. Authors who deny Paul's ministry in Galatia are inclined to make the term *anōterika merē* refer to the last phase of Paul's journey to Ephesus, in which case he would have entered the city not via the Lycus Valley but through the more northerly Cayster Valley. The comment in Acts 18:23 then no longer confirms explicitly that Paul traveled also through the regions of Galatia and Phrygia mentioned earlier. Thus Colin J. Hemer, *The Book of Acts in the Setting of Hellenistic History* (Tübingen: Mohr, 1989),

120; cf. C. K. Barrett, *The Acts of the Apostles* (Edinburgh: T & T Clark, 1994, 1998), 2:892–93. This, however, is not a plausible interpretation: (1) What benefit is there in knowing from which side the apostle approached the city of Ephesus? (2) Why would Luke, of the whole journey from Antioch to Ephesus, report only something about the final phase?

3. For a description and analysis of recent publications about the city of Ephesus and the arrival of Christianity there, see Schnabel, "Die ersten Christen in Ephesus," 349–82.

4. The complications of reconstructing a journey in the east after release in Rome are demonstrated by Wolfgang Metzger, *Die letzte Reise des Apostels Paulus: Beobachtungen und Erwägungen zu seinem Itinerar nach den Pastoralbriefen* (Stuttgart: Calwer Verlag, 1976). John A. T. Robinson (*Redating the New Testament* [Philadelphia: Westminster; London: SCM Press, 1976], 71 n. 147) argues that this complexity shows the hypothetical nature of the reconstruction. Robert L. Reymond (*Paul: Missionary Theologian* [Fearn: Christian Focus Publications, 2000], 247) reconstructs what he calls "the fifth missionary journey" as follows: Rome-Crete-Ephesus-Macedonia-Nicopolis in Epirus-Troas-Corinth-Miletus- (arrested again)-Rome.

5. In more recent times a dating during the third journey is encountered only sporadically. Thus Robinson, *Redating the New Testament*, 82–84.

6. See chapter 8.1.

7. See Anthony Kenny, *A Stylometric Study of the New Testament* (Oxford: Clarendon Press, 1986), 80–100. Concerning the letters of Paul (with the exception of Titus) he concludes, "On the basis of the evidence in this chapter for my part I see no reason to reject the hypothesis that twelve of the Pauline Epistles are the work of a single, unusually versatile writer" (p. 100).

8. Strelan, *Paul, Artemis and the Jews*, 155: "The heresies and associated practices opposed in *Timothy* can be better understood on a Jewish background. That is not to say that they did not have a [distinctive] Ephesian flavor or that they were totally isolated from the influence of the Artemis cult."

9. H. Mills, "Greek Clothing Regulations: Sacred and Profane?" *Zeitschrift für Papyrologie und Epigraphik* 55 (1984): 255–65.

10. Richard Oster ("The Ephesian Artemis as an Opponent of Early Christianity," *Jahrbuch für Antike und Christentum* 19 [1976]: 24–44) is of the opinion that the hymn in 1 Timothy 3:16 is formulated as a conscious attack on the claims of Artemis. Strelan (*Paul, Artemis and the Jews in Ephesus*, 153–54) argues against this: "The best that one can conclude is that an ex-Artemis follower may have had felt [*sic*] *some* affinity with the language of the Christian hymn, but would not have seen it as an attack on his/her former goddess, and probably would have had to learn the meaning of the hymn from Jews familiar with its language and its worldview."

Chapter 9: Long-Distance Pastorate

1. Some manuscripts use *apoleipein* for "leaving" Titus behind on Crete, while the majority read *kataleipein*. These are not, however, two verbs with different meanings

but interchangeable synonyms (cf. Josephus *Jewish Wars* 1.259 with *Antiquities* 14.346). These verbs are often used for "leaving behind" someone when one's own travels continue, but on occasion also for leaving persons posted somewhere via instructions from a distance. Thus a king can "leave" garrisons in strategic strongholds (Josephus *Contra Apionem* 1.77), and one can "leave behind and therefore not take along" a brother on an island without having been there oneself (Josephus *Antiquities* 17.324–35, esp. 335). See also Luke Timothy Johnson, *Letters to Paul's Delegates: 1 Timothy, 2 Timothy, Titus* (Valley Forge, Pa.: Trinity Press International, 1996), 212 (cf. 221): "It is possible to take the phrase 'I left you in Crete' . . . not in a geographical sense but in an administrative sense, meaning 'I kept you in that place.'"

2. See M. Broadbent, *Studies in Greek Genealogy* (Leiden: Brill, 1968); W. Speyer, "Genealogie," in *Reallexicon für Antike und Christentum*, vol. 9, cols. 1145–1268.

3. During the third missionary journey Paul wrote regularly to Corinth. Only two of his letters have been preserved; at least two have been lost. One of the latter was written before our 1 Corinthians; in this letter the apostle already gave instructions on dealing with adulterers within the community (see 1 Cor. 5:9–11). Another lost letter was sent after 1 Corinthians and before 2 Corinthians; in this letter the apostle wrote with many tears about the conflict with this community (see 2 Cor. 2:3–4).

4. Ferdinand Christian Baur (*Die sogenannten Pastoralbriefe des Apostels Paulus aufs neue kritisch untersucht* [Stuttgart: Becher and Müller, 1845]) thought that there were two parties, a Jewish Christian party (Peter/Christ) and a Gentile Christian party (Paul/Apollos). Walter Schmithals (*Gnosticism in Corinth: An Investigation of the Letters to the Corinthians* [Nashville: Abingdon, 1971]) sees a gnostic front (the docetic choice for Christ while letting go of the earthly Jesus) versus an ecclesiastic front (Paul, Peter, Apollos). See Jakob Van Bruggen, "W. Schmithals en F. C. Baur," in *Almanak Fides Quadrat Intellectum* (Kampen: Zalsman, 1967), 61–88.

5. The seemingly abrupt transition from a more quiet tone in chapters 1–9 to a passionate section in chapters 10–13 has led many to detach these last chapters from the letter and to consider them the lost "tearful letter" that Paul wrote after his unsuccessful interim visit to Corinth (2 Cor. 2:4). Against this argue the following: (1) There is a difference in intensity between 1–7 and 10–13, but one can find (albeit to a lesser degree) the themes from one section also in the other. For example: confidence in the community as a whole (1:11; 2:3; 7:11; 9:2; 10:15; 11:1), urging to more complete acceptance of Paul (6:12–13; 7:2; 10:7; 11:2–6, 19–23; 12:11, 20–21), and criticism of the pseudoapostles. (2) In 10–13 Paul does not write against the community as a whole, but against those who want to impress and influence them. (3) There is no trace in the textual tradition that the two parts of the letter ever existed separately.

6. Traditionally these pseudoapostles have been understood as having been distinct from the "super apostles" (who are not involved in this conflict at all). But since the nineteenth century the expression "superapostles" (*hyperlian apostoloi*) has often been understood as *ironic* in intent and thus as referring to the pseudoapostles. But against this argue that in the Greek, *hyperlian* does not have an ironic meaning and

that the apostle compares himself *positively* with these *hyperlian apostoloi* while presenting himself in contradistinction to the pseudoapostles in Corinth. For a more detailed discussion, see Jakob Van Bruggen, *Ambten in de apostolische kerk: een exegetisch mozaïek* (Kampen: Kok, 1984), 23–29.

Chapter 10: Absent from Rome

1. See chapter 6.2 for a more detailed discussion of the expulsion of the Jews from Rome (in A.D. 49) and of the effects this had on Paul's opportunities for travel. For the dating of this expulsion, see appendix 1.2.3.

2. Some deny that there is a special relationship between the letter to Rome and the situation of the Christian community there. Thus Günther Bornkamm, "Der Römerbrief als Testament des Paulus," in *Geschichte und Glaube* (Munich: Kaiser Verlag, 1971), 2:120–39. E. P. Sanders (*Paul and Palestinian Judaism: A Comparison of Patterns of Religion* [Philadelphia: Fortress; London: SCM Press, 1977], 488) states: "Romans had a specific occasion, but the occasion was not a debate within Rome." Jerome Murphy-O'Connor (*Paul: A Critical Life* [Oxford: Clarendon Press, 1996], 334) agrees: "Paul's focus on the relationship between Judaism and Christianity is more likely to have been directly inspired by the problems he encountered with the Judaizers during the winter in Corinth, and by his concern as to how the collection would be accepted in Jerusalem."

3. For a survey of the various questions and hypotheses surrounding Romans, see Karl P. Donfried, ed., *The Romans Debate* (Peabody, Mass.: Hendrickson, 1991).

4. See also Jakob Van Bruggen, *Het raadsel van Romeinen 16* (Groningen: De Vuurbaak, 1970). Cf. F. Godet, *Commentaire sur l'Épitre aux Romains*, 2 vols. (Paris: Sandoz & Fischbacher, 1879–80), 2:568, 581–83, 592–93). See also chapter 13, section 1.

5. Calvin J. Roetzel (*The Letters of Paul: Conversations in Context* [Louisville: Westminster/John Knox, 1998], 104): "But the return of these Jewish Christians brought new tensions to the Roman church." Joseph Shulam (*A Commentary on the Jewish Roots of Romans* [Baltimore: Messianic Jewish Publishers, 1997], 14): "Claudius' banishment of the Jewish community from the city in 52 C.E. may therefore have left a vacuum in the early community which the Gentile believers came to fill. This might have created rivalry over leadership when the Jewish believers began returning."

6. Thus, among others, J. Christiaan Beker (*Paul the Apostle: The Triumph of God in Life and Thought* [Philadelphia: Fortress, 1980], 61): "It is possible that Romans 14 and 15 reflect a church in which returning Jewish Christians found a preponderance of Gentile Christians, a situation that led to friction among them." See also Thomas Jacob Oosterhuis, *The "Weak" and the "Strong" in Paul's Epistle to the Romans: An Exegetical Study of Romans 14.1–15.13* (Edmonton: Elkon Press, 1992). Oosterhuis also considers vegetarianism and abstinence from wine (Rom. 14:21) to be Jewish characteristics, because some people in Judaism were adherents of total abstinence and vegetarianism.

7. Mark D. Nanos, *The Mystery of Romans: The Jewish Context of Paul's Letter* (Minneapolis: Fortress, 1996), 85–165.

8. Suetonius, *Claudius* 25.4. Many see in this passage from Suetonius indirect proof for an early arrival of the gospel concerning *Christus* in Rome. Already around A.D. 49 it is thought to have created so much unrest among the Jews that the emperor intervened to expel the Jews. For a recent defense of this hypothesis, see Helga Boterman, *Das Judenedikt des Kaisers Claudius: Römischer Staat und Christiani im 1. Jahrhundert* (Stuttgart: Franz Steiner, 1996); and Pieter Lalleman, "Keizer Claudius en de christenen in Rome," *Bijbel en Wetenschap* 23 (1998): 43–45.

9. In *Nero* 16, Suetonius correctly uses the spelling *christiani.*

10. In *Claudius* 25, Suetonius discusses the measures Claudius took against the inhabitants of Lycia, Rhodos, Ilium, and Judea in the East, after which he continues with the peoples in the West (Germans and Gauls). See Jakob Van Bruggen, *De oorsprong van de kerk te Rome* (Groningen: De Vuurbaak, 1967). Cf. Thomas Lewin, *Fasti Sacri or a Key to the Chronology of the New Testament* (London: Longmans, Green, and Co., 1865), lxii–lxiv, 295–96.

11. Josephus (*Antiquities* 20.130) mentions how Quadratus, during his intervention in Palestine via a judicial inquiry (20. 131–32), discovered that there were five revolutionary leaders who incited the population to insurrection against Rome. Of these five, Josephus mentions only Doetius. In Rome, by contrast, it was apparently especially the name *Chrestus* that stood out on the basis of reports received. He may be one of the four leaders Josephus does not mention by name. Striking is the theory of S. Benko, who believes that Chrestus was a Jewish zealot in Rome ("The Edict of Claudius of A.D. 49 and the Instigator Chrestus," *Theologische Zeitschrift* 25 [1969]: 406–18).

12. E. Mary Smallwood, *The Jews under Roman Rule: From Pompey to Diocletian* (Leiden: Brill, 1976), 201–19; Harry J. Leon, *The Jews of Ancient Rome* (Peabody, Mass.: Hendrickson, 1995); Leonard Victor Rutgers, "Roman Policy toward the Jews: Expulsions from the City of Rome during the First Century C.E.," in: *Judaism and Christianity in First-Century Rome*, ed. Karl P. Donfried and Peter Richardson (Grand Rapids: Eerdmans, 1998), 93–116.

13. For the history of the collection, see chapter 7.1, and for its significance, chapter 16.1 (conclusion), as well as the footnotes in both these sections.

Chapter 11: Prisoner of His Countrymen

1. That this impression is incorrect is apparent from, among other things, the manner in which Paul writes in Romans 11 about the grafting of the Gentile Christians into the olive tree of Israel.

2. Eusebius, *Historia Ecclesiastica* 2.23.1.

3. We will not consider here the idea that the letter was sent from Ephesus, because the underlying assumption of this view is difficult to substantiate. It is possible to speak of a lengthy imprisonment in that city only in hypothetical terms. The data in Acts do not point in that direction (Acts 19:9–10, 21–22), and both passages in Paul's

letters that speak of a threat to his life in Asia cannot refer to a period of imprisonment. (1) In 1 Cor. 15:32 Paul says that in Ephesus he fought wild beasts. But this cannot have been true in a literal sense because a Roman citizen could not be condemned to fighting in the arena with large carnivores such as lions. Furthermore, Paul says that he fought wild beasts "after the manner of men" (KJV; *kata anthrōpon*), indicating that this statement is metaphorical in intent. (The NIV paraphrases *kata anthrōpon* as "for merely human reasons.") He endured conflicts with people that were comparable to fighting wild animals in the arena! (2) In 2 Cor. 1:8 Paul speaks of a life-threatening pressure in Asia: he was under so much pressure that his survival was at risk. The choice of words here is not reminiscent of imprisonment but rather of potentially lethal opposition—which is what Paul experienced at the end of his stay in Asia (Acts 19:22) during the riot instigated by Demetrius (Acts 19:29–31).

4. See E. E. Ellis, *The Making of the New Testament Documents* (Leiden: Brill, 1999), 245. For Colossae (and Laodicea, which is mentioned in the letter), see Colin J. Hemer, *The Letters to the Seven Churches of Asia in Their Local Setting* (Sheffield: JSOT Press, 1986), 179–82.

Chapter 12: Sent in Shackles to the Emperor

1. For the circumstances and details of this imprisonment, see Brian Rapske, *The Book of Acts and Paul in Roman Custody* (Grand Rapids: Eerdmans, 1994).

2. It is preferable not to view Paul's imprisonment from the perspective of Roman procedural law until after the moment when Paul appeals to Caesar. Up to that point, Paul had been kept in protective custody against the attacks of the Jews, which fell outside the parameters of Roman procedural law. The advocate for the Jews, Tertullus, brings charges against Paul before Felix, but he tries to explain that Paul should be tried in accordance with Jewish temple law (since he was supposed to have brought Gentiles into the temple; Acts 24:6–8). The Roman authorities are asked to turn Paul over for trial (Acts 25:11, 16, 20). Felix considers the case "your case," not a case of the Roman authorities against Paul; see Acts 24:22 (*ta kath' hymas*).

For an extensive description of the manner in which Paul came in contact with Roman procedural law, see Adrian Nicolas Sherwin-White, *Roman Society and Roman Law in the New Testament* (Oxford: Clarendon Press, 1963); and Harry W. Tajra, *The Trial of St. Paul: A Juridical Exegesis of the Second Half of the Acts of the Apostles* (Tübingen: Mohr, 1989). In these studies the period of custody under Felix is treated as falling under Roman procedural law (*extra ordinem*: see Tajra, *Trial*, 114–15).

3. Dennis R. MacDonald ("The Shipwrecks of Odysseus and Paul," *New Testament Studies* 45 [1999]: 88–107) suggests that Luke, by the way he describes the sea voyage and the shipwreck, intentionally invites a comparison between Paul and the hero Odysseus.

4. Remarkable is Heinz Warnecke's opinion that Paul did not wash ashore on Malta but on the island of Cephalonia, off the west coast of Greece (*Die tatsächliche Romfahrt des Apostels Paulus* [Stuttgart: Verlag Katholisches Bibelwerk, 1987]).

5. The "afflictions" are part of life on earth, rather than of dying. Thus Joseph was rescued from all his "afflictions" (Acts 7:10). Paul's experience of suffering (2 Tim. 3:11) and that of other Christians (2 Cor. 1:7) are part of what is experienced in terms of affliction and adversity during this life on earth. It is suffering in this world (Rom. 8:18). For all believers this can be characterized as "the sufferings of Christ" (2 Cor. 1:5). Jesus himself was made perfect through what he suffered (Heb. 2:10). Although Jesus' death also involved "suffering," his death was at the same time an act in which he gave his body and blood for those who are his. On this point there never is an analogy between Christ and the Christian. Paul does not fill up Christ's sacrificial death, but only Christ's suffering on behalf of his people and humanity. On this topic, see also Gerrit De Ru, *Heeft het lijden van Christus aanvulling nodig: Onderzoek naar de interpretatie van Colossenzen 1:24* (Amsterdam: Bolland, 1981).

Chapter 13: Coworkers Coming and Going

1. The theme of collegiality in the spread of the gospel is discussed by Gottfried Schille, *Die urchristliche Kollegialmission* (Zürich: Zwingli Verlag, 1967). For the circle of Paul's friends and colleagues, see also F. F. Bruce, *The Pauline Circle* (Grand Rapids: Eerdmans, 1985), and for a comparison with the role of envoys in the Hellenistic world, see Margaret M. Mitchell, "New Testament Envoys in the Context of Greco-Roman Diplomatic and Epistolary Conventions: The Example of Timothy and Titus," *Journal of Biblical Literature* 111 (1992): 641–62.

2. The Majority Text reads *Achaia*, some older manuscripts read *Asia*.

3. The word *aparchē* is often understood to refer to the "firstfruits" (Epenetus then would have been one of the first converts in Asia or Achaia; cf. NIV, Rom. 16:5; 1 Cor. 16:15). However, in the Septuagint the word *prōtogennēma* is more frequently used for "firstfruits." And in the Greek temples everyone would read the word *aparchē* as an inscription on votive offerings to the deity (see H. Beer, *Aparchee und verwandte Ausdrücke in griechischen Weihinschriften* [unpub. thesis, Würzburg, 1914]). Furthermore, early conversion was not considered a special privilege in the church. It is therefore well possible to see Epenetus as a "votive offering of Achaia for Christ." The churches in Achaia apparently relinquished this brother for the service of the gospel in Rome. In 1 Corinthians 16:15–18 the "household of Stephanas" appear to have given themselves to service to the saints as "*aparchē* of Achaia," and Paul expresses his gratitude for this in a letter to Corinth.

4. According to Richard S. Cervin ("A Note regarding the Name 'Junia(s)' in Romans 16.7," *New Testament Studies* 40 [1994]: 464–470), *Iunia* is a (Latin) woman's name, not a shortened form of *Iunianus*, a man's name. The male name *Iunius* would have been written in Greek as *Iounios* (not *Iounias*). See also John Thorley, "Junia, a Woman Apostle" (*Novum Testamentum* 38 [1996]: 18–29). It is, however, open to question whether Andronicus and Junia were apostles (see following note). The reading *Julia* is attested by only a few manuscripts (among them one papyrus).

5. The expression *episēmoi en tois apostolois* (Rom. 16:7) indicates that these two individuals were well known to the apostles or that they themselves belonged to the apostles. In the latter case they probably belonged to the seventy who were once sent out by Jesus (Luke 10). Because Paul says that they are also ahead of him (see note 7 below), it seems probable that Andronicus and Junia were well known among the apostles as a couple who were active in the gospel.

6. They are not called "fellow prisoners"—Paul was not in prison when he wrote this letter. They are *sunaichmalōtoi*: fellow "prisoners of war." The apostle sees himself as a prisoner of war of Christ, who leads him in a triumphal procession (2 Cor. 2:14), and his colleagues in the gospel then share in that status (Col. 4:10; Philem. 23). Because they have become prisoners of war, they are *slaves* (not prisoners).

7. The phrase *hoi kai pro emou gegonan en Christōi* is often understood as indicating that these people were already converts before Paul became a Christian (*pro emou* is then connected with *en Christōi*). But immediately preceding this phrase we read that they are "famous among the apostles," and in this respect they also appear to have an advantage over Paul (*kai pro emou*). In Greek, *ginomai pro* can mean that one is ahead of someone else on the road. Because Paul still is not in Rome and his "relatives" Andronicus and Junia are already there, the apostle can say with a touch of humor, "in Christ they have pulled away and left me in their dust."

8. The usual translation appears to be supported by a fragment of a biography of Philonides, found in Herculaneum: "for the best-loved of relatives or friends one might perhaps be willing to risk his neck" (*parabaloi an hetoimōs ton trachēlon*). See Adolf Deissmann, *Light from the Ancient East: The New Testament Illustrated by Recently Discovered Texts of the Graeco-Roman World*, 4th ed., 1923 (reprint, Grand Rapids: Baker, 1965), 94–95. However, the verb *paraballein* is used there, whereas Paul writes *hypotithenai*. This latter verb does not allude to the "giving up" or "risking" of one's neck, but rather to "subordinating, placing under." This is not about risk but about servitude (cf. Sirach 51:26: "put [*hypothete*] your neck [*trachēlon*] under the yoke"; 1 Clement 63.1 and Acts 15:1).

9. Paul uses the image of working under a yoke for service in the gospel also elsewhere (1 Cor. 9:9–10; Phil. 4:3).

10. The expression "my soul" (*hē psychē mou*) can mean "I myself" (1 Thess. 2:8; cf. 2 Cor. 12:15). For the idea of working in someone else's place, see also Philem. 13 and Col. 1:7.

11. *diakonon*; see Rom. 16:1 NIV footnote.

12. Concerning Phoebe, see Jakob van Bruggen, "Een vrouw waar geen woorden voor te vinden zijn," in *Ambt en aktualiteit*, ed. F. H. Folkerts et al. (Haarlem: Vijlbrief, 1992), 51–60.

13. When the apostle asks Timothy to bring the cloak which he left with Carpus in Troas (2 Tim. 4:13), he does so because he needs this cloak because of the cold, which suggests that at this point he had not yet spent many winters in Rome. Apparently the cloak was left in Troas in the spring, at the end of the third missionary jour-

ney (Acts 20:5–6), and Paul did not need it in the years he spent in Caesarea. But in Rome, where the temperatures drop lower, he misses his cloak. He hopes that Timothy can bring it with him before the beginning of the next winter (2 Tim. 4:21).

14. The apostle also asks for books (2 Tim. 4:13). This indicates that he is prepared for a lengthy imprisonment. In Caesarea there were continually hope and fear, and it became clear only gradually that his imprisonment there would last for years. In Rome the situation is more stable, so that Paul in this situation is preparing himself for a long stay.

15. When Paul writes that he "left Trophimus sick in Miletus" (2 Tim. 4:20), he does not mean that he himself had recently been in Miletus. The apostle sends his collaborators to serve in various locations, but he can lose their active collaboration when they are under way. Thus he had to accept the fact that Trophimus remained in Miletus and could no longer be deployed. Paul lost him through his illness in Miletus.

Chapter 14: Given Up as Missing

1. J. van Eck also calls the "meeting with the emperor" the "goal to which the last part of Acts points" (*Paulus en de koningen: politieke aspecten van het boek Handelingen* [Franeker: Van Wijnen, 1989], 21–22, 86).

2. See, among others, W. M. Ramsay, *St. Paul: The Traveller and the Roman Citizen* (London: Hodder and Stoughton, 1905; reprint, Grand Rapids: Baker, 1963), 23, 27–28.

3. For this hypothesis, see Nicolaas G. Veldhoen, *Het proces van den apostel Paulus* (Alphen aan den Rijn: Samsom, 1924); and Henry J. Cadbury, "Roman Law and the Trial of Paul," in *The Beginnings of Christianity*, ed. Kirsopp Lake and Henry J. Cadbury (London: Macmillan, 1933), 5:297–338. The hypothesis is challenged by Adrian Nicolas Sherwin-White, *Roman Society and Roman Law in the New Testament* (Oxford: Clarendon Press, 1963), 108–19. According to Harry W. Tajra (*The Trial of St. Paul: A Juridical Exegesis of the Second Half of the Acts of the Apostles* [Tübingen: Mohr, 1989], 193–96), Paul had to be released after two years, but when he was released he did not receive a declaration of innocence, so that his position could remain suspect in the eyes of the Roman authorities.

4. Colin J. Hemer (*The Book of Acts in the Setting of Hellenistic History* [Tübingen: Mohr, 1989], 365–410) gives a detailed description of the various theories that have been proposed to explain the puzzling ending of Acts. Hemer himself links the ending to the dating of Acts: When Luke finished Acts 28, he did not yet know the further events of Paul's life and he also did not know yet that the somber expectations pronounced by the elders in Miletus (Acts 20:38) would not be fulfilled because the apostle (against expectations) would travel once again in the east. The book of Acts would have been concluded "before Paul's renewed travels had falsified the expectation" (p. 407). Against this solution stands that Paul in Acts 20:20–29 did not voice personal expectations but rather reported what the Holy Spirit revealed to him.

5. For an overview of the earliest sources concerning Paul's martyrdom, see Harry W. Tajra, *The Martyrdom of St. Paul: Historical and Judicial Context, Traditions, and Legends* (Tübingen: Mohr, 1994), 118–97.

6. Tacitus, *Annales* 15.44.

7. George Ogg (*The Odyssey of Paul* [Old Tappan, N.J.: Revell, 1968]; U.K. edition: *The Chronology of the Life of Paul* [London: Epworth Press, 1968], 194) speaks of the Neronian persecution of A.D. 64. The persecution actually lasted longer. The first immediate cause was the fire of Rome (A.D. 64), but the persecutions continued until the end of Nero's reign (in A.D. 68) and did not remain limited to only one year. See Jakob van Bruggen, "Na vele jaren: Stadhouder Felix en de jaren van Paulus," in *Almanak Fides Quadrat Intellectum* (Kampen: Zalsman, 1979), 119–54, esp. 145–48.

8. See Ernest Best, "Recipients and Title of the Letter to the Ephesians: Why and When the Designation 'Ephesians'?" in *Aufstieg und Niedergang der Römischen Welt* 2.25.4: *Religion*, ed. Wolfgang Haase (Berlin: Walter de Gruyter, 1987), 3245–79.

9. Thus Ernest Best, "Ephesians 1.1" and "Ephesians 1.1 Again," in *Essays on Ephesians* (Edinburgh: T & T Clark, 1997), 1–24.

10. (1) In only five of our manuscripts are the words "in Ephesus" missing in Ephesians 1:1 (in two of the five—Vaticanus and Sinaiticus—the phrase was added later).

(2) In all manuscripts, "To the Ephesians" stands above the text as the address. These superscriptions date, like those above the Gospels, from the first century (Martin Hengel, *Die Evangelienüberschriften* [Heidelberg: Winter, 1984]).

(3) Marcion did not change the address at the beginning of the letter, but he interpolated the text of 1:1, and thus in the second century he found there the words "in Ephesus." (See Tertullian, *Adversus Marcionem* 5.17.1: "Marcion et titulum aliquando interpolare gestit," where *titulus* refers, in accordance with the classical meaning of the word, to the introductory paragraph and not to the title or superscription.)

(4) It would appear that Origen used a text that omitted "in Ephesus." (See the fragments published by J. A. F. Gregg, "The Commentary of Origen upon the Epistle to the Ephesians," *Journal of Theological Studies* 3 [1902]: 233–44, 398–420, 551–76.) However, he does view the letter as having been addressed to the Ephesians (see fragment 119.11, 120.4). According to some, the statement in fragment 102.2 that in the letter to the Ephesians only the words "to the saints who are" are found indicates that "in Ephesus" is missing. However, the statement should be translated "[The letter to] the Ephesians is the only one in which we find the expression 'to the saints' " (*epi monōn Ephesiōn heuromen keimenon to tois hagiois tois ousi*). Origen notes that only in this letter, between the words "to the saints" and "in Ephesus," are two words that at first glance seem to be redundant, viz., "who are." Origen takes these words in an absolute sense, which leads him to an elaboration on the "being" of the Christians. His comment is based on the fact that this expression about "the being saints" is found in conjunction with the mention of the Ephesians at the beginning of the letter (Eph. 1:1). Origen knew only a text that included the phrase "in Ephesus" in 1:1.

11. Tychicus is mentioned in both Colossians 4:7 and Ephesians 6:21 as the person who will further inform the Christian community about Paul. Because this name appears in both letters, the letters to Ephesus and Colossae are often viewed as having been sent at the same time and delivered to the churches by Tychicus. This coworker is also mentioned in 2 Timothy 4:12 ("I sent Tychicus to Ephesus"). It is, however, not possible that Tychicus would have taken the letter to the Colossians with him on this occasion, for two reasons. (1) Colossians was sent at the same time as the letter to Philemon, at a time when Paul considered the possibility of visiting the church in Colossae soon (Philem. 22). (2) At the time when Paul sent the letters to the Colossians and to Philemon there were a large number of coworkers with Paul, but when 2 Timothy was written these coworkers were not present, or different names are mentioned.

It is therefore more plausible that Tychicus left from Caesarea with the letters to the Colossians and to Philemon to go to Asia, and that many years later he is sent again from Rome to the region with which he was so familiar (he came from Asia; see Acts 20:4). He then took the letter to the Ephesians with him on this later journey.

Chapter 15: Paul in the Constellation of the Apostles

1. According to some interpreters Paul's words "whatever they were" do not refer to their uninfluential social background but rather to their personal relationship with Jesus during his life on earth. Paul then indicates that he does not consider this especially important (Donald Guthrie, *Galatians* [London: Oliphants, 1974; Grand Rapids: Eerdmans, 1981]). But this interpretation does not do justice to the fact that being "ear- and eyewitnesses" is not only something out of the past, but lends permanent special status.

2. According to Calvin J. Roetzel (*Paul: The Man and the Myth* [Minneapolis: Fortress Press, 1999], 135–51), Paul's celibacy was an expression of his ascetic piety in which he was a sign of the approaching cosmic crisis. But such a theological framing of his being unmarried as an apostle makes it difficult to explain why the apostle accepts with ease that the other apostles *are* married. His life as an unmarried man would appear, therefore, to have more to do with his special sense of duty as the least of the apostles.

3. Herman N. Ridderbos, *Paul: An Outline of His Theology* (Grand Rapids: Eerdmans, 1975). See also the section on Paul in George Eldon Ladd, *A Theology of the New Testament* (Grand Rapids: Eerdmans, 1974). Ridderbos looks for the genius of Paul's theology in his eschatology, in which there is a tension between the "already" and the "not yet" of the salvation in Jesus Christ. Ladd sees the core of Paul's thinking in the conviction that the center of salvation history lies in the redeeming work of God in Jesus Christ, by which a new era was ushered in. Robert L. Reymond, *Paul: Missionary Theologian* (Fearn: Christian Focus Publications, 2000), prefers to speak about Paul's "missionary theology": "I intend to present Paul's theology in the form of a 'mini' systematic theology which takes into account Paul's perception of the triune God's gracious work of saving the elect and restoring the cosmos to its paradi-

saical state by the cross-work of Christ. I see no real profit in trying to capture his thought by a 'biblical theology' method of presentation" (p. 309).

4. For a detailed description of Räisänen's convictions and his place in New Testament theology, see T. E. van Spanje, *Inconsistency in Paul? A Critique of the Work of Heikki Räisänen* (Tübingen: Mohr Siebeck, 1999).

5. See, for example, Alan F. Segal, *Paul the Convert: The Apostolate and Apostasy of Saul the Pharisee* (New Haven: Yale University Press, 1990).

6. J. Christiaan Beker, *Paul the Apostle: The Triumph of God in Life and Thought* (Philadelphia: Fortress Press, 1980).

7. Society of Biblical Literature Symposium Series 1–4 (Minneapolis: Fortress Press, 1991–97): Jouette M. Bassler, ed., *Pauline Theology: Thessalonians, Philippians, Galatians, Philemon* (1991); David M. Hay, ed., *Pauline Theology: 1 and 2 Corinthians* (1993); David M. Hay and E. Elizabeth Johnson, eds., *Pauline Theology: Romans* (1995); E. Elizabeth Johnson and David M. Hay, eds., *Pauline Theology: Looking Back, Pressing On* (1997).

8. Paul W. Meyer, "Pauline Theology: A Proposal for a Pause in Its Pursuit," in Johnson and Hay, *Looking Back, Pressing On*, 140–60. Meyer writes, "Paul's theology in particular is not the *father* of his 'theologizing' but its *child*" (p. 152).

9. Thus James D. G. Dunn, "In Quest of Paul's Theology: Retrospect and Prospect," in Johnson and Hay, *Looking Back, Pressing On*, 95–115.

10. The idea of E. Haenchen, P. Vielhauer, and others that there are drastic differences between Paul as he is presented in Acts and Paul as he is known from his own letters is refuted in detail by Stanley E. Porter, *The Paul of Acts: Essays in Literary Criticism, Rhetoric, and Theology* (Tübingen: Mohr Siebeck, 1999).

11. Paul himself gives in Romans 1:3 the earth-born Jesus the title "Son of God," and in 1:4 he delineates in what way Jesus' exaltation showed him to be "Son of God" (*horizesthai* does not mean "appoint" but "demarcate, clearly delineate"). In the text itself we find no reason for the hypothesis of an older, more adoptionist stratum, against which the Pauline Christology then stands as a renewal. For a detailed discussion of the opinions concerning an alleged pre-Pauline confession in this passage, see J. P. Versteeg, *Christus en de Geest: Een exegetisch onderzoek naar de verhouding van de opgestane Christus en de Geest van God volgens de brieven van Paulus* (Kampen: Kok, 1971), 97–130.

12. See C. H. Dodd, *The Apostolic Preaching and Its Developments* (London: Hodder & Stoughton, 1936; New York: Harper & Brothers, 1944, 1951).

13. See George W. Knight, *The Faithful Sayings in the Pastoral Letters* (Kampen: Kok, 1968).

14. See Jakob van Bruggen, "Vaste grond onder de voeten: De formule *pistos ho logos* in de Pastorale Brieven," in *Bezield verband: Opstellen aangeboden aan Prof. J. Kamphuis* (Kampen: Van den Berg, 1984), 38–45.

15. The NIV paraphrases, "So from now on we regard no one from a worldly point of view. Though we once regarded Christ in this way, we do so no longer."

16. For 2 Corinthians 5:16, see also B. C. Lategan, *Die aardse Jesus in die prediking van Paulus volgens sy briewe* (Rotterdam: Bronder-offset, 1967), 200–218.

17. See David Wenham, *Paul: Follower of Jesus or Founder of Christianity?* (Grand Rapids: Eerdmans, 1995); Paul W. Barnett, *Jesus and the Logic of History* (Grand Rapids: Eerdmans; Leicester: Apollos, 1997), 39–58.

18. See Jonggil Byun, *The Holy Spirit Was Not Yet: A Study on the Relationship between the Coming of the Holy Spirit and the Glorification of Jesus according to John 7:39* (Kampen: Kok, 1992).

19. For a more detailed discussion of the central points in Jesus' preaching that follow, see Jakob van Bruggen, *Jesus the Son of God: The Gospel Narratives as Message* (Grand Rapids: Baker, 1999).

20. For Paul and the law, see chapters 16 and 17.

Chapter 16: God's Envoy to the Nations

1. For a description of the current state of affairs on this issue, see Terence L. Donaldson, *Paul and the Gentiles: Remapping the Apostle's Convictional World* (Minneapolis: Fortress, 1997).

2. Otfried Hofius ("Paulus—Missionar und Theologe," in Jostein Adna et al., eds., *Evangelium, Schriftauslegung, Kirche* [Göttingen: Vandenhoeck & Ruprecht, 1997], 224–37) thinks that Paul, after long theological reflection on the event near Damascus, finally came to the conviction that he had to put the primary emphasis on preaching to the Gentiles. This conviction is thought to have developed especially through a reinterpretation of Isaiah 40–55.

3. James D. G. Dunn (*The Epistle to the Galatians* [Peabody, Mass.: Hendrickson, 1993], 111–12) wants to limit the agreement to the responsibility for the Christians among the Gentiles and the Jews respectively. The agreement then is not so much related to the spread of the gospel as to the care for the converted Christians. But this limited agreement runs counter to the deliberations that are the basis for the agreement: "They saw that I had been entrusted with the task of preaching the gospel to the Gentiles, just as Peter had been to the Jews" (Gal. 2:7).

4. T. E. van Spanje, *Inconsistency in Paul? A Critique of the Work of Heikki Räisänen* (Tübingen: Mohr Siebeck, 1999), 178.

5. Ernest de Witt Burton, *A Critical and Exegetical Commentary on the Epistle to the Galatians* (Edinburgh: T & T Clark, 1921), 96–99, esp. 98: "The meaning of the agreement was that Paul and Barnabas were to preach the gospel in Gentile lands, the other apostles in Jewish lands." J. Munck, *Paulus und die Heilsgeschichte* (Aarhus: Universitetsforlaget, 1954), 112: ". . . in this division, Peter received Palestine, Syria, and probably also the eastern regions in- and outside the Roman Empire. Paul was allotted all of the Greek Diaspora, stretching westward from Syria as far as Roman rule extended." See also F. Mussner, *Der Galaterbrief* (Freiburg: Herder, 1974), 122–23; Frank J. Matera, *Galatians* (Collegeville, Minn.: Liturgical Press, 1992), 77–78.

6. Richard N. Longenecker, *Galatians* (Dallas: Word, 1990), 58–59.

7. J. Louis Martyn (*Galatians: A New Translation with Introduction and Commentary* [New York: Doubleday, 1997], 213) speaks of "two simultaneous lines of mission distinguished from one another ethnically." Ben Witherington III (*Grace in Galatia: A Commentary on Paul's Letter to the Galatians* [Edinburgh: T & T Clark, 1998], 141) writes, "There was probably considerably more overlap in these Petrine and Pauline spheres of ministry than one might suspect on a superficial inspection of the matter."

8. See P. H. R. van Houwelingen, *1 Petrus: Rondzendbrief uit Babylon* (Kampen: Kok, 1991), 26–27.

9. Peter Stuhlmacher (*Das paulinische Evangelium, Vol. 1, Vorgeschichte* [Göttingen: Vandenhoeck & Ruprecht, 1968], 100) is of the opinion that the Jerusalem agreement soon appeared to be impossible to carry out in practice, since it did not contain provisions (1) for mixed regions and (2) for mutual communication.

10. 1 Cor. 16:1–4; 2 Cor. 8–9; Rom. 15:25–28. The *ptōchoi* (poor) mentioned in the collection-agreement (Gal. 2:10) are not identical with "the saints in Jerusalem." At issue here is not a juridical recognition of the mother-community, as argued by Karl Holl ("Der Kirchenbegriff des Paulus in seinem Verhältnis zu dem der Urgemeinde," in *Gesammelte Aufsätze zur Kirchengeschichte, vol. 2, Der Osten* [Tübingen: Mohr, 1928], 55–61). Nor is the issue recognition of the eschatological community in Jerusalem, as argued by Dieter Georgi (*Die Geschichte der Kollekte des Paulus für Jerusalem* [Hamburg: Herbert Reich Evangelischer Verlag, 1965], 21–30). The "poor" as a specific group truly in need of assistance are distinguished from the Christian community of circumcised Christians as a whole, which is referred to as "the circumcision" in Galatians 2:9. See also Leander E. Keck, "The Poor among the Saints in the New Testament," *Zeitschrift für die neutestamentliche Wissenschaft* 56 (1965): 100–129, and "The Poor among the Saints in Jewish Christianity and Qumran," *Zeitschrift für die neutestamentliche Wissenschaft* 57 (1966): 54–78. The material gift for the poor among the circumcised is a demonstration of the fact that the Gentile Christians now share the spiritual gifts with the Jewish mother-church (Rom. 15:27).

11. Georgi (*Die Geschichte der Kollekte*, 22) and K. F. Nickle (*The Collection: A Study in Paul's Strategy* [London: SCM Press, 1966], 129–42) incorrectly view the collection as a means to bring about harmony between Jewish Christians and Gentile Christians. It is, rather, a means to confirm that unity. They do state correctly, however, that this collection is proof of "the real and full inclusion of Gentile believers into the Body of Christ" (Nickle, *Collection*, 129). For the collection, see also Burkhard Beckheuer, *Paulus und Jerusalem: Kollekte und Mission im theologischen Denken des Heidenapostels* (Frankfurt: Peter Lang, 1997); S. Janse, *Paulus en Jeruzalem: Een onderzoek naar de heilshistorische betekenis van Jeruzalem in de brieven van Paulus* (Zoetermeer: Boekencentrum, 2000).

12. See chapter 18.2.3 for a discussion of the question why Paul often begins with preaching in synagogues, even though he wants to reach the Gentiles.

13. 2 Cor. 4:3; 1 Thess. 1:5; 2 Thess. 2:14.

14. See also Daniel J.-S. Chae, *Paul as Apostle to the Gentiles* (Carlisle: Paternoster Press, 1997), 297–99, 302–7.

15. In *Contra Apionem* 2.145–296, Josephus describes in a summary statement the lofty qualities of the laws of Moses. In these laws, all of human life is absorbed into religion, reverence for the one God (2.165–71, 190–92), and the virtue of solidarity with humanity (2.211–14). Thus the laws of Moses have given humanity most of their good ideas (2.281–86). On the other hand, Josephus describes these laws as a coherent system of national-religious laws, given by the national lawgiver Moses. These laws established a nation and lent a special quality to that nation (2.179–89). The unifying concept is that of the Jewish theocracy in contrast to the monarchy, oligarchy, or democracy among other nations (2.164–67). For a more detailed discussion, see appendix 3 in this book.

16. See Abraham J. Malherbe, "Conversion to Paul's Gospel," in Abraham J. Malherbe, Frederick W. Norris, and James W. Thompson, eds., *The Early Church and Its Context: Essays in Honor of Everett Ferguson* (Leiden: Brill, 1998), 237–41.

17. Morna D. Hooker ("1 Thessalonians 1.9–10: A Nutshell—But What Kind of Nut?" in *Geschichte—Tradition—Reflexion*, ed. Hermann Lichtenberger [Tübingen: Mohr, 1996], 435–48) challenges the widespread idea that these verses present a summary of the gospel. She views them as a summary of what Paul is going to write in the next chapter. Nevertheless these verses remain (also) a summary indication of the central effects the basic preaching has had.

18. Thus Josephus criticizes (along with the enlightened Greek philosophers) the anthropomorphic idol-images of polytheism (*Contra Apionem* 2.236–54). They are in conflict with what can be seen of God in creation: "By His works and bounties He is plainly seen, indeed more manifest than ought else. . . . We behold His works: the light, the heaven, the earth, the sun, the waters, the reproductive creatures, the sprouting crops. . . . Him must we worship by the practice of virtue; for that is the most saintly manner of worshipping God" (*Contra Apionem* 2.190–92 [trans. H. St. J. Thackeray, Loeb edition]); cf. Paul's words in Rom. 1:18–32.

19. Although most Bible versions put it at the end of chapter 16, a great many manuscripts put this doxology at the conclusion of chapter 14 (Rom. 14:24–26). The phrase in question is found as Romans 14:24 in the edition of the Majority Text by Zane C. Hodges and Arthur L. Farstad, *The Greek New Testament according to the Majority Text*, 2d ed. (Nashville: Nelson, 1985).

20. In Acts 6:7 we read of "being obedient *to* the faith." Here "faith" is not a further aspect of being obedient ("obeying in faith"), but rather an indication of the content of the gospel to which one submits in faith ("*the* faith").

21. The link between faith and obedience is much less clear in other versions: "But not all the Israelites accepted the good news" (NIV); "They did not all heed the glad tidings" (NASB).

22. In general it involves taking captive every thought "to make it obedient to Christ" (2 Cor. 10:5–6); being obedient "always" (Phil. 2:12); not obeying the gospel

(2 Thess. 1:8). For its application in concrete situations, see 2 Cor. 7:15; 2 Thess. 3:14; Philem. 21 (Paul's obedience).

23. Gerhard Friedrich, "Muss *hypakoē pisteōs* Röm 1,5 mit 'Glaubensgehorsam' übersetzt werden?" *Zeitschrift für die neutestamentliche Wissenschaft* 72 [1981]: 118–23).

24. The grammatical terminology varies considerably in the treatment of this point in the commentaries. For a more extensive discussion of this aspect, see Jakob van Bruggen, "Geloofsgehoorzaamheid: De betekenis van een paulinische formulering voor de ethiek," in *Nuchtere noodzaak: ethiek tussen navolging en compromis*, ed. J. H. F. Schaeffer, J. H. Smit, and Th. Tromp (Kampen: Kok, 1997), 85–86.

25. Thus, for example, the commentaries by Murray (1959), Käsemann (1974), Cranfield (1975); Schmithals (1988).

26. Glenn N. Davies, *Faith and Obedience in Romans: A Study in Romans 1–4* (Sheffield: Academic Press, 1990), 30.

27. See the commentary by Krimmer (1983).

28. See the commentaries on Romans 1:5 by J. D. G. Dunn (1988), John Ziesler (1989), Douglas Moo (1991), Robert H. Mounce (1995). Don B. Garlington (*Faith, Obedience and Perseverance* [Tübingen: Mohr, 1994], 30) writes, "Paul has chosen to coin an *ambiguous* phrase expressive of two ideas: the obedience which consists in faith, and the obedience which is the product of faith."

29. See the commentary on Romans by Joseph A. Fitzmyer (1993). For agreement with Fitzmyer's use of the term "commitment," see Garlington, *Faith, Obedience and Perseverance*, 31.

30. Don B. Garlington, "The Obedience of Faith in the Letter to the Romans," *Westminster Theological Journal* 52 (1990): 201–24; 53 (1991): 47–72; 55 (1993): 87–112; idem, *"The Obedience of Faith": A Pauline Phrase in Historical Context* (Tübingen: Mohr, 1991); idem, *Faith, Obedience and Perseverance*. Cf. the commentary on Romans by Heiko Krimmer (1983).

31. Mark D. Nanos, *The Mystery of Romans: The Jewish Context of Paul's Letter* (Minneapolis: Fortress, 1996), 218–38 ("The Obedience of Faith and the Apostolic Decree").

32. See also Brad H. Young, *Paul the Jewish Theologian: A Pharisee among Christians, Jews, and Gentiles* (Peabody, Mass.: Hendrickson, 1997).

33. Carleton Paget ("Jewish Proselytism," *Journal for the Study of the New Testament* 62 [1996]: 65–103) is of the opinion that the non-Christian Jews became jealous of Paul (Acts 17:4–5) because he made converts for Christ among those people whom the Jewish missionaries specifically considered to be their sphere of activity.

34. Josephus, *Antiquities* 13.257, 318 (trans. Ralph Marcus, Loeb edition).

35. Josephus, *Antiquities* 13.258.

36. Josephus, *Jewish War* 2.454 (trans. H. St. J. Thackeray, Loeb edition). D. R. Schwarz ("God, Gentiles, and Jewish Law: On Acts 15 and Josephus' Adiabene Narrative," in *Geschichte—Tradition—Reflexion, Vol. 1, Judentum*, ed. Peter Schäfer

[Tübingen: Mohr, 1996], 263–82) is of the opinion that there was only one choice (becoming a Jew, including circumcision, or standing outside Judaism). This passage about Metilius alone is enough to make Schwarz's interpretation of Josephus's story about Izates debatable.

37. Josephus, *Antiquities* 20.34 (trans. Louis H. Feldman, Loeb edition).

38. Ibid., 20.38.

39. Ibid., 20.39.

40. Ibid., 20.41.

41. Ibid., 20.44–45.

42. Ibid., 20.48.

43. Ibid., 20.49–69.

44. Thus Jonathan Z. Smith ("Fences and Neighbors," in *Approaches to Ancient Judaism*, vol. 2, ed. William Scott Green [Chicago: Scholars Press, 1980], 14): "A convert to Judaism need not be circumcised, but may elect to do so (*Ant.* 20.41,46)."

45. Josephus, *Antiquities* 20.43.

46. Terence L. Donaldson (*Paul and the Gentiles: Remapping the Apostle's Convictional World* [Minneapolis: Fortress Press, 1997], 277–78) is of the opinion that Eleazar can be compared to Saul, who was also involved in converting Gentiles before he was called to Christ, but as a preacher of the circumcision (Gal. 5:11). This comparison between Saul and Eleazar makes sense to the extent that both were uncompromising adherents of Judaism. But it is not convincing historically when mission to the Gentiles is made the point of comparison. First, Josephus never depicts Eleazar as a purposeful preacher among the Gentiles, but rather as a Jew with deep convictions who expresses his opinions openly. Second, there are no traces of any missionary activity, aimed at the Gentiles, on Saul's part in the period before he became a Christian. In Galatians 5:11 ("if I am still preaching circumcision") he does not put himself in line with Jews who want to make Gentiles proselytes through circumcision. Rather, he contrasts himself with Jewish Christians who combine the gospel of Christ with the requirement of circumcision for the Gentiles, because by doing so they abolish the offense of the cross. The word *still* (*eti*) that the apostle uses ("if I am *still* preaching circumcision") does not look back to a period before his conversion to Christ. The apostle Paul expresses himself here somewhat elliptically; his intent is "if as a preacher of the gospel I am still requiring circumcision of the Gentiles. . . ." After all, circumcision as such is never "preached" (not even by the Jews), but is a requirement that either is or is not demanded from people who accept the preaching of the one God and join his people. Paul forms the expression *peritomēn kēryssein* (preaching circumcision) by analogy with *Christon kēryssein* (preaching Christ). See Seyoon Kim, *The Origin of Paul's Gospel* (Tübingen: Mohr, 1981), 40 n. 5. See also Karl-Wilhelm Niebuhr, *Heidenapostel aus Israel: Die jüdische Identität des Paulus nach ihrer Darstellung in seinen Briefen* (Tübingen: Mohr, 1992), 68–69. The apostle expresses himself ironically with a counterfactual statement, and it is incorrect to use this contrary-to-fact statement to draw conclusions concerning the historical reality. Paul merely

wants to emphasize that he is willing to suffer much to preach Christ among the nations and not circumcision (which he at one time defended as a custom that could never be surrendered).

47. It is going too far to say with McEleney that proselytes thus could be exempted from circumcision in some cases (Neil J. McEleney, "Conversion, Circumcision and the Law," *New Testament Studies* 20 [1973–74]: 328ff.). According to J. Nolland ("Uncircumcised Proselytes?" *Journal for the Study of Judaism* 12 [1981]: 192ff.) the uncircumcised individual can never be considered a Jew, although he can be religiously linked to the Jews as God-fearer, because there is an awareness of the great value of spiritual circumcision. See Philo, *De specialibus legibus* 1.1–12 and *Quaestiones et Solutiones in Genesin et Exodum* 2.2; R. Le Déaut, "Le thème de la circoncision du coeur (Dt. XXX 6; Jér. IV 4) dans les versions anciennes (LXX et Targum) et à Qumrân," in *Congress Volume: Vienna 1980*, ed. J. A. Emerton (Leiden: Brill, 1981), 178–205. See also Martin Goodman, "Jewish Proselytizing in the First Century," in *The Jews among Pagans and Christians in the Roman Empire*, ed. Judith Lieu, John North, and Tessa Rajak (London and New York: Routledge, 1992), 68–69.

48. Josephus, *Antiquities* 20.42.

49. According to Martin Hengel and Anna Maria Schwemer (*Paul between Damascus and Antioch: The Unknown Years* [Louisville: Westminster/John Knox, 1997], 64–65) Ananias represents the practice in the Diaspora and Eleazar the strict position in Palestine. But the specific details of Josephus's story preclude the drawing of such generalizing conclusions.

50. Sometimes Ananias is presented incorrectly as a liberal Jew for whom conversion is more important than circumcision. He is then promoted to soul mate of Paul the Christian (F. M. Derwachter, *Preparing the Way for Paul: The Proselyte Movement in Later Judaism* [New York: Macmillan, 1930], 46–48; Derwachter himself later mitigates his thesis [104–5]). Ananias's position vis-à-vis Eleazar is sometimes also compared to the position of Paul and Barnabas with respect to Peter and James (J. Klausner, *From Jesus to Paul* [New York: Macmillan, 1943; London: Allen & Unwin, 1944], 38–40).

Also incorrect is the idea that Ananias represented the Hillelites, who are thought not to have made circumcision an absolute requirement for the proselytes. It is true that in the Judaism of Hillel's time there was discussion on the question as to what must be done with Jewish children who are born without foreskin (are they then in fact already circumcised, or is it still necessary for a drop of blood to flow?), and in later times the discussion shifted to question whether a Gentile who is converted to Judaism and was circumcised before his conversion (perhaps not with an eye to his conversion) must still give drops of blood. With this comes the question whether the ritual bath (which dates from a later time) makes the convert to Judaism who had earlier been circumcised legally a Jew, or whether he should already be considered a Jew after his conversion (on the basis of his prior circumcision) and before the ritual bath. All these discussions involve details of the application of a commandment, but in Izates' case the issue is whether, under certain circumstances, a commandment may and must be subordinated to higher commandments or considerations (Bernard J. Bamberger, *Proselytism in the Talmudic Period* [New York: Ktav, 1968], 45–52).

Chapter 17: Gospel without Law for Gentile Christians

1. Thus, among others, Wilhelm Bousset, *Die Religion des Judentums in spät-hellenistischen Zeitalter*, 3rd ed., ed. Hugo Gressmann (Tübingen: Mohr, 1926).

2. Solomon Schechter, *Aspects of Rabbinic Theology*, new edition, ed. Louis Finkelstein (New York: Schocken, 1961); George Foot Moore, *Judaism in the First Centuries of the Christian Era: The Age of the Tannaim* (Cambridge, Mass.: Harvard University Press, 1927–30).

3. E. P. Sanders, *Paul and Palestinian Judaism: A Comparison of Patterns of Religion* (Philadelphia: Fortress; London: SCM Press, 1977).

4. James D. G. Dunn, *Jesus, Paul and the Law* (Louisville: Westminster/John Knox, 1990).

5. James D. G. Dunn, *Romans* (Dallas: Word, 1988). See also idem, *The Theology of Paul the Apostle* (Edinburgh: T & T Clark; Grand Rapids: Eerdmans, 1998), 354–66: "In sum, then, the 'works' which Paul consistently warns against were, in his view, Israel's misunderstanding of what her covenant law required. That misunderstanding focused most sharply on Jewish attempts to maintain their covenant distinctiveness from Gentiles and on Christian Jews' attempts to require Christian Gentiles to adopt such covenant distinctives. Furthermore, that misunderstanding meant a misunderstanding of God and of God's promised (covenanted) intention to bless also the nations" (p. 366). In this quote it is apparent that for Dunn the accent shifts from a negative perspective on "works" as such to a wrong interpretation of works.

6. In "The New Perspective on Paul" (*Bulletin of the John Rylands Library* 65 [1983]: 95–122), Dunn concentrates on Galatians 2:16: the Jews do not see works as meritorious but as badges. In his "Works of the Law and the Curse of the Law (Galatians 3,10–14)" (*New Testament Studies* 31 [1985]: 523–42) he elaborates this opinion.

7. In his commentary on Romans, Dunn interprets Romans 3:20 as follows: the works of the law are demarcating "identity markers" through which the Gentiles are denied justification by Israel's God. Cranfield presents a series of arguments against this exegesis, as well as against Dunn's exegesis of Romans 3:28 and of instances where *erga* occurs without *nomou*, such as Romans 9:11–12 (C. E. B. Cranfield, "The Works of the Law in the Epistle to the Romans," *Journal for the Study of the New Testament* 43 [1991]: 89–101; idem, *On Romans and Other New Testament Essays* [Edinburgh: T & T Clark, 1998], 1–14).

8. James D. G. Dunn ("Paul's Conversion—A Light to Twentieth Century Disputes," in *Evangelium, Schriftauslegung, Kirche*, ed. Jostein Adna et al. [Göttingen: Vandenhoeck & Ruprecht, 1997], 77–93) characterizes Paul's conversion as a conversion from a separatist Judaism focused on boundaries to a Judaism that wanted to fulfill its eschatological mission among the nations (92). See also Dunn, *Theology of*

Paul the Apostle, 346–54: the Judaism Paul broke with was a specific form of Judaism, viz., the inwardly focused Judaism that stood in opposition to Hellenistic Judaism, which had a more open attitude toward the nations.

9. Michael Winger, "Meaning and Law," *Journal of Biblical Literature* 117 (1998): 105–10; Harm W. Hollander, "The Meaning of the Term 'Law' (*Nomos*) in 1 Corinthians," *Novum Testamentum* 40 (1998): 117–35. Winger posits in general that *nomos* can point to the Jewish law referentially, but not in terms of sense and denotation.

10. See H. W. Hollander and J. Holleman, "The Relationship of Death, Sin and Law in 1 Cor. 15:56," *Novum Testamentum* 35 (1993): 270–91. They discuss the phrase "the power of sin is the law" and defend the thesis that this refers to laws in general. Laws do not in fact improve society; rather, they lead to an increase in violence and war. However, the context of this phrase is full of references to the Old Testament (1 Cor. 15:54–55); in the Hellenistic world death is more a natural phenomenon or a liberator than a punishment for sin; and finally the singular *nomos* is striking and unexpected if Paul did indeed have "laws in general" in mind here.

11. Alan F. Segal, *Paul the Convert: The Apostolate and Apostasy of Saul the Pharisee* (New Haven/London: Yale University Press, 1990), 34–71.

12. Ibid., 187–223.

13. Mark D. Nanos, *The Mystery of Romans: The Jewish Context of Paul's Letter* (Minneapolis: Fortress, 1996), 3–40.

14. Ibid., 166–238.

15. Peter J. Tomson, *Paul and the Jewish Law*: Halakha *in the Letters of the Apostle to the Gentiles* (Assen/Minneapolis: Van Gorcum/Fortress, 1990).

16. Karin Finsterbusch, *Die Thora als Lebensweisung für Heidenchristen: Studien zur Bedeutung der Thora für die paulinische Ethik* (Göttingen: Vandenhoeck & Ruprecht, 1996).

17. Matthias Klinghardt, *Gesetz und Volk Gottes: Das lukanische Verständnis des Gesetzes nach Herkunft, Funktion und seinem Ort in der Geschichte des Urchristentums* (Tübingen: Mohr, 1988); Jacob Jervell, *Die Apostelgeschichte* (Göttingen: Vandenhoeck & Ruprecht, 1998).

18. Heikki Räisänen, *Paul and the Law* (Tübingen: Mohr, 1983). For a discussion of this work, see T. E. van Spanje, *Inconsistency in Paul? A Critique of the Work of Heikki Räisänen* (Tübingen: Mohr Siebeck, 1999).

19. For a survey of the recent discussions concerning Paul, Judaism, and the law, see Hans Hübner, "Paulusforschung seit 1945: ein kritischer Literaturbericht," in *Aufstieg und Niedergang der Römischen Welt*, 2.25.4: *Religion*, ed. Wolfgang Haase (Berlin: Walter de Gruyter, 1987), 2649–2840; R. Barry Matlock, "A Future for Paul?" in *Auguries: The Jubilee Volume of the Sheffield Department of Biblical Studies*, ed. David J. A. Clines and Stephen D. Moore (Sheffield: Sheffield Academic Press, 1998), 144–83; Frank Thielman, *From Plight to Solution: A Jewish Framework for Understanding Paul's View of the Law in Galatians and Romans* (Leiden: Brill, 1989), 1–27;

and idem, *Paul and the Law: A Contextual Approach* (Downers Grove, Ill.: Inter-Varsity Press, 1994), 14–47.

20. *Morphōsis tēs gnōseōs kai tēs alētheias.*

21. Michael Bachmann ("4QMMT und Galaterbrief: *ma'ase ha-torah* und *erga nomou*," *Zeitschrift für die neutestamentliche Wissenschaft* 89 [1998]: 100) relates the expression to the Jewish law, but he understands *erga* as "rules of life" (*halakhot*); it then concerns not so much human fulfillment of the law as the particularized rules for living that flow from the law. Greek linguistic usage makes such a limiting of the meaning of "works" (*erga*) to the rules of the law (as separate from their fulfillment) not plausible.

22. Vincent M. Smiles, *The Gospel and the Law in Galatia: Paul's Response to Jewish-Christian Separatism and the Threat of Galatian Apostasy* (Collegeville, Minn.: the Liturgical Press, 1998), 119: "*erga* can sometimes stand alone as an abbreviation for the whole phrase."

23. If Paul were thinking here of the Jewish works of the law, his choice of words would make sense only as a possible anticipation. Later Paul would then be able to come back to this when warding off intruding Judaism. But there is no trace in this letter of such a heresy. The apostle thus does not write in anticipation of a threatening heresy within the Christian community. He only looks back to the past. But how could there have been "works of the law" in paganism?

24. See Gal. 4:8–10, where Paul describes life in accordance with the Jewish ethos in terms of the pagan system of deeds.

25. In most manuscripts we find another phrase, which is difficult to translate: *ei de ex ergōn, ouketi esti charis, epei to ergon ouketi estin ergon* ("But if it be of works, then is it no more grace: otherwise work is no more work," KJV).

26. For the law in Galatians, see Thielman, *From Plight to Solution*, 46–86; and idem, *Paul and the Law*, 119–44. Thielman emphasizes that within Judaism (specifically in its eschatology) there was an awareness that the law could be fulfilled only in the age to come, with the help of the Spirit. The immediate cause for Paul's sometimes negative statements in Galatians about the law lies in the situation in Galatia, but the underlying conviction that leads to these negative statements Paul owes to his Jewish background. Thus he did not develop his vision only after he came to faith in Christ.

27. P. C. Böttger ("Paulus und Petrus in Antiochien. Zum Verständnis von Galater 2.11–21," *New Testament Studies* 37 [1991]: 77–100) calls this the "historical dimension of Paul's doctrine of justification."

28. The phrase "by the works of the law" was introduced in 3:2 in contrast to the "hearing of faith."

29. Cf. Bachmann, "4QMMT und Galaterbrief."

30. For the law in Romans, see Thielman, *From Plight to Solution*, 87–116; idem, *Paul and the Law*, 160–213. According to Thielman the position of the law has changed because of the coming of the eschatological era: the condemning function of the law is now past, and the factors that limited the law to the nation of Israel have

been transcended. This process is in line with the history of the Torah (including Israel's failure) and the Jewish eschatological expectations within Judaism.

Chapter 18: In Prayer for Israel

1. In the nineteenth century and the first half of the twentieth, Paul was viewed especially by Jewish writers such as Graetz, Hirsch, Kohler, Baeck, Klausner, and (somewhat later) also Maccoby as a Hellenistic apostate (see Stefan Meissner, *Die Heimholung des Ketzers: Studien zur jüdischen Auseinandersetzung mit Paulus* [Tübingen: Mohr, 1996], 12–71, 112–16).

2. See Rainer Kampling, "Eine auslegungsgeschichtliche Skizze zu 1 Thess 2,14–16," in *Begegnungen zwischen Christentum und Judentum in Antike und Mittelalter*, ed. Dietrich-Alex Koch and Hermann Lichtenberger (Göttingen: Vandenhoeck & Ruprecht, 1993), 183–213.

3. Heikki Räisänen, "Römer 9–11: Analyse eines geistigen Ringens," in *Aufstieg und Niedergang der Römischen Welt*, 2.25.4: *Religion*, ed. Wolfgang Haase, (Berlin: Walter de Gruyter, 1987), 2924–25. See also T. E. van Spanje, *Inconsistency in Paul? A Critique of the Work of Heikki Räisänen* (Tübingen: Mohr Siebeck, 1999), 101, 173–76.

4. Earl J. Richard treats these verses as an interpolation (*First and Second Thessalonians* [Collegeville, Minn.: Glazier, 1995], 119–27): "The author is post-Pauline and is writing from a Gentile-Christian perspective which one should characterize as anti-Jewish" (p. 127). For an in-depth discussion of this topic, see Ingo Broer, "Der ganze Zorn ist schon über Sie gekommen: Bemerkungen zur Interpolationshypothese und zur Interpretation von 1 Thess 2,14–16," in *The Thessalonian Correspondence*, ed. Raymond F. Collins (Leuven: Peeters, 1990), 137–59. See also Jon A. Weatherly, "The Authenticity of 1 Thessalonians 2.13–16: Additional Evidence," *Journal for the Study of the New Testament* 42 (1991): 79–98; Simon Légasse, "Paul et les Juifs d'après 1 Thessaloniciens 2,13–16," *Revue Biblique* 104.4 (1997): 572–91. For possible earlier traditions behind Paul's words, see Jon A. Weatherly, "Responsibility for the Death of Jesus in Paul: 1 Thessalonians 2.14–16," in *Jewish Responsibility for the Death of Jesus in Luke-Acts* (Sheffield: Sheffield Academic Press, 1994), 176–94.

5. Eduard Verhoef (*De brieven aan de Tessalonicenzen* [Kampen: Kok, 1998], 128–29) views 1 Thessalonians 2:16b as an example of apocalyptic language that should not be toned down by comparison with other epistles. The resultant discrepancy is not so much logical as emotional and vague. Carol J. Schlueter (*Filling Up the Measure: Polemical Hyperbole in 1 Thessalonians 2.14–16* [Sheffield: Sheffield Academic Press, 1994], 197) speaks of "exaggerated language": "Paul's statements in 1 Thess. 2.14–16 are, to be sure, an unfortunate set of accusations. Seen in the context of denunciations against others, however, they reflect not his final and absolute view but his way of dealing with the conflict.") Ingo Broer ("Antijudaismus im Neuen Testament? Versuch einer Annäherung anhand von zwei Texten (1 Thess 2,14–16 und Mt 27,24f)," in *Salz der Erde—Licht der Welt: Exegetische Studien zum Matthäus-*

evangelium, ed. Lorenz Oberlinner and Peter Fiedler [Stuttgart: Verlag Katholisches Bibelwerk, 1991], 321–55) explains the vehemence of the language from the fact that what is involved is a family conflict (the Jewish family).

6. Charles A. Wanamaker (*Commentary on 1 & 2 Thessalonians: A Commentary on the Greek Text* [Grand Rapids: Eerdmans, 1990], 117–18) takes the words *eis telos* ("to the utmost") as if they read *heōs telous* ("until the end comes"). It is then a temporal statement, not a definitive one.

7. That the Greek phrase *ephthasen de ep'autous hē orgē eis telos* ("the wrath came upon them in full") can be used for God's wrath in time is apparent from the fact that almost the same phrase is found in the *Testament of Levi* 6.11(*ephthase de hē orgē kuriou ep'autous eis telos*). There these words are used to refer to the judgment on the Shechemites executed by Simeon and Levi. It is possible that Paul in fact quotes these words; see Otto Michel, "Fragen zu 1 Thessalonicher 2,14–16: Antijüdische Polemik bei Paulus" (in *Antijudaismus im Neuen Testament? Exegetische und systematische Beiträge*, ed. W. Eckert, N. P. Levinson and M. Stöhr, 50–59 [Munich: Kaiser Verlag, 1967], 50–59). It is also possible that they were later added as a Christian interpolation (derived from Paul) to the *Testament of Levi*. But in both cases it appears that the words allude to expressions of God's wrath in time (in contradistinction to the final judgment) or that they can easily be construed as such.

8. E. Stegemann, "Zur antijüdischen Polemik in 1.Thess 2,14–16," *Kirche und Israel* 1 (1990): 54–64; Peter Wick, "Ist I Thess 2,13–16 antijüdisch? Der rhetorische Gesamtzusammenhang des Briefes als Interpretationshilfe für eine einzelne Perikope," *Theologische Zeitschrift* 50.1 (1994): 9–23.

9. Alan F. Segal, *Paul the Convert: The Apostolate and Apostasy of Saul the Pharisee* (New Haven: Yale University Press, 1990).

10. Mark D. Nanos, *The Mystery of Romans: The Jewish Context of Paul's Letter* (Minneapolis: Fortress, 1996).

11. See chapter 16.5.

12. Some Bible versions give the impression that in Acts 13:33 Paul is speaking about Jesus' resurrection from the dead and that Psalm 2 is cited as proof for that resurrection. But the argument of Paul's speech indicates that in Acts 13:33 the apostle points to the fact that Jesus as a prophet "arose" in Israel and worked there. Thus God has "begotten" him in Israel (Ps. 2 KJV, NASB).

(1) The verb *anistēmi* can be used for the "raising up" of a prophet (see Acts 3:22; 7:37 KJV, NASB).

(2) This verb is used in Acts 3:26 for Jesus' appearing on earth ("When God raised up his servant, he sent him first to you to bless you").

(3) In Acts 13:34 the verb *anistēmi* is used for the resurrection from the dead, as is specifically stated there ("The fact that God raised him from the dead").

(4) In Acts 13:23–29 Paul speaks of Jesus' coming to Israel and in 13:30–31 of his resurrection from the dead. The scriptural proof follows in 13:32–37 (in 13:32–33 for his coming, and in 13:34–37 for his resurrection).

(5) Psalm 2 does not refer to the resurrection but rather to the begetting of the royal Son (the words "You are my Son" were heard at the baptism of Jesus!).

13. N. T. Wright (*The Climax of the Covenant: Christ and the Law in Pauline Theology* [Edinburgh: T & T Clark, 1991], 156): "The covenant is now the renewed covenant; and the badge of membership is faith." Wright sees continuity. The nation of Israel as a whole could not fulfill the law, it was oppressed by foreign rulers, and its national history ends in the destruction of the Messiah *and* in a rebirth of the covenant people of this Messiah. This leads (pp. 15–16) to a redefinition of election (Israel; Christ's people) and of monotheism (the one and only God presents himself in later times as the Spirit who comes via the Messiah).

14. See chapter 16.4.

15. In most Bible translations the word "covenant" is used here: "this is my covenant [with them]" (NIV, NASB, KJV, NRSV). But Paul writes, with the Septuagint, "and this is for them the *arrangement* from my side" (*kai hautē autois hē par' emou diathēkē*). In view here is an arrangement or disposition within the relationship between God and his people.

16. In Romans 11:27b the words "when I take away their sins" are reminiscent of another Bible passage that deals with God establishing a new dispensation for Israel. In Jeremiah 31:31–34, the Lord announces a "new covenant" with the house of Israel and with the house of Judah (a new arrangement for them). He will write the law on their hearts and forgive their wickedness. It is well possible that Paul conflated the two passages from Isaiah and Jeremiah because of the word *diathēkē*; both passages deal with the new way God will open up for his people (not like the way he opened up from Egypt to Canaan, Jer. 31:32).

17. The KJV has added to this problem by translating *tēs palaias diathēkēs* in 2 Cor. 3:14 as "the reading of the old testament."

Appendix 1: The Chronology of Paul's Life

1. In 1807 Friedrich Schleiermacher wrote a book in which he questioned the authenticity of 1 Timothy, partly on the basis of linguistic differences between this letter and 2 Timothy and Titus (!), which he considered genuine: *Über den sogenannten ersten Brief des Paulos an den Timotheus: Ein kritisches Sendschreiben an J. C. Gass* (Berlin: Realschulbuchhandlung, 1807).

2. A mere five years after Schleiermacher questioned the authenticity of 1 Timothy, a New Testament introduction appeared that considered both letters to Timothy and the letter to Titus to be spurious (J. G. Eichhorn, *Einleitung in das Neue Testament*, 3.1 [Leipzig: Weidman, 1812], 315–410). And in 1835 F. C. Baur published a book whose title alluded to Schleiermacher's 1807 volume: Baur, *Die sogenannten Pastoralbriefe des Apostels Paulus aufs neue kritisch untersucht* (Stuttgart-Tübingen: Cotta'sche Verlagshandlung, 1835).

3. To this school belonged, among others, A. D. Pierson, S. A. Naber, W. C. van Manen, and G. A. van den Bergh van Eysinga. See Hermann Detering, *Paulusbriefe*

ohne Paulus? Die Paulusbriefe in der holländischen Radikalkritik (Frankfurt am Main: Peter Lang, 1992).

4. John Knox, *Chapters in a Life of Paul* (New York: Abingdon-Cokesbury, 1950). See also D. W. Riddle, *Paul, Man of Conflict: A Modern Biographical Sketch* (Nashville: Cokesbury Press, 1940); and John Coolidge Hurd, *The Origin of 1 Corinthians* (London: SPCK, 1965).

5. As early as 1936, John Knox published an article on this topic: "Fourteen Years Later: A Note on the Pauline Chronology," *Journal of Religion* 16 (1936): 341–49. See also his article "The Pauline Chronology," *Journal of Biblical Literature* 58 (1939): 15–29.

6. Robert Jewett, *A Chronology of Paul's Life* (Philadelphia: Fortress, 1979).

7. Gerd Lüdemann, *Paul, Apostle to the Gentiles: Studies in Chronology* (Philadelphia: Fortress, 1984). For the continuing effect of this study, see also Joachim Gnilka, *Paulus von Tarsus: Apostel und Zeuge* (Freiburg: Herder, 1996), 64–71.

8. Jerome Murphy-O'Connor, *Paul: A Critical Life* (Oxford: Clarendon Press, 1996).

9. Karl P. Donfried and I. Howard Marshall, *The Theology of the Shorter Pauline Letters* (Cambridge: Cambridge University Press, 1993), 7–12, 64–72: "[1 Thessalonians] contains the key to the theology of the early Paul, and therefore, we would insist, also the key to understanding the theology of the late Paul" (p. 64).

10. The identification of Galatians 2:1 with Acts 18:22 and the simultanous rejection of the historicity of Acts is also found in, among others, J. W. Straatman, *Paulus, de apostel van Jezus Christus: Zijn leven en werken, zijne leer en zijne persoonlijkheid; een historisch onderzoek* (Amsterdam: Loman, 1874); Gustav Volkmar, *Paulus von Damascus bis zum Galaterbrief* (Zürich: Schröter & Meyer, 1887); E. Barnikol, *Die drei Jerusalemreisen des Paulus* (Kiel: Mühlau Verlag, 1929).

11. W. M. Ramsay, *The Cities of St. Paul: Their Influence on His Life and Thought; The Cities of Eastern Asia Minor* (London: Hodder and Stoughton, 1907; reprint Grand Rapids: Baker, 1963); *St. Paul: The Traveller and the Roman Citizen* (London: Hodder and Stoughton, 1905; reprint Grand Rapids: Baker, 1963).

12. Compare the wide-ranging, detailed studies of Colin J. Hemer, *The Book of Acts in the Setting of Hellenistic History* (Tübingen: Mohr, 1989). E. E. Ellis (*The Making of the New Testament Documents* [Leiden: Brill, 1999], 253) concludes: "The book of Acts together with the Pauline epistles also provides the best and indeed the only sequential reconstruction of the Apostle Paul's ministry."

13. For a discussion on Luke 1:1–4 compared with the pretensions of the professional Greek historians, see Armin D. Baum, *Lukas als Historiker der letzten Jesusreise* (Wuppertal: Brockhaus, 1993), 103–49. For Luke as Paul's traveling companion, see Jakob van Bruggen, *Lucas: Het evangelie als voorgeschiedenis* (Kampen: Kok, 1993), 11–19.

14. Thus, for example, John C. Lentz (*Luke's Portrait of Paul* [Cambridge: Cambridge University Press, 1993]) claims that the portrait of Paul in Acts is a creation of

Luke, who wanted to portray a figure of high social and ethical quality in order to appeal to the higher social groupings in Roman society. Only a limited portion of what Luke writes fits in such a hypothesis, and it does not explain why Luke, if this were indeed his purpose, wrote so much more about Paul that is entirely irrelevant to this purpose. For the idea that Luke portrays the apostle in accordance with the group norms of that era, see also Bruce J. Malina and Jerome H. Neyrey, *Portraits of Paul: An Archeology of Ancient Personality* (Louisville: Westminster/John Knox Press, 1996), 203.

15. See Jakob van Bruggen, *Christ on Earth: The Gospel Narratives as History* (Grand Rapids: Baker, 1998), 106–9; Harold W. Hoehner, *Chronological Aspects of the Life of Christ* (Grand Rapids: Zondervan, 1977).

16. See chapter 3.5.

17. George Ogg, *The Odyssey of Paul* (Old Tappan, N. J.: Revell, 1968; U.K. edition, *Chronology of the Life of Paul* [London: Epworth Press, 1968]), 16.

18. For further details, see Jakob Van Bruggen, *"Na veertien jaren": De datering van het in Galaten 2 genoemde overleg te Jeruzalem* (Kampen: Kok, 1973), 13–19.

19. For a description and commentary, see A. Deissmann, *Paul: A Study in Social and Religious History* (reprint Gloucester, Mass.: Peter Smith, 1972), 265–71; L. Hennequin, "Inscription de Delphes," in *Dictionnaire de la Bible: Supplément*, vol. 2 (Paris : Letouzey et Ané, 1934), cols. 355–68; A. Plassart, "L'Inscription de Delphes mentionnant le proconsul Gallion," *Revue des Etudes Grecques* 80 (1967): 372–78; Murphy-O'Connor, *Paul*, 15–22.

20. For the various options see van Bruggen, *"Na veertien jaren,"* 50–51.

21. The church historian Orosius mentions "the ninth year" of Claudius (*Historiae* 7.6.15) and refers to Josephus as his source. This date, however, is not found in any of the writings of Josephus known to us. On the other hand, Orosius mentions this date in passing, and it is not otherwise significant for him. This argues for taking this detail seriously, since it is mentioned without any ulterior motive, even though Orosius attributes it, perhaps incorrectly, to Josephus. Helga Botermann (*Das Judenedikt des Kaisers Claudius* [Stuttgart: Franz Steiner Verlag, 1996], 54–57) is of the opinion that Orosius's date has no value because it is thought to have been derived from the combination of this expulsion and the mention of Gallio in Acts 18:1–2. Two objections argue against this: (1) Orosius appeals to a source outside Acts, even though he is in error about the name of the author (Josephus). (2) If Orosius did not get the "ninth year" from an external source but rather from his own calculations on the basis of the first year of Gallio's tenure, then he is an independent witness for this first year. In this case he apparently had access to sources that could inform him as to the dates of Gallio's governorship. See also Rainer Riesner, *Paul's Early Period: Chronology, Mission Strategy, Theology* (Grand Rapids: Eerdmans, 1998), 180–87.

22. See Jakob van Bruggen, *De oorsprong van de kerk te Rome* (Groningen: De Vuurbaak, 1967), 16–20; and Dixon Slingerland, "Suetonius *Claudius* 25,4 and the Account in Cassius Dio," *Jewish Quarterly Review* 79 (1989): 305–22, for a detailed

discussion of Cassius Dio (*Historiarum Romanarum quae supersunt* 60.6.6). According to Cassius Dio, Claudius did not expel the Jews from Rome but isolated them somewhat by forbidding them to attend public gatherings and meetings of non-Jews. In this respect Claudius differed from his predecessor, Tiberius, who did expel the Jews from Rome (Cassius Dio 57.18.5). At the beginning of his reign, in A.D. 41, Claudius chose to treat the Jews with a measure of circumspection (Cassius Dio 60.3–60.9 describes the first year of his reign). It is incorrect to ignore the difference between the initial isolation of the Jews and their later expulsion and to date the latter as if it were the initial isolation described by Dio, as is done by, among others, Murphy-O'Connor, *Paul*, 9–15. Lüdemann (*Paul, Apostle to the Gentiles*, 164–71) even draws the conclusion that Paul founded the Christian community in Corinth shortly after A.D. 41 and that he visited this church again during the Gallio era (in Acts 18:1–2 Luke then incorrectly conflates these two events). For the distinction between the action of Claudius in A.D. 41 and that in A.D. 49, see also Dixon Slingerland, "Acts 18:1–17 and Luedemann's Pauline Chronology," *Journal of Biblical Literature* 109 (1990): 686–90; and Riesner, *Paul's Early Period*, 167–79.

23. See Vegetius, *Epitoma Rei Militaris* 4.39 ("Ex die ergo tertio idus Nouembres usque in diem sextum idus Martias maria clauduntur"). According to S. Dockx ("Chronologie de la vie de saint Paul, depuis sa conversion jusqu'à son sejour à Rome," *Novum Testamentum* 13 [1971]: 261–304), the voyage was resumed as early as February 7. But Dockx does not adequately distinguish between the opening of the commercial shipping season for vessels that also took passengers and the risk that imperial couriers, wealthy entrepreneurs who wanted to evade pirates, and ships that had been forced to winter sometimes took by leaving before the season started. It is likely that Paul had to make use of the regular means of sea transport. For more details, see van Bruggen, "*Na veertien jaren,*" 52 n. 52.

24. Cassius Dio 57.14.5; 60.11.6; 60.17.3.

25. Thus Adolf von Harnack, *Geschichte der altchristlichen Literatur bis Eusebius*, II.1, *Die Chronologie der Literatur bis Irenäus* (Leipzig: Hinrichs Verlag, 1897), 233–38. See Ogg, *Odyssey of Paul*, 146–59, for a detailed discussion of the so-called antedated chronology.

26. See Jakob van Bruggen, "Na vele jaren: Stadhouder Felix en de jaren van Paulus," in *Almanak Fides Quadrat Intellectum* (Kampen: Zalsman, 1979), 126–33.

27. Ibid., 121–25.

28. Josephus, *Vita* 13–16.

29. See George Ogg, *Odyssey of Paul*, 161–62.

30. See van Bruggen, "Na vele jaren," 151 n. 28.

31. Josephus, *Antiquities* 20.137–97; *War* 2.247–72.

32. For the possible significance of Pallas, brother of Felix, for this chronology, see Jakob van Bruggen, "Na vele jaren, 137–39.

33. Because Paul writes "after three years" (*meta etē tria*), we must think of an interval of three full years; he does not write "in the third year," in which case the partial year with which the three-year period began could be counted as the first year.

34. Chrysostom, *Commentary on Galatians*, on 2:1 (*MSG* 61.633–34). Valentin Weber (*Die antiochenische Kollekte* [Würzburg: Bauch, 1917], 80) gives a different interpretation of the passage in Chrysostom. For a refutation of that interpretation, see van Bruggen, "*Na veertien jaren,*" 167 n. 7.

35. In his 1535 Commentary on Galatians (Weimar edition, 40.1.151–52) Luther locates the visit of Galatians 2:1 in an event several years after that of Acts 15. From the lecture notes by Rörer it appears that he probably thought of an identification with Acts 18:22 (ibid.). This is confirmed by the way Luther writes in his commentary about the sequence of the circumcision of Titus, the shaving of Paul's head in Cenchrea, and the going up to Jerusalem (ibid., 1.155).

36. We can reconstruct Iacobus Cappellus's train of thought on the basis of the extensive tables his brother Ludovicus included at the beginning of his own *Historia Apostolica*.

37. Ludovicus Cappellus, *Historia Apostolica illustrata* (Geneva, 1634; reissued, Saumur: De Tournes & De la Pierre, 1683), 53–57.

38. Salomo van Til, *Opus Analyticum*, vol. 2 (Basel: Brandmüller, 1724), 588–89.

39. Johann Jakob Hess wrote *Geschichte und Schriften der Apostel Jesu* in the beginning of the nineteenth century, and I. F. Köhler wrote *Versuch über die Abfassungszeit der epistolischen Schriften im Neuen Testament und der Apokalypse* in 1830. Both of these works are difficult to find in libraries. They are incorporated and cited in Karl Schrader, *Der Apostel Paulus*, 5 vols. (Leipzig: Kollmann, 1830–36), 1:79–81. The most extensive contemporary critical discussion of the position of these authors can be found in Rudolph Anger, *De temporum in Actis Apostolorum ratione* (Leipzig: Baumgärtner, 1833), 142, 153–59, 182.

40. Leopold Immanuel Rückert, *Commentar über den Brief Pauli an die Galater* (Leipzig: Köhler, 1833), 321–36.

41. Karl Wieseler, *Chronologie des apostolischen Zeitalters bis zum Tode der Apostel Paulus und Petrus* (Göttingen: Vandenhoeck & Ruprecht, 1848), 181–205.

42. J. W. Straatman, *Paulus, de apostel van Jezus Christus*; Gustav Volkmar, *Paulus von Damascus*; E. Barnikol, *Die drei Jerusalemreisen.*

43. E. E. Ellis, *The Making of the New Testament Documents* (Leiden: Brill, 1999), 255: "When Gal 2:1–10 is identified with the famine visit of Acts 11:27–30; 12:25, these differences virtually disappear and a notable agreement is produced, not only between those passages in particular but also generally between the events of the Apostle's ministry presented in his correspondence and those presented in Acts." Robert L. Reymond (*Paul: Missionary Theologian* [Fearn: Christian Focus Publications, 2000], 101–14) defends the South Galatia hypothesis to promote the identification of Galatians 2:1–10 with the famine visit of Acts 11 and 12.

44. See A. Suhl, "Der Beginn der selbständigen Mission des Paulus," *New Testament Studies* 38 (1992): 430–47; Ben Witherington III, *The Paul Quest: The Renewed Search for the Jew of Tarsus* (Downers Grove, Ill.: InterVarsity Press, 1998), 314–16.

45. John J. Gunther (*Paul, Messenger and Exile: A Study in the Chronology of His Life and Letters* [Valley Forge, Pa.: Judson Press, 1972]) identifies Galatians 2:1–10 with Acts 11:27–12:25 and dates Christ's death in A.D. 30. The same is true of Witherington, *The Paul Quest*, 304–31.

46. Joachim Jeremias ("Sabbathjahr und neutestamentliche Chronologie," in *Abba: Studien zur neutestamentlichen Theologie und Zeitgeschichte* [Göttingen: Vandenhoeck & Ruprecht, 1966], 235–37) is of the opinion that Luke doubled this journey. In reality there were not both a journey to Jerusalem before the first missionary journey (the collection journey of Acts 11–12) *and* a journey to Jerusalem after the first journey (the apostolic convention of Acts 15). Rather, there was only one journey to Jerusalem, which took place after the first missionary journey. The collection journey thus coincided with the apostolic convention.

47. Cf. Murphy-O'Connor, *Paul*, 1–4. Supposing a very early date for Philemon (A.D. 53), Murphy-O'Connor arrives at a date several years before the beginning of the Christian Era.

Appendix 3: Jewish Religion and the Law

1. Friedrich Avemarie, *Tora und Leben: Untersuchungen zur Heilsbedeutung der Tora in der frühen rabbinischen Literatur* (Tübingen: Mohr, 1996).

2. Avemarie (*Tora und Leben*, 11–49) discusses authors from F. Weber (1880) to Sanders and Neusner at the end of the twentieth century.

3. Avemarie, *Tora und Leben*, 581–84.

4. Ibid., 575–76. The reason for the keeping of commandments differs depending on the chosen point of view. In relation to God, it is the keeping of an unconditional command. In relation to Israel, it is living with the gift of grace and salvation. In relation to the world as a whole, it is the dissemination of the Torah as mediating and maintaining creation. In relation to the individual and the community, the Torah is useful and protects. In relation to the study of the Torah, the law is a bridle for the evil passions. In relation to retribution, the law is the measure for eternal weal or woe and thus leads to reward or punishment.

5. See also Friedrich Avemarie, "Erwählung und Vergeltung: Zur optionalen Struktur rabbinischer Soteriologie," *New Testament Studies* 45 (1999): 108–26.

6. Quotations from the Mishna in this section are taken from Jacob Neusner, *The Mishna: A New Translation* (New Haven and London: Yale University Press, 1988).

7. George Foot Moore, *Judaism in the First Centuries of the Christian Era: The Age of the Tannaim* (Cambridge: Harvard University Press, 1927–30), 2:92–95.

8. Avemarie, *Tora und Leben*, 296–99. Maimonides and Solomon Schechter interpret the passage as follows: Because there are many commandments, there is for each individual a commandment that will acquit him or her. According to Avemarie, the

issue is increasing righteousness rather than acquittal. The quote from Isaiah refers according to Avemarie (p. 299) either to justification by God (we have here, then, a Pauline idea, although justification here is brought about through human actions rather than through Christ), or to the righteousness of the nation itself (for which a good case can also be made).

9. See ibid., 297.

10. Ibid., 383–86.

11. Avemarie, *Tora und Leben*, does discuss the variations among the manuscripts on p. 384.

12. Illustrative is *'Avot de-Rabbi Nathan* (B 26), which relates an anecdote about Hillel the Elder. He stood at the gate and asked people for how much in anticipated wages they began their daily task. "For one or two denarii," was the answer. "But what use is then this 'dime'? It is good for only one hour! Will you not come and inherit the Torah and inherit life in both this world and the world to come?" What is of little value in the eyes of people (who look upon the Torah as if it were merely a "dime") is in fact the gate to Israel; within that nation God gives life, both for the present and for the world to come. In other words, life under the Torah "pays" better than laboring successfully for wages.

13. In this connection a citation from the Mishnah tractate *Sanhedrin* (10.1) is illustrative: "All Israelites have a share in the world to come."

14. See, for example, Tosephta *Hullin* 10.16: Whoever empties a nest, lets the mother go, and while doing so makes a fatal fall from the tree, must receive the long life promised for letting the mother go [Deut. 22:7] *after* this life.

15. Avemarie, *Tora und Leben*, 378–79: "the promise of life concerns not only the life to come but at the same time also life in this world" and "But what is the life in this world that the Haggadah promises in addition to eternal life as a gift of the Torah?" ("bezieht sich die Verheissung des Lebens nicht allein auf das zukünftige, sondern zugleich auch auf das Leben in dieser Welt" and "Was aber ist das diesseitige Leben, das die Haggada neben dem ewigen als Gabe der Tora verheisst?").

16. E. P. Sanders, *Paul and Palestinian Judaism: A Comparison of Patterns of Religion* (Philadelphia: Fortress; London: SCM Press, 1977), 409–18. He writes, "In IV Ezra, in short, we see an instance in which covenantal nomism has collapsed. All that is left is legalistic perfectionism" (p. 409). On this issue he has been challenged by, among others, Seyoon Kim, in a footnote to the postscript in the second edition of Kim's *Origin of Paul's Gospel* (Tübingen: Mohr, 1984), 347–48. The book of 4 Ezra shows that the legalism that Paul, according to Kim, opposes must indeed have been widespread in Judaism!

17. Philip F. Esler ("The Social Function of 4 Ezra," *Journal for the Study of the New Testament* 53 [1994]: 99–123) sees the document as an attempt to safeguard the corporeal identity of the nation after the fall of Jerusalem in A.D. 70 by recommending the law as linking together the people as a whole. Only thus could be prevented that the nation would lose its identity and be absorbed in the other nations.

18. 1.4–14; 7.22–24.

19. 7.48, 60, 72, 79, 89.

20. In 3.7 we read that God gave Adam only one commandment, which Adam broke. For perishing because of unbelief in the true God, see also 8.55–58.

21. 3.19.

22. All quotes from 4 Ezra (=2 Esdras) are from the NRSV Apocrypha.

23. We leave out of consideration the question to what extent 4 Ezra might be a Jewish-Christian document. There are passages that would seem to fit in the Christian tradition (1.30, 33–40). In 2.47 the "son of God" is mentioned, whom the "great multitude . . . confessed in the world." The inquiry into the unity of the book and its *Sitz im Leben* has not yet been brought to a satisfactory conclusion.

24. The writing should more accurately be called by its older name, *Against the Greeks*, or better yet, *Apologia for the Jews*. Thus F. J. A. M. Meijer and M. A. Wes in their introduction to the translation of Flavius Josephus, *Against the Greeks [Contra Apionem]* (Amsterdam: Ambo, 1999), 15–16. Quotations from *Contra Apionem* are from the Thackeray translation in the Loeb edition.

25. For the thetical description of the greatness of the Jewish laws, see *Contra Apionem* 2.151–296.

26. See the appendix "The Pharisees" in my *Jesus the Son of God: The Gospel Narrative as Message* (Grand Rapids: Baker, 1999), 236–72.

27. There are rabbinic statements about divine acquittal on the basis of a preponderance of good deeds, and a condemnation or acquittal on the basis of a single transgression or a single act of obedience. But the statements are intended to be exhortations and cannot be used to describe Jewish soteriology as a whole (Sanders, *Paul and Palestinian Judaism*, 125–47). When we read these statements we must, furthermore, remember that carrying out a commandment is an expression of acceptance of the one God. Because human beings are imperfect (they exhibit a mixture of good and evil), the great question is whether love for God is decisive in life. This surrender to God can be demonstrated in one act of obedience, but rejection of God can also be shown in a single act of disobedience. For the Jewish Christian James, the rule continues to be valid that "faith without works is dead" (James 2:26 KJV). It is God's mercy that the works of the believing Israelite are weighed and not merely counted.

28. Of an entirely different nature is the question whether the evil of human pride or self-confidence was not found among the Jews. The Gospels show that not even the Pharisees were immune to this evil (Matt. 3:9; Luke 18:9–14), and Paul often warns against the danger of "glorying." But deformed spirituality is not something that is found uniquely in Judaism, and it is difficult to extrapolate actual pride and turn it into a soteriological dogma.

BIBLIOGRAPHY

Anger, Rudolph. *De temporum in Actis Apostolorum ratione*. Leipzig: Baumgärtner, 1833.

Avemarie, Friedrich. *Tora und Leben: Untersuchungen zur Heilsbedeutung der Tora in der frühen rabbinischen Literatur*. Texte und Studien zum Antiken Judentum 55. Tübingen: Mohr, 1996.

———. "Erwählung und Vergeltung: Zur optionalen Struktur rabbinischer Soteriologie." *New Testament Studies* 45 (1999): 108–26.

Bachmann, Michael. "4QMMT und Galaterbrief: *ma'aśe ha-torah* und *erga nomou.*" *Zeitschrift für die neutestamentliche Wissenschaft* 89 (1998): 91–113.

Bamberger, Bernard J. *Proselytism in the Talmudic Period*. New York: Ktav Publishing House, 1968 (original publication: Cincinnati: Hebrew Union College Press, 1939).

Barnett, Paul W. *Jesus and the Logic of History*. New Studies in Biblical Theology 3. Grand Rapids: Eerdmans; Leicester: Apollos, 1997.

———. *Jesus and the Rise of Early Christianity: A History of New Testament Times*. Downers Grove, Ill.: InterVarsity Press, 1999.

Barnikol, E. *Die drei Jerusalemreisen des Paulus: Die echte Konkordanz der Paulusbriefe mit der Wir-Quelle der Apostelgeschichte*. Forschungen zur Entstehung des Urchristentums des Neuen Testaments und der Kirche 2. Kiel: Mühlau Verlag, 1929.

Barrett, C. K. *A Critical and Exegetical Commentary on the Acts of the Apostles*. 2 vols. International Critical Commentary. Edinburgh: T & T Clark, 1994, 1998.

Bassler, Jouette M., ed. *Pauline Theology: Thessalonians, Philippians, Galatians, Philemon*. SBL Symposium Series 1. Minneapolis: Fortress Press, 1991.

Baum, Armin D. *Lukas als Historiker der letzten Jesusreise*. Monographien und Studienbücher 379. Wuppertal: Brockhaus, 1993.

Baur, Ferdinand Christian. *Die sogenannten Pastoralbriefe des Apostels Paulus aufs neue kritisch untersucht*. Stuttgart-Tübingen: Cotta'sche Verlagshandlung, 1835.

———. *Paulus, der Apostel Jesu Christi. Sein Leben und Wirken, seine Briefe und seine Lehre. Ein Beitrag zu einer kritischen Geschichte des Urchristenthums*. Stuttgart: Becher und Müller, 1845.

Becker, Jürgen. *Paul: Apostle to the Gentiles*. Louisville: Westminster/John Knox, 1993. (German edition: *Paulus: Der Apostel der Völker*. Uni-Taschenbücher 2014. Tübingen: Mohr Siebeck, 1998.)

Beckheuer, Burkhard. *Paulus und Jerusalem: Kollekte und Mission im theologischen Denken des Heidenapostels*. Europäische Hochschulschriften 23,611. Frankfurt am Main: Peter Lang, 1997.

Beer, H. *Aparchē und verwandte Ausdrücke in griechischen Weihinschriften*. Würzburg (thesis), 1914.

Beker, J. Christiaan. *Paul the Apostle: The Triumph of God in Life and Thought*. Philadelphia: Fortress Press, 1980.

Benko, S. "The Edict of Claudius of A.D. 49 and the Instigator Chrestus." *Theologische Zeitschrift* 25 (1969): 406–18.

Best, Ernest. "Recipients and Title of the Letter to the Ephesians: Why and When the Designation 'Ephesians'?" In *Aufstieg und Niedergang der Römischen Welt*, 2.25.4. *Religion*, edited by Wolfgang Haase, 3245–79. Berlin: Walter de Gruyter, 1987.

———. "Ephesians 1.1" and "Ephesians 1.1 Again." In *Essays on Ephesians*, 1–24. Edinburgh: T & T Clark, 1997.

Böcher, Otto. "Das sogenannte Aposteldekret." In *Vom Urchristentum zu Jesus*, edited by Hubert Frankemölle and Karl Kertelge, 325–36. Freiburg: Herder, 1989.

Bockmuehl, Markus. "The Noachide Commandments and New Testament Ethics, with Special Reference to Acts 15 and Pauline Halakha." *Revue Biblique* 102 (1995): 72–101.

Boismard, M.-É., and A. Lamouille. *Les Actes des deux apôtres*. 3 vols. Études Bibliques NS 12–14. Paris: Gabalda, 1990.

Borgen, Peder. *Early Christianity and Hellenistic Judaism*. Edinburgh: T & T Clark, 1996.

Bornkamm, Günther. "Der Römerbrief als Testament des Paulus." In *Geschichte und Glaube*, 2:120–39. Beiträge zur evangelischen Theologie 53. Munich: Kaiser Verlag, 1971.

Boterman, Helga. *Das Judenedikt des Kaisers Claudius: Römischer Staat und Christiani im 1. Jahrhundert*. Hermes Einzelschriften 71. Stuttgart: Franz Steiner Verlag, 1996.

Böttger, P. C. "Paulus und Petrus in Antiochien. Zum Verständnis von Galater 2.11–21." *New Testament Studies* 37 (1991): 77–100.

Bousset, Wilhelm. *Die Religion des Judentums im spät-hellenistischen Zeitalter*. 3rd ed. Edited by Hugo Gressmann. Handbuch zum Neuen Testament 21. Tübingen: Mohr, 1926.

Breytenbach, Cilliers. *Paulus und Barnabas in der Provinz Galatien: Studien zu Apostelgeschichte 13f.; 16,6; 18,23 und den Adressaten des Galaterbriefes*. Arbeiten zur Geschichte des antiken Judentums und des Urchristentums 38. Leiden: Brill, 1996.

Broadbent, M. *Studies in Greek Genealogy*. Leiden: Brill, 1968.

Broer, Ingo. "Der ganze Zorn ist schon über Sie gekommen: Bemerkungen zur Interpolationshypothese und zur Interpretation von 1 Thess 2,14–16." In *The Thessalonian Correspondence*, edited by Raymond F. Collins, 137–59. Bibliotheca Ephemeridum Theologicarum Lovaniensium 87. Leuven: Peeters, 1990.

———. "Antijudaismus im Neuen Testament? Versuch einer Annäherung anhand von zwei Texten (1 Thess 2,14–16 und Mt 27,24f)." In *Salz der Erde—Licht der Welt: Exegetische Studien zum Matthäusevangelium*, edited by Lorenz Oberlinner and Peter Fiedler, 321–55. Stuttgart: Verlag Katholisches Bibelwerk, 1991.

Bruce, F. F. *Paul: Apostle of the Heart Set Free*. Grand Rapids: Eerdmans, 1977. (U.K. edition: *Paul: Apostle of the Free Spirit*. Exeter: Paternoster Press, 1977.)

———. *1 and 2 Thessalonians*. Word Biblical Commentary 45. Waco: Word Books, 1982.

———. *The Pauline Circle*. Grand Rapids: Eerdmans, 1985.

———. "The Apostolic Decree of Acts 15." In *Studien zum Text und zur Ethik des Neuen Testaments*, edited by W. Schrage, 115–24. Berlin: Walter de Gruyter, 1986.

Burton, Ernest de Witt. *A Critical and Exegetical Commentary on the Epistle to the Galatians*. International Critical Commentary. Edinburgh: T & T Clark, 1921.

Byun, Jonggil. *The Holy Spirit Was Not Yet: A Study on the Relationship between the Coming of the Holy Spirit and the Glorification of Jesus according to John 7:39*. Kampen: Kok, 1992.

Cadbury, Henry J. "Roman Law and the Trial of Paul." In *The Beginnings of Christianity*, edited by Kirsopp Lake and Henry J. Cadbury, vol. 5, 297–338. London: Macmillan, 1933.

Callan, Terrance. "The Background of the Apostolic Decree (Acts 15:20, 29; 21:25)." *Catholic Biblical Quarterly* 55 (1993): 284–97.

Cappellus, Ludovicus. *Historia Apostolica illustrata, ex Actis Apostolorum et Epistolis Paulinis studiose inter se collatis, collecta etc.* Saumur: De Tournes & De la Pierre, 1683.

Cassius Dio. *Cassii Dionis Cocceiani Historiarum Romanarum Quae Supersunt.* 6 vols. Edited by U. P. Boissevain. Berlin: Weidmann, 1895–1926.

Cervin, Richard S. "A Note regarding the Name 'Junia(s)' in Romans 16.7." *New Testament Studies* 40 (1994): 464–70.

Chae, Daniel Jong-Sang. *Paul as Apostle to the Gentiles: His Apostolic Self-Awareness and Its Influence on the Soteriological Argument in Romans.* Carlisle: Paternoster Press, 1997.

Cheung, Alex T. M. "A Narrative Analysis of Acts 14:27–15:35: Literary Shaping in Luke's Account of the Jerusalem Council." *Westminster Theological Journal* 55 (1993): 137–54.

Cranfield, C. E. B. *A Critical and Exegetical Commentary on the Epistle to the Romans.* Vol. 1, *Introduction and Commentary on Romans I–VIII.* Edinburgh: T & T Clark, 1975.

———. "Changes of Person and Number in Paul's Epistles." In *Paul and Paulinism: Essays in Honour of C. K. Barrett*, edited by M. D. Hooker and S. G. Wilson, 280–89. London: SPCK, 1982.

———. "The Works of the Law in the Epistle to the Romans." *Journal for the Study of the New Testament* 43 (1991): 89–101.

———. *On Romans and Other New Testament Essays.* Edinburgh: T & T Clark, 1998.

Dauer, Anton. *Paulus und die christliche Gemeinde im syrischen Antiochia: Kritische Bestandsaufnahme der modernen Forschung mit einigen weiterführenden Überlegungen.* Bonner Biblische Beiträge 106. Weinheim: Beltz, 1996.

Davies, Glenn N. *Faith and Obedience in Romans: A Study in Romans 1–4.* Journal for the Study of the New Testament Supplement Series 39. Sheffield: Academic Press, 1990.

De Boer, E. A. "Ethiek in de Acta van Jerusalem: Een exegetisch onderzoek naar de betekenis van het besluit van Handelingen XV." In *Almanak Fides Quadrat Intellectum* (Kampen: Zalsman, 1980), 139–68.

Deissmann, Adolf. *Light from the Ancient East: The New Testament Illustrated by Recently Discovered Texts of the Graeco-Roman World.* Grand Rapids: Baker, 1965. (German edition: *Licht vom Osten: Das Neue Testament und die neuentdeckten Texte der hellenistisch-römische Welt.* 4th ed. Tübingen: Mohr, 1923.)

———. *Paul: A Study in Social and Religious History.* Gloucester, Mass.: Peter Smith, 1972. (German edition: *Paulus: Eine kultur- und religionsgeschichtliche Skizze.* 2d ed. Tübingen: Mohr, 1925.)

De Jonge, Marinus. "Notes on Testament of Levi II–VII." In *Studies on the Testaments of the Twelve Patriarchs: Text and Interpretation*, 247–60. Studia in Veteris Testamenti Pseudepigrapha 3. Leiden: Brill, 1975.

Den Heyer, C. J. *Paul: A Man of Two Worlds.* Harrisburg: Trinity Press International, 2000. (Dutch edition: *Paulus: Man van twee werelden.* Zoetermeer: Meinema, 1998.)

Derret, J. Duncan M. "Cursing Jesus (1 Cor XII.3): The Jews as Religious Persecutors." *New Testament Studies* 21 (1975): 244–54.

De Ru, Gerrit. *Heeft het lijden van Christus aanvulling nodig: Onderzoek naar de interpretatie van Colossenzen 1:24.* Exegetica. Amsterdam: Bolland, 1981.

Derwachter, Frederick Milton. *Preparing the Way for Paul: The Proselyte Movement in Later Judaism.* New York: Macmillan, 1930.

Detering, Hermann. *Paulusbriefe ohne Paulus? Die Paulusbriefe in der holländischen Radikalkritik.* Kontexte 10. Frankfurt am Main: Peter Lang, 1992.

Dockx, S. "Chronologie de la vie de saint Paul, depuis sa conversion jusqu'à son séjour à Rome." *Novum Testamentum* 13 (1971): 261–304.

———. "The First Missionary Voyage of Paul: Historical Reality or Literary Creation of Luke?" In *Chronos, Kairos, Christos,* edited by J. Vardaman and E. M. Yamauchi, 209–21. Winona Lake, Ind.: Eisenbrauns, 1989.

Dodd, C. H. *The Apostolic Preaching and Its Developments.* London: Hodder & Stoughton, 1936; New York: Harper & Brothers, 1944, 1951.

Donaldson, Terence L. *Paul and the Gentiles: Remapping the Apostle's Convictional World.* Minneapolis: Fortress Press, 1997.

———. "Israelite, Convert, Apostle to the Gentiles: The Origin of Paul's Gentile Mission." In *The Road from Damascus: The Impact of Paul's Conversion on His Life, Thought, and Ministry*, edited by Richard N. Longenecker, 62–84. Grand Rapids: Eerdmans, 1997.

Donfried, Karl P., and I. Howard Marshall. *The Theology of the Shorter Pauline Letters.* Cambridge: Cambridge University Press, 1993.

Donfried, Karl P., ed. *The Romans Debate*. Rev. ed. Peabody, Mass.: Hendrickson, 1991.

Dunn, James D. G. "The New Perspective on Paul." *Bulletin of the John Rylands Library* 65 (1983): 95–122.

———. "Works of the Law and the Curse of the Law (Galatians 3,10–14)." *New Testament Studies* 31 (1985): 523–42.

———. *Romans*. 2 vols. Word Biblical Commentary 38A-B. Dallas: Word Books, 1988.

———. *Jesus, Paul and the Law*. Louisville: Westminster/John Knox, 1990.

———. *The Epistle to the Galatians*. Black's New Testament Commentaries. Peabody, Mass.: Hendrickson, 1993.

———. "Paul's Conversion—A Light to Twentieth Century Disputes." In *Evangelium, Schriftauslegung, Kirche*, edited by Jostein Adna et al., 77–93. Göttingen: Vandenhoeck & Ruprecht, 1997.

———. *The Theology of Paul the Apostle*. Grand Rapids: Eerdmans; Edinburgh: T & T Clark, 1998.

Du Toit, Andrie B. "A Tale of Two Cities: 'Tarsus or Jerusalem' Revisited." *New Testament Studies* 46 (2000): 375–402.

Eichhorn, J. G. *Einleitung in das Neue Testament*, vol. 3.1. Leipzig: Weidman, 1812.

Ellis, E. E. *The Making of the New Testament Documents*. Biblical Interpretation Series 39. Leiden: Brill, 1999.

Esler, Philip F. "The Social Function of 4 Ezra." *Journal for the Study of the New Testament* 53 (1994): 99–123.

Finsterbusch, Karin. *Die Thora als Lebensweisung für Heidenchristen: Studien zur Bedeutung der Thora für die paulinische Ethik*. Göttingen: Vandenhoeck & Ruprecht, 1996.

Fitzmyer, Joseph A. *Romans: A New Translation with Introduction and Commentary*. Anchor Bible. New York: Doubleday; London: Chapman, 1993.

Friedrich, Gerhard. "Muss *hypakoē pisteōs* Röm 1,5 mit 'Glaubensgehorsam' übersetzt werden?" *Zeitschrift für die neutestamentliche Wissenschaft* 72 (1981): 118–23.

Garlington, Don B. "The Obedience of Faith in the Letter to the Romans." *Westminster Theological Journal* 52 (1990): 201–24; 53 (1991): 47–72; 55 (1993): 87–112.

———. *"The Obedience of Faith": A Pauline Phrase in Historical Context*. Wissenschaftliche Untersuchungen zum Neuen Testament 2.38. Tübingen: Mohr, 1991.

———. *Faith, Obedience and Perseverance: Aspects of Paul's Letter to the Romans*. Wissenschaftliche Untersuchungen zum Neuen Testament 79. Tübingen: Mohr, 1994.

Gasque, W. Ward. *A History of the Interpretation of the Acts of the Apostles*. Peabody, Mass.: Hendrickson, 1989. (2d ed. of *A History of the Criticism of the Acts of the Apostles*. Beiträge zur Geschichte der biblischen Exegese 17. Tübingen: Mohr, 1975.)

Georgi, Dieter. *Die Geschichte der Kollekte des Paulus für Jerusalem*. Theologische Forschung 38. Hamburg: Herbert Reich Evangelischer Verlag, 1965.

Gnilka, Joachim. *Paulus von Tarsus: Apostel und Zeuge*. Freiburg: Herder, 1996.

Godet, F. *Commentaire sur l'Épitre aux Romains*. 2 vols. Paris: Sandoz & Fischbacher, 1879–80.

Goodman, Martin. "Jewish Proselytizing in the First Century." In *The Jews among Pagans and Christians in the Roman Empire*, edited by Judith Lieu, John North, and Tessa Rajak, 53–78. London and New York: Routledge, 1992.

Graetz, H. "Zeit der Anwesenheit der adiabenischen Königin in Jerusalem und der Apostel Paulus." In *Monatsschrift für Geschichte und Wissenschaft des Judenthums* 26 (1877): 241–52, 289–306.

Gregg, J. A. F. "The Commentary of Origen upon the Epistle to the Ephesians." *Journal of Theological Studies* 3 (1902): 233–44, 398–420, 551–76.

Greijdanus, S. *Is Handelingen 9 (met 22 en 26) en 15 in tegenspraak met Galaten 1 en 2? Een vergelijkende, exegetische studie*. Kampen: Kok, 1935.

Gunther, John J. *Paul, Messenger and Exile: A Study in the Chronology of His Life and Letters*. Valley Forge, Pa.: Judson Press, 1972.

Guthrie, Donald. *Galatians*. Rev. ed. The Century Bible, New Series. London: Oliphants, 1974; Grand Rapids: Eerdmans, 1981.

Haacker, Klaus. *Paulus: Der Werdegang eines Apostels*. Stuttgarter Bibelstudien 171. Stuttgart: Verlag Katholisches Bibelwerk, 1997.

Harnack, Adolf von. *Geschichte der altchristlichen Literatur bis Eusebius*. II.1, *Die Chronologie der Literatur bis Irenäus*. Leipzig: Hinrichs Verlag, 1897.

Hay, David M., ed. *Pauline Theology: 1 and 2 Corinthians*. SBL Symposium Series 2. Minneapolis: Fortress Press, 1993.

———, and E. Elizabeth Johnson, eds. *Pauline Theology: Romans*. SBL Symposium Series 3. Minneapolis: Fortress Press, 1995.

Heininger, Bernhard. *Paulus als Visionär: Eine religionsgeschichtliche Studie*. Herders Biblische Studien 9. Freiburg: Herder, 1996.

Hemer, Colin J. *The Letters to the Seven Churches of Asia in Their Local Setting*. Journal for the Study of the New Testament Supplement Series 11. Sheffield: JSOT Press, 1986.

———. *The Book of Acts in the Setting of Hellenistic History*. Edited by Conrad H. Gempf. Wissenschaftliche Untersuchungen zum Neuen Testament 49. Tübingen: Mohr, 1989.

Hengel, Martin. *Die Evangelienüberschriften*. Sitzungsberichte der Heidelberger Akademie der Wissenschaften: Philosophisch-historische Klasse 3. Heidelberg: Winter, 1984.

Hengel, Martin, with Ronald Deines. *The Pre-Christian Paul*. Translated by John Bowden. Philadelphia: Trinity Press International; London: SCM Press, 1991.

Hengel, Martin, and Anna Maria Schwemer. *Paul between Damascus and Antioch: The Unknown Years*. Louisville: Westminster/John Knox, 1997.

Hennequin, L. "Inscription de Delphes." In *Dictionnaire de la Bible: Supplément*. Vol. 2, cols. 355–73. Paris: Letouzey et Ané, 1934.

Hodges, Zane C., and Arthur L. Farstad, eds. *The Greek New Testament according to the Majority Text*. 2d ed. Nashville: Thomas Nelson, 1985.

Hoehner, Harold W. *Chronological Aspects of the Life of Christ*. Grand Rapids: Zondervan, 1977.

Hofius, Otfried. "Paulus—Missionar und Theologe." In *Evangelium, Schriftauslegung, Kirche*, edited by Jostein Adna et al., 224–37. Göttingen: Vandenhoeck & Ruprecht, 1997.

Holl, Karl. "Der Kirchenbegriff des Paulus in seinem Verhältnis zu dem der Urgemeinde." In *Gesammelte Aufsätze zur Kirchengeschichte*. Vol. 2, *Der Osten*, 44–67. Tübingen: Mohr, 1928.

Holland, Glenn S. *The Tradition That You Received from Us: 2 Thessalonians in the Pauline Tradition*. Hermeneutische Untersuchungen zur Theologie 24. Tübingen: Mohr, 1988.

Hollander, Harm W. "The Meaning of the Term 'Law' (Nomos) in 1 Corinthians." *Novum Testamentum* 40 (1998): 117–35.

———, and J. Holleman. "The Relationship of Death, Sin and Law in 1 Cor. 15:56." *Novum Testamentum* 35 (1993): 270–91.

Hooker, Morna D. "1 Thessalonians 1.9–10: A Nutshell—But What Kind of Nut?" In *Geschichte—Tradition—Reflexion*. Vol. 3, *Frühes Chris-*

tentum, edited by Hermann Lichtenberger, 435–48. Tübingen: Mohr, 1996.

Hoppe, Rudolf. "Aufgabenstellung und Konzeption einer 'Einleitung in das Neue Testament': Eine Standortbestimmung." *Biblische Zeitschrift* 43 (1999): 204–11.

Hübner, Hans. "Paulusforschung seit 1945: ein kritischer Literaturbericht." In *Aufstieg und Niedergang der Römischen Welt*, 2.25.4. *Religion*, edited by Wolfgang Haase, 2649–2840. Berlin: Walter de Gruyter, 1987.

Hurd, John Coolidge. *The Origin of 1 Corinthians*. New York: Seabury; London: SPCK, 1965.

Janse, S. *Paulus en Jeruzalem: Een onderzoek naar de heilshistorische betekenis van Jeruzalem in de brieven van Paulus*. Zoetermeer: Boekencentrum, 2000.

Jeremias, Joachim. "Sabbathjahr und neutestamentliche Chronologie." In *Abba: Studien zur neutestamentlichen Theologie und Zeitgeschichte*, 233–38. Göttingen: Vandenhoeck & Ruprecht, 1966 reprint.

Jervell, Jacob. *Die Apostelgeschichte*. Kritisch-exegetischer Kommentar über das Neue Testament. Göttingen: Vandenhoeck & Ruprecht, 1998.

Jewett, Robert. *A Chronology of Paul's Life*. Philadelphia: Fortress Press, 1979.

Johnson, E. Elizabeth, and David M. Hay, eds. *Pauline Theology: Looking Back, Pressing On*. SBL Symposium Series 4. Minneapolis: Fortress Press, 1997.

Johnson, Luke Timothy. *Letters to Paul's Delegates: 1 Timothy, 2 Timothy, Titus*. The New Testament in Context. Valley Forge, Pa.: Trinity Press International, 1996.

Johnson, Sherman E. *Paul the Apostle and His Cities*. Wilmington, Del.: Michael Glazier, 1987.

Kampling, Rainer. "Eine auslegungsgeschichtliche Skizze zu 1 Thess 2,14–16." In *Begegnungen zwischen Christentum und Judentum in Antike und Mittelalter*, edited by Dietrich-Alex Koch and Hermann Lichtenberger, 183–213. Göttingen: Vandenhoeck & Ruprecht, 1993.

Käsemann, Ernst. *Commentary on Romans*. Grand Rapids: Eerdmans, 1980. (German edition: *An die Römer*. Handbuch. Tübingen: Mohr, 1974.)

Keck, Leander E. "The Poor among the Saints in the New Testament." *Zeitschrift für die neutestamentliche Wissenschaft* 56 (1965): 100–129.

———. "The Poor among the Saints in Jewish Christianity and Qumran." *Zeitschrift für die neutestamentliche Wissenschaft* 57 (1966): 54–78.

Kenny, Anthony. *A Stylometric Study of the New Testament.* Oxford: Clarendon Press, 1986.

Kim, Seyoon. *The Origin of Paul's Gospel.* Wissenschaftliche Untersuchungen zum Neuen Testament 2.4. Tübingen: Mohr, 1981.

Klausner, Joseph. *From Jesus to Paul.* Translated by William F. Stinespring. New York: Macmillan, 1943; London: Allen & Unwin, 1944.

Klinghardt, Matthias. *Gesetz und Volk Gottes. Das lukanische Verständnis des Gesetzes nach Herkunft, Funktion und seinem Ort in der Geschichte des Urchristentums.* Wissenschaftliche Untersuchungen zum Neuen Testament 2.32. Tübingen: Mohr, 1988.

Knight, George W. *The Faithful Sayings in the Pastoral Letters.* Kampen: Kok, 1968.

Knox, John. "Fourteen Years Later: A Note on the Pauline Chronology." *Journal of Religion* 16 (1936): 341–49.

———. "The Pauline Chronology." *Journal of Biblical Literature* 58 (1939): 15–29.

———. *Chapters in a Life of Paul.* New York: Abingdon-Cokesbury, 1950.

Koester, Helmut, ed. *Ephesos, Metropolis of Asia: An Interdisciplinary Approach to Its Archaeology, Religion, and Culture.* Valley Forge, Pa.: Trinity Press International, 1995.

Kraft, Heinrich. *Die Entstehung des Christentums.* Darmstadt: Wissenschaftliche Buchgesellschaft, 1981.

Krimmer, Heiko. *Römerbrief.* Neuhausen-Stuttgart: Hänssler, 1983.

Ladd, George Eldon. *A Theology of the New Testament.* Grand Rapids: Eerdmans, 1974.

Lalleman, Pieter. "Keizer Claudius en de Christenen in Rome." *Bijbel en Wetenschap* 23 (1998): 43–45.

Lategan, B. C. *Die aardse Jesus in die prediking van Paulus volgens sy briewe.* Rotterdam: Bronder-offset, 1967.

Le Déaut, R. "Le thème de la circoncision du coeur (Dt. XXX 6; Jér. IV 4) dans les versions anciennes (LXX et Targum) et à Qumrân." In *Congress Volume: Vienna 1980*, edited by J. A. Emerton, 178–205. Supplements to Vetus Testamentum 32. Leiden: Brill, 1981.

Légasse, Simon. "Paul et les Juifs d'après 1 Thessaloniciens 2,13–16." *Revue Biblique* 104.4 (1997): 572–91.

Lentz, John C. *Luke's Portrait of Paul.* Cambridge: Cambridge University Press, 1993.

Leon, Harry J. *The Jews of Ancient Rome.* Rev. ed. Peabody, Mass.: Hendrickson, 1995.

Lewin, Thomas. *Fasti Sacri or a Key to the Chronology of the New Testament*. London: Longmans, Green, and Co., 1865.

Lohse, Eduard. *Paulus: Eine Biographie*. Munich: Beck, 1996.

Longenecker, Richard N. *Galatians*. Word Biblical Commentary. Dallas: Word Books, 1990.

Lüdemann, Gerd. *Paul, Apostle to the Gentiles: Studies in Chronology*. Philadelphia: Fortress, 1984. (German edition: *Paulus, der Heidenapostel*. Vol. 1, *Studien zur Chronologie*. Forschungen zur Religion und Literatur des Alten und Neuen Testaments 123. Göttingen: Vandenhoeck & Ruprecht, 1980.)

MacDonald, Dennis R. "The Shipwrecks of Odysseus and Paul." *New Testament Studies* 45 (1999): 88–107.

McEleney, Neil J. "Conversion, Circumcision and the Law." *New Testament Studies* 20 (1973–74): 319–41.

Malherbe, Abraham J. "Conversion to Paul's Gospel." In *The Early Church and Its Context: Essays in Honor of Everett Ferguson*, edited by Abraham J. Malherbe, Frederick W. Norris, and James W. Thompson, 230–44. Supplements to Novum Testamentum 90. Leiden: Brill, 1998.

Malina, Bruce J., and Jerome H. Neyrey. *Portraits of Paul: An Archeology of Ancient Personality*. Louisville: Westminster/John Knox Press, 1996.

Martyn, J. Louis. *Galatians: A New Translation with Introduction and Commentary*. Anchor Bible. New York: Doubleday, 1997.

Matera, Frank J. *Galatians*. Sacra Pagina. Collegeville, Minn.: Liturgical Press, 1992.

Matlock, R. Barry. "A Future for Paul?" In *Auguries: The Jubilee Volume of the Sheffield Department of Biblical Studies*, edited by David J. A. Clines and Stephen D. Moore, 144–83. Journal for the Study of the Old Testament Supplement Series 269. Sheffield: Sheffield Academic Press, 1998.

Meggitt, Justin J. *Paul, Poverty and Survival*. Edinburgh: T & T Clark, 1998.

Meijer, F. J. A. M., and M. A. Wes. *Flavius Josephus: Tegen de Grieken* (*Contra Apionem*). Translation, introduction, and annotations. Amsterdam: Ambo, 1999.

Meissner, Stefan. *Die Heimholung des Ketzers: Studien zur jüdischen Auseinandersetzung mit Paulus*. Wissenschaftliche Untersuchungen zum Neuen Testament 2.87. Tübingen: Mohr, 1996.

Metzger, Wolfgang. *Die letzte Reise des Apostels Paulus: Beobachtungen und Erwägungen zu seinem Itinerar nach den Pastoralbriefen*. Arbeiten zur Theologie 59. Stuttgart: Calwer Verlag, 1976.

Michel, Otto. "Fragen zu 1 Thessalonicher 2,14–16: Antijüdische Polemik bei Paulus." In *Antijudaismus im Neuen Testament? Exegetische und systematische Beiträge*, edited by W. Eckert, N. P. Levinson, and M. Stöhr, 50–59. Munich: Kaiser Verlag, 1967.

Mills, H. "Greek Clothing Regulations: Sacred and Profane?" *Zeitschrift für Papyrologie und Epigraphik* 55 (1984): 255–65.

Mitchell, Margaret M. "New Testament Envoys in the Context of Greco-Roman Diplomatic and Epistolary Conventions: The Example of Timothy and Titus." *Journal of Biblical Literature* 111 (1992): 641–62.

Moo, Douglas. *Romans 1–8*. Chicago: Moody Press, 1991.

Moore, George Foot. *Judaism in the First Centuries of the Christian Era: The Age of the Tannaim*. 3 vols. Cambridge: Harvard University Press, 1927–30.

Morris, Leon. *The First and Second Epistles to the Thessalonians*. Rev. ed. New International Commentary on the New Testament. Grand Rapids: Eerdmans, 1991.

Mounce, Robert H. *Romans*. New American Commentary. Nashville: Broadman, 1995.

Munck, J. *Paulus und die Heilsgeschichte*. Acta Jutlandica 26.1. Aarhus: Universitetsforlaget, 1954.

Murphy-O'Connor, Jerome. *Paul: A Critical Life*. Oxford: Clarendon Press, 1996.

Murray, John. *The Epistle to the Romans*. 1 vol. ed. Grand Rapids: Eerdmans, 1968.

Mussner, Franz. *Der Galaterbrief*. Herders Theologischer Kommentar 9. Freiburg: Herder, 1974.

Nanos, Mark D. *The Mystery of Romans: The Jewish Context of Paul's Letter*. Minneapolis: Fortress Press, 1996.

Neudorfer, Heinz-Werner. *Der Stephanuskreis in der Forschungsgeschichte seit F. C. Baur*. Giessen: Brunnen Verlag, 1983.

Nickle, Keith F. *The Collection: A Study in Paul's Strategy*. Studies in Biblical Theology 48. London: SCM Press, 1966.

Niebuhr, Karl-Wilhelm. *Heidenapostel aus Israel: Die jüdische Identität des Paulus nach ihrer Darstellung in seinen Briefen*. Wissenschaftliche Untersuchungen zum Neuen Testament 62. Tübingen: Mohr, 1992.

Nolland, John. "Uncircumcised Proselytes?" *Journal for the Study of Judaism* 12 (1981): 173–94.

Ogg, George. *The Odyssey of Paul*. Old Tappan, N. J.: Revell, 1968. (U.K. edition: *The Chronology of the Life of Paul*. London: Epworth Press, 1968.)

Oosterhuis, Thomas Jacob. *The "Weak" and the "Strong" in Paul's Epistle to the Romans: An Exegetical Study of Romans 14.1–15.13*. Dissertation, Free University Amsterdam, 1992. Edmonton: Elkon Press, 1992.

Oster, Richard. "The Ephesian Artemis as an Opponent of Early Christianity." *Jahrbuch für Antike und Christentum* 19 (1976): 24–44.

Paget, Carleton. "Jewish Proselytism at the Time of Christian Origins: Chimera or Reality?" *Journal for the Study of the New Testament* 62 (1996): 65–103.

Philip, Maertens. "Quelques notes sur *pniktos*." *New Testament Studies* 45 (1999): 593–96.

Plassart, A. "L'Inscription de Delphes mentionnant le proconsul Gallion." *Revue des Études Grecques* 80 (1967): 372–78.

Porter, Stanley E. *The Paul of Acts: Essays in Literary Criticism, Rhetoric, and Theology*. Wissenschaftliche Untersuchungen zum Neuen Testament 115. Tübingen: Mohr Siebeck, 1999.

Räisänen, Heikki. *Paul and the Law*. Wissenschaftliche Untersuchungen zum Neuen Testament 29. Tübingen: Mohr, 1983.

———. "Römer 9–11: Analyse eines geistigen Ringens." In *Aufstieg und Niedergang der Römischen Welt*, 2.25.4: *Religion*, edited by Wolfgang Haase, 2891–2939. Berlin: Walter de Gruyter, 1987.

Ramsay, W. M. *St. Paul: The Traveller and the Roman Citizen*. New York: G. P. Putnam's Sons, 1896; London: Hodder and Stoughton, 1905. Reprint, Grand Rapids: Baker, 1963.

———. *The Cities of St. Paul: Their Influence on His Life and Thought; The Cities of Eastern Asia Minor*. London: Hodder and Stoughton, 1907. Reprint, Grand Rapids: Baker, 1963.

Rapske, Brian. *The Book of Acts and Paul in Roman Custody*. The Book of Acts in Its First-century Setting 3. Grand Rapids: Eerdmans, 1994.

Reymond, Robert L. *Paul: Missionary Theologian*. Fearn: Christian Focus Publications, 2000.

Richard, Earl J. *First and Second Thessalonians*. Sacra Pagina 11. Collegeville, Minn.: Michael Glazier, 1995.

Ridderbos, Herman N. *Paul: An Outline of His Theology*. Grand Rapids: Eerdmans, 1975.

Riddle, D. W. *Paul, Man of Conflict: A Modern Biographical Sketch*. Nashville: Cokesbury, 1940.

Riesner, Rainer. *Paul's Early Period: Chronology, Mission Strategy, Theology*. Grand Rapids: Eerdmans, 1998. (German edition: *Die Frühzeit des Apostels Paulus: Studien zur Chronologie, Missionsstrategie und*

Theologie. Wissenschaftliche Untersuchungen zum Neuen Testament 71. Tübingen: Mohr, 1994.)

Robinson, John A. T. *Redating the New Testament.* Philadelphia: Westminster Press; London: SCM Press, 1976.

Roetzel, Calvin J. *The Letters of Paul: Conversations in Context.* 4th ed. Louisville: Westminster/John Knox Press, 1998.

Rückert, Leopold Immanuel. *Commentar über den Brief Pauli an die Galater.* Leipzig: Köhler, 1833.

Rutgers, Leonard Victor. "Roman Policy toward the Jews: Expulsions from the City of Rome during the First Century C.E." In *Judaism and Christianity in First-Century Rome*, ed. Karl P. Donfried and Peter Richardson, 93–116. Grand Rapids: Eerdmans, 1998.

Sanders, E. P. *Paul and Palestinian Judaism: A Comparison of Patterns of Religion.* Philadelphia: Fortress; London: SCM Press, 1977.

Schechter, Solomon. *Aspects of Rabbinic Theology.* Rev. ed. Edited by Louis Finkelstein. New York: Schocken, 1961.

Schille, Gottfried. *Die urchristliche Kollegialmission.* Abhandlungen zur Theologie des Alten und Neuen Testaments 48. Zürich: Zwingli Verlag, 1967.

Schleiermacher, Friedrich. *Über den sogenannten ersten Brief des Paulos an den Timotheus: Ein kritisches Sendschreiben an J. C. Gass.* Berlin: Realschulbuchhandlung, 1807.

Schlueter, Carol J. *Filling Up the Measure: Polemical Hyperbole in 1 Thessalonians 2.14–16.* Journal for the Study of the New Testament Supplement Series 98. Sheffield: Sheffield Academic Press, 1994.

Schmithals, Walter. *Gnosticism in Corinth: An Investigation of the Letters to the Corinthians.* Nashville: Abingdon, 1971. (German edition: *Die Gnosis in Korinth: Eine Untersuchung zu den Korintherbriefen.* 3rd enl. ed. Forschungen zur Religion und Literatur des Alten und Neuen Testaments 66. Göttingen: Vandenhoeck & Ruprecht, 1969.)

———. *Der Römerbrief: Ein Kommentar.* Gütersloh: Mohn, 1988.

Schnabel, Eckhard J. "Die ersten Christen in Ephesus: Neuerscheinungen zur frühchristlichen Missionsgeschichte." *Novum Testamentum* 41 (1999): 349–82.

Schneider, Gerhard. *Die Apostelgeschichte.* 2 vols. Freiburg: Herder, 1980, 1982.

Schrader, Karl. *Der Apostel Paulus.* 5 vols. Leipzig: Kohlmann, 1830–36.

Schwarz, D. R. "God, Gentiles, and Jewish Law: On Acts 15 and Josephus' Adiabene Narrative." In *Geschichte—Tradition—Reflexion.* Vol. 1, *Judentum*, edited by Peter Schäfer, 263–82. Tübingen: Mohr, 1996.

Schwemer, Anna Maria. "Paulus in Antiochien." *Biblische Zeitschrift* 42 (1998): 161–80.

Scott, James M. *Paul and the Nations: The Old Testament and Jewish Background of Paul's Mission to the Nations with Special Reference to the Destination of Galatians*. Wissenschaftliche Untersuchungen zum Neuen Testament 84. Tübingen: Mohr, 1995.

Segal, Alan F. *Paul the Convert: The Apostolate and Apostasy of Saul the Pharisee*. New Haven: Yale University Press, 1990.

Sherwin-White, Adrian Nicolas. *Roman Society and Roman Law in the New Testament*. The Sarum Lectures 1960–1961. Oxford: Clarendon Press, 1963.

Shulam, Joseph, with Hilary Le Cornu. *A Commentary on the Jewish Roots of Romans*. Baltimore: Messianic Jewish Publishers, 1997.

Slingerland, Dixon. "Suetonius *Claudius* 25,4 and the Account in Cassius Dio." *Jewish Quarterly Review* 79 (1989): 305–22.

———. "Acts 18:1–17 and Luedemann's Pauline Chronology." *Journal of Biblical Literature* 109 (1990): 686–90.

Smallwood, E. Mary. *The Jews under Roman Rule: From Pompey to Diocletian*. Studies in Judaism in Late Antiquity 20. Leiden: Brill, 1976.

Smiles, Vincent M. *The Gospel and the Law in Galatia: Paul's Response to Jewish-Christian Separatism and the Threat of Galatian Apostasy*. Collegeville, Minn.: Liturgical Press, 1998.

Smith, Jonathan Z. "Fences and Neighbors: Some Contours of Early Judaism." In *Approaches to Ancient Judaism*, edited by William Scott Green, 2.1–26. Chicago: Scholars Press, 1980.

Speyer, W. "Genealogie." In *Reallexicon für Antike und Christentum*, vol. 9, cols. 1145–1268.

Stegemann, E. "Zur antijüdischen Polemik in 1.Thess 2,14–16." *Kirche und Israel* 1 (1990): 54–64.

Storm, Hans-Martin. *Die Paulusberufung nach Lukas und das Erbe der Propheten: Berufen zu Gottes Dienst*. Arbeiten zum Neuen Testament und Judentum 10. Frankfurt am Main: Peter Lang, 1995.

Straatman, J. W. *Paulus, de apostel van Jezus Christus: Zijn leven en werken, zijne leer en zijne persoonlijkheid; een historisch onderzoek*. Amsterdam: Loman, 1874.

Strelan, Rick. *Paul, Artemis and the Jews in Ephesus*. Zeitschrift für die neutestamentliche Wissenschaft und die Kunde der Älteren Kirche, Supplement 80. Berlin: Walter de Gruyter, 1996.

Stuhlmacher, Peter. *Das paulinische Evangelium.* Vol. I, *Vorgeschichte.* Göttingen: Vandenhoeck & Ruprecht, 1968.

Suhl, A. "Der Beginn der selbständigen Mission des Paulus." *New Testament Studies* 38 (1992): 430–47.

Tajra, Harry W. *The Trial of St. Paul: A Juridical Exegesis of the Second Half of the Acts of the Apostles.* Tübingen: Mohr, 1989.

———. *The Martyrdom of St. Paul: Historical and Judicial Context, Traditions, and Legends.* Wissenschaftliche Untersuchungen zum Neuen Testament 2.67. Tübingen: Mohr, 1994.

Taylor, Justin. *Les Actes des deux apôtres: Commentaire historique (Act. 9,1–18,22).* Études Bibliques NS 23. Paris: Gabalda, 1994.

Taylor, Nicholas. *Paul, Antioch and Jerusalem: A Study in Relationships and Authority in Earliest Christianity.* Journal for the Study of the New Testament Supplement Series 66. Sheffield: Sheffield Academic Press, 1992.

Thielman, Frank. *From Plight to Solution: A Jewish Framework for Understanding Paul's View of the Law in Galatians and Romans.* Supplements to Novum Testamentum 61. Leiden: Brill, 1989.

———. *Paul and the Law: A Contextual Approach.* Downers Grove, Ill.: InterVarsity Press, 1994.

Thiessen, Werner. *Christen in Ephesus: Die historische und theologische Situation in vorpaulinischer und paulinischer Zeit und zur Zeit der Apostelgeschichte und der Pastoralbriefe.* Texte und Arbeiten zum neutestamentlichen Zeitalter 12. Tübingen: Francke Verlag, 1995.

Thorley, John. "Junia, a Woman Apostle." *Novum Testamentum* 38 (1996): 18–29.

Tomson, Peter J. *Paul and the Jewish Law: Halakha in the Letters of the Apostle to the Gentiles.* Compendia Rerum Iudaicarum ad Novum Testamentum III.1. Assen: Van Gorcum; Minneapolis: Fortress, 1990.

Van Bruggen, Jakob. "W. Schmithals en F. C. Baur." In *Almanak Fides Quadrat Intellectum 1964–1967*, 61–88. Kampen: Zalsman, 1967.

———. *De oorsprong van de kerk te Rome.* Kamper Bijdragen 3. Groningen: De Vuurbaak, 1967.

———. *Het raadsel van Romeinen 16.* Kamper Bijdragen 10. Groningen: De Vuurbaak, 1970.

———. *"Na veertien jaren": De datering van het in Galaten 2 genoemde overleg te Jeruzalem.* Thesis, Utrecht 1973, with summary in English. Kampen: Kok, 1973.

———. "Na vele jaren: Stadhouder Felix en de jaren van Paulus." In *Almanak Fides Quadrat Intellectum*, 119–54. Kampen: Zalsman, 1979.

———. *Ambten in de apostolische kerk: een exegetisch mozaïek*. Kampen: Kok, 1984.

———. "Vaste grond onder de voeten: De formule *pistos ho logos* in de Pastorale Brieven." In *Bezield verband: Opstellen aangeboden aan Prof. J. Kamphuis*, 38–45. Kampen: Van den Berg, 1984.

———. "Een vrouw waar geen woorden voor te vinden zijn." In *Ambt en aktualiteit*, ed. F. H. Folkerts, 51–60. Haarlem: Vijlbrief, 1992.

———. *Lucas: Het evangelie als voorgeschiedenis*. Commentaar op het Nieuwe Testament 3. Kampen: Kok, 1993.

———. "Geloofsgehoorzaamheid: De betekenis van een paulinische formulering voor de ethiek." In *Nuchtere noodzaak: ethiek tussen navolging en compromis*, edited by J. H. F. Schaeffer, J. H. Smit, and Th. Tromp, 84–95. Kampen: Kok, 1997.

———. *Christ on Earth: The Gospel Narratives as History*. Grand Rapids: Baker, 1998. (Dutch edition: *Christus op aarde: Zijn levensbeschrijving door leerlingen en tijdgenoten*. Kampen: Kok, 1987.)

———. *Jesus the Son of God: The Gospel Narratives as Message*. Grand Rapids: Baker, 1999. (Dutch edition: *Het evangelie van God's zoon: Persoon en leer van Jesus volgens de vier evangeliën*. Kampen: Kok, 1996.)

Van Eck, J. *Paulus en de koningen: politieke aspecten van het boek Handelingen*. Franeker: Van Wijnen, 1989.

Van Houwelingen, P. H. R. *1 Petrus: Rondzendbrief uit Babylon*. Commentaar op het Nieuwe Testament. Kampen: Kok, 1991.

Van Spanje, T. E. *Inconsistency in Paul? A Critique of the Work of Heikki Räisänen*. Wissenschaftliche Untersuchungen zum Neuen Testament 2.110. Tübingen: Mohr Siebeck, 1999.

Van Til, Salomo. *Opus Analyticum, comprehendens Introductionem in Sacram Scripturam ad Joh. Henrici Heideggeri Enchiridion Biblicum [H]IEROMNHMONIKON concinnatum*. 2 vols. 2d ed. Basel: Brandmüller, 1724.

Van Unnik, W. C. *Tarsus or Jerusalem: The City of Paul's Youth*. Translated by George Ogg. London: Epworth Press, 1962. (Dutch edition: *Tarsus of Jeruzalem: De stad van Paulus' jeugd*. Mededelingen der Koninklijke Nederlandse Akademie van Wetenschappen: Letterkunde, n.s. 15.5. Amsterdam: Noordhollandse Uitgevers Maatschappij, 1952.)

Vegetius. *Flavi Vegeti Renati Epitoma Rei Militaris*. Edited by C. Lang. Rev. ed. Leipzig: Teubner, 1885.

Veldhoen, Nicolaas G. *Het proces van den apostel Paulus*. Alphen aan den Rijn: Samsom, 1924.

Verhoef, Eduard. *De brieven aan de Tessalonicenzen*. Kampen: Kok, 1998.

Versteeg, J. P. *Christus en de Geest: Een exegetisch onderzoek naar de verhouding van de opgestane Christus en de Geest van God volgens de brieven van Paulus*. Kampen: Kok, 1971.

Volkmar, Gustav. *Paulus von Damascus bis zum Galaterbrief*. Zürich: Schröter & Meyer, 1887.

Wallace, Richard, and Wynne Williams. *The Three Worlds of Paul of Tarsus*. London and New York: Routledge, 1998.

Wanamaker, Charles A. *Commentary on 1 & 2 Thessalonians: A Commentary on the Greek Text*. New International Greek Testament Commentary. Grand Rapids: Eerdmans, 1990.

Warnecke, Heinz. *Die tatsächliche Romfahrt des Apostels Paulus*. Stuttgarter Bibelstudien 127. Stuttgart: Verlag Katholisches Bibelwerk, 1987.

Weatherly, Jon A. "The Authenticity of 1 Thessalonians 2.13–16: Additional Evidence." *Journal for the Study of the New Testament* 42 (1991): 79–98.

———. "Responsibility for the Death of Jesus in Paul: 1 Thessalonians 2.14–16." In *Jewish Responsibility for the Death of Jesus in Luke-Acts*, 176–94. Journal for the Study of the New Testament Supplement Series 106. Sheffield: Sheffield Academic Press, 1994.

Weber, Valentin. *Die antiochenische Kollekte, die übersehene Hauptorientierung für die Paulusforschung: Grundlegende Radikalkur zur Geschichte des Urchristentums*. Würzburg: Bauch, 1917.

Wehnert, Jürgen. *Die Reinheit des "christlichen Gottesvolkes" aus Juden und Heiden: Studien zum historischen und theologischen Hintergrund des sogenannten Aposteldekrets*. Göttingen: Vandenhoeck & Ruprecht, 1997.

Welborn, L. L. "Primum tirocinium Pauli (2 Cor 11,32–33)." *Biblische Zeitschrift* 43 (1999): 49–71.

Wenham, David. *Paul: Follower of Jesus or Founder of Christianity?* Grand Rapids: Eerdmans, 1995.

Wick, Peter. "Ist I Thess 2,13–16 antijüdisch? Der rhetorische Gesamtzusammenhang des Briefes als Interpretationshilfe für eine einzelne Perikope." *Theologische Zeitschrift* 50.1 (1994): 9–23.

Wieseler, Karl. *Chronologie des apostolischen Zeitalters bis zum Tode der Apostel Paulus und Petrus: Ein Versuch über die Chronologie und Abfassungszeit der Apostelgeschichte und der paulinischen Briefe. Mit einem Anhange über den Brief an die Hebräer und Excursen über den Aufenthalt der Apostel Paulus und Petrus in Rom*. Göttingen: Vandenhoeck & Ruprecht, 1848.

Wilson, A. N. *Paul: The Mind of the Apostle*. New York: Norton, 1997.

Winger, Michael. "Meaning and Law." *Journal of Biblical Literature* 117 (1998): 105–10.

Witherington, Ben, III. *Grace in Galatia: A Commentary on Paul's Letter to the Galatians*. Edinburgh: T & T Clark, 1998.

———. *The Paul Quest: The Renewed Search for the Jew of Tarsus*. Downers Grove, Ill.: InterVarsity Press, 1998.

Wright, N. T. *The Climax of the Covenant: Christ and the Law in Pauline Theology*. Edinburgh: T & T Clark, 1991.

———. "Paul, Arabia, and Elijah (Galatians 1:17)." *Journal of Biblical Literature* 115 (1996): 683–92.

Young, Brad H. *Paul the Jewish Theologian: A Pharisee among Christians, Jews, and Gentiles*. Peabody, Mass.: Hendrickson, 1997.

Ziesler, John. *Paul's Letter to the Romans*. TPI New Testament Commentaries. Philadelphia: Trinity Press International; London: SCM Press, 1989.

INDEX OF BIBLICAL AND EXTRABIBLICAL REFERENCES

Acts

1 Corinthians

Ephesians

Philippians

INDEX OF SUBJECTS AND NAMES

Jakob van Bruggen (Th.D., Utrecht University) is research professor of New Testament at the Theological University in Kampen, Netherlands, where he taught from 1967 until 2001. He is the author of more than fifteen commentaries and monographs in Dutch and English, including *Christ on Earth: The Gospel Narratives as History*, *Jesus the Son of God: The Gospel Narratives as Message*, and *The Future of the Bible*. He is the general editor of a major New Testament commentary series published by J. H. Kok, Kampen. He has lectured at seminaries and colleges in several countries and has presented papers at the annual meeting of the Evangelical Theological Society.